Women, Quotas and Politics

Although highly controversial, electoral gender quotas have been introduced recently in a large number of countries around the world to improve women's representation in national parliaments.

Women, Quotas and Politics offers the first global comparative analysis of the new trend to introduce gender quotas in public elections – written by researchers from all major regions in the world. This book presents cutting-edge research about the discursive controversies and actual implementation processes in countries with quota provisions. Providing a quantitative and qualitative assessment of these quotas in a variety of political systems, from developing nations and new democracies to established democracies, the contributors evaluate how they have been implemented; where these quotas have succeeded and failed; and how they can contribute to the political empowerment of women.

Making an important contribution to our knowledge about gender politics worldwide, this book will be of interest to NGOs, to students and scholars of democracy, electoral systems, policy-making, comparative politics and gender studies.

Drude Dahlerup is Professor of Political Science at Stockholm University, Sweden. She has written extensively on feminist theory, women's political representation and the history of the women's movement.

Routledge research in comparative politics

Women, Quotas and Politics

Edited by Drude Dahlerup

Routledge
Taylor & Francis Group

LONDON AND NEW YORK

First published 2006
by Routledge
2 Park Square, Milton Park, Abingdon, Oxon OX14 4RN

Simultaneously published in the USA and Canada
by Routledge
270 Madison Ave, New York, NY 10016

Reprinted 2006, 2007

Routledge is an imprint of the Taylor & Francis Group, an informa business

© 2006 Drude Dahlerup for selection and editorial matter,
individual contributors, their contributions

Typeset in Baskerville by Wearset Ltd, Boldon, Tyne and Wear
Printed and bound in Great Britain by MPG Books Ltd, Bodmin

British Library Cataloguing in Publication Data
A catalogue record for this book is available from the British Library

Library of Congress Cataloging in Publication Data
A catalog record for this book has been requested

ISBN 10: 0-415-37549-5
ISBN 13: 978-0-415-37549-8

Contents

Illustrations

Figures

Tables

Contributors

Gihan Abou-Zeid is the Regional Director of Gerbil for Training and Consultancy Center, Senior Researcher and board member in NGOs forum for Women in Development, Cairo, Egypt.

Milica G. Antić is a Professor of Sociology and Sociology of Genders in the Department of Sociology, Faculty of Arts, University of Ljubljana, Slovenia.

Clara Araújo is a Professor in the Department of Social Science at the University Estado de Rio de Janeiro, Brazil.

Carol Bacchi is an Associate Professor in Politics, School of History and Politics, University of Adelaide, South Australia.

Julie Ballington was Programme Officer, Women in Parliament, International Idea, Stockholm, until September 2005 when she joined the Inter-Parliamentary Union, Geneva.

Farzana Bari is the Director of the Women's Studies Centre, at the Quaid-i-Azam University, Islamabad, Pakistan.

Cecilia Bylesjö is a temporary Programme Officer, Women in Politics, Political Parties Programme, International Idea, Stockholm, Sweden.

Drude Dahlerup is a Professor in the Department of Political Science, Stockholm University, Sweden.

Lenita Freidenvall is a PhD student in the Department of Political Science, Stockholm University, Sweden.

Ana Isabel García is the Executive Director of the Gender and Society Foundation (GESO), Costa Rica.

Kareen Jabre is Manager, Programme for partnership between men and women, Inter-Parliamentary Union, Geneva.

Dior Konaté is a PhD student in the Department of History at the University of Wisconsin-Madison, USA. She earned her BA and MA in Senegal.

Mona Lena Krook is an assistant Professor in the Department of Political Science and Women and Gender Studies Program at Washington University, St Louis, USA.

Sonja Lokar is Chair of the Stability Pact Gender Task Force for South Eastern Europe.

Joni Lovenduski is a Professor at the School of Politics and Sociology, at Birkbeck, University of London, UK.

Colleen Lowe-Morna is the Director of Gender Links in Johannesburg, South Africa.

Nazmunessa Mahtab is Chair and Professor in the Department of Women's Studies, University of Dhaka, Bangladesh.

Richard E. Matland is a Professor in the Political Science Department at the University of Houston, USA.

Bidyut Mohanty is a Doctor and Head of the Women's Studies Department at the Institute of Social Sciences, New Delhi, India.

Shirin M. Rai is a Professor in the Department of Politics and International Studies at the University of Warwick, UK.

Francisia S.S.E. Seda is a Professor in the Department of Law and Sociology, Faculty of Social Policy, University of Indonesia.

Hege Skjeie is a Professor in the Department of Political Science at Oslo University, Norway.

Judith Squires is a Professor in the Department of Politics at the University of Bristol, UK.

Aili Tripp is the Associate Dean of International Studies and an Associate Professor in the Department of Political Science & Women's Studies at the University of Wisconsin-Madison, USA.

Acknowledgements

'No democracy without women!' Today, this phrase is heard all over the world. Consequently, there is a strong demand for new tools that can rapidly break the historical male dominance in political life. Electoral gender quotas are one such tool, and during just one decade gender quotas have been introduced in an amazing number of countries.

This book is the first world-wide comparative analysis of the introduction and implementation of electoral gender quotas, based on research from all major regions of the world. The Swedish Research Council has supported this research and by a special grant made it possible for us to convene and discuss the drafts of the book at a seminar in Stockholm in June 2004. Diane Sainsbury and Monica Erwer gave valuable comments on various parts of the manuscript at the Stockholm seminar. Two master students, later masters of political science, Åsa Fredell and Emma Frankl, have worked as research assistants for this book, and I am sure that I speak on behalf of all authors in thanking them both for their competent and insisting work with the bibliography and the tables. Emma Frankl also worked as research assistant for the chapter on South Asia, while Dina Obied was Research Assistant for the Arab chapter.

I want to thank my colleagues at the Department of Political Science at Stockholm University for all their help to me and the Quota Research Group, which has consisted of Christina Alnevall, Emma Frankl, Åsa Fredell, Lenita Freidenvall and Anja Taarup Nordlund. During her one year fellowship at Stockholm University, Mona Lena Krook, Columbia University, joined the research group. The working paper series of the research project can be found on www.statsvet.su.se/quotas.

I also want to thank International IDEA, and especially Julie Ballington and Yee-Yin Yap for several years of fruitful co-operation around the establishment of the global web site on the use of gender quotas in politics: www.quotaproject.org and for organizing very stimulating conferences for researchers, politicians and NGOs on the introduction and implementation of electoral gender quotas: Jakarta (2002), Lima (2002), Pretoria (2003), Budapest and Cairo (both 2004). Reports from all these conferences are available on www.idea.int.

It would be impossible for me to mention all the enthusiastic and inspiring people we have met and had discussions with at seminars and conferences on gender quotas around the world. There is a great demand for more knowledge about the experiences with various types of quota regimes – for good and bad. I hope that this book will give new and useful knowledge to all those people and organizations around the world who share the belief that democracy cannot function without the full inclusion of women in all parts of political life.

Drude Dahlerup
Stockholm July 2005

Abbreviations

ANC	African National Congress
APEC	Asia-Pacific Economic Cooperation
AU	African Union
CEDAW	Convention on the Elimination of All Forms of Discrimination against Women (1979)
CEE	Central and Eastern European (Network for Gender Issues)
CIS	Commonwealth of Independent States (former Soviet states)
EP	European Parliament
EU	European Union
FWCW	United Nations Fourth World Conference on Women (Beijing 1995)
GDI	Gender related Development Index
GL	Gender Links (South Africa)
IDASA	Institute for Democratic Alternatives in South Africa
IDB	Inter-American Development Bank
IMF	International Monetary Fund
IPU	Inter-Parliamentary Union
MEP	Member of the European Parliament
MP	Member of Parliament
NGO	Non-Governmental Organization
OSCE	Organization for Security and Co-operation in Europe
SADC	Southern African Development Community
SP	Stability Pact for South Eastern Europe
SP GTF	Stability Pact Gender Task Force
SWAPO	South West African People's Organization
UN	United Nations
UNDP	United Nations Development Programme
UNIFEM	United Nations Development Fund for Women
UNMIK	United Nations Interim Administration Mission in Kosovo
WID	Women in Development

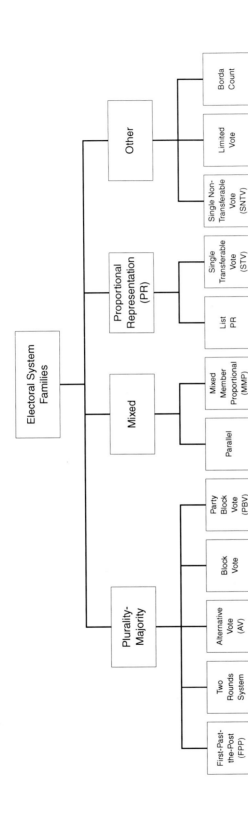

Figure 1 The applied typology of electoral systems, after *Electoral System Design: The New International IDEA Handbook.* Stockholm, 2005, see www.idea.int.

Notes

Plurality/majority systems: in an FPP system, or single-member districts, the winner is the candidate with the most votes, however, not necessarily an absolute majority. When used in multi-member districts it becomes Block Vote. If voters vote for party lists instead of individual candidates, it becomes Party Block Vote. Majoritarian systems, such as the Alternative Vote or the Two-Round System, try to ensure that the winning candidate receives an absolute majority.

Mixed systems: parallel systems that use both a PR element and a plurality/majority (or other) element. Usually voters have two votes, one for each element.

Proportional representations systems: the wanted proportionality is usually based on the use of party lists, where political parties present lists of candidates to the voters. Such party lists can be closed (unchangeable) or open to preferential voting by the voters. In Single Transferable Vote, voters rank-order candidates in multi-member districts.

Part I
Introductory chapters

1 Introduction

Drude Dahlerup

Gender quotas – a new global trend

In the autumn of 2003, Rwanda unexpectedly surpassed Sweden as the number one country in the world in terms of women's parliamentary representation. In the election to the newly constituted Rwandan parliament, women received 48.8 percent of the seats as opposed to 45.3 percent in Sweden. For decades, a Scandinavian country, be it Finland, Norway or most recently Sweden, was at the top with the highest percentage of women elected to parliament. With this extraordinary result, Rwanda came to represent a new trend in world politics, which we in this study have conceptualized as *the fast track to gender balance in politics.* During just a decade-and-a-half, countries as different as Argentina, Uganda, South Africa, Bosnia and Herzegovina, France and Costa Rica have, through the use of gender quotas, attempted to rapidly change women's historical under-representation in political institutions. This book is the first world-wide comparative analysis of the introduction of electoral gender quotas, based on in-depth case studies from all major regions of the world.[1]

Gender balance among political representatives is important for many reasons. Today, only about 16 percent of the world's parliamentarians are women, and according to feminist movements as well as to feminist theory this shortage of women in political institutions may have serious consequences for the political agenda, for the articulation of women's interests and for the legitimacy of democratic institutions (Phillips 1995; Norris 2004). Furthermore, the under-representation of women as well as that of other groups may influence how various categories of people are constructed in our minds.

Today, around 40 countries have introduced gender quotas in elections to national parliaments, either by means of constitutional amendment or by changing the electoral laws (legal quotas). In more than 50 other countries major political parties have voluntarily set out quota provisions in their own statutes (party quotas). Even if quota provisions are often very controversial, the use of the quota tool to make historical leaps or jump starts in women's representation is becoming a global trend.

Having gathered data on the use of quotas globally,[2] it is time to formulate new research questions. The use of electoral gender quotas challenges our ideas and theories about the relationship between women's political representation and their socio-economic position, since quotas may lead to unprecedented historical leaps in women's representation without simultaneous changes in women's socio-economic position. What are the arguments for and against gender quotas in various regions of the world? What types of quotas are actually applied, and how do they match various electoral systems? What are the effects of gender quotas in terms of numbers as well as the empowerment of women? Are women politicians that are elected on the basis of quotas actually empowered if they have no power base in political parties or civil society? Does the inclusion of women further democratization? How can we explain the apparent paradox that an increasing number of countries with very traditional gender regimes and almost totally male-dominated parliaments provide opportunities for women through the introduction of electoral gender quotas? Why are electoral gender quotas popular in some regions of the world while highly contested in others? These are all crucial questions that need to be addressed by feminist research as well as by international institutions and non-governmental organizations (NGOs).

In this book we will argue that a country's image in the international community is of growing importance today. This aspect of globalization has increased the opportunities for women's movements to play the international card in their lobbying on the national level. This trend may also, however, result in the mere symbolic inclusion of women in politics in order to make the country appear 'modern'. For better or worse, the international community is strongly involved in most processes of nation-building and reconstruction today, and many international organizations are involved in the promotion of gender quotas, especially in post-conflict societies. On the global level, UN conferences and the CEDAW convention have been especially important for the issue of women's political representation (Krook 2004a). In this introduction recent discursive changes involving women's political representation are discussed. This is followed by a discussion of the theoretical framework for analyzing electoral gender quotas and definitions of various types of electoral gender quotas. Lastly, the research design and contents of this book are presented.

The Beijing World Conference on Women – New Discourses

Several new discourses, while contested, are gaining influence in the world today. On the global level, the *Platform for Action*, agreed upon at the Fourth UN World Conference on Women in Beijing in 1995, may be seen as representing a discursive shift in relation to women in politics (FWCW

1995). As this book will show, the Beijing Platform has been very influential, and women's movements all over the world have attempted to give the controversial demand for gender quotas legitimacy by referring to the Platform for Action.[3] A discourse is here defined as interlinked constructions of meanings, which includes perceptions of possible actions (but not actual actions). The relationship between general assumptions and possible political actions is central to the field of policy analysis (Bacchi 1999).

First, the Beijing Platform talks about 'discriminatory attitudes and practices' and 'unequal power relations' that lead to the under-representation of women in arenas of political decision-making. This may be labeled *a discourse of exclusion.* Whereas previously the focus was on women's lack of resources or lack of will to participate in politics, attention is now directed towards those institutional and cultural mechanisms of exclusion that prevent women from obtaining an equal share of political positions in most political institutions in the world. Importantly, in this new discourse, the responsibility for promoting change is shifted from the individual woman to those institutions that are, consequently, expected to take action to identify and correct the causes of women's under-representation.

Second, the demand for a certain minimum level of representation for women is being challenged by a new discourse of equal representation, often expressed by the term *gender balance.* WeDo's 50–50 campaign is a good example of this new discourse (WeDo 2005). Thus, the goal is no longer described as 'more women in politics' but as 'equal participation' and 'equitable distribution of power and decision-making at all levels'. Somewhat contradictorily, however, the Beijing Platform also speaks of securing a 'critical mass', the latter often associated with figures of 20 or 30 percent women (Dahlerup 1988; FWCW 1995: Art. 181–95).

Third, affirmative action is suggested as a possible means of attaining the goal of women's equal participation in political decision-making, although the controversial word 'quotas' is not used. For governmental and public administration positions, it is recommended that the world's governments use 'specific targets and implementing measures . . . if necessary through positive action' (FWCW 1995: Art. 190.a). Concerning elections, it is stated that governments should commit themselves to 'Take measures, including, where appropriate, in electoral systems that encourage political parties to integrate women in elective and non-elective public positions in the same proportion and at the same levels as men' (FWCW 1995: Art. 190.b). Political parties should 'Consider examining party structures and procedures to remove all barriers that directly or indirectly discriminate against the participation of women' (FWCW 1995: Art. 191.a).

Even if the language is cautious, the Beijing Platform represents on the whole a new discourse, focusing on the mechanisms of exclusion through institutional practices, setting gender balance as the goal and demanding that governments and political parties commit themselves to affirmative action. In this book we identify what we call the fast track discourse and the fast track policy as an important part of the new directions set out in the Beijing Platform.

Theoretical perspectives on electoral gender quotas

In a narrow, technical sense, electoral gender quotas are simply a type of equal opportunity measure that force the nominating bodies, in most political systems the political parties, to recruit, nominate or select more women for political positions. However, as this study will show, quotas touch upon many fundamental principles in feminist theory, in political science and in contemporary political debates: the contested construction of women as a politically relevant category and principles of representation and of equality, vital questions that are discussed by Carol Bacchi in Chapter 2. Also involved are different types of equality policies, how quotas influence the relation between voters, political parties and their representatives, the effectiveness and value of representation as well as the possible link between women's representation and the legitimacy of democracy. But first, the notion of the fast track versus the incremental track is developed.

The 'fast track' versus the 'incremental track'

Electoral gender quotas represent *'the fast track'* to equal representation of women and men in politics in contrast to *'the incremental track'*. Behind the fast track model is growing impatience with the slow pace of change of the position of women. The notion of the fast track versus the incremental track can be viewed as involving first two discourses, second different types of actual equality policies, and third an account of the actual speed of historical development in women's representation (Dahlerup and Frei-denvall 2003, 2005). The Beijing Platform clearly represents the fast track discourse. This distinction between the two tracks may be relevant for many other policy areas but has been developed with respect to gender and political institutions.

In 1990 the United Nation's Economic and Social Council endorsed a target of 30 percent women in decision-making positions in the world by 1995 (United Nations Commission on the Status of Women 1995). This target was far from being met. In 1995, only 10 percent of the world's parliamentarians were women. In 2005, around 16 percent of the world's parliamentarians are women, still far from the target of 30 percent. This figure implies that politics is still predominantly a men's business, with men making up 84 percent of parliamentarians. The difference between various regions of the world is, however, substantial, as Table 1.1 shows.

Table 1.1 Women in national parliaments – regional differences[a]

	Percent
Americas	18.8
Arab States	8.2
Asia	15.2
Europe (OSCE member states, excluding the Nordic countries)	17.0
Nordic countries	39.9
Pacific	11.3
Sub-Saharan Africa	16.5
World average	**16.0**

Source: IPU (2005).

Note
a Lower or single houses.

The Nordic countries, Denmark, Finland, Iceland, Norway and Sweden, have for a long time displayed the highest share of female politicians, consistently exceeding the 20 percent threshold since the 1970s and 1980s (see Table 1.1 and the Nordic chapter in this book). The rest of Europe, the Americas, Asia and Sub-Saharan Africa are all close to the world average, while the figure for the Pacific is only 11.3 percent and in Arab countries 8.2 percent. However, there are also great variations within regions, and today countries like Costa Rica, South Africa, Rwanda and Mozambique have overtaken industrialized nations like the United States and the United Kingdom, which in the House of Representatives and the House of Commons only have 15 and 18 percent women, respectively. Today, we witness a challenge to the Nordic countries, which, together with the Netherlands, used to be very much alone at the top of the world ranking.

In the debate in Latin America, in South Africa and in many other countries, the extraordinarily high representation of women in Scandinavian parliaments has been used as an argument in support of the introduction of electoral gender quotas.[4] This argument is, however, somewhat misleading, since the real boom for women's representation in Denmark, Finland, Norway and Sweden occurred in the 1970s and in Iceland in the 1980s, all before the introduction of any quotas. Gender quotas were introduced when women already comprised 20 to 30 percent in these parliaments. Moreover, in the Nordic countries electoral quotas have always been voluntary, never a legal requirement, and are only used by some of the political parties at the centre and at the left (see Chapter 3). In general, the Nordic countries come close to what we label *the incremental track* towards equal political representation for women and men. It took approximately 60 years from women's enfranchisement for Denmark, Norway and Sweden to cross the 20 percent threshold and 70 years to reach 30 percent. *This means that the Nordic countries, in spite of the high level of women's representation, can no longer be considered the model, or at any rate the only model, for increasing women's representation.*

Constructed as an analytical distinction between discourses, the two tracks include different assumptions about historical development, different problem identifications with regard to the causes of women's under-representation as well as differences in choice of strategy (Dahlerup and Freidenvall 2005).

The primary problem, according to *the incremental track discourse*, is that women do not have the same political resources as men. While prejudice against women is recognized, it is assumed that this will eventually disappear as society develops. There is thus an inherent notion of gradualism, often embedded in an optimistic, linear view of progress. In Chapter 2, Carol Bacchi further discusses this predominantly liberal perspective and its scepticism of quotas.

In contrast, *the fast track discourse* rejects the idea of gradual improvement in women's representation. It is even assumed that an increase in resources might not automatically lead to equal representation. Exclusion and discrimination are regarded as the core of the problem identification and understanding, the solution to which could very well be affirmative action. Based on the new diagnosis of the problem associated with the fast track discourse, according to which gender balance will not come about 'by itself', there is a growing impatience among contemporary feminists, who are not willing to wait 70 to 80 years in order to achieve their goals. A linear projection predicts that at the current rate, gender balance among parliamentarians will not be reached until the turn of the twenty-second Century (Norris 2004: 180). The responsibility for dealing with the under-representation of women rests with the political institutions. In line with this conception of women's under-representation, mandated quotas for the recruitment and election of female candidates are needed.

Additional discourses

The goal of gender balance in politics, common to both the incremental and the fast track discourses, is, however, not shared all over the world. Consequently, several additional discourses can be identified: According to the third, *the gender-blind discourse*, gender is irrelevant when it comes to political representation, from which follows that no action should to be taken. In contrast, the fourth, *the politics-is-a-men's-business discourse* is strongly preoccupied with gender but assumes that women are unfit and unqualified for political positions. In the fourth discourse women belong in the home, and any involvement of women in electoral politics threatens to undermine their presumed roles as mothers and housewives.

Discourses and actual policy

Discourses found in empirical studies like the present may approximate more or less closely to one of these constructed types. In addition, the logical connection implied in the Beijing Platform discourse between the understanding of the problem (actual exclusion of women) and the measures advocated (affirmative actions, quotas) is not always present. When it comes to actual policy making, this link may be even weaker. When equality policy is passed in consensus, which is often the case in many parts of the world, one may see political parties vote for the same law from very different discursive positions.

Nevertheless, discourses are key structures that influence actions. Consequently, the discursive frames are very important to the quota debate. To the feminist movement as well as to all other social movements, it is well-known that attempts to change the discursive frames are an essential part of the activities of all movements and that this basically involves a power struggle (Dahlerup 1998a; della Porta and Diani 1999).

'Fast track' equality policy

Gender quotas are part of a new type of equality policy, representing a shift from 'equal opportunity' to 'equality of result'. Building on the first generation of national and international equality policy, the anti-discrimination laws, is a second generation labeled affirmative-action or positive-action policies. Affirmative action implies measures that target structural discrimination or that make it possible to leap over the barriers, as in the case of gender quotas. There is no doubt that affirmative action has the potential for contributing to substantial changes, which is probably why it is so controversial, especially in the Western world (Bacchi 1996; Dahlerup 1998b; Teigen 2000; Klausen and Maier 2001). This shift in equality policy has been supported by recommendations on the use of affirmative action set out in the Beijing Platform, UN Resolution 1325, the CEDAW convention and many other international declarations (Krook 2004a).

During the last two decades equal opportunity 'machineries' (institutions) and equality legislation have emerged in most countries in the world, usually promoted by the feminist movement. Recently, 'mainstreaming', which entails that all policy must include a 'gender perspective', has become a new tool, nationally as well as in regional and international organizations such as the AU, the EU, APEC and the UN. It remains to be seen whether this approach will actually help to develop new perspectives on public policy or just bury the special Equal Opportunity Units that have been important in the promotion and implementation of equality policies (Pollack and Hafner-Burton 2000; ABANTU *et al.* 2003; Borchorst and Dahlerup 2003; Rai 2003).

Seen as a policy field, equality policy is characterized by a lack of established partners or adversaries, like the historical organizing of workers versus employers. It is a policy area that involves feelings and ambiguities and in which rigorous analysis of goals and means are rare and symbolic policies widespread (Stetson and Mazur 1995; Borchorst and Dahlerup 2003). It has been argued that even in the Scandinavian countries, well-known for their comprehensive equality policies, policies aiming at changing gender relations and gender structures in general have had to 'yield' when in conflict with other goals and means (Skjeie and Teigen 2003). The degree of conflict over equality policy varies considerably, but it has been argued that the widespread appeal to consensus, the fear of conflict in equality policies, derives from a search for harmony between the sexes in the private sphere that is now being transferred into public sphere policy (Eduards 2002: 154). Equality policies have historically been promoted by parties on the left and by social-liberal parties. The question is whether electoral gender quotas follow this pattern. In this book we ask why some countries have chosen to introduce quotas while others have not, and why the introduction of quotas are subject to significant and vehement controversies in some countries while passing almost unanimously and without much discussion in others.

Contrary to what is usually expected, a quota provision of, say, 30 percent does not automatically lead to a considerable and rapid increase in women's representation. In public debates as well as in research, the focus is mainly on the passionate debates over the introduction of quotas, while the no less important implementation process is often neglected. In this study we will follow the entire process, from the discussions of gender quotas over the decision on actual quota rules to the implementation process and the discussion of the effects of quota provisions. In general, there is a need for in-depth studies of the implementation and outcome of equality policies. Does equality policy work? What are the experiences of various types of affirmative action policies? Can affirmative action policies affect structural discrimination and lead to substantial changes? When do we see unintended consequences? These crucial questions will be addressed through the study of electoral gender quotas.[5]

Parties, electoral systems and gender quotas

The point of departure for any quota analysis is that political parties are the gatekeepers when it comes to nominations and elections to political posts (Norris and Lovenduski 1995). In most systems based on competition between parties, but of course also in one-party systems, it is the parties that dominate the recruitment and selection of candidates. The introduction of electoral quotas goes to the very core of the relationship between voters, parties and representatives. The substantial resistance to gender quotas in older democracies illustrates the extent to which the electoral systems are considered to be 'natural', even if there are significant variations between countries. In contrast, in the many contemporary post-conflict societies and societies in transition to democracy, the electoral systems are open for discussion, and national as well as international forces are engaged in the art of 'electoral engineering'.

As the electoral system constitutes one of the most important entrances to public decision-making, it is vital to the functioning of democracy. The opponents of quotas argue that quotas contradict the principle of merit – let the best man (sic) win after meeting the voters. But since political parties normally control who is nominated and where (in more or less safe seats), one may ask whether the limits imposed by quotas do not restrict the free scope of the party leadership more than that of the voters. Seen from a different perspective, gender quotas may in fact expand the choices of the voters.

By making historical leaps in women's representation possible, quotas potentially change the links established in electoral studies between women's position in parliaments, on one hand, and their socio-economic position and the political structures, especially the electoral system, on the other. Studies have found that a high level of political representation for women is correlated with a high level of gainful employment among women, a high level of education among women as compared to men, secularization, a longer period of time since enfranchisement and, not least, an electoral system based on proportional representation rather than plurality-majority systems. Women's representation also tends to be greater in parties on the left than in parties on the right, although there are many exceptions. Cultural factors and 'contagion' from one country to another are also seen as increasingly important (Sainsbury 1993; Nelson and Chowdhury 1994; Norris and Lovenduski 1995; Matland and Studlar 1996; Bergqvist 1999; Caul 1999; Matland and Montgomery 2003; Norris 2004).

Most research in this field has dealt with Western countries, and, consequently, there is an urgent need to view the actual scope of previous theories critically. It is obvious that, among other things, the established link between secularization and women's representation will change with actual leaps in the number of women in politics in the Catholic countries of Latin America and may do so in the future in Muslim countries like Indonesia (see Chapter 12). According to Matland, a threshold of development seems to exist for less developed, non-Western countries. Only after that threshold is passed do proportional representation, labor force participation and cultural standing exert positive influences on the representation of women (1998). However, the use of quotas might change all established patterns in the future.

The next step is to analyze which factors lead to the introduction of quotas and to what extent the prevailing electoral system influences the probability of having quota provisions introduced. Do we see today more quota systems being introduced in proportional systems than in plurality-majority systems? One reason could be that it is quite complicated to get quotas to work in a plurality-majority system in which each party has only one candidate and in which the winner takes all (FPP).

This study will ask what type of quota systems are being introduced in various parts of the world and how they match different electoral systems. If the chosen quota type does not match the electoral system in a given country, it may be a case of pure symbolic policy (Borchorst and Dahlerup 2003). Symbolic policy is traditionally defined as policy that develops as a response to demands from the outside but that is not intended to make any real difference. When it comes to equality policy, the concept of symbolic policies should be redefined so as to include policy measures that rest on a lack of understanding of means and ends and on a lack of interest in finding out how to get measures such as quotas to actually have an effect. In his study of the introduction of quotas in Peru, Gregory Smidt found absolutely no evidence that any attention was paid to how quotas would actually work in conjunction with the very different rules that are used in municipal and congressional elections (2003: 3).

In studying the diffusion of electoral gender quotas, the concept of 'contagion' (Matland and Studlar 1996) may not be fully adequate, since it might lead us to underestimate the transformation necessary for making the new international discourse of gender balance acceptable in various national contexts. Even in an era of globalization, political debates are conducted primarily within national boundaries, and the decision to introduce electoral gender quotas are usually taken by national parliaments or national political parties. In this book we will study regional patterns of diffusion of quotas.

Substantive and numerical representation

The difference between numerical representation of women (women's share of the representatives) and substantive representation (attention to women's interests, however defined) is a well-known theme in feminist theory. Empirical analyses have tried to answer the question of to what extent and under what conditions women politicians 'make a difference' in politics. Goetz and Hassim ask to what extent increasing numbers of women in politics will help produce 'gender-sensitive politics' and better 'public accountability' to women (2003: 5). Those familiar with this field of research know how complicated it is to evaluate the impact of women's increased representation. However, research from all over the world has shown that even if party affiliation is usually more important than gender, it has been women politicians that have initiated equality policies, often in cross-party women's alliances (Skjeie 1992; Lovenduski and Norris 1993; Lovenduski and Randall 1993; Wängnerud 2000; Hassim 2003). The concept of a critical mass, the notion that women will only be able to start making a difference when their numbers exceed about 30 percent, is a point of contention in feminist theory, though widely used by women politicians themselves and by proponents of quotas (Dahlerup 1988). Women politicians themselves are, however, often caught between contradictory expectations: on the one hand, feminist movements often accuse elected women of not representing women and of not pursuing women's issues, that is, of not making a difference, while, on the other hand, women politicians are accused of not behaving like 'real' politicians, of not being like or as good as men, that is, of being too different.

The question of substantial representation is extremely important, although methodologically complicated because at the macro level it is difficult to distinguish the effect of an increasing number of women politicians from other factors influencing legislation – factors which may have caused the increase in women's representation in the first place. Also, if no differences are found in micro level analyses between the attitudes and parliamentary actions of women and men politicians (from the same party), it might in fact be a result of women politicians having influenced their male colleagues, an accomplishment that would require other methodologies to recognize than those looking for gender differences.

Despite all of the academic controversies about whom women represent (see the discussion in Chapter 2), and in spite of all of the attempts to focus entirely on the classic argument of justice, we cannot, as Marian Sawer argues, expect campaigns for more women in politics to give up on 'making a difference' discourse (Sawer 2000: 377). As we shall show in this book, such arguments are frequently used in the quota debate as well, and this book will illuminate how stories of past and future records of women politicians are often crucial in quota debates all over the world.

The effectiveness of representation

Research on women's political representation should also deal with the question of what one could label the *effectiveness* of women's representation, an issue that is highly relevant to the research about gender quotas.[6] Under what conditions are women politicians able to make use of their positions as elected politicians? Seen from such a perspective, the focus shifts to the electoral system and to political institutions seen as workplaces, that is the institutional routines, norms and culture that frame women's and men's abilities to actually work as politicians. Significantly, in these contexts women are often met with double standards: women politicians are accused of lacking knowledge and education but at the same time criticized for only representing a small group of educated elite women; women politicians are often accused of being tokens of their clans, families and parties, as if men never are.

In the case of electoral gender quotas, these debates become even tougher. The concept of 'tokenism', or in India 'proxy' women, is often used against women elected on the basis of quota regulations. The argument is that 'quota women' are dependent on their husbands and families and/or on their political party or an autocratic leader both before and after their election. Even if problems of tokenism and patronage do limit women's opportunities to act for change, as several chapters in this book will show, double standards are also at play here. In these heated debates about token quota women, there is a failure to mention that in clientelist systems most men politicians also belong to political families and that they are also dependent on the political leadership for their (re)nomination.

It is important to state the obvious: that quota provisions do not solve all problems for women in politics and that they may even create new ones. If there is prejudice against women in a society, as is often the case, quotas do not remove these barriers for women to full citizenship. If women have trouble combining family responsibilities and political work, quotas do not in themselves overcome this difficulty. However, quota provisions might make it possible for women to surmount some of the barriers that prevent their access to certain opportunities. They could, it is claimed, enable a 'jump start' in places where women have almost no representation at all.

The fast track discourse rejects the accusations that women's low representation is primarily caused by women's lack of resources. Rather, women are as competent as men (and how competent are male politicians, it is polemically asked?). The real problem is that women's experiences are not recognized and, after all, the counter-argument goes, being a politician is about *representing*, not a matter of university education.

Nevertheless, the fast track policy does reopen the question of women's resources, but in a different sense. While women in Nordic politics, the very model of the incremental track, had developed a rather solid power base in the political parties prior to the introduction of any party quotas, one may ask if fast track policy, so important for the rapid increase in women's representation, may result in the election of women politicians with very limited power bases in society and in the parties. Consequently, the question of 'tokens' should be rephrased: Do quotas under certain circumstances have the unintended consequence that under certain conditions women politicians will lack a power base of their own and thus have difficulties using their elected position as they want? If the quota rules do not match the electoral system, as is the case where women politicians lack their own constituency because their seats are 'added', then tokenism might in fact be a consequence.

This study of the introduction of quotas rests on research on women in politics during the last decade, and the authors of this book have all worked with these themes in their research. In this book we will not study whether the increased number of women politicians makes a difference, only how this very subject is debated among opponents and advocates of gender quotas. Aside from this, the book will concentrate on the implication for women politicians of being elected by means of quotas. Thus, it is *the consequences of being elected via quotas – being a 'quota woman'*, not the effect of women politicians in general that this book sets out to analyze. However, this cannot be studied in isolation from the development of the political institutions themselves.

The new trend to introduce gender quotas points to a renewed interest in representation in political institutions, even if the women's movement's relation to the state has always been ambiguous. We have witnessed several historical shifts between stressing the empowerment of women at the grass roots level and demands for increased representation in the political institutions, although research has shown that these two kinds of empowerment may in fact supplement each other (Dahlerup 1998a). The focus here is on the *value of representation*.

The concept of empowerment will play a central role throughout this book. In feminist debates about empowerment, especially in a development setting, 'empowerment over' has been replaced by a concept of 'empowerment to' or 'empowerment to choose'. Empowerment is thus not defined as a process nor as a result but as a tool (Kabeer 2000; Parpart *et al.* 2002). This is highly relevant for the quota debate, since being a representative may give previously excluded groups not only the right to choose as far as their own life is concerned but the right to participate in what David Easton once labeled 'those interactions through which values are authoritatively allocated for a society' (Easton 1965: 21). By their 'critical acts', women politicians may make serious attempts to change the position of women or groups of women at large (Dahlerup 1988). This is what makes political representation so special and so potentially important.

Even if representation in political institutions might be an important tool, the value of gender quotas and political representation are closely linked to socio-economic changes in women's position and in society at large, as all of the following chapters will argue. The contested concepts of recognition versus redistribution are central to this debate (Fraser 1995; Young 1997; Hoskyns and Rai 1998).

Further, the political empowerment of women in political institutions cannot be discussed in isolation from the importance of these institutions themselves. Even if 'the theory of shrinking institutions'– that women enter institutions with diminishing power (Skjeie 1992) – should not be seen as an immutable law of nature, the present neo-liberal trend to move decision-making power away from polities and towards the market is of utmost importance for the discussion of gender balance in political institutions. This notion of the value of representation in contemporary society is discussed in several chapters of this book and highlights the debate about the relationship between women's empowerment and the development of democracy.

Gender quotas and democratization

While equal *participation* of both women and men in political parties and social movements is stated as a general goal, equal *representation* was for a long time not seen as equally important to address, as Anne Phillips rightly observes (1995: 31). Outside feminist circles, all-male political assemblies were previously not considered undemocratic. No international boycott was ever launched against Switzerland before 1971 or against Kuwait for excluding women from political citizenship until 2005.

In modern feminism, however, a link is established between women's political empowerment and democratization. When a group of Nordic feminist scholars in 1985 entitled their book *Unfinished Democracy*, it was a deliberate challenge to the prevailing scientific discourses that do not hesitate to label a country 'democratic', even if women are de jure or de facto excluded from political representation (Haavio-Mannila 1985). Previously, even feminists had been reluctant to challenge the democratic character of a country, even if women lacked representation.[7] While the demand for more women in politics has rested primarily on arguments of justice, of women's interests that men cannot safeguard or on a wish to include women's experiences on the political agenda, gender balance in political decision-making is increasingly seen as a prerequisite for democracy itself. But what is the link between the inclusion of women and democratization?

Newer international declarations are often ambiguous on this point. In a rather radical resolution from the Council of the Interparliamentary Union, IPU, as early as 1992, it is stated:

> The concept of democracy will only assume true and dynamic significance when political policies and national legislation are decided upon jointly by men and women with equitable regard for the interests and aptitudes of both halves of the population.
>
> (IPU 1994)

However, in a 1994 declaration women's involvement is said to 'strengthen' democracy, and gender neutral affirmative action measures are recommended on a 'strictly interim basis' (IPU 1994). Does this imply that democracy is possible without women? The Beijing Platform for Action is even weaker and does not posit a direct casual link between democratization and gender equity in political decision-making. Rather, the link is stated to be one between development and the active involvement of women:[8]

> Achieving the goal of equal participation of women and men in decision-making will provide a balance that more accurately reflects the composition of society and is needed in order to strengthen

democracy and promote its proper functioning ... Without the active
participation of women and the incorporation of women's perspective
at all levels of decision-making, the goals of equality, development and
peace cannot be achieved.

(FWCW 1995: Art. 181)

The link between the empowerment of women and democratic development is more in focus in *post-conflict countries* and in countries that are in a
process of *transition to democracy* than in the old democracies. The latter
tend to consider democracy to be fully established once and for all – even
before women had any right to participate. This book will show how
gender quotas have been introduced in post-conflict societies, such as
Bosnia & Herzegovina, Afghanistan and Rwanda, as well as in countries in
transition to democracy, such as in Latin America. The hypothesis is that
even if armed conflicts used to strengthened patriarchal structures
through systematic rapes and degradation of women, the following period
of total reconstruction might in fact under certain conditions lead to new
openings for women and for other previously marginalized groups. It is
only during very recent years that it has become practically impossible to
disregard the gender perspective in processes of reconstruction. With its
global perspective, this book can contribute to our understanding of the
conditions under which such openings occur and of the importance of
national and international feminist pressure.

Are quotas for women in non-democratic countries without competitive
elections worth working for? In many Arab and African countries, this is
exactly what women's movements are demanding. In patronage systems,
the means of women's access seem to be very important for their legitimacy and effectiveness (Goetz 2003: 110). To reject any relevance of such
a project is to deny that there might be a link between the exclusion of
women and the lack of democratic development as well as development in
general. In newer development discourses equality between women and
men is not just seen as something that will eventually follow from 'development'. Rather, the liberation of women and women's active involvement is seen as a prerequisite for social and economic development. In
this way, the 'patriarchy' or the exclusion of women is seen as one of the
three main obstacles to development in the Arab world (Joseph and Sly-
omovics 2001; UNDP 2003).

Similar discursive changes can be identified in relation to the under-
representation of ethnic minorities and immigrants in politics. This book
focuses on women's political representation, and the intersection between
gender, ethnicity, religion or caste is only discussed when relevant to a
gender perspective.

The link between democratization and inclusion of women in political
decisions-making is framed in terms of two empirical questions in this
study: First, to what extent are such arguments used in quota debates in

various parts of the world today? Second, under what conditions have post-conflict situations actually entailed an opening for the inclusion of women in politics?

The implementation of quotas

The outcome of quota provisions should be evaluated in qualitative as well as quantitative terms. The first perspective deals with the complicated question of the possibility for the elected 'quota women' to perform their task as politicians and, if they so wish, to make a difference, as discussed above. The second perspective directs our attention to the actual number of women nominated and elected after the introduction of electoral gender quotas.

Table 1.2 shows all countries that had passed the 30 percent threshold for women in parliament in 2005.[9] The table reveals that not all countries have reached the global top ranking in terms of women's representation in parliament with the help of quota provisions. Major historical increases in women's parliamentary representation can occur without quota provisions, just as the mere introduction of quotas has not resulted in uniform increases in the numbers of women parliamentarians worldwide, as this

Table 1.2 The top of the world rank order[a]

Country	Women in national parliament (%)	Quota type	Electoral system
Rwanda	48.8 (2003)	Legal quotas (C)	List PR
Sweden	45.3 (2002)	Party quotas	List PR
Norway	37.9 (2005)	Party quotas	List PR
Finland	37.5 (2003)	No quota	List PR
Denmark	36.9 (2005)	No quota	List PR
Netherlands	36.7 (2003)	Party quotas	List PR
Cuba	36.0 (2003)	No quota	Two Rounds
Mozambique	36.0 (2004)	Party quotas	List PR
Spain	36.0 (2004)	Party quotas	List PR
Costa Rica	35.5 (2002)	Legal quotas (L)	List PR
Belgium	35.3 (2003)	Legal quotas (L)	List PR
Argentina	33.5 (2003)	Legal quotas (C)	List PR
Austria	33.3 (2002)	Party quotas	List PR
South Africa	32.8 (2004)	Party quotas	List PR
Germany	31.8 (2005)	Party quotas	MMP
Burundi	30.5 (2005)	Legal quotas (L)	List PR
Iceland	30.2 (2003)	Party quotas	List PR

Source: International IDEA and Stockholm University (2005); official statistics. Changes after the election not included.

Notes
a Parliaments with more than 30 percent women.
Key Electoral Systems: *Proportional Representation*: List PR. *Mixed*: MMP = Mixed Member Proportional. Key Quota Type: Legal quotas: Constitutional (C) or Law (L).

book will show. However, electoral gender quotas are no doubt an affirmative action measure that, properly implemented, has the potential to increase women's representation rapidly, as the new high rankings of South Africa, Mozambique and Costa Rice bare out. Proportional representation systems are the most prevalent among these top ranking countries, both those with and those without quota provisions. In Chapter 13, Richard Matland will illuminate the connection between the electoral system and the introduction of quotas.

Today, quotas are introduced in countries in which women only constitute a very small minority in parliament, and we are now witnessing historical leaps in women's representation, e.g. from 19 to 35 percent women in parliament in one election (Costa Rica), 30 percent women elected in the very first democratic parliamentary election (South Africa). For some countries in the Arab and African regions, a 'jump start' is the appropriate expression, since almost no women held political office before the quotas. By including all major regions of the world, this book will be able to study to what extent and under what circumstances quota provisions may lead to substantial increases and actual leaps in women's representation.

Defining electoral gender quotas

Quota is not an unambiguous concept. The term 'quota' sometimes refers only to party nominations, leaving 'reserved seats' outside the quota family. This book works with a more comprehensive definition of quotas, more apt to include the many different ways in which countries today try to increase women's political representation through affirmative action measures.

Quotas in politics involve setting up a percentage or number for the representation of a specific group, here women, most often in the form of a minimum percentage, for instance 20, 30 or 40 percent. Quotas are used as a measure to increase the representation of historically excluded or under-represented groups. Gender quotas may be constructed so as to require a minimum representation for women or may state a maximum-minimum representation for both sexes, for instance no more than 60 and no less than 40 percent for each sex. In the case of the latter, gender neutral regulation, the quota provision sets a maximum for both sexes, which quotas for women do not.

At what level? In the study of different quota regimes in politics, a distinction must be made between regulations aiming at changing the composition of: (1) the pool of potential candidates, here called the aspirants; (2) the candidates who stand for election; and (3) those elected. *Electoral quotas may be defined as regulations that in public elections require a certain minimum in numbers or percentage of a specific group at one of these levels.*

There are examples of quota requirements on all three levels, but most quota systems concern the second level, setting up minimum requirements of representation of certain groups on the electoral ballots (candidate quotas). The partly unsuccessful 'women's short lists' in England is an example of a type of quota system targeting the first level (aspirant quotas). At this level, the aim of quotas is to broaden the pool from which the selection committee or the primary will chose candidates. Quotas in the form of 'reserved seats' operate on the third level. Here certain groups are warranted or guaranteed a certain number of seats among the elected (reserved seat quotas).

One might argue that reserved seats should not be counted among electoral quotas. However, as it will be shown in this book, reserved seats today come in many different types some excluding, others including, elections, as in the Ugandan case in which certain seats, elected regionally by a special electorate, are reserved for women. In fact, variations in reserved seat systems are an important new field of study. The term 'elect-oral gender quotas' is used to describe quota systems that are designed to operate in public elections.

The mandate. Quotas may be mandated in a country's constitution or by law, usually in the electoral law. In both cases we can speak of *legal quotas*. Legal quotas regulate the proceedings of all political parties in a country and may also prescribe sanctions in case of non-compliance. Quotas may, however, be voluntarily decided by one or more political parties in a country, in which case we can speak of *party quotas*. In such cases some political parties may have quotas, while others in the same country reject the idea. Countries with legal quotas are categorized as legal quota coun-tries, whether the individual parties in the country have actually inscribed gender quotas in their statutes or not. When a law is in place, all parties have to comply. When legal quotas are in place, party quotas are only of interest if a party has voluntarily decided on a higher percentage than the percentage mandated or if a party has introduced other special rules not inscribed in the law (like the ranking of the candidates).

The relation between quota level and mandating is not unambiguous, as this book will show (see Table 1.3). While quotas to enlarge the pool of aspirants (first level) are usually decided on by the parties themselves, can-didate quotas for party lists at elections (second level) may be mandated either by the parties themselves (party quotas) or by the constitution or law (legal quotas). The third level of quotas, the reserved seats, is usually legal quota systems, mandated by the constitution and/or law, by decree from the ruling party in a one-party system or from the monarch. However, there are examples such as Morocco, in which a 'gentlemen's agreement' reserved all 30 seats on the so-called national list for women candidates. By analyzing the many new types of gender reserved seat systems, this book will be able to shed light on the selection mechanism often used in semi-democratic and non-democratic systems. Quotas for internal organizations in political parties, like steering committees or nominations committees, are, although important, only included in this study when relevant for the introduction of electoral gender quotas. More-

Table 1.3 Types of electoral quotas

Mandated by	Aspirants	At what level? Candidates	Elected
Legal quotas (constitutional or electoral law)	n/a	Candidate quotas	Reserved seats
Voluntary party quotas	Aspirant quotas (short lists)	Candidate quotas	Reserved seats[a]

Note
a Informal agreements among political parties reserving a certain number of seats for women.

over, many parties and even governments operate with more or less speci-fied *targets and recommendations (sometimes labeled 'soft' quotas)*. A target might be just as effective as a written quota provision that is not followed. For the sake of clarity, however, the focus here is, with a few exceptions, on formally decided and recorded quotas.

Quota systems on all three levels and of different kinds may also be in use in relation to the selection of different ethnic groups, castes, clans and religious groups for political office. Quotas or reserved seats for ethnic and religious groups do exist, as in Jordan and Lebanon. Moreover, all electoral systems include some kinds of quotas, though usually under dif-ferent labels, as when densely populated areas are given a disproportion-ate number of seats in parliament or when electoral districts are designed in order to favor, or disfavor, specific groups. Mala Htun's interesting argument that ethnic groups receive reserved seats while women, because gender is cross-cutting and women are parts of all social groupings, receive candidate quotas is discussed and challenged in this book (Htun 2004).

The research design of the book

With a few exceptions, research on quotas to date has concentrated pri-marily on single country studies or in some rare cases studies covering one region.[10] It seems essential to broaden the analysis.

The regional and global comparative perspective

It is a challenge to study what appear to be the same phenomena, elect-oral gender quotas introduced within a short historical period in so many different political systems all over the globe. This book is based on new research. Obviously, it is impossible for one researcher to have in-depth knowledge about the implementation of quotas all over the world. Thus, the regional chapters in the book are written by researchers who have conducted extensive studies of women in politics in their respective countries and regions and who were invited to conduct new research on the recent use of quotas in their regions. For all of the authors the production of this book involved a challenge in confronting regional or presumably 'universal' theories with the empirical realities of countries from different corners of the world.

In the seven regional chapters in the book, the introduction of electoral gender quotas is studied in a regional perspective. With the selection of the seven regions, this book covers the introduction of quotas in large parts of the world. The regional chapters can be read separately, each having its own profile derived from the regional context. The selected regions are: the Nordic countries, Latin America, Sub-Saharan Africa, the Balkans, the Arab region, Western Europe, North America, Australia and New Zealand (the 'West') and South Asia.

These regions are selected for analysis because they represent interesting cases of the use of gender quotas. The five small Nordic countries, well-known for very high levels of women's representation illustrate what is here labeled the incremental track. The chapter on 'The West' shows the strong resistance among liberal democracies to introducing quotas through legal means. In sharp contrast, Latin America is the continent with the most widespread use of legal quota provisions, all introduced during the last decade. Many countries in Sub-Saharan Africa have also recently introduced quotas, although of different types from those in Latin America. With the introduction of quotas in the Arab countries in Northern Africa and the Middle East, the democraticizing potential of the inclusion of women and other previously excluded groups is raised. In the Balkan region we see crucial examples of the inclusion of a gender perspective in a post-conflict restructuring of society, something also being attempted with varying degrees of success in countries like Rwanda, Afghanistan and Iraq. While the main focus is on the parliamentary level, a chapter on the astounding case of introducing 30 percent quotas for women at the local level in India, Bangladesh and Pakistan is included.

The comparison *between regions* that is made possible by the inclusion of so many major regions of the world is based on our analyses of the use of quotas in individual countries and systematic comparisons *within the regions*. The most dissimilar research design – encompassing most of the world – is thus based on research using a most similar design, comparing within regions. The seven regional chapters offer a unique collection of new research. This regional approach is chosen in order to study the diffusion of the idea of quotas among neighboring countries and in order to be able to focus on the contextuality of quota discourses and regulations.

The notion of region employed in the book is an analytic construct. While regions are often geographically identifiable, this is not always the case, as the region of 'The West' exemplifies. Here 'region' captures a shared intellectual history, a common cultural heritage, and common or quite similar languages. This allows the United Kingdom, Canada, the United States, New Zealand and Australia to be considered together. On the same basis, the Latin American region is confined to former Spanish and Portuguese colonies.[11]

With the selection of the seven regions, we do not cover the whole world. There are other areas that would have been interesting to include, such as the part of Oceania that is left out and South East Asia, where the Philippines and Taiwan represent interesting quota cases. Other interesting cases for future research are the CIS countries Armenia and Uzbekistan (International IDEA and Stockholm University 2005). Eastern Europe and Russia are also interesting cases, but mostly because of the widespread rejection of quotas, which – not always correctly – are associated with the period of Soviet rule. A recent book on women's representation in this area makes a chapter in this book superfluous (Matland and Montgomery 2003).

In Section III, however, we include a number of shorter studies of cases of special interest.

A catalogue of questions for all regional chapters

Even if each chapter tells its own story, the same set of analytical problems is raised in all of the main regional chapters. To date, research on quotas has tended to concentrate on the discursive controversies surrounding quotas. These form an essential part of this research project. However, in addition we investigate three often neglected issues: the types of quota systems in use, the implementation or lack of implementation of quotas and questions of the consequences of introducing quotas. The main questions raised in all the empirical studies in this large scale comparative analysis are the following:

– *Diffusion:* What are the factors behind the recent trend to introduce gender quotas in so many countries in the world?
– *Quota discourses:* What are the main arguments used for and against electoral gender quotas? How are the quota discourses constructed in the different political systems and cultures around the world?
– *Types of quotas:* What types of quota regulations are in use in various parts of the world, and how do they match different electoral systems?
– *Implementation result:* Are quota regulations actually implemented? Are there sanctions in case of non-compliance, and are there law enforcing agencies? Is it impossible to find a sufficient number of qualified women candidates, as opponents of quota provisions have often argued?
– *Outcome:* How can we evaluate the outcome of various quota types in different political and cultural contexts? Have quotas actually increased the number of women in parliaments? Is it possible to reach

conclusions regarding the conditions under which electoral gender quotas have contributed to the empowerment of women in political institutions?

The content of the book

In Chapter 2, Carol Bacchi analyzes contemporary feminist theory debates on key concepts in political analysis: equality, representation, citizenship and rights, all of which are central to the quota debate. Even if quota debates are contextually framed, it is surprising to see to what extent these same contested concepts form part of the quota debates all over the world today, even though the emphasis may vary. According to Bacchi, affirmative action like quotas should not be characterized as 'preferential treatment' or 'special help', since this language tends to stigmatize affirmative action targets, women in this case, and as a result may undermine the effectiveness of the reform. To locate affirmative action as an exemption within anti-discrimination legislation to compensate for past discrimination wrongly implies that present social rules are generally fair. Consequently, Bacchi argues for shifting the focus in equality debates from women's disadvantage to men's privilege. It is Bacchi's conclusion that challenging dominant norms in this field reduces concerns that quotas rely upon a homogeneous category 'women', which might downplay the significance of the diversity of women's experiences.

Part II of the book contains the seven regional chapters. In Chapter 3, 'The Nordic countries: an incremental model', Lenita Freidenvall, Hege Skjeie and Drude Dahlerup discuss the factors behind the world famous high representation of women in Denmark, Finland, Iceland, Norway and Sweden (30 to 45 percent women in parliament). The authors identify a Nordic *incremental discourse* on women's representation according to which gender equality will continue to develop gradually with the help of the benevolent state. Contrary to what is commonly believed, no legal quotas for elections were ever passed in the Nordic countries. Quotas in these small, stable welfare states have the form of voluntary party quotas and are used predominantly by parties on the left, with the exception of Norway where quotas in general are an accepted measure. But quotas were not introduced until women had already attained 20 to 30 percent of the seats in the parliament and local councils. Consequently, in spite of the many discursive controversies over quotas in the Nordic countries, these *high echelon quotas* have proven to be a continuation of Nordic incrementalism rather than a break with the past. The Nordic countries are taken up first because they are seen to represent the incremental track that is to be contrasted with the many representatives of the fast track, first Latin America.

In Chapter 4, Clara Araújo and Ana Isabel García analyze the rapid dissemination of gender quotas in Latin America during the last ten years, following Argentina as the pioneer country (1991). The introduction of gender quotas is placed in the context of contemporary transition to democracy, where quotas became associated with the issue of modernization. The epicenter of Latin American women's struggles in the 1990's was the process of redemocratization, and during this process the women's movement contributed to the strengthening of the language of human rights in the region. The authors show that gender quotas in this region come in the form of legal quotas and that the most successful cases, such as Costa Rica and Argentina, are those in which the judiciary intervenes in case of non-compliance. The acquired judicial norms may either be interpreted as the result of the strength of the women's movement or as a symptom of the absence of ideological commitment on the part of the political parties, the authors argue.

In Chapter 5, Sub-Saharan Africa, the authors, Aili Tripp, Dior Konate and Colleen Lowe-Morna, discuss why Africa today has some of the highest rates of female political representation in the world. Africa is another very interesting example of the use of fast track policies for women's political representation, but here both voluntary party quotas, as in South Africa, and reserved seat quotas, as in Rwanda, are in use. The chapter points to the impact of the women's movement, post-conflict factors, state objectives and the movement towards democratization and political liberation throughout Africa. Quotas were often introduced in situations in which constitutions were being rewritten, which made it easier to place gender on the agenda. In many post-conflict societies women found it easier to make inroads through reserved seats, where they do not have to contend with male incumbents. The change in women's political representation is, according to the authors, occurring within a broader context of women making bids for power in a number of arenas.

In Chapter 6, Milica G. Antic and Sonja Lokar analyze the exclusion and inclusion of women in the reconstruction phase after the collapse of the state socialist regime and the subsequent ethnic conflicts and war in the Balkans. The authors argue that the post-conflict situation made it extremely difficult for women in the political parties and for women NGOs to be heard. However, some windows of opportunity were opened, which women's organizations were skillfully able to use. In the first period after the first free elections, there was an open conservative setback, and gender quotas were rejected, whereas the second period saw some 'unwilling acceptance', influenced by the international and national women's movements. In the present third stage within the framework of the Stability Pact for South Eastern Europe, women have, according to the authors, become a distinct, novel political subject in the Balkans. In this first overview of the many attempts to include women in the post-conflict process in the individual Balkan countries, a move is traced away from 'gentlemen's agreements' that are not honored to the acceptance of legal gender quotas.

In Chapter 7, Gihan Abou-Zeid analyzes the many new demands for women's access to political decision-making in the Arab region. With the exception of Kuwait, Arab women have formal political rights, but only around 7 percent of the parliamentarians in the region are women, the lowest in the world. The author analyzes the background to and the effect of the introduction of quota provisions today in many Arab countries, often in the form of reserved seats. For the author there is no doubt that it is important to try to create access for women even in countries with non-competitive elections. In many of the Arab countries, quotas may represent a jump start for women into politics. However, the author points out that women, once elected, are often met with prejudice, and their qualifications are questioned, perhaps more so if they have obtained their seats because of gender quotas. In many Arab states the fourth discourse, 'politics is-a-men's-business', prevails, but the author is able to show that changes may be underway in some parts of the Arab nation.

Chapter 8, written by Mona Lena Krook, Joni Lovenduski and Judith Squires, covers a constructed region, the 'Western world', located on three continents. The authors show that there is a connection between different models of citizenship, the likelihood that quotas are adopted and what types of quotas are in use. In the liberal citizenship model, with its emphasis on individualism, quotas are often 'soft', that is, just recommendations and informal targets but never legal. In corporatist or consociational European models of citizenship, with their commitment to social partnership, voluntary party quotas prevail. In the republican citizenship model, with the philosophical commitment to universalism and centralized forms of government, legal quotas have been possible (France), however, they have had limited success during the implementation stage on the national level. The authors stress that a particular model of citizenship does not guarantee any specific outcome, either negative or positive. Rather, awareness of these models sheds light on the opportunities and constraints for quota campaigns in specific contexts.

In the last of the regional chapters, Chapter 9, the focus is on the local level. Shirin M. Rai, Farzana Bari, Nazmunessa Mahtab and Bidyut Mohanty analyze the extraordinary experiments to introduce 33 percent quotas for women in local politics in India, Pakistan and Bangladesh. In India, which has a long tradition of reserved seats for the scheduled castes, gender quotas have brought several million women into local politics, sometimes just as tokens, sometimes empowered, supported by capacity-building programs for the elected women. It is the conclusion of this chapter that quotas in politics can only form one part of a multi-facetted strategy for empowering women, involving not just recognition but also redistribution of socio-economic resources within a society. The authors show that the implementation of gender quotas in South Asia form part of a long history of constructing post-colonial citizenship but that they are also part of current governmental strategies for addressing issues relating to the status of the nation within the international community.

Chapters 10, 11 and 12 are three smaller chapters on selected cases. The ambiguous role of the international community in post-conflict societies are discussed by Julie Ballington and Drude Dahlerup in Chapter 10 on Timor-Leste, Iraq and Afghanistan. Chapter 11, which is written by Cecilia Bylesjö and Francisia SSE Seda, tells the story about the introduction with mixed results of gender quotas in Indonesia. Finally the quite radical implementation of gender quotas in the world parliaments' own organization, the Interparliamentary Union, IPU, is discussed in Chapter 12 by Kareen Jabre.

In Chapter 13, Richard Matland analyzes the effectiveness of various types of quota provisions at all three levels of the electoral process: the aspirants, the candidates and the elected. Only under certain conditions do gender quotas actually increase women's representation. An electoral system with high district magnitude, closed-list proportional representation, rules about the ranking of the candidates and good-faith compliance from the political parties are sufficient, but not necessary conditions for gender quotas to work, Matland concludes. Chapter 14 brings the conclusion of the book.

Notes

1 This book is one of the results of the research project 'Electoral Gender Quotas – a Key to Equality?', supported by the Swedish Research Council, see www.statsvet.su.se/quotas. The research team has consisted of Christina Alnevall, Drude Dahlerup, Emma Frankl, Åsa Fredell, Lenita Freidenvall and Anja Taarup Nordlund, in 2001–2 joined by Mona Lena Krook, Columbia University. We thank International IDEA, especially Julie Ballington and Yee-Yin Yap for years of fruitful co-operation. The concept of fast track versus incremental track discourses as ideal types were first developed in Dahlerup and Feidenvall (2003, 2005), see also Dahlerup and Nordlund (2004).
2 See www.quotaproject.org, a Global Database of Quotas for Women, established and maintained by the International Institute for Democracy and Electoral Assistance (IDEA) in co-operation with the Research Project 'Electoral Gender Quotas – a Key to Equality?', Stockholm University, Department of Political Science.
3 Some of these new formulations may in fact be found in the CEDAW convention from 1979. The convention recommends the states to adopt 'temporary special measures' (UN 1979: Art. 4). Also, the Interparliamentary Union, IPU, and other international and regional organizations formulated early on new claims for women's representation. However, it is the Beijing Platform that is most often referred to in the quota debate.
4 For Argentina, the leading Latin American country concerning quotas: Oral communication from Mariá José Lubertino, president of the Instituto Social y Politica de la Mujer. Professor of Human Rights and Guarantees at the Universidad de Buenos Aires (see also Phillips 1995: 57).
5 The possible effect of equality policy in the Western world is being analyzed by the international research program, RNGS (Research Network on Gender Politics and the State).
6 The term 'effectiveness' is used differently by Goetz and Hassim, namely as more directly linked to the discussion of substantial representation (2003: 5).

7 Only after an internal debate did the Danish Women's Society dare to introduce a poster in 1909 stating that 'there is no universal suffrage when women do not have the right to vote', since this challenged the general perception that democracy and universal suffrage were introduced in Denmark already in 1849 with extended male suffrage. Not until 1915 did Danish women get the right to vote for parliament (Dahlerup 2002: 341).

8 Thanks to Christina Alnevall for pointing this out to me.

9 There are a few minor variations in the percentages for individual countries, because some of the authors of the following chapters have chosen to show the present number of women in parliament (changes following death and retirement) and not the numbers at Election Day. The table of the world rank order published by the Inter-Parliamentary Union, IPU, contains both election day figures and figures that reflect the present day situation. Consequently, there may be some, however insignificant, differences between our figures and those of IPU.

10 Marques-Pereira and Nolasco (2000); Htun and Jones (2002); Stockholm University (working paper series) (2002–) (www.statsvet.su.se/quotas); International IDEA's Quota Workshop Report Series no. 1–3 (2003a, b, 2004); Lowe-Morna (2003); European Political Science (symposium: gender quotas) (2004); Norris (2004). For an excellent overview, see Krook (2004b).

11 Comoros and Mauritania are dealt with in both Chapters 5 and 7, because they geographically belong to Sub-Saharan Africa, but are members of the Arab League.

Bibliography

ABANTU *et al.* (2003) 'Maputo Declaration on Gender Mainstreaming and the Effective Participation of Women in the African Union', 24 June. Online. Available at: http://www.sarpn.org.za/documents/d0000480/P405_Gender_AU.pdf (accessed 21 February 2005).

Bacchi, C.L. (1996) *The Politics of Affirmative Action. 'Women', Equality and Category Politics*, London: Sage.

—— (1999) *Women, Policy and Politics*, London: Sage.

Bergqvist, C. (ed.) (1999) *Equal Democracies? Gender and Politics in the Nordic Countries*, Oslo: Scandinavian University Press.

Borchorst, A. and Dahlerup, D. (eds) (2003) *Ligestillingspolitik som diskurs og praksis*, Frederiksberg: Samfundslitteratur.

Caul, M. (1999) 'Women's representation in parliament: the role of political parties', *Party Politics*, 5, 1: 79–98.

Dahlerup, D. (1988) 'From a Small to a Large Minority: Women in Scandinavian Politics', *Scandinavian Political Studies*, 11, 4: 275–98.

—— (1998a) *Rødstrømperne. Den danske Rødstrømpebevægelses udvikling, nytænkning og gennemslag, Vol. I–II*, Copenhagen: Gyldendal.

—— (1998b) 'Using Quotas to Increase Women's Political Representation', in A. Karam (ed.) *Women in Parliament. Beyond Numbers*, Stockholm: International IDEA, pp. 91–106.

—— (2002) 'Three Waves of Feminism in Denmark', in G. Griffin and R. Braidotti (eds) *Thinking differently. A reader in European Women's Studies*, London & New York: Zed Books, pp. 341–50.

Dahlerup, D. and Freidenvall, L. 'Quotas as a "Fast Track" to Equal Political Representation for Women: Why Scandinavia is No Longer the Model', paper presented at the American Political Science Association's Annual Meeting, Philadelphia, August 2003.

——— (2005) 'Quotas as a Fast Track to Equal Representation for Women', *International Feminist Journal of Politics*, 7, 1: 26–48.

Dahlerup, D. and Nordlund, A.T. (2004) 'Gender Quotas: a Key to Equality? A Case Study of Iraq and Afghanistan', *European Political Science*, 3, 3: 91–8.

della Porta, D. and Diani, M. (1999) *Social movements. An introduction*, Oxford: Blackwell.

Eduards, M. (2002) *Förbjuden handling: om kvinnors organisering och feministisk teori*, Malmö: Liber.

Easton, D. (1965) *A Systems Analysis of Political Life*, New York: Wiley.

European Political Science (2004) 'Symposium: Gender Quotas', *European Political Science*, 3, 3: 51–105.

FWCW Beijing 1995, see under UN.

Fraser, N. (1995) 'Recognition or Redistribution? Dilemmas of Justice in a "Post-Socialist" Age', *New Left Review*, 212: 68–93.

Goetz, A.M. (2003) 'The Problem with Patronage: Constraints on Women's Political Effectiveness in Uganda', in A.M. Goetz and S. Hassim (eds) *No Shortcuts to Power: African Women in Politics and Policy Making*, London: Zed Books, pp. 110–39.

Goetz, A.M. and Hassim, S. (2003) 'Introduction: Women in Power in Uganda and South Africa', in A.M. Goetz and S. Hassim (eds) *No Shortcuts to Power: African Women in Politics and Policy Making*, London: Zed Books, pp. 1–28.

Haavio-Mannila, E. *et al.* (eds) (1985) *Unfinished Democracy: Women in Nordic Politics*, New York: Pergamon.

Hassim, S. (2003) 'Representation, Participation and Democratic Effectiveness: Feminist Challenges to Representative Democracy in South Africa', in A.M. Goetz and S. Hassim (eds) *No Shortcuts to Power: African Women in Politics and Policy Making*, London: Zed Books, pp. 81–109.

Hoskyns, C. and Rai, S.M. (1998) 'Gender, Class and Representation: India and the European Union', *The European Journal of Women's Studies*, 5, 3–4: 345–66.

Htun, M. (2004) 'Is gender like ethnicity? The political representation of identity groups', *Perspectives on Politics*, 2, 3: 439–58.

Htun, M.N. and Jones, M.P. (2002) 'Engendering the Right to Participate in Decision-making: Electoral Quotas and Women's Leadership in Latin America', in N. Craske and M. Molyneux (eds) *Gender and the Politics of Rights and Democracy in Latin America*, Houndmills: Palgrave, pp. 32–56.

Inter-Parliamentary Union (IPU) (1994) 'Plan of Action', 26 March. Online. Available at: http://www.ipu.org/wmn-e/planactn.htm (accessed 7 February 2005).

——— (IPU) (2005) 'Women in National Parliaments', situation as of 15 August. Online. Available at: http://www.ipu.org/wmn-e/world.htm (accessed 6 October 2005).

International IDEA (2003a) *The Implementation of Quotas: Asian Experiences*, Quota Workshop Report Series no. 1, Stockholm: International IDEA.

——— (2003b) *The Implementation of Quotas: Latin American Experiences*, Quota Workshop Report Series no. 2, Stockholm: International IDEA.

——— (2004) *The Implementation of Quotas: African Experiences*, Quota Workshop Report Series no. 3, Stockholm: International IDEA.

International IDEA and Stockholm University (2005) 'Global Database of Quotas for Women'. Online. Available at: http://www.quotaproject.org (accessed 17 February 2005).

Joseph, S. and Slymovics, S. (2001) *Women and Power in the Middle East*, University of Pennsylvania Press.

Kabeer, N. (2000) *The Power to Choose: Bangladeshi Women and Labour Market Decisions in London and Dhaka*, London: Verso.

Klausen, J. and Maier, C.S. (eds) (2001) *Has Liberalism Failed Women? Assuring Equal Representation in Europe and the United States*, New York: Palgrave.

Krook, M.L. (2004a) 'Promoting gender-balanced decision-making: the role of international fora and transnational networks', in H.R. Christensen, B. Halsaa and A. Saarinen (eds) *Crossing Borders: Re-Mapping Women's Movements at the Turn of the 21st Century*, Odense: Odense University Press, pp. 205–20.

Krook, M.L. (2004b) 'Reforming Representation: The Diffusion of Candidate Gender Quotas Worldwide', paper presented at the International Studies Association Annual International Convention, Montreal, March.

Lovenduski, J. and Norris, P. (eds) (1993) *Gender and Party Politics*, Thousand Oaks: Sage.

Lovenduski, J. and Randall, V. (1993) *Contemporary Feminist politics: Women and Power in Britain*, Oxford: Oxford University Press.

Lowe-Morna, C. (2003) 'Beyond Numbers: Quotas in Practice', in International IDEA *The Implementation of Quotas: African Experiences*, Quota Workshop Report Series no. 3, Stockholm: International IDEA, pp. 114–19.

Marques-Pereira, B. and Nolasco, P. (eds) (2000) *La représentation politique des femmes en Amérique latine*, Bruxelles: GELA-IS/L'Harmattan.

Matland, R.E. (1998) 'Women's Representation in National Legislatures: Developed and Developing Countries', *Legislative Studies Quarterly*, 23, 1: 109–25.

Matland, R.E. and Montgomery, K.A. (eds) (2003) *Women's access to political power in post-communist Europe*, New York: Oxford University Press.

Matland, R. and Studlar, D.T. (1996) 'The Contagion of Women Candidates in Single-Member District and Proportional Representation Electoral Systems: Canada and Norway', *The Journal of Politics*, 58, 3: 707–33.

Nelson, B.J. and Chowdhhury, N. (eds) (1994) *Women and Politics Worldwide*, New Haven & London: Yale University Press.

Norris, P. (2004) *Electoral Engineering. Voting Rules and Political Behaviour*, Cambridge: Cambridge University Press.

Norris, P. and Lovenduski, J. (1995) *Political Recruitment. Gender, Race and Class in the British Parliament*, Cambridge: Cambridge University Press.

Parpart, J., Rai, S. and Staudt, K. (eds) (2002) *Rethinking Empowerment: gender and development in a global/local world*, London: Routledge.

Phillips, A. (1995) *The Politics of Presence: The Political Representation of Gender, Ethnicity and Race*, Oxford: Oxford University Press.

Pollack, M.A. and Hafner-Burton, E. (2000) 'Mainstreaming Gender in the European Union', *Journal of European Policy*, 7, 3: 432–56.

Rai, S.M. (ed.) (2003) *Mainstreaming gender, democratizing the state? Institutionel mechanisms for the advancement of women*, Manchester, NY: Manchester University Press.

Sainsbury, D. (1993) 'The Politics of Increased Women's Representation: The Swedish Case', in J. Lovenduski and P. Norris (eds) *Gender and Party Politics*, Thousand Oaks: Sage, pp. 263–90.

Sawer, M. (2000) 'Parliamentary Representation of Women: From Discourses of Justice to Strategies of Accountability', *International Political Science Review*, 21, 4: 361–80.

Skjeie, H. (1992) *Den politiske betydningen av kjønn: En studie av norsk topp-politikk*, Oslo: Institute for Social Research.

Skjeie, H. and Teigen, M. (2003) *Menn imellom. Mannsdominans og likestillingspolitikk*, Oslo: Gyldendal Akademisk.

Smidt, G. 'The Implementation of Gender Quotas in Peru: Legal Reform, Discourses, and Impacts', paper presented at the Regional Workshop on The Implementation of Quotas: Latin American Experience, International IDEA, Lima, February 2003.

Stetson, D.M. and Mazur, A. (eds) (1995) *Comparative State Feminism*, Thousand Oaks/London/New Delhi: Sage.

Stockholm University (2002-) *The Research Program on Gender Quotas*. Working Paper Series, Stockholm University: Department of Political Science. Online. Available at: www.statsvet.su.se/quotas.

Teigen, M. (2000) 'The Affirmative Action Controversy', *NORA – Nordic Journal of Women's Studies*, 8, 2: 63–77.

United Nations (UN) (1979) 'Convention on the Elimination of All Forms of Discrimination Against Women', *UN Treaty Series*, 1249: 13.

United Nations Commission on the Status of Women (1995) 'Monitoring the Implementation of the Nairobi Forward-looking Strategies for the Advancement of Women', E/CN.6/1995/3/Add.6. Online. Available at: http://www.un.org/documents/ecosoc/cn6/1995/ecn61995-3add6.htm (accessed 21 February 2005).

United Nations Development Program (UNDP) (2003) *Arab Human Development Report 2003*, New York: UNDP.

United Nations Fourth World Conference on Women (FWCW) (1995) 'Beijing Declaration and Platform for Action', 15 September. Online. Available at: http://www.unesco.org/education/information/nfsunesco/pdf/BEIJIN_E.PDF (accessed 17 February 2005).

Women's Environment & Development Organization (WeDo) (2005) '50/50 Campaign. Get the Balance Right!'. Online. Available at: http://www.wedo.org/campaigns.aspx?mode=5050main (accessed 18 February 2005).

Wängnerud, L. (2000) 'Representing Women', in P. Esaiasson and K. Heidar (eds) *Beyond Westminster and Congress. The Nordic Experience*, Columbus: Ohio State University Press, pp. 132–54.

Young, I.M. (1997) 'Unruly Categories: A Critique of Nancy Fraser's Dual Systems Theory', *New Left Review*, 222: 147–60.

2 Arguing for and against quotas
Theoretical issues

Carol Bacchi

Debates about electoral quotas for women can be acrimonious. Not all women support them; nor do all feminists. This is the case in both older and newer democracies. At stake in these debates are the meanings of some key concepts in political analysis – equality, representation, citizenship and rights. In the first three sections of this chapter, I elaborate the ways in which these concepts relate to the quota issue, the bases of disagreements, and theoretical developments that attempt to shift the issue past some theoretical sticking points. In particular I draw attention to interventions that suggest the importance of challenging dominant norms in the concepts under consideration. In the last section on gender, I suggest that mounting these challenges reduces concerns that quotas rely upon a homogeneous category 'women', which tends to downplay the significance of the diversity of women's experiences.

Context is clearly crucial when reflecting on these issues. It is impossible, for example, to talk about notions of citizenship without considering country-specific institutions and particular political situations. Points will be raised drawing attention to exactly this dimension of the problem. At the same time, one is struck by the ways in which debates on these issues travel across borders, often employing common terms of reference.

Equality

Electoral quotas for women are a form of affirmative action, aimed at increasing women's representation in elected legislative bodies. Other kinds of reforms with the same ultimate goal are sometimes advanced. Some place their hope in the form of electoral system. It has been pointed out, for example, that proportional representation has a better track record than simple majority systems in getting women elected (Rule and Zimmerman 1994; Squires 1996: 86; Matland 1998). More commonly, there is support for a range of equal opportunity measures, including reforms such as skills training for women, financial aid, and forms of 'caring' leave, such as maternity leave (Norris 2003: 3). By way of contrast affirmative action measures are described as aiming at equality of result, rather than equality of opportunity. That is, they consist of measures designed to *guarantee* an increased representation of women.

The idea of guaranteeing selection of women representatives has produced a good deal of controversy in countries like the United States and Britain, countries overtly committed to equal opportunity, and in many European countries (Klausen and Maier 2001). Affirmative action and hence electoral quotas are described as bypassing competitive processes and hence as ignoring the merit principle which, it is argued, ensures that the best person will be selected for the job. This form of argument against electoral quotas for women appears in many different contexts (Htun and Jones 2002: 35; Rai 2002: 141).

Some theorists make the case that electoral quotas are more easily defended than employment quotas, since the issue of political representation makes a crucial distinction (Bacchi 1996: 15). The argument is that quotas in political representation are more clearly justifiable than quotas in numbers of lawyers or university professors, for example, because government should be tied to the people to some degree. There are links here with arguments about the character of representation in democracies, addressed in the next section. Despite this claim, the same types of arguments raised against labour-market affirmative action tend to get raised against electoral quotas – for example, that women lack the appropriate qualifications or that a better-qualified man will lose out in order to meet a quota for women. Electoral quotas for women, in this argument, become a form of discrimination against men.

A case in point is the challenge in Britain to the implementation of All Women Shortlists, introduced by the Labour Party in 1993, and discussed in greater detail in a later chapter (see Krook, Lovenduski and Squires). In the 1996 decision overturning this policy, the courts ruled that:

> Although a Member of Parliament is an office holder, s.13 [of the Sex Discrimination Act 1975] is not restricted to discrimination in employment. Section 13 was widely drafted to cover all kinds of professions, vocations, occupations and trades in which persons may engage, whether paid or unpaid, and whether or not they be 'employment' as defined in s.82 (for example doctors, lawyers and judges) including thereby persons who hold public office. (Jepson and Dyas-Elliott [applicants] v. The Labour Party and others [respondents] [1996] IRLR 119).

As to whether or not there were grounds under the EEC Equal Treatment Directive (76/207: Art. 2(4)) for 'positive discrimination', the courts followed the lead of Kalanke v Freie Hansestadt Bremen (Case C-450/93 [1995] ECR I-3051) and declared that 'That Article cannot have intended a total block on one sex'.

A key concept in this debate is merit. Those opposed to quotas for women argue that positions should be filled on merit and that this is easily measured. Those in favour of quotas argue either that existing systems are unfair in the ways they assess women – that they discriminate and ignore women's merit – or that the understanding of merit is too narrow. It is sometimes claimed that gender constitutes a form of merit since political systems ought to reflect the views of the whole population. Many forms of electoral quota, of course, retain aspects of the merit principle. Even the so-called zipper system, where men and women are listed alternately in party lists, incorporates a test of merit in the first round (Teigen 2000: 73).

The debate about merit ties into understandings of discrimination. Those opposed to quotas argue that all that is needed for an equal society is equal treatment of different people, a classical liberal position. The goal here is a gender-blind (and race-blind) polity.[1] Discrimination is understood as different treatment of equals, and affirmative action is represented as a form of discrimination, albeit positive discrimination. As a consequence, in countries grounded in equal opportunity premises, affirmative action proposals tend to be located as exemptions within anti-discrimination statutes (Bacchi 1999: 99).

Locating affirmative action as an exemption within anti-discrimination law has a number of effects. First, as exemptions, affirmative action reforms are consistently subject to contestation and the threat of removal. In addition, arguments which defend the need to use the exemption commonly take the form that affirmative action is an exceptional intervention, a form of 'special treatment' or 'specific advantage', to compensate for past or present discrimination. In other work (Bacchi 2004) I have described the dominance of this understanding, both among opponents and supporters, that affirmative action is a form of 'preferential treatment' for women and other outgroups.

Characterizing affirmative action as 'preferential treatment' or 'special help' for those described as 'disadvantaged' tends to stigmatize affirmative action targets, leading some to disassociate from the reform, and as a result undermining the effectiveness of the reform. In response some feminists question the usefulness of affirmative action as a reform mechanism. For example, Nancy Fraser (1997: 115) argues that the reform is limited in its potential since it marks 'the most disadvantaged class as inherently deficient, insatiable, as needing more and more'.

One response to this dilemma is to challenge the dominant representation of affirmative action as 'special help' or 'preferential treatment'. To accomplish this it is necessary to point out that locating affirmative action as an exemption within anti-discrimination law represents the 'problem' in limited ways (Bacchi 1999: Chapter 5). It suggests that social rules are generally fair but that some people face prejudicial attitudes and/or incidental blockages (barriers) that hold them back. In this understanding, discrimination is an aberration in a generally fairly functioning society. By way of contrast it is possible to highlight the numerous levels at which 'social differentials pervade law' (Black 1989). With this understanding of the problem, affirmative action is not 'special help' for outgroups but an attempt to redress entrenched privilege (see Eveline 1994). Hence, affirmative action measures are not discrimination, positive or otherwise, or 'preferential treatment', but attempts to do justice. At a recent expert meeting organized to develop building blocks for a General Recommendation on Article 4(1) of the CEDAW Convention, the Rapporteur, Rikki Holtmaat (2003: 14) attempted to alter the terms of the debate around affirmative action with exactly this form of intervention:

> The drafters must carefully choose their words to overcome the dominant view of 'positive action' or 'affirmative action' measures as special favours or preferential treatment of women, or which otherwise portray women as the problem and as the ones needing to change. To avoid these understandings the term disadvantage should be used judiciously in the GR [General Recommendation]. More accurate language, e.g. 'underrepresented' or 'excluded' ought to be used where appropriate. The GR should clearly reflect that the central problem is the existing privilege of men, rather than the 'disadvantage' (too often constructed as the 'impairment') of women.

Along related lines Mari Teigen (2000) usefully argues that it is important to reframe affirmative action so that it is removed from the discrimination/anti-discrimination controversy. She offers three strategies to accomplish this goal: first, a shift in focus from non-discrimination to a 'right to be treated as an equal'; second, stressing the special contribution of women in male-dominated fields, transferring the focus from discrimination against women to the benefits of including women; third, transferring the 'burden of proof' from those advocating equality to those defending the status quo. The last of these is a version of the shift outlined above from a focus on women needing 'help' to a focus on the generally unfair character of social rules. In Teigen's view the question should not be 'why women?' but 'why not women?', articulating a version of what Anne Phillips (1995: 81) calls a negative justice argument.

Each of these strategies is relevant to debates about electoral quotas for women. The suggestion that women be treated as equal individuals could prove useful to some women. The second argument, that women will bring specific virtues, values and experience to politics, is a commonplace defence of electoral quotas in many settings, and will be addressed more fully in the last section on gender. The third suggestion that current political systems are unjust usefully shifts the focus from women to the inadequacies of current electoral systems. This theme is pursed in the next two sections.

Representation

Above we saw that some people argue that gender can be considered a form of merit on the grounds that legislatures should reflect the views of the whole population. This is the same argument mounted to suggest that electoral quotas are more defensible than labour-market quotas. This argument rests upon a conviction that women's views are currently not adequately represented in existing democracies. It is certainly clear that there is no necessary correlation between length of experience of democracy and numbers of women in political office. Anne Marie Goetz (2003: 49) argues on these grounds that established democracies are facing not simply a 'deficit', but that they are built upon deeply gendered conditions for political participation.

To evaluate the claim that there is a need for more women in political office, it is useful to reflect upon different understandings of representation. Hannah Pitkin (1967) distinguished between an understanding of representation as 'acting on behalf of' and an understanding of representation as 'standing in for'. In the first model the elected representative is a trustee, authorized to use her judgement when acting on behalf of electors; in the second she is a delegate, strictly accountable to those who elect her.

Anne Phillips (1995: 28) notes that, if there were binding mandates, as appears to be assumed in the 'delegate' model, it would not matter so much who our representatives are, because we could count on them to represent our views. However, as she points out, in contemporary electoral politics, there are no binding mandates, and representatives exercise judgement. The question then becomes – what are the grounds for expecting elected representatives to reflect women's views and address their needs?

Phillips (1995) points out that generally in established democracies it is assumed that elected representatives express the full variety of opinions of their electors and hence that women's views are automatically included. She calls this model a 'politics of ideas'. Elected representatives are expected to display a degree of impartiality because of their distance from the particular commitments of any specific group. Members of underrepresented groups have challenged this position. They make the argument that the majority of elected representatives represent the views of the select portion of the population from which they come, commonly middle-class men. This provides the grounds for defending a 'politics of presence', which holds that political representatives should display the characteristics (sex, 'race', etc.) of members of underrepresented groups in order to counter the partiality of those who currently dominate elected bodies. Commonly, quotas are aligned with a politics of presence.

Recent developments in democratic theory, arguing for deliberative democratic models to replace aggregative models, add nuance to this claim. Aggregative models, it is suggested, underpin both the trustee and delegate conceptions of elected representatives. In both cases electors are assumed to hold pre-formed interests which are then either taken on board by delegates or which provide the backdrop to trustees' behaviours. By way of contrast, supporters of deliberative democracy conceptualize political representation as the negotiation of 'problems, conflicts and claims of need or interest' (Young 2000: 22), not as the representation of pre-formed interests.

Envisioning democracy as 'collective problem-solving' in this way reopens debates about meanings of representation. Representation is reconceptualized as a process over space and time, with representatives moving between authorization and accountability. This increases the importance of representatives' descriptive characteristics. According to Iris Marion Young, in order for deliberative models to win legitimacy, they require 'the expression and criticism of the diverse opinions of all the members of society' (Young 2000: 6). Anne Phillips (2001: 29) agrees: 'If there were hardly any women involved in the discussion . . . most deliberative democrats would have to distrust the results'.

There is therefore a space within the deliberative tradition to demand full representation (Gargarella 1998), though it is unclear if this position necessarily challenges a 'politics of ideas'. Many in the deliberative tradition, for example, invest their hope in rational communication leading to the development of a 'common good'. They are critical of any suggestion that politics is about self-interest or group interest, and oppose quotas on the grounds that they reflect group interests. In this view quotas promote factionalism and undermine dispassionate deliberation.

There are two kinds of response to this argument. The commitment to rational communication, it can be argued, shows a reliance on the abstract, disembodied individuals of liberal theory, ignoring the embodiedness and embeddedness of both electors and their representatives (Cohen 1998; Beasley and Bacchi 2000). Along related lines it can be argued that group-based claims are not just assertions of 'self-regarding interest' or claims to identity, but reflect the 'experiences of people located in structurally or culturally differentiated social groups' (Young 2000: 7). In addition, it is possible to challenge the supposed neutrality of a 'common good' and hence to contest the implication that those demanding group forms of representation are destabilizers of an assumed harmony. Susan Bickford (1996: 104) usefully points out how this argument ignores the group-status of dominant groups:

> Groups that are marked out as groups are seen as self-interested in pursuing group-specific claims, whereas dominant groups, precisely because they are not marked out as groups, can speak their own claims in the language of impartiality and 'the common good'.

Going further, Iris Marion Young (2000: 7) makes the case that the 'difference' of underrepresented groups represents a resource for, rather than a threat to, 'community'. In her view democracies should encourage dissensus over consensus, and should create the space for 'agonistic' deliberation over competing claims.

As in the challenge to an understanding of discrimination as an aberration in a fairly functioning work, an argument for quotas along these lines points to the elitist character of existing electoral systems, where those who command authority on the basis of conventional social values will be the ones who will be elected (see Manin 1997). It claims that representatives should be people 'like us', supporting a kinds of grassroots democracy that aims at reducing the degree of political mediation (Gidengil 1996: 25). Roberto Gargarella (1998: 274) makes this point forcefully: 'We need to know who deliberates, and we should be worried if most people are kept at the margins of political deliberation'.

There is certainly evidence that supporters of quotas are increasingly employing this form of argument, criticizing existing democracies. In 1998 a bureau meeting of Socialist International Women declared that 'A true democracy cannot and does not exclude women' (Socialist International Women 1998). A 2001 Asia-Pacific forum on gender balance in political representation echoed this comment: 'The legitimacy of a democratic, representative system is open to challenge and question when half of the electorate is not equally represented' (Asia Pacific Workshop 2001: 3). A Brazilian congresswoman Marta Suplicy declared: 'In Brazil today, [the quota] is more than a new instrument in women's struggle for equality and the construction of a true democracy, it is an imperative of justice' (cited in Htun and Jones 2002: 34). In these accounts political participation is defended as a human right.

However, pointing out that women are underrepresented and that this matters, leaves out of consideration a range of crucial issues about democratic processes. For example, just as it is important to reflect on the overrepresentation of middle-class men in electoral positions, so it is crucial to consider which women manage to gain political office. Hoskyns and Rai (1998), for example, found in their survey of women Parliamentarians in India and the European Union that the vast majority is middle class, do not have families and were not connected to the women's movement. They take this as evidence of the 'globalization of elite politics'.

On a related issue Goetz and Hassim (2003: 5–6) consider to what extent increasing the numbers of women in elected legislatures will help to produce gender-sensitive policies and better accountability to women. Their goal is to identify the conditions required to move beyond a simply numerical or 'descriptive' representation to a more substantive one.[2] To this end they identify three sets of inter-related conditions necessary to encourage and allow women in elected office to advocate a gender equity agenda in policy debates: (1) the nature of civil society and the place and power of the gender equity lobby in civil society; (2) the nature of the political system (the depth of procedural and substantive democracy) and the organization of political competition (for example the number and nature of parties); and (3) the nature and power of the state (for example whether it is a developmental state; whether or not there is decentralization). They offer the example of Uganda to illustrate the limitations of quotas in specific contexts, pointing out how new seats were created for women, removing them from normal competition for ward councillor seats, and making them 'seem lesser politicians'. They insist that it is important to assess institutional changes to increase numbers of women in politics in terms of whether they are 'simply a legitimation exercise for the state, enabling officials to listen to previously excluded groups but with no obligation to act upon what they hear'.[3] These issues are also crucially important in parts of Latin America where there are concerns that 'collaboration with flawed democracies might serve to arrest rather than to advance more general democratic reform' (Molyneux and Craske 2002: 12).

Because of the need for facilitating conditions to produce effective participation, some feminist theorists fear that quotas represent a shift in feminist politics towards a more moderate, less confrontational mode, focusing simply on inclusion rather than substantive change. They ask: will women simply be incorporated? Will they be turned into 'political men'? (Das 1998; Lovenduski and Stephenson 1999: 10; Siim 2000: 41). These are familiar concerns. The issue of co-option and the limits of procedural reforms have been fraught issues for feminists since at least the 1970s. Some also draw attention to the limited scope of quota proposals, which tend to target national legislatures, in an 'increasingly global and interdependent' world (Squires 1996: 87; Molyneux and Craske 2002: 6). Molyneux and Craske (2002: 7), for example, insist that the political agendas of the women's movement 'cannot ignore the painful reality of deepening socioeconomic inequalities and the limited scope offered for addressing them by neoliberal policies'. Some insist that, for meaningful change to occur, there is a need for quotas for women in a range of sites, including the judiciary, the media, employer associations and corporate boards (Young 2000: 152–3).

These analyses reflect understandable concerns that a focus on electoral quotas, or rather on electoral quotas alone, constructs the problem in ways that are limited. At the same time there is a good deal of support for the claim that raising women's representation is a necessary, if not a sufficient, reform. Goetz and Hassim (2003: 5) are clear that in their view 'descriptive representation may be a necessary first step to the institutional representation that is required if "substantive" representation is to be achieved'. Susan Bickford (1999: 92) agrees that 'electoral arrangements should be one element of a radical democratic pluralist politics'. To produce effective participation, it is argued, other changes are needed.

Shireen Hassim (2003: 83–4) identifies the need for two developments – 'a broadening of democratic commitment in the political system as a whole and the strengthening of the women's movement outside the state' – establishing links to the next two sections.

Citizenship and rights

A key argument used by defenders of quotas is that women are entitled to equal citizenship and equal rights. This is becoming a popular argument in a number of places, indicated in the endorsement above by the 2001 Asia Pacific Forum that political participation is a human right. In new democracies this argument has considerable purchase with governments keen to be recognized as 'modern' and legitimate.

There are, however, long-standing debates in Western liberal democracies, and more recent debates in newer democracies, about the content both of citizenship and of rights. Both these concepts have proved problematic for women making claims to inclusion. In a later chapter Krook, Lovenduski and Squires illustrate that different conceptions of citizenship create different kinds of opening for quota demands. For example, they show that the consociational model in Belgium, where group representation is well established, provided conditions conducive to quotas for women (see also Meier 2000; Diaz 2002). This highlights the importance of context in relationship to the issue of citizenship. In this section I start from this insight to reflect upon the connection between quotas and current debates on the meaning of citizenship in feminist theory. More specifically I want to reflect upon how the issue of quotas produces new and useful perspectives on citizenship and rights, moving feminists past some intractable dilemmas.

In Western feminist theory, Carole Pateman (1989) was among the first to draw attention to the male norm operating within conceptions of citizenship. She pointed out that it was no coincidence that women had a long, hard battle to win voting rights. This was because political participation was tied to expectations about citizenship behaviours conventionally preformed by men. The emphasis was upon the role of citizens as defenders of the realm and on the contribution of labour defined as 'productive'. Productive labour in this understanding consists of employment in paid labour and ignores all the useful things we do that are unpaid (see Narayan 1997). In particular it ignores the operation of the sexual division of labour that leaves women responsible for the care of children and other 'citizens', often including men.

This starting point in how citizenship has been defined has created a dilemma for feminists trying to argue for equal citizenship status for women. Ruth Lister (2000: 35) asks, can 'a concept originally predicated on the very exclusion of women' be 'reformulated so as satisfactorily to include (and not simply add) them (on)'? And can it, in so doing 'give full recognition to the different and shifting identities that women simultaneously hold'? A difficulty here is that feminist attempts to demand inclusion are often constrained by context to operate within the original terms of debate. The frameworks shaping feminist citizenship theory frequently include at their heart debates about: women's public activities versus their 'private' lives; women's status relative to men's – should they press for 'equality' or demand recognition of their 'difference'? – should they press for a single standard of 'gender-neutral' citizenship or demand a gender-differentiated model? The difficulty for women in the citizenship debate is that in each instance one of these poles is established as the norm, compelling them either to aspire to it or to set themselves apart as 'different'. From the time of the suffrage movement there have been debates within the women's movement over whether women should press for 'equality' with men or try to have their 'difference' revalued upwards (Bacchi 1990). In a model that treats 'difference' as lesser, as incidental, these options are fraught

For example, a recurring issue for women making claims to full and equal citizenship has been whether to insist that women's unpaid domestic contribution be valued, or to demand that women be given access to paid labour (Lister 2000: 49). At times the American women's movement has divided sharply over this issue. One strategy developed in the United States and in some other Western liberal democracies has been to press for recognition of something called 'maternal citizenship'. This has meant demanding that women's maternal contributions be valued equally with conventional forms of citizenship contribution, military service and paid employment. Other feminists have noted that any concessions to maternal feminism have been inadequate, inevitably produce women as second-class citizens, and have serious repercussions for women who do not fit the assumed heterosexual and 'paired' model behind this claim (Lister 2000: 47).

To move past the equal/different, domestic contributions/paid labour dilemmas it is useful to put in question the original term, the starting point for the comparison. As in the cases of discrimination and representation discussed above, it is possible to challenge the established norms of citizenship participation as public and as necessarily involved in paid labour. This is not an easy challenge to mount, particularly in the current political climate where economic contribution is privileged, and where in many settings a distinction is being inscribed between 'passive' and 'active' citizenship. For example, in the United States, there are two broad contemporary approaches to citizenship, a liberal rights model that sees political, civil and some social rights as due to citizens by their very status as citizens (characterized by critics as 'passive'), and a civic republican model that ties these rights to performance of forms of citizenship activity. The latter participation model is particularly popular there at the moment, explaining in part the emphasis in American feminist theorizing on women's public participation over their private, domestic activities (see Dietz 1985).

Elsewhere strategies for recognizing women's citizenship take different forms. For example, some Western European feminists contrast welfare regimes, using as their chief point of differentiation whether or not a male breadwinner model of social organization is in place (Orloff 1993). Some Scandinavian feminists (Hernes 1987; Siim 1990) insist that 'an adequate account of contemporary citizenship' must grasp 'the interplay between material rights, multi-level participation, and political identities' (Lister 2000: 40). In Eastern Europe, where the dismantling of communism has meant the reduction of social rights and increasing reliance on family, women are trying to establish a claim for recognition in the domestic sphere (Havelkova 2000). In Latin America, Virginia Vargas (2002: 215), a prominent feminist activist, argues that '[t]hose who campaign for political rights while neglecting or ignoring social or cultural rights ... sustain and legitimize the exclusionary character of existing democracies and formulations of citizenship'.

These examples illustrate the role of context in shaping citizenship demands. Some authors make the case that illustrating this very point can assist in challenging the equal/different, public/private, active/passive dichotomies structuring these debates (Scott 1988; Bacchi 1990). Pateman (1989: 204), for example, insists that 'the opposition between men's independence and women's dependence has to be broken down, and a new understanding and practice of citizenship developed'. Along similar lines Bettina Cass (1994: 114) maintains that there is a need to problematize 'men's independence, with the negation of welfare that it implies and which is its consequence'. Ruth Lister (2000: 49) concludes that the objective should be refusing to try 'to shape women to accommodate the practice of citizenship as it traditionally has been defined', reiterating the theme in this chapter of a strategic challenging of entrenched norms in dominant concepts and practices. A question here is – to what extent do electoral quotas fit rather than challenge dominant conceptions of citizenship?

Electoral quotas for women clearly involve a demand for women's increased participation in public-sphere activities. This, of course, explains in part the ambivalence of many Eastern European women about this strategy (see Havelkova 2000). However, in at least two ways quotas cut across the dichotomies that have produced difficulties for women's citizenship claims. First, they straddle the public/private divide by insisting that women, because they are women, deserve representation; second, they draw attention to the importance of having a voice in defining the nature of citizenship rights and responsibilities.

The suggestion that quotas cut across public/private boundaries rests upon a challenge to the mind/body dichotomy implicit in the 'politics of ideas'. Feminists have pointed out that numbers of people are treated as second-class citizens or are denied citizenship status altogether precisely because of their bodies. The ways in which the disabled and members of different 'races' have been treated in terms of citizenship in many places at different times supports this contention. It follows that bodies matter to citizenship (Beasley and Bacchi 2000). Because quotas rely at some level upon the contention that embodied experience requires representation, they challenge the disembodied model that has dominated Western liberal thought. In this way a 'politics of presence' compels a rethinking of conventional citizenship norms.

This is not to deny the intense contestation accompanying this claim. Indeed, feminist citizenship debates reveal the essentially contested nature of the key terms of reference around citizenship and rights (Charlesworth and Chinkin 2000: Chapter 7; Lister 2000: 44). Vargas (2002: 204), for example, emphasizes the 'shifting nature' of rights and the need for feminists to develop and defend a concept of citizenship that incorporates a social dimension (economic rights) and sexual rights. It can be argued that, in order for understandings of citizenship to be developed in these ways, women need to be present where contestation over political meaning takes place. This kind of argument can provide a rationale for quotas.[4]

Arguing for quotas in this way does not mean denying the context-specific conditions that may well mean that women in some situations will see no immediate urgency for them. Nor does it mean that demands for quotas are the end-point of claims for citizenship rights. As argued in the previous section, analysis then turns to the necessary conditions for producing effective participation. Susan Bickford (1999: 106) makes the point that 'the institutional contexts in which citizenship are performed are themselves (partially) formative of citizen identity'. This insight shifts the focus to the adequacy/inadequacy of those institutions. New questions emerge: are existing political institutions producing/enabling adequate forms of citizenship? Supporters of quotas for women contend that they are inadequate if they largely exclude women from crucial negotiations over meanings of citizenship and over desirable institutional arrangements for social life.

Given the identified significance of the 'power to define' associated with these debates, supporters of quotas stress the importance of making women's voices a part of democratic deliberation. With all this there remain important concerns, raised earlier, about which women's voices will be heard and whether or not it is possible to think about women as a constituency (Goetz and Hassim 2003: 6), an issue addressed in the next section.

Gender

The argument that numbers of women are needed to represent women is hotly contested. The classical liberal view, captured in the notion of a politics of ideas, is that women are already represented. Those who defend quotas offer several different rationales for contending that women require greater representation. Often the suggestion is that women have common interests, based on historical disadvantage and the 'characteristics of gender relations' (Goetz 2003: 38). Some argue that women share common concerns, because of the kinds of social roles they tend to fill, with an emphasis on their domestic and child-rearing responsibilities (Htun and Jones 2002: 35). At times there is a more utilitarian argument that, because of common experiences, women will bring something positive to politics, a love of peace for example or an awareness of the importance of caring activities (Teigen 2000: 73).[5] A related argument is that because women have not been associated with conventional political systems they may well have 'unrealized potential for creating change' and may, to an extent, be less corrupt than men (Dahlerup 2001: 105; Htun and Jones 2002: 51; Rai 2002: 144). Finally, a less common argument, but one that shares a conviction that women constitute a collective, is that there is a need for women role models.

These arguments have come under increasing scrutiny in some recent feminist theory that expresses concerns about the essentialist assumptions that appear to underpin this understanding of 'woman'. Over the past 20 years feminist theory in Western countries and in many other parts of the world has paid increasing attention to 'differences among women' (Siim 1993: 30; Bacchi 1996: 9; Rai 2002: 135). This trend has been reinforced by developments in feminist post-structuralist theory. Questions are raised about the viability and usefulness of reform strategies that, in this interpretation, tend to accentuate and freeze existing, constructed identity groups, instead of looking for ways to cut across these identities (Butler 1990). A case is made that progressive politics requires challenging and working across 'fabricated identities' (Mouffe 1992; Fraser 1995, 1997).

Context is important here. In some settings making claims about women's specific contributions seems to be less politically contentious than in others. In many developing countries, for example, women appear to have a clear agenda, with a focus on cash crops and with education, child welfare and health, and violence against women as priorities. Pramila Dandravate, campaigning for quotas at the national level in India, describes 'a woman's perspective of development' as 'totally different from men'. To support her claim she refers to surveys which show 'that 100 per cent of a woman's income goes towards the welfare of the family while in the case of men a substantial proportion goes towards satisfying his own whims' (Nath 1996: 15). However, at the same time, the proposal in India for national quotas for women has foundered on demands that a sub-quota for 'untouchable women' be included in the legislation (see Narasimhan 2002; Rai 2002: 139).

In the West extended debates around the viability of a category 'women' have been prompted in part by attacks from several quarters on so-called 'identity politics', attacks targeting groups that mobilize around race/ethnicity, sexuality, disability, as well as 'women'. I have already mentioned that some deliberative democrats argue that identity-based 'interests' threaten to undermine the 'common good'. Many social conservatives share this view and label identity groups 'special interests'. Some on the left, such as Nancy Fraser (1995), have also expressed concern that an emphasis on identity (or 'recognition') undermines the goal of universal levelling (or 'redistribution'). In this view (political) representation 'would be a strategy of recognition rather than redistribution, thus limiting its transformative potential' (Rai 2002: 137).

In contrast Iris Marion Young challenges the constructed dichotomy between recognition and redistribution, insisting that 'for most social movements, what Fraser calls "recognition" is a means to the economic and social equality and freedom that she brings under the category of redistribution' (Young 1997: 152; see also Rai 2002: 137).[6] Using Sartre's conception of a 'series', Young argues that 'membership in the group called "women" is the product of a loose combination of different structural factors' that produce common 'perspectives' (Young 2002: 421; see also Young 1994, 2000; Dhanda 1998–9). Perspectives, says Young, are looser than interests. They denote a way of regarding situations, moving us past the problem of 'attributing to all members of those groups common opinions or interests'. This argument underpins her insistence that women's voices and the voices of other outgroups need to be included in deliberative proceedings (Young 2000: 133, 8).

According to Susan Bickford (1999: 104), Young's notion of seriality provides a basis for arguing for quotas: 'Instituting descriptive representation can be seen as an attempt to foster the articulation of diverse perspectives from members of the series'.[7] Bickford emphasizes the role of political institutions in shaping identities. In this understanding identities are not essences; they are partly the cultural products of institutional practices (see also Rose 1999). We exist as political beings, Bickford argues, in a world that has made our social identities matter. Hence, it stands to reason that we need to resist 'in terms of the identity under attack' (Bickford 1996: 133).

Anne Phillips (1995: 68, 168) is unwilling to surrender the notion of 'interests'. In her view, recognizing that women have diverse interests does not refute the claim that 'interests are gendered'. Still, she shares the conviction that gender quotas do not presume any unified 'women's position': 'indeed, the shift from a more token representation of women opens up space for a wide variety of female politicians'. Defenders of French parity offer a similar rebuttal to the charge of essentialism – that the full range of opinions among women will gain representation when women make up 50 per cent of representatives (Teigen 2000: 63; see also Gaspard 1998). This would be so, of course, only if that 50 per cent consisted of women from a wide variety of class, ethnic/racial and family backgrounds, which on existing evidence is not yet occurring (Hoskyns and Rai 1998; Rai 2002).

Still, the shift to looser descriptors of group membership (series) reduces the tendency to make claims on the basis of group membership, claims about what 'women' are like or what they will do. Rather, as in challenges to dominant understandings of discrimination and citizenship traced earlier in the paper, the focus of attack is shifted from 'women' to the structural inequalities affecting members of particular groups, the material structures shaping them as a series. Context, however, will affect the particular shape of any argument. For example, Shirin Rai (2002: 144) makes the case that in India 'women's groups demanding quotas for women should have taken into account the long-standing caste-based quotas'. As Shireen Hassim (2003: 104) explains, the complexities in women's lives necessitate conducting politics 'simultaneously at two levels' – 'At an external level of politics, a narrow terrain of common purpose is mapped out, articulated and defended, while at an internal level there is vigorous contestation over specific policies and party political manifestos'. This 'dual politics' reflects the need 'to present the illusion of a united constituency' all the while articulating 'the diverse interests of women arising from the intersection of race, class and gender inequalities'.

Conclusion

Electoral quotas for women are being introduced in many countries, countries with vastly different experiences of democracy and feminist mobilization. The purpose of this chapter has been to elaborate some of the key debates that surface over quota proposals and to outline forms of argument that attempt to move these debates forward. A common theme has been the increasing tendency to direct attention away from rationales that focus on women's 'differences' to those that highlight the existence of gendered norms in key political concepts including equality/ discrimination, representation and citizenship/rights.

In equality debates, Rikki Holtmaat (2003) suggests shifting the focus from women's disadvantage to men's privilege (see also Eveline 1994). In debates about forms of democracy Young (2000) and Bickford (1996) insist that 'true' democracies need to create space for the voices of out-groups. Other feminist theorists (Pateman 1989; Cass 1994; Lister 2000) draw attention to the male norm operating in dominant understandings of citizenship and rights, shifting attention from women's dependence to men's independence and questioning men's lack of participation in care-giving activities. Context will affect the possibility of mounting these challenges. In addition, to capture the full diversity of women's lives, these theoretical interventions must attend to the ways in which existing norms are 'classed', 'raced', 'sexualized' and formed around assumptions of physical 'normalcy'. With this critical perspective, 'the "minimal" demand for a numerical increase in women's representation can become the grounds upon which a deeper struggle may be fought' (Hassim 2003: 104).

Notes

1 Arguments against affirmative action for women share many of the characteristics of arguments against affirmative action for other outgroups, including for example Blacks in the United States.
2 Goetz and Hassim (2003: 5) are careful to qualify the distinction between 'descriptive' and 'substantive' representation. They note that the distinction may overstate the role of political agency, and neglects the way in which 'descriptive' representation may be 'a necessary first step in institutional transformation'.
3 See Kawamara-Mishambi and Ovonji-Odida (2003) for a more positive account of developments in Uganda.
4 Here it is important to pay heed to Vargas's (2002. 209) concern that, in Latin America, 'feminist incursions into the sphere of formal politics privileged strategies that aimed at strengthening some of the political dimensions of citizenship, whereas little attention was paid to the contents of what was "under discussion"'.
5 These arguments were well rehearsed in campaigns for woman suffrage in a number of sites (see Bacchi 1983; Dahlerup 2001: 110).
6 In a 2003 interview, Nancy Fraser articulates a revised three-dimensional theory of justice including redistribution, recognition and representation. The latter, she argues, 'allows us to problematize governance structures and decision-making procedures', suggesting possible support for some forms of electoral quota (Fraser and Naples 2004: 9).
7 Young (2000: 149–50) prefers 'quotas for women in party lists' to reserved seats as a means of increasing representation of outgroups. She expresses concerns that the latter, as in the case of seats for Maoris in New Zealand, 'can tend to freeze both the identity of that group and its relation with other groups in the party'.

Bibliography

Asia Pacific Workshop in Gender Balance in Political Representation (2001) 'Women in Government – 50/50: Get the Balance Right!' Online. Available at: http://www.cld.org/ManilaConference.html (accessed 2 March 2004).
Bacchi, C. (1983) *Liberation Deferred? The Ideas of the English-Canadian Suffragists, 1877–1918*, reprinted in 1985, 1987, Toronto: University of Toronto Press.
—— (1990) *Same Difference: Feminism and Sexual Difference*, Sydney: Allen and Unwin.
—— (1996) *The Politics of Affirmative Action: 'Women', Equality and Category Politics*, London: Sage.
—— (1999) *Women, Politics and Policy: the construction of policy problems*, London: Sage.
—— (2004) 'Policy and Discourse: challenging the construction of affirmative action as preferential treatment', *Journal of European Public Policy*, 11, 2: 128–46.

Beasley, C. and Bacchi, C. (2000) 'Citizen Bodies: embodying citizens – a feminist analysis', *International Feminist Journal of Politics*, 2, 3: 337–58.

Bickford, S. (1996) *The Dissonance of Democracy: Listening, Conflict, and Citizenship*, Ithaca: Cornell University Press.

—— (1999) 'Reconfiguring Pluralism: Identity and Institutions in the Inegalitarian Polity', *American Journal of Political Science*, 43, 1: 86–108.

Black, D. (1989) *Sociological Justice*, New York: Oxford University Press.

Butler, J. (1990) *Gender Trouble*, New York: Routledge.

Cass, B. (1994) 'Citizenship, work and welfare: the dilemma for Australian women', *Social Politics: International Studies in Gender, State, and Society*, 1, 1: 106–24.

Charlesworth, H. and Chinkin, C. (2000) *The boundaries of international law: A feminist analysis*, Manchester: Manchester University Press.

Cohen, S. (1998) 'Body, Space and Presence: Women's Social Exclusion in the Politics of the European Union', *The European Journal of Women's Studies*, 5, 3–4: 367–80.

Dahlerup, D. (2001) 'Women in Political Decisionmaking: From Critical Mass to Critical Acts in Scandinavia', in I. Skjelsbaek and D. Smith (eds) *Gender, Peace and Conflict*, London: Sage, pp. 104–21.

Das, S. (1998) *The Times of India*, 22 July, p. 5.

Dhanda, M. (1998–9) 'Justifications for Gender Quotas in Legislative Bodies: A Consideration of Identity and Representation', *Women's Philosophy Review*, 20: 44–62.

Diaz, M.M. (2002) 'Do Quotas Matter? Positive Actions in the Belgian Parliament', *Res Publica*, 44, 1: 49–72.

Dietz, M. (1985) 'Citizenship with a Feminist Face: The problem with maternal thinking', *Political Theory*, 13, 1: 19–37.

EEC, *Equal Treatment Directive* (76/207: Article 2(4)).

Eveline, J. (1994) 'The Politics of Advantage', *Australian Feminist Studies*, Special Issue: *Women and Citizenship*, 19: 129–54.

Fraser, N. (1995) 'Recognition or Redistribution? Dilemmas of Justice in a "Post-Socialist" Age', *New Left Review*, 212: 68–93.

—— (1997) *Justice Interruptus*, New York: Routledge.

Fraser, N. and Naples, N. (2004) 'To interpret the world and to change it: an interview with Nancy Fraser', *Signs*, 29, 4: 1103–25.

Gargarella, R. (1998) 'Full Representation, Deliberation, and Impartiality', in J. Elster (ed.) *Deliberative Democracy*, Cambridge, UK: Cambridge University Press, pp. 260–76.

Gaspard, F. (1998) 'Parity: Why Not?', trans. by Jennifer Curtis Gage, *differences: A Journal of Feminist Cultural Studies*, 9, 2: 93–103.

Gidengil, E. (1996) 'Gender and Attitudes Toward Quotas for Women Candidates in Canada', *Women & Politics*, 16, 4: 21–44.

Goetz, A.M. (2003) 'Women's Political Effectiveness: A Conceptual Framework', in A.M. Goetz and S. Hassim (eds) *No Shortcuts to Power: African Women in Politics and Policy Making*, London: Zed Books, pp. 29–80.

Goetz, A.M. and Hassim, S. (2003) 'Introduction: Women in Power in Uganda and South Africa', in A.M. Goetz and S. Hassim (eds) *No Shortcuts to Power: African Women in Politics and Policy Making*, London: Zed Books, pp. 1–28.

Hassim, S. (2003) 'Representation, Participation and Democratic Effectiveness:

Feminist Challenges to Representative Democracy in South Africa', in A.M. Goetz and S. Hassim (eds) *No Shortcuts to Power: African Women in Politics and Policy Making*, London: Zed Books, pp. 81–109.

Havelkova, H. (2000) 'Abstract Citizenship? Women and Power in the Czech Republic', in B. Hobson (ed.) *Gender and Citizenship in Transition*, Houndmills: Macmillan, pp. 118–38.

Hernes, H. (1987) *Welfare State and Women Power*, Oslo: Norwegian University Press.

Holtmaat, R. (2003) 'Building Blocks for a General Recommendation on Article 4(1) of the CEDAW Convention', in I. Boerefinj, F. Coomans, J. Goldschmidt, R. Holtmaat and R. Wolleswinkel (eds) *Temporary Special Measures: Accelerating De Facto Equality of Women Under Article 4(1) UN Convention on the Elimination of All Forms of Discrimination Against Women*, Antwerpen: Intersentia, pp. 213–30.

Hoskyns, C. and Rai, S.M. (1998) 'Gender, Class and Representation: India and the European Union', *The European Journal of Women's Studies*, 5, 3–4: 345–66.

Htun, M.N. and Jones, M.P. (2002) 'Engendering the Right to Participate in Decision-making: Electoral Quotas and Women's Leadership in Latin America', in N. Craske and M. Molyneux (eds) *Gender and the Politics of Rights and Democracy in Latin America*, Houndmills: Palgrave, pp. 32–56.

Jepson and Dyas-Elliott [applicants] v The Labour Party and others [respondents] [1996] IRLR 119.

Kalanke v Freie Hansestadt Bremen (Case C-450/93 [1995] ECR I-3051).

Kawamara-Mishambi, S. and Ovonji-Odida, I. (2003) 'The "Lost Clause": The Campaign to Advance Women's Property Rights in the Uganda 1998 Land Act', in A.M. Goetz and S. Hassim (eds) *No Shortcuts to Power: African Women in Politics and Policy Making*, London: Zed Books, pp. 160–87.

Klausen, J. and Maier, C.S. (eds) (2001) *Has Liberalism Failed Women? Assuring Equal Representation in Europe and the U.S.*, New York: Palgrave.

Lister, R. (2000) 'Dilemmas in Engendering Citizenship', in B. Hobson (ed.) *Gender and Citizenship in Transition*, Houndmills: Macmillan, pp. 33–76.

Lovenduski, J. and Stephenson, S. (1999) *Women in decision-making: Report on existing research in the European Union*, Luxembourg: Office for Official Publications of the European Communities.

Manin, B. (1997) *The principles of representative government*, Cambridge: Cambridge University Press.

Matland, R.E. (1998) 'Women's Representation in National Legislatures: Developed and Developing Countries', *Legislative Studies Quarterly*, 23, 1: 109–25.

Meier, P. (2000) 'From theory to practice and back again: Gender quota and the politics of presence in Belgium', in M. Saward (ed.) *Democratic Innovation*, London: Routledge, pp. 106–16.

Molyneux, M. and Craske, N. (2002) 'The Local, the Regional and the Global: Transforming the Politics of Rights', in N. Craske and M. Molyneux (eds) *Gender and the Politics of Rights and Democracy in Latin America*, Houndmills: Palgrave, pp. 1–31.

Mouffe, C. (1992) 'Democratic Citizenship and the Political Community', in C. Mouffe (ed.) *Dimensions of Radical Democracy*, London: Verso, pp. 225–39.

Narasimhan, S. (2002) 'Gender, Class, and Caste Schisms in Affirmative Action Policies: The Curious Case of India's Women's Reservation Bill', *Feminist Economics*, 8, 2: 183–90.

Narayan, U. (1997) 'Towards a Feminist Vision of Citizenship: Rethinking the implications of Dignity, Political Participation, and Nationality', in M. Shanley and U. Narayan (eds) *Reconstructing Political Theory: Feminism Perspectives*, Cambridge: Polity Press, pp. 48–67.

Nath, M. (1996) 'Cutting Across Party Lines: Women Members of Parliament Explain their Stand on Reservations Quotas', *Manushi*, 96, 15: 7–19.

Norris, P. (2003) *Increasing Women's Representation in Government: What strategies would work best for Afghanistan?* Prepared by the Afghanistan Reconstruction Project. New York: Center on International Cooperation, New York University.

Orloff, A. (1993) 'Gender and the social rights of citizenship: the comparative analysis of gender relations and the welfare state', *American Sociological Review*, 58: 303–28.

Pateman, C. (1989) *The Disorder of Women: Democracy, Feminism and Political Theory*, Cambridge: Polity Press.

Phillips, A. (1995) *The Politics of Presence*, Oxford: Clarendon Press.

—— (2001) 'Representation Renewed', in M. Sawer and G. Zappalà (eds) *Speaking for the People: Representation in Australian Politics*, Melbourne: Melbourne University Press, pp. 19–35.

Pitkin, H. (1967) *The Concept of Representation*, Berkeley: University of California Press.

Rai, S. (2002) 'Political representation, democratic institutions and women's empowerment: the quota debate in India', in J.L. Parpart, S.M. Rai and K. Staudt (eds) *Rethinking Empowerment: Gender and development in a global/local world*, London: Routledge, pp. 133–46.

Rose, N. (1999) *Powers of Freedom: Reframing political thought*, Cambridge, UK: Cambridge University Press.

Rule, W. and Zimmerman, J.F. (1994) *Electoral Systems in Comparative Perspective: Their Impact on Women and Minorities*, Westport, CT: Greenwood Press.

Scott, J. (1988) 'Deconstructing Equality Versus Difference: Or, the Uses of Post-structuralist Theory for Feminism', *Feminist Studies*, 14, 1: 33–50.

Siim, B. (1990) *Models of Citizenship – Gender Relations, Citizenship and Democracy in the Scandinavian Welfare States*, Bochum: ECPR Joint Sessions.

—— (1993) 'The gendered Scandinavian welfare states: The interplay between women's roles as mothers, workers and citizens in Denmark', in J. Lewis (ed.) *Women and Social Policies in Europe*, Aldershot: Edward Elgar, pp. 25–48.

—— (2000) *Gender and Citizenship: Politics and Agency in France, Britain and Denmark*, Cambridge, UK: Cambridge University Press.

Socialist International Women (1998) 'Women and Power-Sharing: Leadership and Strategies', Bureau Meeting Statement, 15–16 May. Oslo, Norway. Online. Available at: http://www.socintwomen.org.uk/RESOLUTIONS-ENGLISH/Norway%201998/Oslo.html (accessed 2 March 2004).

Squires, J. (1996) 'Quotas for Women: Fair Representation?', *Parliamentary Affairs: A Journal of Comparative Politics*, 49, 1: 71–88.

Teigen, M. (2000) 'The affirmative action controversy', *NORA* (*Nordic Journal of Women's Studies*), 8, 2: 63–77.

Vargas, V. (2002) 'The Struggle by Latin American Feminisms for Rights and Autonomy', in N. Craske and M. Molyneux (eds) *Gender and the Politics of Rights and Democracy in Latin America*, Houndmills: Palgrave, pp. 199–221.

Young, I.M. (1994) 'Gender as Seriality: Thinking about Women as a Social Collective', *Signs*, 19: 713–38.

—— (1997) 'Unruly Categories: A Critique of Nancy Fraser's Dual Systems Theory', *New Left Review*, 222: 147–60.

—— (2000) *Inclusion and Democracy*, Oxford: Oxford University Press.

—— (2002) 'Lived Body vs Gender: Reflections on Social Structure and Subjectivity', *Ratio*, 15, 4: 410–28.

Part II
Regional chapters

3 The Nordic countries

An incremental model

Lenita Freidenvall, Drude Dahlerup and Hege Skjeie

Nordic incrementalism

The five Nordic countries, Denmark, Finland, Iceland, Norway and Sweden, are well-known for their extraordinarily high women's representation in politics and their extended welfare states. Until Rwanda recently overtook Sweden's place as number one, the Nordic countries have alternated at the top of the world rank order of countries according to the representation of women in national parliaments. On the GDI, the Gender related Development Index, they are all among the top countries (UNDP 2004). The specificity of the Nordic countries in terms of women in politics is the reason for having a special chapter on these five small countries. In this chapter common empirical and discursive traits in a Nordic model of governance and its importance for women's political representation will be discussed. The limited role of quota provisions for this development is highlighted.

Largely, the Nordic discourse may be characterized as an *incrementalist discourse* of empowerment. According to this discourse gender equality develops gradually, step wise, and as a concerted effort where state intervention may assist in moving equality in the right direction. The discourse leans heavily on a modernist belief in gradual progress, a 'travel metaphor of equality' (Dahlerup and Freidenvall 2003; Skjeie and Teigen 2003). However, it took 70 to 80 years after the enfranchisement for women to reach 30 to 40 percent of the parliamentary seats. Consequently, this discourse has recently been challenged, especially by the women's movements, urging the political parties to act. We conclude that in spite of their celebrated high representation of women in politics and the inspiration this no doubt has rendered to many countries around the world, the Nordic countries should not be considered the only model for women's political empowerment. Today, *the fast track* discourse and practice is challenging the Nordic incremental model, also from within.

Democratic stability, secularism, egalitarianism, a large public sector and an extended welfare state as well as high standards of living and a long tradition for popular participation are among the characteristics usually attached to the Nordic countries (Castles and Sainsbury 1990). Long-term stability, reformism and incrementalism seem to be interdependent. In terms of gender, the Nordic countries have been labeled 'women friendly', and a 'laboratory of gender equality' (Hernes 1982; Gomard and Krogstad 2001). We know it has surprised many observers, that the Nordic gender political model from within have been continuously criticized by Nordic feminist activists and scholars. But maybe this critique of the 'gender power system' in the Nordic countries (Hirdman 1990), in itself has been important for the development of the Nordic model. In this chapter we discuss a number of paradoxes in the development of the Nordic countries from a gender perspective, contrasting the incremental practice and discourse with the new quota debate of the last two decades.

No legal quotas

In international literature on women in politics, one can find the argument, that women's representation reached a historical and world-wide high in the Scandinavian countries, Denmark, Norway and Sweden due to quotas (Phillips 1995: 57). In the Latin American discussion on quotas, the women's movement has referred to the Nordic example in its advocacy for the introduction of legal quota regulations.

This narrative, however, ignores several facts: With regard to representation in elected political assemblies, no legal quotas, forcing all political parties to nominate a certain minimum of women on their lists, have ever been in use. Neither is the mere principle of equality between women and men inscribed in the constitutions. Second, only some political parties and today only in Norway, Iceland and Sweden have quotas for public election (party quotas), whereas other political parties strongly reject the idea. Third, voluntary party quotas were not introduced until the 1980s, when women already occupied 20 to 30 percent of seats in parliament, at that time also the highest in the world.[1] In the Nordic countries, electoral quotas have been seen as a *critical act* made by an already large minority of women, using their acquired power position in the political parties (Dahlerup 1988a, b). Nordic quota provisions for political institutions may be seen as 'quotas for gender balance', not minimum requirements. All in all, electoral gender quotas in the Nordic countries could be labelled *high echelon quotas.*

Nordic paradoxes

To be 'on top' in terms of equality has been an integrated part of the Nordic countries self-image for decades. However, there are several remarkable paradoxes: First, given the high number of women in the political institutions, the overwhelming male dominance of leadership in private business and in academia is surprising. In these spheres men occupy 85 to 95 percent of the positions (Togeby *et al.* 2003; Skjeie and Teigen 2003). Second, a curious gap persists between the political unwillingness to regulate representation by means of the law in elected institutions as compared to other public institutions, and here, most notably, public committees and boards (appointed bodies). Third, given the fact that 'gender equality' is an official state ideology in all five countries, and that a number of political parties, most widespread in Sweden, label themselves 'feminist', public equality policy is rather limited and reluctant, always seeking consensus and most often based on the principle of gender neutrality (Bergqvist *et al.* 1999; Hirdman 2001; Pincus 2002; Raevaara 2003; Borchorst and Dahlerup 2003; Skjeie and Teigen 2003).

Historical development

The Nordic discourse of incrementalism leans on actual historical development. Table 3.1 shows the historical development in women's representation in the national parliaments of the five Nordic countries. The table, based on the Norwegian theorist of nation-building, Stein Rokkan's famous concept of developmental thresholds, is in itself illustrative of the discourse of incrementalism.

Table 3.1 shows that apart from Finland, women's representation remained very low, no higher than 3 to 4 percent in the first 20 years after women's enfranchisement. The Finnish development is extraordinary, first because women got the right to vote as early as 1906 and at the same time as men, second because women's representation in the Finnish parliament from the start reached almost 10 percent and remained a worldwide high.

An increase occurred around World War II, followed by a period of gradual improvements. A take-off came in the 1970s, where the 20 percent threshold was overcome. Iceland lags behind the other Nordic countries, but had its take-off in the 1980s, when the new Women's Party (1983–99) sparked a debate about women's low representation. The gradualism of the Nordic development since 1945 is shown by the steady increase of usually 2 to 4 percent, with only few historical jumps. A parallel slow, and until recently steady increase in women's representation has occurred at the local level, which is important in the Nordic countries, because of the independent taxation authority and large budgets of the communes.

In recent years, the unbroken line of increase in women's representation has, however, come to a stop. In Norway, the representation rates in parliament have remained unchanged since the mid-1980s (around 35/65). Denmark has seen a similar standstill, even a reduction in the percentage of elected women in some local and national elections. Also in Finland the previous gradual increase seems to have come to a halt, and in the 2004 election in Iceland women's representation dropped from 35

Table 3.1 Four institutional thresholds for women in Nordic parliamentary politics

Thresholds	Denmark	Finland	Iceland	Norway	Sweden
1. Legitimization					
Founding of feminist organizations	1871	1884	1894	1884	1884
Founding of suffrage societies	1889	a	1907	1885	1903
2. Incorporation					
Universal suffrage, enacted	1915	1906	1920	1913	1919
3. Representation (Parliamentary)					
1st election, ordinary representatives	1918	1907	1922	1921	1921
1st election, over 10% of representatives	1966	1907	1983	1973	1953
1st election, over 20% of representatives	1979	1970	1987	1977	1973
1st election, over 30% of representatives	1988	1983	1999	1985	1985
1st election, over 40% of representatives	never	never	never	never	1994
Proportion of women 2005 in %[b]	36.9	37.5	30.2	37.9	45.3
Highest proportion of women in any election %	37.9	38.5	34.9	39.4	45.3
4. Executive Power (Government)					
1st ordinary minister[c]	1924	1926	1970	1945	1947
1st Cabinet, at least 10% of ministers	1953	1953	1983	1965	1966
1st Cabinet, at least 20% of ministers	1981	1987	1999	1973	1976
1st Cabinet, at least 30% of ministers	1994	1991	never	1986	1991
1st Cabinet, at least 40% of ministers	never	1991	never	1986	1994[d]
1st Cabinet, at least 50% of ministers	never	never	never	never	1994
Proportion of women 2005 in %[b]	26.3	44.4	20.0	42.1	50.0
1st Prime Minister	never	2003	never	1981	never
1st President (Iceland, Finland)	n/a	2003	1980	n/a	n/a

Source: Bergqvist *et al.* (1999) (updated figures).

Notes
a In Finland no societies were founded with the explicit purpose of campaigning for the right to vote.
b Representation: last election. Cabinet ministers as of 10 Oct 2005.
c The world's first female minister outside the Soviet Union was the Dane Nina Bang in the first, but short Social Democratic government 1924–6. Finland's first female minister, Miina Sillanpää, maintained a place in the government for 20 years.
d When a social democratic government replaced a non-socialist government in 1994, the proportion of women increased from 38 to 50 percent.

to 30 percent. The reactions to these new trends have, however, varied considerably from country to country. In Denmark this standstill was hardly noticed outside feminist circles, whereas in Sweden at the other extreme, a drop in women's representation at the 1991 election, the first drop since the 1920s, resulted in uproar and quota regulations.

Only recently has the very low political representation of the growing number of immigrants to the Nordic countries been subject to public discussion, revealing the same controversies between advocates of incrementalism versus those who favor an affirmative action policy. No immigrants are seated in the Finnish, Norwegian and Icelandic parliaments, whereas the Swedish parliament has 3.4 percent immigrants, the Danish 1.1 percent (2004), defined as MPs born outside the country to parents with non-Nordic citizenship. In general, the historical and present day exclusionary practices within the self-expressed homogenous Nordic communities, which now face new demands from minority groups and a growing number of immigrants from other parts of the world, have come into focus (de los Reyes *et al.* 2002).

Structural explanations: the Nordic model

Since gender quotas were mainly introduced in the 1980s and 1990s and then only in some of the countries and in a selected number of parties, other factors must be found to explain the high representation of women in Nordic parliaments. In the following sections, women's political representation is discussed in relation to the specific Nordic tradition and ideology of state-society interaction in terms of political mobilization. In this endeavor the dynamics between institutional factors and the many actors in play are stressed. The strong Social Democratic parties, ruling for most of the last 50 years in Norway and Sweden, and often being part of coalition governments in the rest of the Nordic countries, have strongly influenced the development of the Nordic countries, also in terms of gender, after eventually yielding for a gender perspective.

The electoral system

The proportional system (List PR) contributes to explaining the high representation of women in the Nordic countries. Proportional representation and large multimember constituencies are factors associated with high representation of women. However, as Diane Sainsbury has rightly noted, the proportional representation system can hardly explain the increase, since it has been an integrated part of the political system of all five countries from the first democratic elections in the nineteenth century (Sainsbury 1996). Consequently, it might be adequate to reformulate the theory of the importance of the proportional system for women's representation: Because of its multiple numbers of candidates, the proportional representation system is less resistant to change than the plurality-majority system, where each party only has one candidate. The question of closed versus open lists does not serve much as a factor of explanation, since the five Nordic countries differ a great deal in this respect. Whereas Finland has a compulsory personal voting system and Denmark and Iceland have voluntary personal voting systems, parties in Sweden (until 1998) present closed lists. Norway has practiced a mixed system with closed lists in parliamentary elections and open, changeable lists in local elections.

Socio-economic and cultural factors

The correlation between women's political representation and their level of education and labor force participation should also be emphasized (Andersen 1975; Rule 1981, 1987; Sainsbury 1993; Matland 1998; Kaiser 2001; McDonagh 2002). The lower female representation in Iceland which has been associated with the dominant social structure of agriculture and fishery, only recently changed. In general, women representation is higher in rural than urban areas for both national and local levels of decision-making (Haavio-Mannila *et al.* 1985; Bergqvist *et al.* 1999). Cultural factors can also to a certain extent be highlighted. *Political culture*, for example, has been used to explain women's representation in the Nordic countries, where a strong emphasis on social and economic equality coexists with a relatively high proportion of women in parliament. Similarly, the impact of religion can be stressed, based on studies showing that protestant or secular countries have more women in politics than Catholic countries. This does not however explain the change in representation patterns in the 1970s (Norris 1987; Bystydzienski 1995).

Nordic competition

Another factor is the competition among Nordic governments on issues of equality and social welfare. Exchange within the Nordic countries has been the case for the social movements, notably the women's movements, but also political parties and equal opportunity units have exchanged knowledge and experiences, for instance within the framework of the Nordic Council of Ministers and the Nordic Council. This has given the feminist movement the opportunities to 'play the Nordic card', by constantly referring to measures and progresses in the other countries (Raevaara 2003). Also, Nordic gender research has repeatedly published Nordic comparative analyses, revealing which country is 'lagging behind' the others within a special area. This Nordic competition has, however, diminished today, because of the countries' different affiliations to the European Union (Borchorst and Dahlerup 2003).

State feminism

One main interpretation of Scandinavian representation politics over the last 30 years is that the key to changes in women's citizenship status has been the interaction of women's political mobilization 'from below' in social movements and voluntary organizations, with political integration 'from above' in political parties and political institutions. This double tendency has been incorporated in the concept of state feminism (Hernes 1987).

The concept of state feminism and, more largely, the Scandinavian feminist debates on gendered citizenship are strongly influenced by what we call a social democratic legitimization model of participation and governance. Broadly speaking, such debates have been embodied in a general notion of social movements being democracy's primary 'actors' and 'agents' of change. This stress on movements is important for several reasons. Conceptually, it maintains the importance of collective action – and of close and integrative alliances between movements, parties and the state. Ideologically, movements are granted a kind of 'instant' – if only diffuse – legitimacy for those claims of social and political rights they make on behalf of the groups they 'carry'/care about. Such claims are seen to define society's ongoing processes of political mobilization; they represent – so to speak – popular democracy at work (Skjeie and Siim 2000).

Second, the notion of social democratic citizenship, dominating since World War II, implies that questions of social and political inclusions and exclusions are usually discussed in relation to two distinct, institutionally defined channels of political influence and power, what Stein Rokkan, called the numerical-democratic and the corporate-pluralist channel for the formulation and representation of interests (Rokkan 1987). In countries where social democratic parties maintained governance hegemony for more than a quarter of a century, and often successfully remained in power after their hegemony was broken, the ideology of 'movement democracy' thus contributed to shape the structure of national decision making at large (Skjeie and Siim 2000).

It seems fair to maintain that the increasingly strong feminist criticism of party-based political exclusions in the Nordic countries during the 1970s and early 1980s rarely contained a normative-based rejection of participation within traditional political institutions as such, as was a distinctive trend in much American and European feminism. Instead, it was a criticism of the actual practices of 'democracy' followed by a demand for inclusion. Men's monopolization of party-based politics was stated more as a problem for democracy than party politics were for women. Given this integrationist perspective on gendered political power, there is little doubt that also feminist activism could benefit considerably from a long legacy of diffuse movement legitimacy (Skjeie 1992; Skjeie and Siim 2000).

Legal quotas for public committees

Although corporatism has changed its pattern of composition since the late 1980s, there is still a strong feminist critique of the influence of corporatism in social democratic governance (Skjeie 2003; Skjeie and Teigen 2003). This criticism has led to legislation that has improved the representation of women in the corporatist system. A concrete example was the drive to increase women's representation in appointed positions in the state administration of Sweden in 1985–7. Feminists were not only involved in agenda setting and in framing the debate, but were also in charge of the inquiry commission leading to legislation and the eventual evaluation of the outcome (Bergqvist 1995; Sainsbury 2004). This commission also spurred a debate on women's representation in the political parties. Another example is the elaborate system of quota policies in Norway, which was in fact initiated to reform the gender participation patterns in negotiations through corporate bodies. After a phase of soft 'recommendations' for appointing more women, new legislation was passed first in Norway in the 1980s, soon to be followed by the other Nordic countries (Dahlerup 1988b). These laws demand that the appointing minister or organ shall see that all public committees rather vaguely acquire a 'gender balance', or set up a minimum-maximum of 40/60 for both sexes. In spite of heavy protests from trade unions and industry, all appointing organizations and institutions, including both private and public institutions, must nominate both a woman and a man for each post, thereafter the gender balance is for the appointing minister to secure. Implementation of these rules has not been easy, and not all ministers – especially not those in transport, agriculture and fishery – have complied with the law.

Recently, Finland and Norway have taken the extraordinary step of passing laws that demand a minimum of 40 percent of either sex in *all local public committees and boards*. It is surprising that this provision not only encompasses appointed members of committees, but also the steering boards of the local council, elected by and among the members of the popular elected local assemblies (Pikkala 2000; Teigen 2003; Holli 2004). The quota regulation of the local boards in Norway and Finland combined with the regulations for public committees in all five countries since the 1980s shows that legal quotas in case of appointment to public bodies are considered more legitimate than regulations interfering with the electoral process.

Strategic factors: campaigns and movements

The feminist movement

The Women's Movement in the Nordic countries has a long and continuous history of activities to promote equality between women and men, even if individual organizations have had their ups and downs, as illustrated by the wave metaphor of first, second and maybe third wave of feminism (Dahlerup 2004). Unlike most other countries, the original feminist organizations that fought for women's access to education, for the legal rights of married women, and later for suffrage, still exist, albeit at a low level of activity. More than 100-year-old feminist magazines are still being issued.

The Nordic countries were leading in the so called 'Sex Role Debate' of the 1960s, which stressed the importance of socialization into female and male sex roles (Holter 1981; Hagemann 2003). Soon a new, socialist and radical Women's Liberation Movement followed, mobilizing thousands of young women during the 1970s and 1980s. These movements varied in their views of the state and formal political institutions, from the Icelandic movement that transformed itself into a successful political party to the predominantly grass root character of the Danish 'Redstockings'. However, the movement in all five countries challenged the traditional male concept of citizenship, resulting in what might be seen as a new hegemonic discourse, according to which an all male political assembly is considered undemocratic and unacceptable. Thus, the 'acceptable minimum of women' on electoral lists in committees or in government has steadily increased (Dahlerup 1998a).

The women's sections

The high level of women in the Nordic parliaments and local councils depends heavily on the support and mobilization of women's organizations and groups inside the political parties. Although the focus on sex roles in the 1960s led to calls inside parties to disband their women's sections in the name of gender equality, women pointed to the increased attention to gender issues in society to demonstrate the need to retain the women's sections to continue to attract women voters. Also, by distancing themselves from the 'feminists' in the new, radical women's movement, they managed to make their claims on equal opportunity and a higher women's representation more acceptable, albeit by more or less internalizing the ideas of the 'feminists'. By drawing on the increased attention to gender equality, they pointed to the gains made by women in rivaling parties to press for additional measures within their own. By demanding and acquiring seats in nomination committees, women actively nominated women, pressed for women candidates and overviewed the overall nomination process with a gender perspective. Women's sections have actively recruited women candidates, even if not all women politicians have wanted to associate themselves with the women's sections.

Joyce Gelb's remarkable statement of 'feminism without feminists' in Sweden seems to rest on a negligence of the women's groups and organizations working within the political parties. Previously, these women's sections were mass organizations, organizing tens of thousands of women, especially in labour and farmers' parties (Haavio-Mannila *et al.* 1985; Gelb 1989). Today, most parties have equality committees and/or feminist groups, functioning as pressure groups within the parties on gender issues. The strongest and still active women's organizations within the political parties are found in Finland and Sweden.

Party strategies for women

Continuous claims by party women as well as by the autonomous feminist movements for an increased women's representation have also successfully resulted in parties introducing measures to promote women. Since the 1970s individual parties have made use of a number of strategies to increase the number of women candidates, among them recommendations to the local party organizations to nominate more women, capacity building for potential women candidates, and network activities. In general, critique has been raised against the way politics are conducted in order to make the political workplace more gender sensitive. For instance, many parties have assisted politicians with children by organizing babysitting at meetings and family activities at conferences as well as accommodating meeting hours. In several cases, the state has supported cross-party actions to help more women come forward as candidates. The autonomous feminist movements have had 'Vote for Women' campaigns, even if such actions were often met with resistance from the parties, who argue that gender can never be more important than party ideology. However, surveys show that during the last decades the voters have responded positively to such appeals. Investigations have revealed a gender gap in voter's preferences according to the sex of the candidate. Thus, ever since the 1970s, the Nordic political parties have been exposed to internal as well as external criticism for lacking women on electoral lists. For nominating bodies, a 'gender balance' has been a stated goal in most parties. However, 'equality' may be perceived differently, as 25, 40 or 50 percent, by respective parties.

The discourses on quotas in the Nordic countries

In contrast to legislative quotas used in many other parts of the world, quotas in the Nordic countries have only been introduced voluntarily by individual parties, primarily by left, social democratic, centrist and green parties. However, no Finnish party has quota provisions, and two Danish political parties decided after just a few years to abandon them again, partly by the request of young women party members who argued that such 'special measures' for women were no longer necessary (Dahlerup 1998a; Borchorst and Christensen 2003). Consequently, the Nordic countries do not present a unified model on the use of quotas. In the Nordic countries, the debate on women's (low) representation started already after the first election following enfranchisement, whereas the quota debate unfolded only during the last two decades. The Nordic quota debate thus started when women had already obtained 20 to 30 percent representation in parliament, and in a political climate supportive of equality in principle. *Consequently, in the Nordic quota debate, the conflicts have evolved around means rather than goals.*

Incrementalism versus the fast track

First of all, a discourse and practice of incrementalism can be identified. This discourse is based on a firm belief in a steady and unbroken line of progress, a typical modernist outlook. It is implicitly framed in a notion of time or historical development as a linear process. As society develops and new, more gender equal generations succeed gender equality will be gradually attained. The focus is on women's (lack of) resources, and a subsequent increase in women's labor market participation and educational level is expected to more or less automatically result in more women candidates. The historical steady increase in women's representation has no doubt contributed to the endurance of this discourse of incrementalism.

The Nordic incremental discourse is thus embedded in an optimistic view of future progress. However, important variations arc found as to how much intervention is needed to reach 'equality' in various sectors. While parties on the right in general have favored limited intervention, the Social Democrats have emphasized the need for intervention, illustrated by the opening speech of the Swedish prime minister, Göran Persson, in parliament in 1998, when he stated that 'this is the most equal parliament in the world', however adding that 'gender equality is not obtained in Sweden' (Dahlerup 2004: 234).

Also the historical demands by Nordic feminists for 'more women in politics' are embedded in an incremental discourse, however, with a strong emphasis on the need for actions by the parties combined with the need for educating women to be better prepared for political positions. But following the strong feminist mobilization of the late 1960s, the 1970s and 1980s, Nordic feminism took a discursive shift, now stressing processes of *exclusion*, expressed in a new language of 'male dominance', 'patriarchy' and 'the male society'. In this context, demands for quotas for women have become more and more widespread, even if not all feminists accept this idea.

Thus during the last two decades, the discourse of incrementalism has been challenged by a concept of radicalization – what we might call *a fast track discourse.* In their pure forms, the two discourses rest on two different sets of assumptions about historical development, different problem identification of the causes of women's under-representation, as well as differences in the choice of strategy (Dahlerup and Freidenvall 2005). According to the fast track discourse, the power hierarchy between the sexes is constantly being reproduced also in younger generations and backlash is seen as possible with regard to gender equality and the number of women in parliament. Thus, within this competing frame gender equality (and women's political representation), will not improve automatically as time goes by with new gen(d)erations, and men will not voluntarily give up powers attained. With a growing impatience on integrative strategies never becoming fully accomplished, radical actions, such as quota provisions implying a fast change are then argued for.

In Denmark, after a few years of quota debates and limited numbers of quota experiments, the discourse of incrementalism in the 1990s returned to the scene, but through the widespread notion that equality is more or less achieved, and consequently no more action is necessary. Researchers have spoken of 'saturation' in the equality debate (Kjær 2000). Warnings against a future 'dominance' of women in certain areas are now being heard (Borchorst and Dahlerup 2003; Dahlerup 2004). With reference to this discursive frame, it is not surprising that the lack of increase in Danish women's representation in recent years has not been followed by active measures to change the situation as had been the case in Sweden.

A recent analysis of gender equality politics in Norway pinpoints the paradox of how an extreme male dominance in elite positions in business, state administration, media, the church, the arts, academia, etc. combines with verbal commitment to equality values through a dominant *travel metaphor of equality*. This travel metaphor suggests a nationally encapsulated 'equality journey' where gender equality is seen as a kind of developmental process which continuously 'evolve' towards a common goal. The analysis reveals and problematizes the 'self-evidence' of equality policy as a consensus among the national elite, which is called the problem of benevolent non-committal. When equality is treated as a field of negotiable compromises, principles of equality often have to '*yield a little*' (Skjeie and Teigen 2003).

Why more women in politics? Why quotas?

The demands for more women in Nordic politics, later expressed as a demand for 'gender balance' have rested on a variety of arguments concerning women's rights, women's contribution and interests as well as discriminatory practices in the parties. With the justice argument, the unjust exclusion of women from the political sphere is in focus. The justice argument, however, has always in the Nordic countries been combined with arguments that women should and can make a difference in politics. In a 1984 survey among all women's sections and equality committees within the Nordic political parties all, except for one 'may be', expressed the view that more women in politics would change the political agenda as well as the climate and working procedures of political institutions. However, many added: 'but only if there are a sufficient number of women' (Dahlerup 1988b). Ever since the first women were elected, feminist groups have criticized the women politicians for not making more of a difference. Women politicians have in return argued that more women are needed to make a difference. It is evident, that feminist attempts to construct women as a politically relevant group has influenced women politicians, and opened up cross-party alliances among women, in spite of resistance from their parties (Wängnerud 1998).

The debate on gender in the Nordic countries varies, however. The Norwegian discussion on women in politics and on quotas in the 1970s and early 1980s largely made use of a 'rhetoric of difference' (Skjeie 1992) either underscoring 'women's contributions' to politics, or arguing 'women's conflicting interests'. In contrast, the Swedish debate has to a greater extent been centered on concepts of discrimination and exclusion. In both cases the arguments have been largely based on constructing the category of 'women' as a single entity. The Women's Party in Iceland, represented in the Icelandic parliament from 1983–95 with 5 to 10 percent of the votes, stood for election on the most unambiguous women's platform, containing an interesting combination of radical feminism and a revaluation of traditional women's work, still prevailing in the fishing and agricultural communities in Iceland (Styrkársdóttir 1986; Bergqvist *et al.* 1999).

Based on research in the five countries, the arguments used in the Nordic countries for and against electoral gender quotas can be summarized as follows (Dahlerup 1988b, 1998a; Pikkala 2000; Teigen 2000; Skjeie 2001; Freidenvall 2003; Holli 2004).

Arguments used for gender quotas

- quotas will ensure that both women and men will be part of the political decision-making
- quotas will force the political parties to recruit and include more women
- women constitute half of the population – it is therefore a democratic right for women to have half of the seats in parliaments
- quotas make it possible for women to enter as a group, ensure a critical mass, not just a token few
- women are just as qualified as men, but women's qualifications have been downgraded
- quotas are not discrimination of men, but an answer to the discrimination of women
- introduction of quotas may cause conflict, but only temporarily
- men in fact tend to select other men – 'the Huey, Dewey, Louie-effect'
- it is good for the image of the party

Arguments used against gender quotas

- unqualified women will displace qualified men; quotas violate the merit principle
- politicians should not be elected because of their sex, but on their qualifications and political beliefs

- quotas are undemocratic; they distort the democratic process
- quotas discriminate against men
- quotas are unliberal; it is a 'free ride' which is against the principle of free competition (liberal argument)
- quotas place gender before class (left argument)
- nominations should remain the prerogative of the local party organizations
- quotas infringe on women's rights, women do not want to be chosen because of their sex
- quotas are 'coercion'; it creates permanent conflicts between men and women
- what counts is 'what you have in your head, not what you have between your legs!'
- quotas are not necessary; women can do it on their own (especially women opponents)
- women do not constitute a group; women have different opinions
- quotas do not solve the crucial problems for women in politics, such as family obligations

As this list reveals, the arguments for and against quotas in the Nordic countries are very similar to the arguments found in other non-post-conflict countries in the world. But the argument that women can do it without quotas of course has greater value in the Nordic countries because of the historical increase in women's representation. Consequently, when it became clear that there was a lack – to many observers a *surprising* lack – of increase in women's share of the top positions in academia and private business, a new vehement discussion about the need for intervention has recently begun in the Nordic countries, followed by demands for quotas in academia as well as the corporate board rooms. In Norway, where quotas are now 'business as usual', actual legal intervention has been the result.

Gender equality as equal opportunity or equality of result

Another significant frame, very much related to the other frames, is gender equality. Equality discourses may be classified according to whether equality is defined in terms of processes of equal opportunity or participatory equality (equality of result). These two discourses seem to have split the Nordic political parties into two divisions, one to the right and one to the left of the political spectrum.

The prevailing view in parties to the right concurs that individual women might face problems (in terms of lack of education, experience and self-confidence), in the competition for parliamentary seats. They should thus be provided with assistance such as political candidate schools, mentor programs, and network activities. These measures will provide women with the necessary prerequisites in terms of competence and expertise to compete on equal terms with men.

A competing discourse – today expressed most clearly by parties to the left and by feminists in the Nordic countries – is the one of participatory justice. This discourse claims both structural and individual discrimination. Equal opportunity does not exist just due to the removal of formal barriers. Direct discrimination and complex patterns of hidden barriers prevent women from participating on equal terms and from attaining a fair share of political power and influence. The political parties are seen as responsible for actions taken, not individual women.

Gender neutrality: avoiding conflict

Also apparent in the debate on women's representation in politics and quotas is the quest for gender equality as a joint project. In this discourse, the promotion of gender equality is seen as a collective project, based on mutual understanding and co-operation between the sexes. In the Nordic countries, equality policies are typically formulated in gender neutral terms, and so are all quota rules. Gender neutrality is conceived in terms of fairness for both sexes, but has in fact functioned as a conflict-avoiding measure. Because of the many women in recent Nordic politics, quotas in the left parties have, in a few instances, worked to the benefit of male candidates.

A new discourse of profitability

While the previous arguments on women's 'contribution' still prevail, discourses on conflict of interest between women and men are often being substituted by 'profitability talk' – that is by arguments about how profitable integration politics in fact would be to a whole range of institutions – ranging from higher education to boards of private businesses. This is interpreted as the attempt by state feminism to adapt to an expanding liberalist market ideology in public affairs (Skjeie and Teigen 2003; Teigen 2003). The increasingly influential rhetoric of gender profitability adjusted to a market ideology makes it, however, difficult to maintain a perspective of rights and justice. When paid work free from discrimination is emphasized as important in so far as it is profitable for the employer, the principle is for sale – such as when women are to enter boardrooms, judicial offices and professorships in order to better serve students, to advance the climate in the workplace, to improve risk assessments, and/or to enhance the image (Skjeie and Teigen 2003).

When gender equality is argued as a means to secure competitiveness, the category of 'women' accordingly becomes a representation of 'means' for companies and organizations to use. This rhetoric of profitability puts equality on the defensive, as a field that must be defended with something else than its own value. Such discussions circle around a far too old – and endlessly patriarchal – requirement that women should contribute 'as gender' – with their collective empathy, talent, and reason. Do 'we' have something to contribute? If not, what are we nagging about? Both the travel metaphor and the rhetoric of profitability add to the construction of a seeming consensus on gender equality, a new analysis concludes. They simply bypass problems of individual and structural discrimination and misrecognition (Skjeie and Teigen 2003).

The use of voluntary party quotas in the Nordic countries

When it comes to the actual adoption of quotas in the Nordic countries, the attention was first turned to women's political representation in internal boards and committees. Supported by the general feminist mobilization of the 1970s and 1980s, women within the political parties started a heavy critique of the parties' male dominance, which resulted in the first quota regulations, usually for both local and central party organizations.[2] Having broken the pattern of historical male dominance within the parties, the active feminist women in many parties used their new power base to push for party quotas at nominations. Gradually initiatives were raised to increase women's representation at the electoral level, introducing a 40/60 principle or the zipper system for candidates at national, county and municipal level. In general quotas were first introduced by parties to the left, to be followed by rivaling parties (cp. Matland and Studlar 1996). Quotas in use have primarily been gender neutral, setting a minimum and maximum for both women and men. Table 3.2 shows the voluntary party quotas in use in the Nordic countries over the years.

In *Denmark*, two of the parties represented in parliament, the Socialist People's Party and the large Social Democratic Party introduced internal party quotas of 40 percent in 1977 and 1983 after long and vehement debates. Electoral quotas were introduced by the same parties in the mid-1980s and abandoned again in the mid-1990s. At the general elections of 1981 and 1984, the Socialist People's party elected 43 percent women to parliament. At the first election prior to and after the adoption of the quota rule, however, women's representation decreased to 33 percent. The Social Democrats never had quotas for national parliament elections, only for local and European elections and only for a very short period of time. Today, no political party in Denmark has electoral quotas inscribed in their party rules.

In *Finland*, where the party system traditionally has been very strong and women's party organizations are still functioning, no party quotas have been adopted for public election, in contrast to the widespread use of quotas for appointed office, both nationally and locally. Nomination of candidates is highly regulated by law, delegating the selection to the local

Table 3.2 The result of party quotas in the Nordic countries: Party by party

Country	Party	Quota	Year of introduction	Women MPs of the party[a]
Denmark Party Quotas	Socialist People's Party *Socialistisk Folkeparti*	40%	National 1988–90 EU Parliament 1983–90	(1987: 33%) 33%, 50%, 0
	Social Democratic Party *Socialdemokratiet*	40%	EU Parliament 1988–96	50%, 33%
Finland No quotas				
Iceland Party Quotas	People's Alliance *Althydubandalag*	40%	Party dissolved in 1999[b]	
	Social Democratic Party *Althyduflokkur*	40%	Party dissolved in 1999	
	The Women's Party *Kvinnalistinn*	100%	1983–99 Party dissolved	All women's party
	United Front *amfylkingin*	40%	2002	(1999: 53%) 45%
	Progressive Party *Framsóknarflokkur*	40%	1996	(1995: 20%) 25%, 33%
Norway Party Quotas	Socialist Left Party *Socialistisk Venstreparti*	40%	1975	(1973: 19%) 50%, 50%, 50%, 41%, 31%, 33%, 48%, 47%
	Norwegian Labour Party *Det Norske Arbeiderparti*	40%	1983	(1981: 33%) 42%, 51%, 49%, 49%, 47%, 52%
	Centre Party *Senterpartiet*	40%	1989	(1985: 17%) 27%, 44%, 36%, 60%, 45%
	Christian People's Party *Kristelig Folkeparti*	40%	1993	(1989: 36%) 38%, 44%, 36%, 45%
	Liberal Party *Venstre*	40%	1975	(1973: 0) 0, 0, 0, 0, 0, 17%, 0, 40%
Sweden Party Quotas	Swedish Social Democratic Party *Socialdemokratiska Arbetarepartiet*	50% zipper-system	1993	(1991: 41%) 48%, 50%, 47%
	Left Party *Vänsterpartiet*	50%	1987	(1985: 16%) 38%, 31%, 46%, 42%, 47%

Table 3.2 Continued

Country	Party	Quota	Year of introduction	Women MPs of the party[a]
	Green Party *Miljöpartiet de Gröna*	50%	1987	(new party) 45%, N/A, 56%, 50%, 59%

Sources: Official electoral statistics.

Notes

a The percentage of women in each party's parliamentary fraction for all election years after the introduction of quotas (in parentheses the percentage of women in the last election previous to the introduction of quotas).

b Before the parliamentary election of 1999, a new electoral alliance, the United Front was formed, composed of four political parties: the PA, the SDP, the WA, and the People's Movement.

parties. National quota legislation is seen as rocking the very foundation of the party system (Holli 2004).

In *Iceland*, the Left Party introduced a 40 percent quota for internal party structures in the 1980s. One may call the successful Women's Party a radical quota system, since only women stood for election on the party's lists, 1983–99. Since then many Icelandic parties have passed recommendations to increase women's representation and some have introduced party quotas with various degrees of formalization. However, when the party leaderships do not control the nominations process because of the open primaries, the contagion effect from the Women's Party and from the smaller parties with party quotas has not been permanently decisive (Kristjánsson 2002, 2003).

In *Norway*, party quotas were simultaneously introduced by the Socialist Left Party and the Liberal Party (1975), to be followed in the 1980s by all other main parties, except the Conservatives and the right-wing Progress Party. The largest party, the Labour party introduced a 40 percent quota in 1983, which established a minimum representation of 40 percent for 'each sex', for both the composition of internal party organizations and for nominations for public elections. In 1986 the new Labour Prime Minister, Gro Harlem Brundtland, made this a regulatory norm also for cabinet appointments when she formed the world's first 'Women's Cabinet' – as the international media immediately named it. Today, quotas have become an institutional norm in Norway and also in other areas of public life.

In *Sweden*, almost all parties have adopted special measures to increase women's political representation ranging from goals, non-mandatory recommendations and quotas. Quotas were first introduced by the Green Party (1987) and the Left Party (1987). The Green Party adopted quotas, upon its founding in 1981, involving a minimum of 40 percent of either sex in boards and committees as well as a joint male/female chair of the party. This provision was extended in 1987 to include a minimum of 40 percent of either sex on electoral lists as well. In 1997, the quota provision was extended to 50 percent, plus or minus one person. The Left Party implemented in 1987 a policy of at least the same proportion of women on party lists as women members in the constituency. This strategy was extended in 1990 to a minimum of 40 percent of either sex, and in 1993 to a minimum of 50 percent women.

The development from recommendations and targets (soft quotas) to actual quota regulations in political parties on the left can be illustrated by the Swedish development: It was not until 1993 that the largest party, the Social Democratic Party, introduced 'Every second for the ladies' ('Varannan Damernas'), where women and men alternate on the electoral ballot. This party had previously preferred party targets such as the recommendation from 1987 of a minimum representation of 40 percent of either sex at all levels within the party. In 1990, this policy was extended to 'an equal representation of the sexes'. An unprecedented decrease from 38 to 33 percent in the 1991 general election contributed to a renewed discussion of women's political representation in Sweden. This decrease together with the threat posed by the feminist pressure group, the 'Support Stockings', who threatened to form a women's only party, as in Iceland, if the women's representation did not improve, challenged the political parties. More specifically it offered women, especially within the Social Democratic Party a window of opportunity to press for additional measures, i.e. quotas.

In Sweden, many parties have adopted recommendations, instead of quotas, to increase the number of women in politics. The Liberal party was first to do so, when the party congress in 1972 passed a regulation that all party boards and committees be composed of at least 40 percent of members of each sex. This recommendation was extended in 1974 to cover electoral lists as well and in 1984 extended to include alternated lists at general elections. The Christian Democratic Party has followed a similar path, with its introduction in 1987 of a minimum of 40 percent of members of each sex in electoral ballots. The Conservative Party decided in 1993 on a goal of equal representation between the sexes, but leaving the final decision of the list composition to the nomination committees. The same goes for the Centre Party that decided on a goal of equal representation between the sexes in 1996.

The fact that no legal quota requirements have been in use in the Nordic countries reflects the resistance especially within the bourgeois parties against quotas. However, as the high representation of women even in Nordic liberal and conservative parties indicates, the rejection of quotas has been followed by various actions in non-quota parties to improve women's representation – and thereby prove that quotas are unnecessary! The women's sections used quotas as a threat if better representation for women was not accomplished (Dahlerup 1988b: 86).

Until recently there has been little public concern about those practices which largely have kept the parliament closed to ethnic minorities. No legal affirmative action provisions have been introduced in the Nordic countries in order to further the inclusion of recent immigrants in the political institutions. In accordance with Mala Htun's argument, the few affirmative action regulations for ethnic minorities are geographically defined, as the Sami Parliaments in both Norway and Sweden, and the previous affirmative action measure to secure a minimum representation of one seat for the German minority in the Danish parliament. Quotas for ethnic minorities are generally rejected (Togeby 2003; Htun 2004). The recruitment of minority women within the quota for 'women' has been scarce, and not until recently did the political parties start active recruitment of minority women.

The implementation and effects of quotas

The Swedish parliament today is close to an actual 50–50 gender balance with 45 percent women. In the Norwegian parliament with 38 percent women, the overall representation figures have not changed much since the mid-1980s. Denmark and Finland with no quota provisions are number four and five on the world rank order with 37 and 38 percent women, while Iceland recently dropped from 35 to 30 percent women in the Althing. Formal regulations of integration politics by use of quotas have clearly been most prominent in Norwegian and Swedish party politics.

As Table 3.2 shows, however, there are many discrepancies between the actual quota provision in a party and the number of women elected. The effect of party quota provisions should therefore be evaluated party-by-party, as well as in terms of an increased competition among parties for women's votes, which brings the implementation processes into focus.[3]

Implementation agents and implementation obstacles

Party quotas might work very similarly to legal quotas. When it comes to implementation and sanctions for non-compliance, however, the two quota systems differ. Party quotas are decided upon by the national party organization and are usually not subject to referenda among party members. In the Nordic countries, the decision to introduce party quotas has been taken by the central committee of the parties or at the annual party convention. In many cases the local party organizations have felt that quotas have been imposed from above. Since nomination in Nordic political parties is usually the prerogative of the local branches, there is an inbuilt conflict between the central and the local party organization when it comes to implementing quota provisions.

Especially in the case of small parties, who may only expect one seat in their constituency, one finds a similar need for interventions by the central party to meet quota requirements as in plurality-majority electoral systems. The 40 percent quota in the Norwegian Socialist Left party is usually implemented by nominating a woman and a man as the two first names on the party's list in each constituency. The central party overlooks the joint nominations results and may intervene, especially for the safe seats in order to prevent that the party ends up with an all male parliamentary group, in case all the top candidates turn out to be men. This was the case of the Left party in Sweden in 2002, when many constituencies with only one safe seat selected a man to top the list.

Research has also shown that incumbent MPs are seldom rejected if he or she wants to stand for reelection. In the stable Nordic countries, the main factor behind replacement of politicians is not the electoral result, but voluntary retreat (Wallin *et al.* 1981; Narud *et al.* 2002). Given the strong wish for consensus in Nordic equality politics, quotas often clash with incumbency. When the Danish Social Democratic party after a long discussion eventually introduced a 40 percent minimum for each sex in all party committees (except for the steering committee), the number of seats in all committees were expanded as a conflict-preventing measure (Dahlerup 1998b).

Even if the Danish Social Democratic Party never introduced quotas for parliamentary elections, the central party in the 1980s and early 1990s in a few cases forced a so-called 'supplementary female candidate' upon the local party organization, if only male candidates had been nominated in a constituency. The central party feared that women voters might desert the party if there were no women candidates on the party's list at the election. However, these supplementary candidates did not do well because they lacked their own base in the constituency.

Implementation results

The introduction of quotas has, as Table 3.2 reveals, mostly contributed to a continuation of the gradual increase in women's representation. Only a few jumps in women's share of the parliamentary seats have occurred due to the introduction of quotas. As Table 3.2 also shows, the actual percentage alters both up and down for individual parties. Far from the jump starts of many other countries, the Nordic *high echelon quotas* have continued the historical incrementalism and protected the already high level of representation against backlash.

In Sweden, women's representation within the parliamentary fraction of the Social Democratic Party increased from 41 percent in 1991 to 48 percent in 1994, the first election with quotas. In the subsequent elections women got 50 percent (1998) and 47 percent (2002). In general, at the 2002 election the political parties with 40 to 50 percent quotas had a higher representation of women compared to parties without quotas: 51

to 42. However, so was also the case *before* the introduction of quotas, since quotas were introduced in the parties that already then had the highest women's representation. At the crucial election of 1991, when women's representation dropped for the first time since 1928, the difference was 36 compared to 28. However, a 2002 national survey of Swedish nomination committee chairs shows that only 23 percent of them believe that quotas are fair, while 33 percent believe they are 'necessary evils', and 43 percent believe they are 'principally unacceptable'. More women chairs than men chairs support quotas (29 vs 20 percent). Control for party, however, shows that while 78 percent of the bourgeois nomination committee chairs believe quotas are 'principally unacceptable' none of the socialist chairs oppose them, although more than half of them believe they are 'necessary evils' (Freidenvall forthcoming).

The introduction of quotas in the Norwegian Labour Party in 1983, see Table 3.2, was followed by an increase in the parliamentary fraction in the 1985 election from 33 to 42 percent. In the subsequent elections the percentage was 51, 49, 49, 47 and 52. The increase followed the adoption of quotas within the Socialist Left Party, coincided with a drop from 16 seats (hereof three women) to only two (hereof one woman) in 1977. In two elections during the 1990s, women's representation came just above the 30 percent mark. In the two latest elections, it again came close to 50 percent. In the Center Party, the 40–60 regulation today reflects 45 percent women and 55 percent men within the parliamentary delegation. In general, the political parties without quotas have a lower representation of women than the parties with quotas.

In Denmark, after the Social Democratic Party's introduction of 40 percent quota for municipal elections, the party nominated 33 percent women in 1989 and 32 percent in 1993, with the result of 29 respectively 31 percent women actually elected against 26 percent previously. This result also reveals the lack of correspondence between women's share of the nominated and the elected when the quota provisions do not include placement requirements and the lists are open to voters' preferences. In the first election after the party had abandoned quotas, the number of nominated women in fact dropped to 30 percent in 1997 and 29 percent in 2001; however 31 percent of women were elected for the party in both elections. Thus, the effect of the quota systems was limited for the municipal elections. For the elections to the European Parliament, quotas did seem to have had some effects, for the nomination as well as the election of women. Most interesting, after the quota was abandoned, because they were no longer considered 'necessary' by a majority in the party, the result of the nomination process came as a shock: Even if 40 percent of women were nominated by the party (six out of 15), four middle aged men topped the list. Only by public appeal to the voters by leading feminists was one young woman elected as one out of three. Later, in 2005, this young woman was elected leader of the whole party!

For the Danish Socialist People's Party the quota requirement ensured the election to the European Parliament of a man, who was moved up as number two on the electoral list because of the quota rules, after an internal primary in the party had placed four women at the top. As a result, one woman and one man were sent to Brussels (Dahlerup 1988b).

This analysis reveals that for some of the political parties, the introduction of quotas resulted in jumps in women's representation, notably in Norway. In other cases, not least in Denmark, quotas rules were only used half-heartedly and only for a short time and had little effect. In Sweden large jumps in women's representation after the introduction of quotas failed to appear, simply because women's representation was already high in those parties where quotas were adopted.

In a system with almost no institutionalized sanctions, not even in the political parties themselves, for non-compliance with quota rules, the question is what the incentives have been for the local branches to comply with centrally imposed quota rules? Our investigations show that it is not the sanctions by the central party organization that make the local party organizations comply with the quota rules. Rather, parties have gradually nominated more women because they fear the sanction of the voters, especially the female voters, if they do not have a sufficient number of women among their candidates. However, what is considered a sufficient share of women has gradually increased in the Nordic countries from just one woman in the 1940–60s, to one third in the 1970s and 1980s, to a new demand for de facto gender balance, notably in Sweden and Norway today.

In the debates on quotas, the prediction has often been expressed, especially among opponents that it would be impossible to find enough women candidates to stand for election. With the exception of some shortage of women candidates at the local level, this prediction has not come true. The main effect of recommendations, targets as well as quotas has been that the political parties at all levels have been forced to seriously recruit women.

The danger of stigmatization of 'quota women' has not been confirmed by the Nordic experiences. High echelon quotas imply that individual politicians are usually not singled out. Concerning 50–50 percent quotas with the use of a zipper system, alternating women and men on the list, two lists are made up and combined, one list for men and one list for women. The only decision left is whether the list should be topped by the number one from the women's or the men's lists. In such a system, women are no more 'quota women' than men are 'quota men'.

It has been subject to vehement discussions in the Nordic countries whether all these elected women have made a difference in politics. There is no agreement on this issue. However, research has shown that ever since women won the suffrage, it has primarily been women politicians who have raised issues of gender equality and in alliances with men have

succeeded in changing the political agenda of the Nordic countries somewhat (Skjeie 1992; Dahlerup 1998a; Wängnerud 1998).

Conclusions

Although women's political representation in the Nordic countries is very
high by international standards, quota provisions play only a limited role.
Instead a combination of structural factors such as institutional, socio-
economic and cultural factors, and strategic factors such as the activities
and campaigns launched by parties and the women's movement explains
patterns of women's representation.

Generally, the Nordic ambivalence towards quota politics can be interpreted as an effect of the various discursive frames that quota debates have
been embedded in. Incrementalism first implies an understanding of
historical development as gradual and progressive, implying a view where
improvements will evolve more or less automatically with changes in
women's position in society at large. In accordance with this notion of lin-
earity, time is seen in terms of a natural and self-regulatory process. Voluntary strategies are instead seen as preferable. Equal opportunities, second,
imply an understanding of men and women's equal rights to take part in
politics and in the competition for electoral posts. According to this logic
it is assumed to let 'the best person' win. Gender equality avoiding conflicts, finally, suggests that women and men must work in concerted action
to improve gender imbalances in parliament. The use of quotas would in
this perspective insinuate that there might be a conflict between men and
women, in contrast to the ideal of consensus.

However, the introduction of electoral quotas in various parties can be
seen as a discursive shift, starting in Norway, partly taking place in Iceland
and Sweden, to a certain extent having influenced Finland by the recent
implementation of quotas for local committees, including the steering
board of the local council, but not having influenced Denmark. This shift
is emphasized by a critique of the voluntary strategies used to increase
women's representation and a growing impatience about improvements
not being made within the anticipated time frame. The discursive shift
that has taken place in some parties is a product of the women's movements' continuous struggle to emphasize structural barriers to women's
inclusion in politics, and their ability to bend the discursive frames, supported by important structural and strategic factors mentioned above.
That electoral gender quotas have always been framed as gender neutral is
part of the continuous attempts in the Nordic countries to promote
gender equality without spurring gender conflicts.

The Nordic *high echelon quotas* were introduced when women already
had 20 to 30 percent of the parliamentary and local council seats. The
analysis reveals that, despite the many discursive controversies in its implementation and effects, quota provisions in the Nordic countries in

practice have proved to be a continuation of Nordic incrementalism rather than a break with the past.

The apparent paradox, that the Danish parliament with 37 percent women is seen as gender equal, while the Swedish one with 45 percent is seen as unequal, highlights the fact that equality is subject to interpretation, also within the Nordic countries.

Notes

1 A few parties did introduce quotas in the 1970s, for example in Norway the Socialist Left Party and the Liberal Party.
2 The Women's sections within the older Nordic political parties were created in the inter-war period or before. They often had the right to send a few representatives to the party leadership at various levels.
3 Research in the Nordic countries has shown that voters are sensitive to the sex of the candidates, although to a limited extent and with variations between left and right parties (Dahl *et al.* 1989).

Bibliography

Andersen, K. (1975) 'Working Women and Political Participation, 1952–1972', *American Journal of Political Science*, 19: 439–55.

Bergqvist, C. (1995) 'The Declining corporatist state and the political gender dimension', in L. Karvonen and P. Selle (eds) *Women in Nordic Politics: Closing the Gap*, Aldershot: Dartmouth, pp. 205–28.

Bergqvist, C. *et al.* (eds) (1999) *Equal Democracies? Gender and Politics in the Nordic Countries*, Oslo: Scandinavian University Press.

Borchorst, A. and Christensen, A.D. (2003) 'Könskvotering i SF og i forskerstillinger – diskursiv praksis og forändring', in A. Borchorst and D. Dahlerup (eds) *Ligestillingspolitik som diskurs og praksis*, Frederiksberg: Samfundslitteratur, pp. 101–23.

Borchorst, A. and Dahlerup, D. (eds) (2003) *Ligestillingspolitik som diskurs og praksis*, Frederiksberg: Samfundslitteratur.

Bystydzienski, J.M. (1995) *Women in Electoral Politics: Lessons from Norway*, Westport: Praeger.

Castles, F.G. and Sainsbury, D. (1990) 'Politics in Scandinavia', in R.C. Macridis (ed.) *Modern Political Systems: Europe*, 7th edn, Englewood Cliffs, New Jersey: Prentice Hall, pp. 281–327.

Dahl, H.M. *et al.* (1989) *Hvorfor stiger kvinderepræsentationen? En analyse af folketingsvalget i september 1987*, University of Aarhus: Department of Political Science.

Dahlerup, D. (1988a) 'From a Small to a Large Minority: Women in Scandinavian Politics', *Scandinavian Political Studies*, 11, 4: 275–98.

—— (1988b) *Vi har ventet længe nok – håndbog i kvinderepræsentation*, Copenhagen: Nordisk Ministerråd.

—— (1998a) *Rødstrømperne. Den danske Rødstrømpebevægelses udvikling, nytænkning og gennemslag, Vol. I–II*, Copenhagen: Gyldendal.

—— (1998b) 'Using Quotas to Increase Women's Political Representation', in A. Karam (ed.) *Women in Parliament. Beyond Numbers*, Stockholm: International IDEA, pp. 91–106.

—— (2004) 'Continuity and Waves in the Feminist Movement – A Challenge to Social Movement Theory', in H. Römer Christensen, B. Halsaa and A. Saarinen (eds) *Crossing Borders: Remapping Women's Movements at the Turn of the 21st Century*, Odense: University Press of Southern Denmark, pp. 59–78.

Dahlerup, D. and Freidenvall, L. 'Quotas as a "Fast Track" to Equal Political Representation for Women: Why Scandinavia is No Longer the Model', paper presented at the 19th International Political Science Association World Congress, Durban, South Africa, June–July 2003.

Dahlerup, D. and Freidenvall, L. (2005) 'Quotas as a Fast Track to Equal Representation for Women', *International Feminist Journal of Politics*, 7, 1: 1–22.

de los Reyes, P., Molina, I. and Mulinari, D. (eds) (2002) *Maktens (o)lika förklädnader: kön, klass och etnicitet i det postkoloniala Sverige: en festskrift till Wuokko Knocke*, Stockholm: Atlas.

Freidenvall, L. (2003) 'Women's political representation and gender quotas – the Swedish case.' The Research Program on Gender Quotas. Working Paper Series 2003: 3, Stockholm University: Department of Political Science.

—— (forthcoming), *Vägen till varannan damernas. Om kvinnorepresentation, kvotering och politiska partier i Sverige 1970–2002*, PhD dissertation, Stockholm University: Department of Political Science.

Gelb, J. (1989) *Feminism and Politics: A Comparative Perspective*, Berkeley: University of California Press.

Gomard, K. and Krogstad, A. (eds) (2001) *Instead of the Ideal Debate. Doing Politics and Doing Gender in Nordic Political Campaign Discourse*, Gylling: Aarhus University Press.

Haavio-Mannila, E. *et al.* (eds) (1985) *Unfinished Democracy: Women in Nordic Politics*, New York: Pergamon.

Hagemann, G. (2003) *Feminisme og historieskriving – inntrykk fra en reise*, Oslo: Universitetsforlaget.

Hernes, H. (1982) *Staten – kvinner ingen adgang?* Oslo: Universitetsforlaget.

—— (1987) *Welfare State and Women Power: Essays in State Feminism*, Oslo: Norwegian University Press.

Hirdman, Y. (1990) 'Genussystemet', in *Demokrati och makt i Sverige*, SOU 1990: 44, Stockholm: Statens offentliga utredningar, pp. 73–116.

—— (2001) *Genus – om det stabilas föränderliga former*, Malmö: Liber.

Holli, A.M. (2004) 'Quotas for Indirectly Elected Bodies: A Tailor-Made Solution for Finland', *European Political Science*, 3, 3: 81–9.

Holter, H. (1981) 'Om kvinneundertrykkelse, mannsundertrykkelse og hersketeknikker', in K. Andenaes, T. Johansen and T. Mathisen (eds) *Maktens ansikter: perspektiver på makt og maktforskning*, Oslo: Gyldendal, pp. 216–35.

Htun, M. (2004) 'Is Gender like Ethnicity? The Political Representation of Identity Groups', *Perspectives on Politics*, 2, 3: 439–58.

Kaiser, P. (2001) *Strategic Predictors of Women's Parliamentary Participation: A Comparative Study of Twenty-Three Democracies*, PhD dissertation, Los Angeles: University of California.

Kjær, U. (2000) 'Saturation without parity: The stagnating number of female councillors in Denmark', in N. Rao (ed.) *Representation and Community in Western Democracies*, Houndmills: MacMillan, pp. 149–66.

Kristjánsson, S. (2002) 'Iceland: From Party Rule to Pluralist Political Society', in H.M. Narud, M.N. Pedersen and H. Valen (eds) *Party Sovereignty and Citizen*

Control. Selecting Candidates for Parliamentary Elections in Denmark, Finland, Iceland and Norway, Odense: University Press of Southern Denmark, pp. 107–66.

——— (2003) 'Iceland: A Parliamentary Democracy with a Semi-presidential Constitution', in K. Ström, W.C. Muller and T. Bergman (eds) *Delegation and Accountability in Parliamentary Democracies*, Oxford: Oxford University Press, pp. 399–417.

Matland, R. (1998) 'Enhancing Women's Political Participation: Legislative Recruitment and Electoral Systems', in A. Karam (ed.) *Women in Parliament: Beyond Numbers*, Stockholm: International IDEA, pp. 65–88.

Matland, R. and Studlar, D.T. (1996) 'The Contagion of Women Candidates in Single-Member District and Proportional Representation Electoral Systems: Canada and Norway', *The Journal of Politics*, 58, 3: 707–33.

McDonagh, E. (2002) 'Political Citizenship and Democratization: The Gender Paradox', *American Political Science Review*, 96, 3: 535–52.

Narud, H.M., Pedersen, M.N. and Valen, H. (eds) (2002) *Party Sovereignty and Citizen Control. Selecting Candidates for Parliamentary Elections in Denmark, Finland, Iceland and Norway*, Odense: University Press of Southern Denmark.

Norris, P. (1987) *Politics and Sexual Equality: The Comparative Position of Women in Western Democracies*, Boulder: Lynne Rienner.

Phillips, A. (1995) *The Politics of Presence: The Political Representation of Gender, Ethnicity and Race*, Oxford: Oxford University Press.

Pikkala, S. 'Representations of Women in Finnish Local Government: Effects of the 1995 Gender Quota Legislation', paper presented to the Joint Session Workshops of the European Consortium for Political Research, Copenhagen, April 2000.

Pincus, I. (2002) *The Politics of Gender Equality Policy*, PhD dissertation, Örebro University: Department of Political Science.

Raevaara, E. 'Talking about Equality, Acting for Change: Conceptualisations of Gender Equality in Parliamentary Debates in Finland and France', paper presented at the General Conference of the European Consortium for Political Research, Marburg, Germany, September 2003.

Rokkan, S. (1987) *Stat, nasjon, klasse*, Oslo: Universitetsforlaget.

Rule, W. (1981) 'The Critical Contextual Factors in Women's Legislative Recruitment', *Western Political Quarterly*, 34: 60–77.

——— (1987) 'Electoral Systems, Contextual Factors and Women's Opportunity for Elections to Parliament in Twenty-three Democracies', *The Western Political Quarterly*, 40, 3: 477–98.

Sainsbury, D. (1993) 'The Politics of Increased Women's Representation: The Swedish Case', in J. Lovenduski and P. Norris (eds) *Gender and Party Politics*, Thousand Oaks: Sage, pp. 263–90.

——— (1996) *Gender, Equality and Welfare States*, Cambridge: Cambridge University Press.

——— (2004) 'Women's Political Representation in Sweden: Discursive Politics and Institutional Presence', *Scandinavian Political Studies*, 27, 1: 65–87.

Skjeie, H. (1992) *Den politiske betydningen av kjønn: En studie av norsk topp-politikk*, Oslo: Institute for Social Research.

——— (2001) 'Quotas, Parity and the Discursive Dangers of Difference' in C.S. Maier and J. Klausen (eds) *Has Liberalism Failed Women? Assuring Equal Representation in Europe and in the United States*, New York: Palgrave, pp. 165–76.

Skjeie, H. (2003) 'Særuttalelse: Demokrati, makt og menneskerettigheter', in *Sluttrapport fra Makt- og demokratiutredningen*, NOU 2003: 19, Oslo: Statens forvaltningstjeneste, Informasjonsforvaltning, pp. 74–87.

Skjeie, H. and Siim, B. (2000) 'Scandinavian Feminist Debates on Citizenship', *International Political Science Review*, 21, 4: 345–60.

Skjeie, H. and Teigen, M. (2003) *Menn imellom. Mannsdominans og likestillingspolitikk*, Oslo: Gyldendal Akademisk.

Styrkársdóttir, A. (1986) 'From social movement to political power: the new women's movement in Iceland', in D. Dahlerup (ed.) *The New Women's Movement: Feminism and Political Power in Europe and the US*, Newbury Park: Sage, pp. 140–57.

Teigen, M. (2000) 'The Affirmative action controversy', *NORA* (*Nordic Journal of Women's Studies*), 8, 2: 63–77.

—— (2003) *Kvotering og kontrovers*, Oslo: Pax.

Togeby, L. (2003) *Fra fremmedarbejdere til etniske minoriteter*, Aarhus: Aarhus University Press.

Togeby, L., Andersen, J.G., Munk Christiansen, P., Jørgensen, T.B. and Vallgårda, S. (2003) *Magt og demokrati i Danmark. Hovedresultater fra Magtudredningen*, Aarhus: Aarhus University Press.

United Nations Development Programme (UNDP) (2004) 'Human Development Report 2004'. Online. Available at: http://hdr.undp.org (accessed 25 January 2005).

Wallin, G. *et al.* (1981) *Kommunalpolitikerna. Del 1 och 2.* Ds Kn 1981: 17–18.

Wängnerud, L. (1998) *Politikens andra sida. Om kvinnorepresentation i Sveriges riksdag*, PhD dissertation, Göteborg: Göteborgs universitet.

4 Latin America

The experience and the impact of quotas in Latin America

Clara Araújo and Ana Isabel García

Latin America is the leading continent when it comes to the introduction of gender quotas in politics. This chapter analyses the many experiences of gender quota policies in the region.[1] It seeks to understand the general background – the main features and conditions that led to the adoption of these policies – to identify the main characteristics of the adopted legislation, as well as to evaluate its subsequent results and impacts on women's representation in legislative branches throughout the region.

Eleven out of 19 Latin American countries have approved the quota system in legal or constitutional acts aiming at promoting greater gender equality in political parliamentary representation. In countries that have not adopted quota legislation, many political parties have changed their rules and approved similar types of affirmative action policies.[2] These changes occurred over a relatively short period of time. All countries adopted them between 1996 and 2000, with the exception of Argentina, which acted earlier, in 1991. The geographic concentration of countries that adopted quota systems in the region and their rapid dissemination as an official policy throughout Latin America had a positive impact on the adoption of similar policies in the rest of the world.

On the basis of previous contributions and on other data, our analysis intends to highlight some aspects.[3] In the case of Latin America, the role of various factors related to the political transitions to democratic regimes in the last two decades should be considered: the need for international legitimacy on the part of newly born democracies; the socio-economic changes that have affected women in the region; and the role of women's movements throughout the process. There are also broader issues usually considered in studies on international quota experiences.

The Latin American socio-political context

The modernization process in Latin America occurred in a complex and unbalanced way, conferring a distinct character to the socio-political

systems in the region in comparison to other developing societies
(Brunner 1989). Most Latin America states acquired their independence
relatively early, in the beginning of the nineteenth century (Kaplan 1966;
Gomáriz 1977). This early independence was faced with a singular contra-
diction: its political systems bore the burden of their colonial heritage,
while, at the same time, suffered the impact of modern ideas, mostly from
the French and American Revolutions meant to shatter that same old
order. As a result, the region has always been characterized by an ongoing
tension – on one side, political ideas, constitutions, institutions and even
middle class bureaucracies with markedly modernizing and progressive
views, and on the other, traces of *clientelism, patronage* and authoritarianism inherited from the colonial past.

This tension, established in the context of societies structurally dependent on a global market dominated by countries in the Northern Hemi-
sphere, has manifested itself in a pendulum motion, swinging, back and
forth between progressive periods and authoritarian ones (Gomáriz
1977). There are some exceptions, first and foremost, Costa Rica. During
the 1960s and 1970s the region was hit by a wave of military coups and by
the establishment of authoritarian regimes in many of its countries. This
historical record left a legacy of tension, currently reflected by the co-
existence of democratic political systems and extremely unbalanced and
unfair socio-economical realities.

The last two decades were particularly important in Latin American
history. Numerous countries under authoritarian or dictatorial regimes
initiated processes of democratization or re-democratization in the 1980s.
Argentina, Brazil, Uruguay, Paraguay, Peru, Panama, Dominican Republic, El Salvador, Guatemala, Nicaragua, Chile, and Bolivia had their dictatorial governments replaced, through revolutionary processes or
democratic reforms. Democratic reforms were also initiated in countries
with *caudilho* and oligarchic tradition, such as Mexico. However, the Latin
American democratic transition was accompanied by IMF-presided economic reforms that impacted the region's socio-economic development.
Economic reforms were geared towards privatization, reinforcement of
the idea of limited state, reduction of social expenses and an emphasis on
the market. Thus, during the 1990s, a 'two-way' movement took place: (1)
in the political sphere, there were some democratic changes and many
countries in the region moved towards the consolidation and broadening
of civil and political rights. Political systems in the region adopted a more
democratic design, with regular elections and institutional and normative
rules associated to the law; (2) in the economic sphere, reforms generated
recession and an increase in poverty and inequality. Thus, Latin American
countries went through contradictory and tense processes, combining
political advances and socio-economic setbacks.

The presence of women in the region's politics

Each country went through its own particular process of female inclusion. By the end of the nineteenth century Mexico, Peru and the nations of the Southern Cone of South America had already witnessed the emergence of women's groups and associations. By the mid-twentieth century, feminist organizations had appeared in the remaining Latin American countries. The first organized political action of Latin American women was the suffragist movement (late nineteenth century), following the example of women's movements in other parts of the world. Several feminine political parties were founded, some organized movements, such as the Brazilian Feminine League (1920s) and the Costa Rican Feminist League (1943) also appeared. But the region only began its slow march towards recognizing women's right to vote and to be elected in the 1920s. Ecuador was the first country to adopt a law addressing this issue in 1929. The last country to do so was Paraguay, in 1961, see Table 4.1.

Women first established their presence in the Executive Power by occupying positions in the Ministries. However, the process of female inclusion in ministerial positions has been slow in many countries. For example, Ecuador, Brazil and Argentina had their first female ministers in 1979, 1982, and 1989, respectively.

Up to now, only four women in these countries have served as President: Lydia Gueiler in Bolivia (1979–80) and Estela Martínez, Perón's widow, in Argentina (1974–6); Violeta Barrios, Chamorro's widow, in Nicaragua (1990–6) and Mireya Moscoso in Panama (1999–2004). Again, Latin America followed a general pattern – these women rose to power by inheriting political capital from husbands or brothers. Presidents' wives have also played significant political roles with respect to women in some countries. This was the case of Eva Peron, the first wife of President Perón in Argentina.

In general, women were elected to legislative posts after their political citizenship was acknowledged. However, the proportion of elected women

Table 4.1 The right to vote for women

1929	1932	1934	1942	1945	1956	1947
Ecuador	Brazil Uruguay	Cuba	Dominican Republic	Guatemala	Panama	Argentina Venezuela

1949	1950	1952	1953	1954	1955	1962
Costa Rica Chile	El Salvador	Bolivia	Mexico	Colombia	Honduras Peru Nicaragua	Paraguay

Source: Valdés and Gomáriz (1995).

remained low in most countries, with the exception of Cuba, Costa Rica and Nicaragua. Up until the quota system was established, this percentage was usually less than 15 per cent.

Women's relations to power and the State, however, were not unilateral. In numerous occasions, feminist movements were engaged in popular protests against governments. In fact, Latin American women's political action during the 1970s and 1980s was characterized by its strong grassroots organization, as well as its active participation in the democratic transition in a region that was starting to experience.

Social movements were a crucial part in the struggle for democracy in the region. Women, in turn, were key figures in denouncing authoritarianism and in protests against the economic reforms of the 1980s (Álvarez 1998; Polanco 1999; Htun and Jones 2002; Molyneux and Craske 2002; Vargas 2002; Molyneux 2003). Collective forms of resistance began to appear, such as neighbourhood associations, mothers' clubs, amongst others. The 'Mothers of the *Plaza de Mayo*' became the symbol of the struggle against dictatorship in Argentina. Mothers' clubs in Brazil and Nicaraguan associations were other examples of resistance and organization for a return to democratic rule. These movements reflected both the strong tradition of community mobilization for provision of basic needs (involving, mostly, women), and the possibilities for mobilization at the time.

By the end of the 1980s and the beginning of the 1990s in Latin America, the main focus was on achieving political rights and guaranteeing constitutional civil rights. At the same time, the demand for a more substantive form of democracy emerged, which involved not only formal and electoral tasks, but also collective participation and the defence of social rights curtailed by the neo-liberal economic policies imposed during the 1980s and 1990s. Although some important changes had occurred in the social and economic profile of women in the region – such as increase in life expectancy, educational levels, employment and non-discrimination laws – economic reforms aimed at reduced public spending had a significantly negative impact on women's living conditions.[4]

Thus, the epicentre of Latin American women's struggles in the 1990s was the process of re-democratization, strategically focused on enforcing their rights as women and as citizens in the political and social dimensions. The political environment was a crucial factor. For women, the aspiration for citizenship started with the 'the right to have rights'. The focus on 'rights' covered both the guarantee of 'formal' rights and the demand for broader democratic processes that should include a participative dimension and the defence of social rights. The absence of women in the decision making process was an example of the limits of existing political democracy. In short, the women's movement[5] during the processes of re-democratization expressed itself in many ways and contributed to the strengthening of the language of human rights in the region.[6]

As new democratic processes were being established in Latin America, new feminist strategies emerged focusing on the access to power and the increase of women's representation and participation in institutional politics. The concern was to 'enter wherever possible' (Carrasco 1999) and to move 'from protest to proposal' (Molyneux 2003). This implied a combination of pressure from below, by autonomous organizations, with pressure from above, or from within the state. Quota strategies became an important focus of women's organizations. Part of the feminist movement, however, preferred to keep away from the state, in order to preserve and protect the movement's autonomy. The tension between these perspectives and the risk of women's movement being captured by a minimalist concept of democracy and by a governmental agenda, dominated the movement's debates throughout the 1990s.

The emergence of quota policies in Latin America: political and institutional context

A number of political factors contributed to the emergence of quota proposals in Latin America throughout the 1990s. Some of them are linked to the institutional dimension, while others are associated to the women's movement collective action. Both are related to the processes of re-democratization in the region. In the items below, we shortly address some aspects that seem to be directly or indirectly relevant for quota policy adoption in the region.

The re-democratization process during the 1980s and 1990s decades and its association with the issue of modernization

Many new governments, after dictatorial period, had been elected with the compromise of promoting more political equality also in terms of gender and race or ethnicity. The gap between women and men in the decision-making process was an indicator of the weakness of the regimes. The improvement of women's situation in the society became part of the political agenda of re-democratization. This process was carried out by two kinds of political reasons – ideological and/or pragmatic – not necessarily contradictory, but in some cases more oriented by one or another motivation. As the countries recently freed from dictatorial or authoritarian regimes needed external legitimacy, the new civilian governments were keen to build a positive and modern image associated to the prevalence of constitutional rights and democratic and transparent institutions. In this context, the extension of women's rights was seen as a means of overcoming traits that gave these countries a less modern image vis-à-vis the international community. New governments were eager to distance themselves from the traditional image of Latin American politics, associated with the predominance of *clientelism* and personal leadership, widespread corruption in institutions and authoritarian rule. This is also a period in which women's rights were being incorporated in a broader political institutional agenda in the international context. The adoption of specific policies for women was associated to the concept of 'good governance' in the global market, as part of the very idea of 'modernization'. This new interpretation could be found in the international organs linked to the UN and in economic institutions that monitored reforms in the region. It was included in various international agreements and also adopted by many local governments. In the 1990s, many Latin American leaders including Eduardo Frei in Chile, Fujimori in Peru, Cardoso in Brazil and Zedillo in Mexico adopted pro-women rhetoric and special government agencies were created to develop gender or women's policies (Álvarez 1998: 270; Molyneux 2003). Women occupied this space mainly due to their struggle, as was previously noted. In some cases, however, these measures were adopted for pragmatic reasons, such as meeting conditionality requirements of multilateral finance agencies.[7] Defence of women's rights in public discourse became a proof of 'good will' and commitment to a modern society.

The new institutional design of the re-democratization processes implied important changes in normative and constitutional aspects

The processes of re-democratization in Latin America permitted the inclusion of new actors and new proposals in the decision-making process, such as the quota policy proposals. The inclusion of the new political players – as in the case of women – tends to broaden the basis of legitimacy in the political system, a relevant factor when considering the civilian context of political crisis (García and Gomáriz 2000). As it was observed, (Krook 2003; Baldez 2004), in a context of transition, the institutional dimension can work as a base for quota policy adoption.

This aspect leads to an additional hypothesis: in the context of the region's re-democratization processes, the institutional weaknesses associated to the presence of 'non-modern' traces in local political may have actually favoured the adoption of changes that may be more difficult to enact in countries with a more consolidated and institutionalized political culture. As it was observed (Ramírez and Eneaney 1997), innovative processes tend to be more easily assimilated by countries with less consolidated institutional structures. Conversely, more mobilization is required for changes in countries with more consolidated forms of democracy, given the importance of their institutions to their political culture. This may explain the relative ease with which quota policies were incorporated into official rhetoric and legal action in Latin America in contrast with the difficulties they have faced in the more consolidated democracies of Europe, for example.

The UN-sponsored international conferences on women's issues and a growing commitment of government to examine the subject, especially after the Beijing Conference

The international conferences that took place in the 1980s and 1990s were important factors in the institutional acknowledgement of the feminist agenda. Their positive effect on the struggle for women's rights is a consensus, especially in the case of the Beijing Conference, but also in relation to Vienna and Cairo Conferences. With respect to Latin America, various authors have highlighted this subject. They focus on three main aspects: the resulting encouragement to regional feminist political articulation; the pressure placed upon governments; and the legitimacy conferred on the feminist struggle by the conferences (García 1997; Araújo 1999, 2003; Htun and Jones 2002; Molyneux and Craske 2002; Vargas 2002; 2003; Bareiro 2003). Supported by the Conferences' resolutions, throughout the 1990s, the 'language of rights' began to include the right to participate in the making of decisions, that is, the right to inclusion in spheres of power. One of the feminist strategies for the acquisition of complete citizenship succeeded in making governments create organs and adopt policies to include women in the decision-making spheres of the State. Faced with the fragility of political institutions – including political parties – and with women's socio-economic disadvantages in an already unequal environment, the feminist movement was able to advance affirmative action measures. Within the framework of the Beijing World Conference on Women, greater advances were made with respect to governmental institutionalization for the promotion of women's rights in the region. National mechanisms were created and a qualitative change took place in their institutional status (García and Ulloa 2004). In Latin America, the international conferences accomplished more than the legitimization of a general political agenda for women. They also legitimized the way women inserted themselves in the re-democratization processes and denounced their difficulties in having access to the spheres of power. New strategies such as quota policies were legitimized in this context.

The organization of women's networks in the region and the struggle for democratization

As it was pointed out, one of the feminist strategies by the end of the 1980s and the beginning of the 1990s consisted of building a wide network in the region. Its period coincides with the international conferences, which worked as a stimulus for many regional meetings under a common agenda: the re-democratization process, the organization of the conference and the situation of women in the region. One specific network for parliamentary women was created through the Parlatino, an inter-parliamentary regional organization. It played an important role in the debate about quotas, before and after the Beijing Conference.[8] Also, women's movements attained legitimacy and popular sympathy as a result of a reasonably expressive history of political activity against dictatorship in many countries. It contributed to the conquest of a positive view from other political sectors, as well as to the inclusion of their organization as relevant collective actors during the restoration of constitutional rights.

The feminist criticism of democracy and its specific appropriation in the region

The point above was linked to an international feminist context and agenda. It also reflected an environment in which the democratization of power was being debated. The limits of inclusion in representative democracies and the need of new ways of recognition led to new proposals, such as that of quotas (Fraser 1995; Phillips 1998; Htun and Jones 2002; Dahlerup 2003). In Latin America, this was incorporated in post-authoritarian context as a way to show new possibilities of democratic experiences of inclusion. In some countries, women's action inside some parties was decisive for the beginning of the debate. However, women's movement isn't a unified block, not all of it was in accordance with the idea that dominant patterns of election would be a way to solve the problem of entering into formal politics; and particularly with the idea of asking for quotas.

The very specific Argentina 'contagion effect'

It has been verified that the positive results that quotas played in Argentina helped to spread this measure to other countries in the region. It was both in terms of the experience of the process of adoption of quotas, the lobby and the mobilization for improving the law, as well as its figures results. Argentina's quota system became a paradigm for other countries going through democratic changes.

In short, some aspects of the political context appear as decisive to the adoption of quotas in the region.

The general characteristics of the process of adopting quotas

The general context outlined above helps in the understanding of the conditions under which the quota system spread in the region. There are some characteristics of this process, which are important to point out. Not all countries accepted the quotas immediately. Some countries, in fact, still do not consider the quota system an official and mandatory policy for the legislature, although they have been discussing it for many years. Colombia has quotas for government jobs and for administrative branches at the legislative level, but not for electoral competition in the legislative sphere. In Uruguay, quotas were first proposed in 1988 and Chile initiated the debate in the early 1990s. Neither country have adopted quotas yet, although some parties as PPD and PS in Chile and PS in Uruguay have been adopting it since the end of the 1980s (D'Albora and Levine 1996; Johnson 2003; Peschard 2003). Other nations that began debating the issue in the late 1980s and early 1990s, such as Costa Rica and Argentina, also rejected the quotas at first. Interestingly enough, these last four Latin American countries have long stood out as a result of their democratic traditions. These traditions include the structure of their institutions, their social organization and the level of their socio-economic development, when compared to the other countries in the region and despite the experiences with dictatorships in Chile, Argentina and Uruguay.

During the 1950s, Argentina had briefly handled quotas for women within the Peronist Party. In the beginning of the 1990s the country was seeking to rebuild its democratic institutions after the military dictatorship. Groups formed by women had an important role in denouncing the dictatorship; they equally presented a previous record of more organized action. The debate on quotas, initiated in 1990, took place in this environment. Quotas were approved in 1991, despite all the controversy that was generated, but with support from the President Menem, seen as a kind of populist politician. Costa Rica, in turn, had always been an exception in the troubled Latin American scenario. It had a long-standing democratic tradition and an institutional culture of preserving institutional practices. In this case, the proposal of quotas did not arise from a need to legitimize an emerging democracy, but rather from a desire to strengthen an existing one.

Peru was perhaps the most emblematic example of the association between quota policies and the quest for legitimacy. Quotas were first proposed by the government of Alberto Fujimori, whose administration was under question since its very beginning in 1992. The quota system had the support of Fujimori's party members, and this led feminist groups to denounce it as demagogical and initially refused to support it (Vargas 2002; Yáñez 2003).

In Mexico, the first proposal was presented in 1993 and was stimulated by the presence of women in the re-democratization process and the creation of MLD (Women Fighting for Democracy). The creation of a political feminist network called 'Diversa', in 1997, (Bartra 2002) helped to improve the law approved in 1996. Equator and the Dominican Republic are also examples of legal reforms boosted by the pressure of women's movement (Pacari 2002).

In many countries, in addition to the general context discussed above, the debate was encouraged by the adoption of policies within the political parties. The parties were pressured by women members or/and needed to improve their performance in elections, as in the case of PRI (Institutional Revolutionary Party), in Mexico or, as in the case of the Worker's Party in Brazil (Suplicy 1996; Araújo 1999; Miguel 1999; Peschard 2002).

The arguments for and against quotas and its discursive framings

Almost every country held numerous debates during the approval processes, thus the lack of consensus on the adoption of quota policies.[9] These differences of opinion and strength and the tension amongst the actors were expressed in the content of the speeches and in the characteristic of first legislations.

It is possible to summarize some points related to the content of speeches from the analysis of literature, although a specific research hasn't been carried out in this paper.[10] The main arguments against the quotas system are centred on: (1) its *unconstitutional character*, which contradicts the principle of equal opportunities; (2) its *discriminatory image*, for women could be stigmatized; and (3) its *undemocratic nature*, since merit would be considered a secondary principle, possibly facilitating the entrance of less qualified women: the risk of fragmentation or a corporative political practice into society. There were further objections, but these were not directly linked to the basis of the proposal or with a democratic liberal perspective. These restrictions appeared to be a warning against the possible rhetoric use of such initiatives. These remarks are associated with the manner that certain governments have spoken of and used quotas during their attempts to gain legitimacy or with the risk of a minimalist approach in relation to the meaning of democracy (Vargas 2002).

The dominating favourable arguments in this process do not differ from those of general experiences reviewed in literature. They can be placed in three basic categories: (a) *normative*: the presence of women is necessary and justified by a sense of *justice*. As it is a positive action, it is a temporary mechanism; (b) *symbolic*: quotas can educate a society and can portray a society as egalitarian and inclusive; (c) *utilitarian:* which can be divided into three arguments: (1) more women in power equals including more female-chosen issues in the political agenda; (2) the presence of women is essential to the legitimacy of democracy; (3) the presence of women is important to improve the quality of democracy since they are more honest, tolerant and less corrupt, an aspect that in Latin America has a particular relevance. Thus, the inclusion of women in the spheres of power could be understood not only as a question of rights, but also, as a question of *usefulness*, due to their honesty and lack of self-interest, as Polanco (1999) and Bareiro (2003) has pointed out. Being able to give an honest contribution to politics (attributing honesty to feminine public conduct) seemed compatible with the ongoing re-democratization process in progress, which was also challenged with changing the prevailing image of corruption and personalization in the region's politics. Probably, due to the political context analyzed above, as well as the political culture, in Latin America utilitarian arguments tended to be more common than the others.

The process and its institutional, collective and individual players

Further examination of these experiences shows that, in most cases, the initial process relied on some core players, although others participated in a less intense or more circumstantial way. One can find female members of political parties, especially congresswomen, in the leading role. Some of these women were linked to women's movement or identified themselves as feminists. These women, supported by the resolutions of the conferences, articulated the support of their parties and of other segments of women, as exemplified by Mexico, Brazil, Argentina, Costa Rica, Peru, Bolivia and Dominican Republic. The networks of women for political participation seem to have played an important role, as for example in Uruguay, in Venezuela, that of the Feminine Politician Forum in Bolivia and WNDC (Women's National Convention for Democracy) in Mexico. The descriptions of some of these processes allow us to infer that the ability to articulate and the political savvy of some of these women were undoubtedly an important, although perhaps not a decisive, factor for the approval of the proposal on a national level. Other important actors were institutional and/or governmental organs in charge of policies for women, as in the cases of Costa Rica, Venezuela, Mexico and Bolivia.

In some cases, direct action undertaken by the President of the Republic, as in Argentina and Peru, or even by the first lady, as in the case of Costa Rica (promoting quotas in the late 1980s) was decisive to the approval of the proposal.

Initially, women's autonomous movements, especially feminist ones, played a secondary role in most countries. In some countries, such as Ecuador, Panama, Mexico, Chile, Argentina, and Uruguay sectors of women's movements were directly involved from the start of the debates. In others, however, it was possible to identify an environment of distrust, associated with a record of government's attempts to co-opt women's movements, as shown by some interpretations of the Dominican Republic's case. There was also resistance to the use of demands on *women's rights*, quotas in particular, as political instruments, exemplified by the Peruvian case (Vargas 2002; Yáñez 2003). This process also revealed a tension within the feminist movement. On one side stood party militants and militants already engaged in government politics supporting quotas. On the other, stood the 'pure' or autonomous feminists, whose trajectories revolved around criticism: of the patriarchal nature of the power of the State; and on the minimalist democracies in process in the region, in distributive and participatory dimensions.

By the 2000s, the quota system had spread and become incorporated into the political agenda of the region. The resulting environment was more open to dialogue and to the involvement of other sectors of women's movements in the further development of these policies. In some cases, the results were very positive, not only for the women involved in the political sphere, but also for the women's movements as a whole, increasing the scope and visibility of their struggle. However, in other countries the attained results were below expectations, generating a demand for a broader evaluation of the subject. These evaluations indicated the need for alliances amongst female members of political parties and women's NGOs. Some stress the need for improving their ability to face the issue of quotas. Others highlight the need of a wider criticism and intervention in relation to the weak mechanisms of democracy, the inequalities that remain plotting against women and most of the population and the limited character of quotas for changing this situation.

The characteristic of quota's law and its legal features in Latin American countries

Table 4.2 shows the countries in Latin America that have adopted quotas for representatives' bodies, the main features of the existing laws and of the electoral systems of each country. As the 4th column shows, in many countries, the quota system is extended to all legislative mandates. However, in this study, we only analyze the cases pertaining to the national parliament.

Some specific observations on individual countries are necessary, given the huge variation in the electoral system, as Table 4.2 reveals.[11]

a   In Argentina, the first law was approved in 1991. However, during the election of 1993, the quota didn't have the awaited impact, due to lack of rules on the rank order and absence of enforcement mandate. The improvement of the law was decisive to the later trajectory of success. Quotas for the Senate in Argentina were approved in 2000 and put into practice in 2001. It is important to stress that before 2001 the senators were elected indirectly. Each list elects two Senators at most. According to some analysis, in fact, by assigning two seats to the majority party and one for the party that comes in second, electoral rules establish quotas of 50 per cent, assuring that at least 33 per cent of the senators will be women (Htun and Jones 2002). This fact was confirmed by the 2001 elections. The national law was suitably regulated in 2001 and the quota is constitutional. However, this improvement is still a process in course and many aspects remain in debate (Lazzaro 2004; Archenti 2004).

b   In Bolivia, part of the members of Congress are elected in majority districts. Quota's law applies only to members elected by means of proportional system and it is compulsory (Benavides 2003). Bolivian's

Table 4.2 General features of quotas to legislative branches in Latin American countries

Country	Quota type	Year of introduction	Legislative branch	Quota provision	Quota at lower levels[a]	Type of list to the chamber[b]	Rules about ranking order	Sanctions for non-compliance	Electoral system
Argentina	Legal quotas (C)	1991 2001	Chamber Senate	30% 30%	P, L	Closed	Yes	Yes	List PR
Bolivia	Legal quotas (L)	1997	Chamber Senate	30%[c] 25%	L (30%)	Closed	Yes	Yes	MMP
Brazil	Legal quotas (L)	1997	Chamber[d]	30%	P, L	Open	No	No	List PR
Chile	No quotas					Open			List PR
Colombia	No quotas								List PR
Costa Rica	Legal quotas (L)	1997	Chamber	40%	L	Closed	Yes	Yes	List PR
Cuba	No quotas								Two Rounds
Dominican Republic	Legal quotas (L)	1997 2000	Chamber Chamber[e]	25% 33%	L (25%) L (50%)	Closed	Yes	Yes	List PR
Ecuador	Legal quotas (L)	1997 2000	Chamber Chamber	20% 30%[c]	P (20%) R, L (30%)[c]	Open	Yes	Yes	List PR
El Salvador	No quotas					Closed			List PR
Guatemala	No quotas					Closed			List PR
Honduras	Legal quotas (L)	2000, 2004	Chamber	30%[c]	R, L	Closed	No	No	List PR
Mexico	Legal quotas (L)	1996 2002	Chamber Senate	30% 30%		Closed to PR	Yes	Yes	MMP
Nicaragua	No quotas					Closed			List PR
Panama	Legal quotas (L)	1997	Chamber	30%	L	Open	No	No	List PR and FPP[f]
Paraguay	Legal quotas (L)	1996	Chamber Senate	20% 20%	P, L	Closed	Yes	Yes	List PR
Peru	Legal quotas (L)	1997 2000	Chamber Chamber	25% 30%	L (25%) P, L (30%)	Open	No	Yes	List PR
Uruguay	No quotas					Closed			List PR
Venezuela	No quotas					Closed			MMP

Sources: Official documents; Htun and Jones (2002), Peschard (2003), Bareiro *et al.* (2004), International IDEA and Stockholm University (2004), IPU (2004).

Notes

a Some countries have quotas for other lower levels: R = Regional or Sub-regional level; P = Provincial level; L = Local level.
b The type of list has a great variation. Closed systems imply that voters can only choose between parties, not candidates. Open are electoral system in multinominal/PR districts in which voter can choose one or more candidates.
c 30 per cent is seen as a minimum, and the goal is to reach 50 per cent.
d In Brazil the present quota provision only applies to the chamber.
e In the Dominican Republic the present quota provision only applies to the chamber.
f Panama has a List PR and FPP proportional system.
Key Quota Type: Legal quotas: Constitutional (C) or Law (L).
Key electoral systems: *Plurality-Majority:* Two Rounds System. *Proportional Representation:* List PR. *Mixed:* MMP = Mixed Member Proportional.

law seems contradictory to the Senate: it establishes that one out of four candidates must be a woman (Art. 112) but at the same time there are only a maximum of three candidates in each district.

c   In Brazil, the quotas initially corresponded to 25 per cent for the State Chambers and the House of Deputies. Currently, it is a minimum of 30 per cent for each sex, requirement for all levels. As the vote is preferential and individualized, there is no rank order. Legislation further defines that percentage belonging to one sex, if not filled or completed, should remain empty. However, in these cases, parties are not prevented from entering their lists, that means that there is no effective sanction.

d   In Colombia, a Quota's Law of 30 per cent was created in 2002 for all 'high posts' in the administrative, legislative and judiciary levels, at national, regional and local levels, too. In the same law, Article 5 established that there are some exceptions, amongst them that one for legislative electoral post, what has been interpreted by the High Court as 'conditionally feasible' and not applicable to legislative representations.

e   Costa Rica has the highest minimum quota in the region, 40 per cent, extended to all legislative positions. The law has been improved since its approval in 1996. The initial compositions were not explicit as to whether quotas were to be applied to eligible positions. The first national election confirmed that the imprecision in the text deterred the fulfilment of the quotas, leading the National Electoral Tribunal to include the term 'eligible positions', to be calculated according to the average results of the previous elections.

f   In the Dominican Republic, quotas of 25 per cent were first legally established in 1997 to Chamber and Senate. However, the same basic types of flaws as other countries were apparent from the start, as no rank order in the list. The Electoral Law was modified in 2000, increasing the minimum percentage of quotas to 33 per cent for deputies and '*regidurías*', and establishing rank order and sanctions. In 2000 the Law of Municipal Organization established a quota of 50 per cent for that level. In 2002 the quota to the Senate was cut down.

g   In Ecuador, the electoral reform in 2000 established a 30 per cent quota. This figure is to be increased by 5 per cent in each election until it reaches a 50 per cent quota for all plurinominal lists for election. This law established rules about rank order (alternating and sequential) and sanctions for non-compliance of both quota provision and rank order. However, in the elections of 2002 (35 per cent) the parties and the Supreme Electoral Tribunal had not fulfilled this mandate, mainly for the rank order rules.

h   Honduras is the most recent country to have passed a new law of quotas, in 2004. Before, in 2000, the 'Law of Equal Opportunities for the Woman', established a 30 per cent quota, 'in a progressive fashion, until equality between men and women is reached', but without sanctions. Furthermore, the rules about rank order established that a candidate's position on the list must conform to a scale based on the results of the three preceding elections. Article 105 of the new law cuts this last problematic rule, but it remains without sanction and a suitable rule about ranking order. The country has not applied the new law yet.

i   In Mexico, the first law didn't have rules about the rank order or mechanisms of sanctions. The present law, from 2002, establishes quotas to Chamber and Senate, to both proportional representation (PR) and single-member districts elections (SMD) and has a mechanism of enforcement mandate and rules about rank order. It was applied for the first time in 2003 and considered an important experience for quotas in single-member districts systems (Baldez 2004). No election has been held for the Senate since the new law.

j   In Panama, a proportional system, the law establishes a quota of at least 30 per cent, but there are no sanctions for non-compliance

k   In Paraguay, the quota percentage is of at least 20 per cent for the Chamber of Deputies and Senate. In case of non-compliance a party is not allowed to enrol for the electoral competition. The law is considered ineffective by women's organization since in the national list the result is less than 20 per cent. A strong debate on changes has occurred and three different proposals have been presented to the parliament during 2004: two argue for 50 per cent and the other for 33 per cent.

l   In Peru, the quota is of 30 per cent for all levels. The law has been implemented with sanctions for non-compliance but as the list is open and preferential, there is no rank order.

m   In Venezuela, a quota of 30 per cent for women was established in 1997. It was applied in 1998 only. In 2000, the National Electoral Council rejected it and didn't apply in the following elections.

As can be noted, most countries approved their first legislation between 1995 and 2000, with the exception of Argentina, which approved it to the Federal Chamber in 1991. In most countries there is Electoral Law. It is possible to notice percentages of about 30 per cent with some of them targeting 50 per cent. Quotas have been applied both in proportional and mixed systems. The experiences have shown that the approval of the law has not resulted in a total and effective compliance with it. In most countries, there were certain flaws during their first electoral experience with quotas, due to the absence of laws with clear rules and sanctions, which made it necessary to alter some aspects of the law. This has occurred due to: a weak and imprecise composition of the norms; political and electoral systems, as well as judicial systems, which have not yet had the time to internalize the recently approved quota system and to modify relevant procedures and culture; in addition to that, one can include the resistance that still remains in the Latin America power structures to the idea of sharing the power between men and women.

Six countries have rules about rank order of the list that corresponds to more than half of the overall countries with quotas. It is important to notice that, in general, we talk about rank order in relation to the closed list. From this perspective more than 60 per cent of countries with quotas have rules about ranking order. The same trend can be found in relation to the existence of enforcement mechanisms directed to the compliance of the political parties with the application of the law, as Table 4.2 shows. Part of the countries have – after their first experience – improved their laws, making them less vague and more precise and effective in terms of sanctions. Yet, not all of them have followed this trend. For example, Honduras has kept the new language vague in terms of sanctions and rules. The improvement of the laws has been working as a kind of 'contagion effect' to the countries that adopted the quota's law later: its laws have been already created with clearer rules and sanctions. Some authors have analyzed this process in 'two stages' – the first was defined 'soft' and the second a more complete in terms of sanctions, in which the improvement of the law worked as a differential to the effectiveness of quotas (Alnevall forthcoming). In fact, as one will see later, the role of these normative mechanisms seems to be decisive to the latter result of quotas. However, its capacity of improving the policy will depend also on other factors.

The impact of the quotas in comparison to Latin American countries without quotas

In what way have quotas worked in Latin America and can changes in the insertion of women be explained by such policies? If so, what have been the features that are responsible for the success? This question can be better analyzed if, in addition to comparing the internal trend in countries that have adopted quotas, we try to compare the evolution between those nations that *do* and *do not* adopt quotas in the region. In this section, we first look at the trends in the presence of women in the legislative powers in Latin American countries, discussing in which sense the quotas have made the difference. After that, we discuss some points that have been identified as key features to explain the efficacy of quotas. In order to give an idea of the trend in the region, Table 4.3 provides a general view of the position of women in the legislative powers in three periods: between the 1970s and the 1980s, around 1995 and in 2004. Before 1995, except for the case of Argentina, all the listed countries did not have quotas. So, 1995 was chosen since it is the year that immediately precedes the process that led to the adoption of quotas and was the year of the Beijing Conference.

The data in the 3rd and 4th columns of Table 4.3 show a growing trend in the participation of women in Latin American legislative representation, despite the wide variation in the electoral years. That period coincides with the end of dictatorship and/or the beginning of re-democratization in many countries, processes that gave a boost in women's representation in parliaments. In general, the data show a growth trend based on two conjugated factors observed during the period: (a) an increasing trend in the participation of women in Latin American parliaments that is independent of the quotas; and (b) the strong impact

Table 4.3 Presence of women in Latin American chambers

Countries with quota	Presence of women			
	1969–83	*1995[a]*	*2001–4*	*Difference in points 1995–2004*
Argentina	7.8 (1973)	5.5	33.5 (2003)	28.0
Bolivia	0.8 (1982)	10.8	18.5 (2002)	7.7
Brazil	0.9 (1982)	6.2	8.2 (2002)	2.0
Costa Rica	7.0 (1970)	16.0	35.5 (2002)	19.5
Dominican Republic	14.3 (1974)	11.7	17.3 (2002)	5.6
Ecuador	0.0 (1979)	4.5	16.0 (2002)	11.5
Honduras	3.6 (1981)	7.0	5.5 (2001)	−1.5
Mexico	11.2 (1976)	14.2	22.6 (2003)	8.4
Panama	5.7 (1972)	8.3	16.7 (2004)	8.4
Paraguay	5.0 (1973)	3.0	10.0 (2003)	7.0
Peru	7.2 (1980)	10.8	18.3 (2001)	7.5
Average	5.8	8.9	18.4	9.5
Countries without quota				
Chile	9.0 (1969)	7.5	12.5 (2001)	5.0
Colombia	6.0 (1974)	10.8	12.0 (2002)	1.2
Cuba	21.8 (1973)	22.8	36.0 (2003)	13.2
El Salvador	11.6 (1983)	10.7	11.0 (2003)	0.3
Guatemala	4.0 (1974)	7.5	8.2 (2003)	0.7
Nicaragua	11.5 (1979)	16.3	20.7 (2001)	4.4
Uruguay	1.0 (1972)	7.1	12.1 (2004)	5.0
Venezuela[b]	4.5 (1978)	6.0	9.7 (2000)	3.7
Average	8.7	11.1	15.3	4.1

Sources: Official statistics; García and Gomáriz (1989), Valdés and Gomáriz (1995), Htun and Jones (2002), Peschard (2003), Bareiro *et al.* (2004), GESO (2004), IPU (2004).

Notes
a This data shows the situation of women in parliaments in 1995, the last year before most countries started to apply quota and the year of Beijing's Conference. However the year of elections in each country vary from 1991 to 1995. In Argentina the percentage is equivalent to that of the pre-quota 1991 election.
b Venezuela approved a Law of Quotas in 1997. It was applied only to the 1998 election and the presence of women increased from 6 per cent to 12 per cent. In 2000 the high court declared it unconstitutional. After the 2000 election the percentage decreased to 9.7 per cent.

caused by quotas in most of the countries where the system had been implemented.

As it is shown, some countries that do not adopt quotas experienced progress in the participation of women in legislature between 1995 and the present – 13 per cent in Cuba, 5 per cent in Chile and 4.4 per cent in Nicaragua for example.[12] However, the most remarkable advances occurred in countries that did adopt quotas as in Argentina, Costa Rica, Ecuador, Mexico and Panama. Countries that have already implemented quotas, with the exception of Brazil and Honduras, witnessed an increase in female participation, which in general is higher than what had occurred in countries under election without quotas. The Argentina's case is still paradigmatic and Costa Rica has one of highest percentages in the world.

The comparison shows that the difference between the averages in the Chambers is small, about 3 per cent. However, what is important is the inversion that has occurred in the average in both types of countries from 1995 to 2004. On the other side, the difference in the Senate is significant at 13.5 per cent.

It is important to note that the growth in Latin America has not been uniform. The variation within the two categories – countries with and without quotas – is remarkable, both, in terms of increment and in terms of its rhythms. There is no pattern of growth among countries with quotas. It varies from almost 30 per cent to a 1.5 per cent decrease as in the case of Honduras. In most countries that already had two or more elections with quotas, the best performances were in the second period. These gains in the second period tend to reflect legislative improvements and a broadening support base for quotas within women's movements, as in the case of Mexico and Costa Rica. However, not all countries that established more precise rules and sanctions kept or increased the growth rate. Ecuador and Dominican Republic, for instance, had a better increment in the first election with quotas. In the second, already possessing an enhanced legislation, the growth rate was smaller. In Brazil in the first election with quotas the percentage decreased from 6.8 per cent to 6.2 per cent. In the second one it increased slowly, only from 6.2 to 8.2 per cent and the legislation remained unaltered throughout this period. Such fact suggests that the improvements in the legislation are mingled with other factors, which might be important for the success of the measure. As an exception, in Panama, there are no signs of significant modifications in the legislation. Notwithstanding, while in the first election with quotas, the percentage of women elected in Panama remained almost the same – 9.9 per cent – in the election of 2004 it rose to 16.7 per cent. This was a substantial increment in the percentage of women elected.

Women's representation in the Senates shows the same trend as the Chamber in terms of general growth. There are variations in terms of increment, but in general, countries with quotas have on average the highest percentages of women senators, see Table 4.4.

Table 4.4 Presence of women in the Senate in some Latin American countries

	Presence of women			
	1969–82	*1995[a]*	*2000–4*	*Difference in points 1995–2004*
Countries with quota				
Argentina	4.3 (1976)	5.6	44.0 (2003)	38.5
Bolívia	7.4 (1982)	3.7	14.8 (2002)	11.1
Paraguay	3.3 (1973)	11.0	8.9 (2003)	−2.1
Average	5.0	6.8	22.6	15.8
Countries without quota				
Brazil	1.5 (1982)	7.4	12.3 (2002)	4.9
Chile	2.0 (1969)	6.5	4.1 (2001)	−2.4
Colombia	0.9 (1974)	6.9	8.8 (2002)	1.9
Dominican Republic	11.1 (1974)	3.3	6.3 (2002)	3.0
Mexico[b]	6.3 (1976)	12.5	15.6 (2000)	3.1
Uruguay	0.0 (1972)	6.7	9.7 (2004)	3.0
Average	3.6	7.2	9.5	2.3

Sources: Official statistics; García and Gomáriz (1989), Valdés and Gomáriz (1995), Htun and Jones (2002), Peschard (2003), Bareiro *et al.* (2004), GESO (2004), IPU (2004).

Notes

a This data shows the situation of women in parliaments in 1995, the last year before most countries started to apply quota and the year of Beijing's Conference. However the election years in each country vary from 1992 to 1995.

b The last quota law approved also applies to the Senate, but there was no election to the Senate in the last election. Therefore, the country is here counted as not having quotas.

In short, when comparing the total number of women in the parliaments of Latin America at the beginning and at the end of this period, it is possible to reach a clear conclusion: there is a general trend of growth in the region; and the most powerful factor for growth of this total seems to be strongly related to the increase of female members of parliament in the countries that adopted quotas. This could be considered as a regional 'fast track effect' (Dahlerup and Freidenvall 2003). However, the internal variation of this effect suggests that it also depends on a conjugation of features.

Features that can explain the consolidation and gains of quotas in the region

The set of factors that influences the efficacy of quotas is still in evaluation due to the recent process. However, it is possible to identify aspects that emerge from this analysis as relevant to the efficacy of quotas in Latin America, some of them already pointed out in other works (Htun and Jones 2002; Bareiro 2003; Krook 2003; Baldez 2004). Those aspects can be categorized as involving *normative, systemic* and *organizational* dimensions. These summarized features tend to corroborate perspective of the multi-causal dimensions of women's access to political representation.

First, from the *normative* stance the efficacy of quotas depends upon whether or not procedures exist that enforce the law and, more importantly, guarantee that women are in positions that enable them to be elected. Argentina, Costa Rica, Bolivia and Mexico are good examples, which also show the importance of a careful composition of these procedures in order to avoid any dubious interpretations. Both Paraguay and Brazil are examples in a contrary way, that is, they show how a non-precise law, without sanctions for its non-fulfilment, incites several interpretations, generally unfavourable to women.

In consolidation of democratic institutions, normative aspects are relevant for legitimization and generate what one may call a 'two-way' effect: institutional fragility can generate awareness of the importance of democratic norms in contrast to personality-dominated political culture. This can create an open environment for new institutional practices. The initial process in some countries with creation of quotas and its subsequent development, suggests that the institutional and normative dimensions may operate as a means of guarantee of changes that the current predominant policy may delay.

Nevertheless, such experiences show that the normative institutional dimension only functions when there are actors – institutional or collective actors – compromised with such changes. In relation to institutional actors, the compromise of governors and legislators seems to be relevant. Besides, the role of the electoral tribunals and judges' opinions that judge and define law's implementation emerges from the experiences as important to define the effective implementation of the law. In Mexico, the existence of members of an electoral judiciary, particularly some women, open to the issue and willing to put the law forward, was considered a decisive factor in the form of quotas' application in the elections of 2003 (Baldez 2004). Ecuador is also an example of the role of this instance in power, in this case, in the opposite sense, that is, put into practice a more fluid interpretation of the law (Pacari 2002).

Second, from the *systemic perspective*, several variables linked to *electoral systems*, previously regarded as important vis-à-vis the access women have to legislative representation, are also taken into account in the case of quotas. The type of electoral system and its interior characteristics – the district size and the format of the list – are also present in many studies of Latin American experiences (Htun and Jones 2002; Matland 2002; Peschard 2003; Schmidt 2003a; Schmidt and Araújo 2004). However, there is no consensus regarding the importance of each of these factors on the efficacy of quotas. From the Latin American experience, some aspects tend to be more visible in the literature, while others still need some research and a better analysis. We will also try to briefly discuss those that seem to be more relevant to the evaluation of this process and its results:

a   The first factor is regarding the type of *electoral system*. It has been discussed that quotas tend to be more easily accepted in a proportional electoral system, since they would allow the inclusion of new players – those included as a result of the quotas – without risking the exclusion of players already present and/or inserted in the political scenario. In fact, Latin America experience shows that the *electoral system as a whole has been important to the adoption of quotas.* Nine out of eleven countries that have adopted quotas have proportional electoral systems, and two have mixed systems. As for the mixed system one notices that in Bolivia the quotas apply only to the proportional election. Note, however that a study on Mexico has shown that women obtained better results in proportional elections than in first-past-the-post elections, in part due to difficulties in the implementation of the law in non-proportional systems (Baldez 2004).

b   *The magnitude of the district* is another aspect discussed in the literature in which the results in countries with quotas appear as controversial. Htun and Jones (2002: 39), in their analysis of the Latin American experience argue that the efficacy of quotas is limited in the case of smaller districts, especially those with a large number of parties. However, some cases, as Brazil and the Senate in Paraguay, cited together with Mexico as examples of high district magnitude, seem to contradict the dominating pattern. In Brazil, the proportion of females elected in smaller districts or medium-sized districts has been greater than those in large ones. The implementation of quotas does not seem to have changed this trend. In the Paraguayan Senate the percentage of women elected in the election of 2003 has decreased from 20 per cent to 8.9 per cent. Analysis on the Peruvian experience with quotas in municipal elections also suggests the opposite: Peruvian women had a better performance in smaller districts due to local electoral logic that guided the choice of candidates, entitled the 'effective quotas' (Schmidt 2003a). The 2004 election in Panama also contradicts the pattern, since the country has very small districts – two seats – and the percentage of women's elected growth from 9.9 per cent in the previous election to 16.7 per cent at present. Thus, while in some larger or middle-sized districts such as Mexico, Bolivia and Costa Rica, the magnitude may be important; the examples above show the need for further examination. This reinforces the Htun and Jones's own analysis on the effect of other factors on the efficacy of quotas.

c   *The type of electoral list:* many studies, based upon comparisons, argue that quotas tend to work better in closed lists, as long as they are distributed on a basis of alternate allocation criteria and placement mandate. In other words, as long as women are guaranteed eligible positions in the lists, a real probability of being elected arises (Polanco 1999; Htun and Jones 2002; García 2003). In general, open lists do not line up candidates for the purpose of eligibility. Thus, women not only face the difficulties of being included in the lists, but also difficulties regarding their competitive positions within the lists. Inclusion in electoral lists, when not accompanied by other measures, tends not to have a major impact. The case of Brazil is emblematic. Another case that needs to be better investigated is the one about Ecuador. Open lists only came into use in Ecuador, after year 2000 electoral reform. Data demonstrate that, in comparative terms, the best increment in Ecuador was a result of the first election following the adoption of quotas and using a closed list (1998), and not the second election, which already featured the open list.

All in all, the various experiences suggest that closed lists produce a more favourable relation but, according to other factors, the variation *intra* list can be more important in same cases. Some studies suggest that there may be a greater variation *intra* list, whether open or closed, than *between* lists of different kinds, considering the fact that other factors may interfere (Schmidt 2003a, 2003b; Schmidt and Araújo 2004). Thus, the logic behind organizing closed and blocked lists may vary considerably between proportional and plurality-majority systems. Likewise, the results obtained by women with the elaboration of open lists may vary significantly between districts, according to a series of institutional and cultural factors. In the case of Peru,[13] Schmidt demonstrated that the results were significant even with open lists and small districts. According to the author, this occurred because of what he called 'effective quotas', that is, quotas that require parties to follow a specific logic, one that includes women given their competitiveness. In the case of Brazil, this strategy is not applicable since their open lists allow for only one vote. In a comparative study between Brazil and Peru, Schmidt and Araújo, showed that the gap between Peru and Brazil is greater than the average difference between open and closed list systems in the last pre-quota and first post-quota elections in Latin America (Schmidt and Araújo 2004: 27). Yet, the case of Panama, which has open list and had a good performance in 2004 needs to be considered on this issue.

d   *Life span of the parties* is another aspect that deserves further examination in regards to the preliminary 'contagious effect' of quotas on legislation. Again, a consensus on this point is inexistent. In some Latin American countries, quotas were adopted and effectively applied by newly formed parties. In other countries, the older parties took on this practice.

Third, from the *organizational political conditions*: resulting gains tend to be associated, also, with pressure from female party members as well as with their capacity to draw support from other organized female sectors, exemplified by Argentina, Costa Rica, Bolivia and Ecuador. The content and scope of the norm will depend on the political strength of its supporters.

Organized action of female party members, especially when involved with other women's movements, can exert pressure on the effectiveness of the law, in regards to both its content and its observance by the parties. Here, it is important to take into account that such political action can interfere in the systemic characteristics of the electoral process. Studies describing the Peruvian process (Vargas 2002; Schmidt 2003a) show how women employed a strategy of appealing to the voters to cast two votes – one for a woman. Indeed, the fact that there were two voting options, as well as a strategy that did not exclude the voter's preferred candidate, seems to have been fundamental for success in the Peruvian case.

Conclusion

An analysis of the adoption of the quotas system, seen as a positive means of increasing the participation of women in Latin American political systems, should begin by highlighting its importance and dimensions: presently, 11 out of 19 countries in the region have adopted legal measures regarding participatory quotas. Furthermore, parties with nationwide influence frequently adopt some form of quota system in countries that lack such national norms. In fact, a general trend of increasing female participation can be observed from the 1980s until the present day. This trend does not depend upon the existence of a quotas system, although its rhythm is considerably slower. Nevertheless, results appear to indicate that the global increment observed at regional level is mainly associated with the adoption of quotas in a significant number of countries.

The concentration in a short time seems to indicate that the importance of circumstantial specific characteristics of the re-democratization process in Latin America, during the 1980s and 1990s, are amongst the principal factors. It is important to note advances made regarding the idea of gender equality in the international community and especially in the UN, as well as the growing presence of the feminist and women's movements in the Latin American scenarios. In this general context, the feminist political agendas, which became part of the public agenda, achieved a noteworthy success, subsequently producing normative and institutional changes.

The process of political openness acted as stimulus to new institutional designs on countries rebuilding their democracies during these two decades. It also provided countries with a greater democratic stability, such as in Costa Rica. The collective action of women during the last decade and its focus on *rights* were very important. Women had to deal not only with the incorporation of their agenda, but also with their direct inclusion as new players in the political system.

It is important to take into account the existence of a complex scenario of interweaving issues. In addition to the previously mentioned contextual and political aspects, normative and institutional conditions should also be considered. Regarding the political system, all in all, in terms of acceptance, the Latin American case reinforces the literature that shows more favourable conditions under PR systems. Quotas seem to work better to the proportionate part of the representation. Another relevant element is related to the type of list – whether open or closed. In general, countries with closed lists have produced the best results, apparently facilitating more effective normative mechanisms. However, some data show that if, on the one hand, in some countries with closed list the results have remained below expectation, on the other, according to other conditions, in open list it is possible to obtain good performance as well.

A dimension that seems to be particularly relevant in Latin America is the normative one: the rules and sanctions of the norms of the quota's law. This factor, in conjunction with the organizational level and political capacity of women within parliament, party structures, as well as the alliance with other organized groups of women, has been critical in the defence and enforcement of more effective legislations and some subsequent results.

The importance that juridical norms acquired in the region tends to reveal two aspects, which could be further explored. On the one hand, the relevance of the compulsory laws with rules and sanctions to the success of this process can be interpreted as an evidence of women's organization strength and the recognition of their issues in the decision-making sphere. On the other, the power and dependence of the juridical norms can also be a symptom of: absence of ideological commitment from the parties with the proposal; its polemic characteristic; or as an evidence of weakness of an egalitarian culture, which would be capable of dispensing strong interventions from juridical sphere in order to promote some measures.

Indeed, effective quotas policies can result from the combination of the strength of the women's movement with a democratic profile of government. Nevertheless, in Latin America as well as in other parts of the world, the approval of quotas is not necessarily an indicator of democracy or even of deeper changes of the women's general status. Other political, economic and social variables must be considered when discussing a wider process of democratization in the region.

Notes

1 The countries that appear in this study are the former colonies of Spain and Portugal: Argentina, Bolivia, Brazil, Colombia, Costa Rica, Cuba, Chile, Ecuador, El Salvador, Guatemala, Honduras, Mexico, Nicaragua, Panama, Paraguay, Peru, Dominican Republic, Uruguay and Venezuela. Haiti was not included. Guiana has had quotas for its national parliament since 2001. However, it is not a part of Latin America, and the lack of data does not allow its inclusion in this analysis.

2 In some countries the quotas apply to all legislative positions. In this paper, we will basically focus the national experiences with quotas and especially those defined as national laws for the legislative level. We are not going to investigate

the quotas within political parties, many of which have preceded national legal adoption. But it should be noted that many political parties in the region adopt internal quotas for direction positions and/or external, for electoral positions. For more details see: http://www.quotaproject.org/ (International IDEA and Stockholm University 2004).

3 Some authors have previously written about this experience. See, for example, Htun and Jones (2002), Bareiro (2003), International IDEA (2003), Peschard (2003).

4 Many studies approached these consequences, like those of Jelin and Hershberg (1996), Álvarez (1998, 1999), Bareiro (1999), Molyneux (2003). Arriagada (1999) showed that although some improvement had happened, in 1997, 4 per cent of the Latin American population was below the poverty line.

5 The concept 'women's movement' expresses the range of existing and active groups within a broader agenda and allows one to consider the agents outside the feminist movements.

6 There was an important debate among feminist movements on the meaning and the type of citizenship, which is not possible to reproduce here, but can be found in, among others, Jelin (1997), Álvarez (1998), Vargas (2002), Bareiro (2003), Molyneux, (2003).

7 Ibid. Aiming to minimize the impact of policies of structural readjustment, institutions such as IDB and the World Bank began to include requirements for conceding financing, such as compensatory policies and/or policies for excluded groups, such as women.

8 See Suplicy (1996), author of quota's law in Brazil and member of women's network in Parlatino.

9 Some authors approached these debates, as for example, Bonder and Nari (1995), Araújo (1999), Polanco (1999), Htun and Jones (2002), Peschard (2002), Bareiro (2003), García (2003), Lubertino (2003).

10 See, D'Albora and Levine (1996), Araújo (1999), García and Gomáriz (2000), Htun and Jones (2002: 35) and Bareiro (2003). In Bareiro (2003), a specific research on this subject involved people that work in electoral offices, at gender or women's offices in governments, as well as women's politicians from nine countries in the region.

11 Nohlen (1995) has showed those variations, which is always in process, as for type of system, type of list or even within each kind of electoral system.

12 Cuba is a particular case since it does not fit within the parameters of a classical representative liberal democracy, which is in focus here.

13 The open list in Peru allows up to two preferential votes for candidates.

Bibliography

Alnevall, C. (forthcoming) 'Cuotas de Género – La Clave de Equidad en América Latina? Un Análisis Comparativo', The Research Program on Gender Quotas, Working Paper Series, Stockholm University: Department of Political Science.

Álvarez, S. (1998) 'Feminismos Latinoamericanos', *Revista Estudios Feministas*, 6, 2: 265–85.

—— (1999) 'Advocating feminism: the Latin American feminist NGO "Boom"', *International Feminist Journal of Politics*, 1, 2: 181–209.

Araújo, C. (1999) 'Cidadania Incompleta – O Impacto da Lei de Cotas sobre a Representação Política das Mulheres Brasileira', unpublished, Rio de Janeiro: Federal University of Rio de Janeiro.

—— (2003) 'Quotas for Women in the Brazilian Legislative System', in International IDEA, *The Implementation of Quotas: Latin American Experiences*, Quota Workshop Report Series no. 2, Stockholm: International IDEA, pp. 72–87.

Archenti, N. 'Qué han hecho las Legisladoras? Impacto de las cuotas en el Congreso Argentino', paper presented at the XXV International Congress of Latin America Studies Association, Las Vegas, October 2004.

Arriagada, I. (1999) 'Limites económicos, sociales y políticos a la participación de las mujeres en América Latina', in Repem/DAWN *Reestructura Política y Transformacion Social*, Montevideo: Repem/DAWN.

Baldez, L. 'Obedecieron y Cumplieran? The Impact of the Gender Quota Law in Mexico', paper presented at the XXV International Congress of Latin America Studies Association, Las Vegas, October 2004.

Bareiro, L. (1999) 'Reestructura Política sin Transformación social', in Repem/ DAWN *Reestructura Política y Transformacion Social*, Montevideo: Repem/DAWN.

—— 'Sistemas Electorales y Representación Femenina', Documento de Trabajo, paper presented at the Reunión sobre gobernabilidad democrática y igualdad de género, Santiago de Chile, October 2003.

Bareiro, L. *et al.* (2004) 'Sistemas electorales y representación femenina en América Latina', *Unidad Mujer y Desarrollo*, Serie Mujer y Desarrollo, 54, Naciones Unidas, Santiago: CEPAL.

Bartra, E. (2002) 'Três Décadas de Neofeminismo en México' in E. Bartra, A. Poncela and A. Lau (eds) *Feminismo en México, Ayer y Hoy*, Colección Molinos de Viento, Serie Mayor 130, Cuidad de México: Universidad Autónoma Metropolitana.

Benavides, J.C. (2003) 'Women's Political Participation in Bolivia: Progress and Obstacles' in International IDEA *The Implementation of Quotas: Latin American Experiences*, Quota Workshop Report Series no. 2, Stockholm: International IDEA, pp. 104–11.

Bonder, G. and Nari, M. (1995) 'The 30 Percent Quota Law – A Turning Point for Women's Political Participation in Argentina', in A. Brill (ed.) *A Rising Public Voice – Women in Politics Worldwide*, New York: The Feminist Press of the City University of New York, pp. 183–93.

Brunner, J.J. (1989) 'Entonces, ¿existe o no la modernidad en América Latina?', in CLACSO *Imágenes Desconocidas, La modernidad en la encrucijada postmoderna*, Buenos Aires: CLACSO.

Carrasco, R. (1999) 'Los procesos de transición y las estrategias de las mujeres', in Repem/DAWN *Reestructura Política y Transformación Social*, Montevideo: Dawn/Repem.

Dahlerup, D. (2003) 'Comparative Studies of Electoral Gender Quotas', in International IDEA *The Implementation of Quotas: Latin American Experiences*, Quota Workshop Report Series no. 2, Stockholm: International IDEA, pp. 10–19.

Dahlerup, D. and Freidenvall, L. 'Quota as a "Fast Track" to Equal Political Representation for Women. Why Scandinavian is no longer the model', paper presented at American Political Association Annual Meeting, Philadelphia, August 2003.

D'Albora, A. and Levine, S. (1996) *Importancia de una ley de cuotas en Chile, Mujer & Ciudadanía*, Santiago: IDEAS Fundación.

Fraser, N. (1995) 'From Redistribution to Recognition? Dilemmas of Justice in a "Post-Socialist" Age', *New Left Review*, 212: 68–93.

Fundación Género y Sociedad (GESO) (2004) *Evolución de la participación sociopolítica de mujeres y hombres en América Latina*, Documento de Trabajo No. 30, San José: GESO.

García, A.I. (1997) 'Mujeres, poder y políticas públicas en el inicio de la era post-Beijing', in *Las Mujeres y el Poder, Colección Ensayo*, San José: Editorial Mujeres.

—— (2003) 'Putting the mandate into practice: legal reform in Costa Rica', in International IDEA *The Implementation of Quotas: Latin American Experiences*, Quota Workshop Report Series no. 2, Stockholm: International IDEA, pp. 88–101.

García, A.I. and Gomáriz, E. (1989) *Mujeres Centroamericanas ante la Crisis, la Guerra y el Proceso de Paz*, San José: FLACSO/CSUCA/UPAZ, Tomos I y II.

—— (2000) 'Género y ciudadanía en América Latina: otra mirada al horizonte', in A. Meentzen and E. Gomáriz (eds) *Democracia de Género, Una propuesta para Mujeres y Hombres del Siglo XXI*, San José: Fundación Heinrich Böll/Fundación Género y Sociedad, pp. 54–76.

García, A.I. and Ulloa, I. (2004) *Las experiencias de presupuestos sensibles al género en el marco general de la experiencia acumulada sobre institucionalización de género y políticas públicas*, San José: Fundación Género y Sociedad.

GESO (2004) see Fundación Género y Sociedad.

Gomáriz, E. (1977) *O Estado nas Sociedades Dependentes. O caso da América Latina*, Lisboa: Editorial Presença.

Htun, M. and Jones, M. (2002) 'Engendering the Right to Participate in Decision-Making: Electoral Quotas and Women's Leadership in Latin America', in N. Craske and M. Molyneux (eds) *Gender and the Politics of Rights and Democracy in Latin America*, New York: Palgrave, pp. 32–56.

International IDEA (2003) *The Implementation of Quotas: Latin American Experiences*, Quota Workshop Report Series no. 2, Stockholm: International IDEA.

International IDEA and Stockholm University (2004) 'Global Database of Quotas for Women'. Online. Available at: http://www.quotaproject.org/ (accessed 28 November 2004).

Inter-Parliamentary Union (IPU) (2004) 'Women in Parliaments'. Online. Available at: http://www.ipu.org/wmn-e/world.htm (accessed 23 November 2004).

Jelin, E. (1997) 'Igualdad y Diferencia: Dilemas de la ciudadanía de las mujeres en América Latina', *Agora*, 7: 189–214.

Jelin, E. and Hershberg, E. (1996) *Constructing democracy: Human Rights, Citizenship and Society in Latin America*, Boulder, CO: Westview Press.

Johnson, N. (2003) 'La Cuota: un mecanismo necesario y efectivo para incrementar la participación de mujeres en cargos políticos relevantes? El caso uruguayo' in A. Nelida (ed.) *Estrategias Políticas de Género, Reformas Institucionales, Identidad y Acción Colectiva*, Proyecto UBACYT, Buenos Aires: Instituto de Investigaciones – Facultad de Ciencias Sociales.

Kaplan, M. (1966) *La formación del Estado Nacional en América Latina*, Santiago: Editorial Universitaria.

Krook, M.L. 'Not All Quotas Are Created Equal: Trajectories of Reform to increase Women's Political Representation', paper presented at European Consortium for Political Research, Edinburgh, March–April 2003.

Lazzaro, A.M. 'Evolucion de La Ley de Cupo Femenino a Traves De la Interpretacion Judicial', paper presented at XXV International Congress of Latin American Studies Association, Las Vegas, October 2004.

Lubertino, M.J. (2003) 'Pioneering Quotas: The Argentine Experience and

Beyond', in International IDEA *The Implementation of Quotas: Latin American Experiences*, Quota Workshop Report Series no. 2, Stockholm: International IDEA, pp. 32–41.

Matland, R.E. (2002) 'Estrategias para ampliar la participación femenina en el parlamento. El proceso de selección de candidatos legislativos y los sistemas electorales', in M. Méndez-Montalvo and J. Ballington (eds) *Mujeres en el Parlamento- más allá de los números*, Stockholm: International IDEA, pp. 111–34.

Miguel, S.M. (1999) *Política de Cotas- Mulheres na Política*, Brasília: CFEMEA.

Molyneux, M. (2003 [2001]) *Women's Movement in International Perspective: Latin America and Beyond*, London: Institute of Latin America Studies.

Molyneux, M. and Craske, N. (2002) 'The Local, the Regional and the Global: Transforming the Politics of Rights', in N. Craske and M. Molyneux (eds) *Gender and the Politics of Rights and Democracy in Latin America*, New York: Palgrave, pp. 1–31.

Nohlen, D. (1995) *Sistemas Electorales y Partidos Políticos*, Cuidad de México: Universidad Nacional Autónoma do México y Fondo de Cultura.

Pacari, N. (2002) 'La Participación Política de la Mujer Indígena en El Congreso Ecuatoriano', in M. Méndez-Montalvo and J. Ballington (eds) *Mujeres en el Parlamento – Más alla de los números*, Stockholm: International IDEA, pp. 45–62.

Peschard, J. (2002) 'El Sistema de cuotas en América Latina. Panorama general', in M. Méndez-Montalvo and J. Ballington (eds) *Mujeres en el Parlamento- Más alla de los números*, Stockholm: International IDEA, pp. 173–86.

—— (2003) 'The Quota System in Latin America: General Overview', in International IDEA *The Implementation of Quotas: Latin American Experiences*, Quota Workshop Report Series no. 2, Stockholm: International IDEA, pp. 20–9.

Phillips, A. (1998) 'Democracy and Representation: Or, Why Should it Matter who our Representative Are?', in A. Phillips (ed.) *Feminism and Politics*, Oxford: Oxford University Press, pp. 224–42.

Polanco, J. (1999) 'La representación política de las mujeres en América Latina: un análisis comparado del caso argentino', unpublished, New York: University of New York.

Ramírez, F. and Eneaney, E. (1997) 'From Women's Suffrage to Reproduction Rights? Cross-National Considerations', *International Journal of Comparative Sociology*, 38, 1: 3–15.

Schmidt, G. (2003a) *Cuotas Efectivas, Magnitud Relativa del Partido Y Éxito de las Candidatas Mujeres*, Lima: Instituto Manuela Ramos.

—— (2003b) 'Unanticipated Successes: Lessons from Peru's Experience with Gender Quotas in Majoritarian Closed List and Open List PR Systems', in International IDEA *The Implementation of Quotas: Latin American Experiences*, Quota Workshop Report Series no. 2, Stockholm: International IDEA, pp. 120–33.

Schmidt, G and Araújo, C. 'The Devil's in the Details: Open List Voting and Gender Quotas in Brazil and Peru', paper presented at the XXV International Congress of Latin American Studies Association, Las Vegas, October 2004.

Suplicy, M. (1996) 'Novos Paradigmas nas esferas de poder', *Revista Estudos feministas*, 4, 1: 126–37.

Valdés, T. and Gomáriz, E. (1995) *Mujeres Latinoamericanas en Cifras*, Santiago: FLACSO/Instituto de la Mujer de España, Tomo Comparativo.

Vargas, V. (2002) 'The Struggle by Latin American Feminism for Rights and Autonomy', in N. Craske and M. Molyneux (eds) *Gender and the Politics of Rights and Democracy in Latin America*, New York: Palgrave, pp. 199–222.

Yáñez, A.M. (2003) 'Cuotas y democracia', in International IDEA *The Implementation of Quotas: Latin American Experiences*, Quota Workshop Report Series no. 2, Stockholm: International IDEA, pp. 114–19.

5   Sub-Saharan Africa

On the fast track to women's political representation

Aili Tripp, Dior Konaté and Colleen Lowe-Morna[1]

Africa has some of the highest rates of female political representation in the world today. In 2003 Rwanda became the country with the highest number of women parliamentarians, surpassing the Nordic countries when women claimed close to 49 per cent of the parliamentary seats. Women in South Africa and Mozambique hold over one-third of parliamentary seats, while women in Namibia claim 42 per cent of seats in local government and women in Uganda one-third. One of the main factors accounting for this increase in female legislative representation has to do with the expanded use of various forms of quotas. No longer is the one-third goal considered sufficient in many parts of Africa. Today active '50/50' movements are pushing for one-half parliamentary seats of women and men in countries as diverse as South Africa, Namibia, Sierra Leone, Kenya, Uganda and Senegal.

These changes are occurring within a broader context of women making bids for power in a number of arenas. Since the early 1990s women have been increasingly forming and heading up political parties, running for the presidency, and they have become active in local politics. There have been four women vice/deputy presidents (in Uganda, Zimbabwe, South Africa and The Gambia), one woman head of state (Liberia), several prime ministers (Rwanda, Burundi, Senegal and Mozambique), and several speakers of the house or deputy speakers. Women make up over half of the electorate in most African countries. Nevertheless women are still excluded from full participation in political decision-making in Africa, as elsewhere in the world. This chapter explores the reasons for the expansion of the use of electoral quotas for women, some of the debates around quotas, types of quotas used and their impact. Although the chapter focuses on national legislatures, quotas have also been introduced at the local level and we briefly discuss the case of Namibia in this regard. Namibia has legislated a 30 per cent quota of women to be included in party candidate lists in local authority elections; Tanzania also has 33 per cent reserved seats in local government elections; Eritrea reserves 30 per cent of its seats in regional assemblies for women as does Uganda. Parties in South Africa are encouraged by law to make sure that women constitute half the candidates on lists for local elections. Table 5.1 shows how many Sub-Saharan African countries have introduced gender quotas recently.

Introduction of quotas

Role of transnational diffusion influences

Quotas were first introduced in Africa, in Ghana after independence, by the Convention People's Party in 1960. Tanzania reserved 15 legislative seats for women in 1975, and Egypt briefly adopted an 8 per cent quota for women parliamentarians between 1979 and 1986. Senegal's Parti Socialiste announced in 1982 that it would reserve one-quarter of its seats for women and Uganda adopted reserved seats for women in 1989. However, the large majority of quotas in Africa were introduced after 1995, the year of the UN Conference on Women held in Beijing, where a Platform of Action adopted by governmental delegations sought to ensure women's equal participation in all forms of 'power structures and decision-making'. These policies adopted at Beijing were heavily influenced by women's NGOs and movements domestically and regionally but also at the international level. After the Beijing Conference, many African countries developed national plans to implement recommendations regarding the status of women and progress was to be monitored over time. The influence of the international women's movement was felt at the regional level as well. Regional organizations, like the Southern African Development Community (SADC), the East African Parliament, and the Economic Community Of West African States (ECOWAS) set targets to improve gender representation and pressured countries that were lagging.

Thus, while much of the impetus for the introduction of quotas came from the international arena, the more immediate pressures came from regional bodies, and the diffusion effects were palpable. Heavy lobbying by civil society organizations and the subsequent establishment of gender structures in the Southern African Development Community (SADC), for example, spurred a vigorous campaign among civil society organizations for greater representation of women in decision-making. In January 1997, government representatives and NGOs held a ground-breaking gender strategy workshop that put forward recommendations for a gender policy and institutional framework in SADC. This was approved by the Council of Ministers that February. In November 1997, SADC Heads of Government adopted a 'Declaration on Gender and Development' at their annual summit in Blantyre. One of the commitments was to achieve a 30 per cent representation of women in politics and decision-making by the year 2005. Soon after, SADC established a Gender Unit, which in May 1999 convened a conference entitled *Beyond 30 per cent in 2005: Women and Decision Making*

Table 5.1 Women and quotas in national legislatures in Africa

Country	Quota type[a]	Levels of political and civil liberties[b]	Women in legislature % (election year)[c]	Electoral system
Angola	No quota	Not free	16.4 (1992)	List PR
Benin	No quota	Free	7.2 (2003)	List PR
Botswana	Party quota[d] Botswana Congress Party: 30% (21%) Botswana National Front: 30% (2%)	Free	11.1 (2004)	FPP
Burkina Faso[e]	Party quota Alliance pour la Démocratie et la Federation: 25% (13%), Congrès pour la Démocratie et le Progrès: 25% (50%)	Partly free	11.7 (2002)	List PR
Burundi	Legal quotas (30%)	Not free	30.5 (2005)	List PR
Cameroon	Party quota Cameroon People's Free Movement: 25–30% (83%) Social Democratic Front: 25% (12%)	Not free	8.9 (2002)	PBV/List PR and FPP[f]
Cape Verde	No quota	Free	11.1 (2001)	List PR
Chad	No quota	Not free	6.5 (2002)	PBV/List PR and TRS[g]
Central African Republic	No quota	Partly free	n/a	Two Rounds
Comoros	No quota	Partly free	3.0 (2004)	Two Rounds
Congo-Brazzaville	No quota	Partly free	8.5 (2002)	Two Rounds
Côte d'Ivoire	Party quota Front Populaire de Cote d'Ivoire: 30% (43%)	Partly free	8.5 (2000)	FPP and PBV[f]
Congo-Kinshasa	No quota	Not free	12.0 (2003)	N
Equatorial Guinea	Party quota Convergencia para la Democracia Social (n/a) Seats held by party: 5.8%	Not free	18.0 (2004)	List PR

Eritrea	*Legal quota* (C) Reserved seats 30% (unicameral)	Not free	22.0 (1994)	Transitional
Ethiopia	*Party quota* Ethiopia People's Revolutionary Democratic Front: 30% (85%)	Partly free	10.7 (2005)	FPP
Gabon	No quota	Partly free	9.2 (2001)	Two Rounds
Gambia	No quota	Partly free	13.2 (2002)	FPP
Ghana	No quota	Free	10.9 (2004)	FPP
Guinea	No quota	Not free	19.3 (2002)	Parallel (List PR and FPP)
Guinea-Bissau	No quota	Partly free	14.0 (2004)	List PR
Kenya	*Legal quota* (C) Executive appointment: 3% (unicameral)	Partly free	7.1 (2002)	FPP
Lesotho	No quota	Partly free	11.7 (2002)	MMP
Liberia	No quota	Partly free	5.3 (2003)	Transitional
Madagascar	No quota	Partly free	6.9 (2001)	FPP and List PR[f]
Malawi	No quota	Partly free	13.6 (2004)	FPP
Mali	*Party quota* Alliance for Democracy: 30% (40%)	Free	10.2 (2002)	Two Rounds
Mauritania	No quota	Partly free	3.7 (2001)	Two Rounds
Mauritius	No quota	Free	17.1 (2005)	Block Vote
Mozambique	*Party quota* Frente de Libertação de Moçambique (Frelimo): 30% (62%)	Partly free	34.8 (2004)	List PR
Namibia	No quota	Free	26.9 (2004)	List PR
Niger	*Legal quota* (L) Elected: 10% Nominated: 25% (unicameral)	Partly free	12.4 (2004)	List PR and FPP[g]
Nigeria	No quota	Partly free	6.4 (2003)	FPP

Table 5.1 Continued

Country	Quota type[a]	Levels of political and civil liberties[b]	Women in legislature % (election year)[c]	Electoral system
Rwanda	*Legal quota (C)* Reserved seats in upper and lower house: 30%	Not free	48.8 (2003)	List PR
Sao Tome & Principe	No quota	Free	9.1 (2002)	List PR
Senegal[h]	*Party quota* Senegal Liberal Party: 33% (Sopi coalition led by SDP: 74%) Parti Socialiste: 25% (8%)	Partly free	19.2 (2001)	Parallel (PBV and List PR)
Seychelles	No quota	Partly free	29.4 (2002)	Parallel (FPP and List PR)
Sierra Leone	No quota	Partly free	14.5 (2002)	List PR
South Africa	*Party quota* African National Congress: 33% (70%)	Free	32.8 (2004)	List PR
Swaziland	Executive appointment (28%)[i]	Not free	10.8 (2003)	FPP
Tanzania	*Legal quota (C)* Reserved seats: 30% (2005)	Partly free	21.4 (2000)	FPP
Togo	No quota	Partly free	7.4 (2002)	Two Rounds
Uganda	*Legal quota (C)* Reserved seats; 18.4% (unicameral)	Partly free	23.9 (2001)	FPP
Zambia	No quota	Partly free	12.7 (2001)	FPP
Zimbabwe	No quota	Not free	16.7 (2005)	FPP

Key Quota Type: Legal Quotas by Constitution (C) or Law (L).

Key electoral systems: *Plurality-Majority*: FPP = First-Past-the-Post, Two-Rounds System, Block Vote, PBV = Party Block Vote. *Proportional Representation*: List PR. *Mixed*: MMP = Mixed Member Proportional, Parallel. T = Transitional (countries that in November 2004 did not have an electoral law). N = No provision for direct elections.

Notes

a Based on Parline database on the Inter-parliamentary Union website www.ipu.org and on data from Global Database of Quotas for Women. A joint project of International IDEA and Stockholm University http://www.quotaproject.org/. Bicameral unless otherwise indicated.

b Based on Freedom House country assessments http://www.freedomhouse.org/ See criteria for categories: http://www.freedomhouse.org/research/freeworld/2003/methodology.htm.

c Based on Inter-Parliamentary Union Data http://www.ipu.org/wmn-e/classif.htm; figures refer to lower house or single house in case of unicameral legislature.

d The party quota figures read as follows: Botswana Congress Party: 30 per cent (21 per cent): The first percentage shows the party's quota provision for women, here 30 per cent, followed by the size of the party fraction in parliament (here 21 per cent).

e Election not yet held under new quota arrangement.

f This is a plurality-majority system.

g Niger has a List PR and FPP proportional system.

h In 1982 Parti Socialiste reserved 25 per cent of all posts in the party for women. In 2001, 14 political parties in Senegal urged political parties to reserve at least 30 per cent of the places on their candidate lists for women.

i The women are appointed by the president (applies only to upper house).

j The special seat quota for women is allocated to political parties based on the proportional number of parliamentary seats won in an election. Each party determines its own mechanism for filling the seats, with some nominating the women and others allowing women party members to elect their candidates.

in SADC that adopted a far-reaching program for achieving gender parity in politics in the region.

Efforts were taken to ensure gender balance within these regional organizations as well. For example, the number of women commissioners in the African Union had been set at five out of ten positions. In 2003 when AU diplomats attempted to reduce this number in a bid to improve regional representativeness, women resisted and were able to hang on to the positions and maintain parity in this institution. Moreover, the Pan-African Parliament of the African Union now has a woman president, Gertrude Mongella, a first in the history of such an Africa-wide body. Mongella had gained international recognition in 1995 as the general secretary of the Fourth UN Conference on Women in Beijing. Clearly, the new measures to increase female political representation were by no means 'gifts' to women, who fought every step of the way for these seats.

Impact of women's movements

The diffusion effects of transnational and regional organizations to encourage the adoption of quotas were closely related to the efforts of national women's movements. These movements that pushed for women's increased political representation demonstrated not only women's awareness of their critical numbers as part of the electorate, but also their aspirations to change the rules of the political game and the face of African politics. Women's movements sought to overcome the social, cultural and religious barriers that prevented them from becoming fully involved in politics. Associational autonomy in women's movements also allowed women to challenge the ways in which political parties conducted politics. In particular, women's organizations often rejected the way in which parties and the state had politicized ethnicity and religion; the way in which politics was based on state patronage, which often excluded women from politics; and the way in which politicians participated in corrupt practices that worked to discourage female participation in politics.

During the 2001 parliamentary elections in Senegal, a non-partisan group of women's organizations, including Senegal's Association of African Women Professionals in Communication (APAC), the Senegalese Women's Council (COSEF), the Reseau Siggil Jigeen (RSJ), and the Association of Female Jurists (AFJ), together with a network of 30 NGOs carried out a citizen's campaign to increase the number of women legislators to at least 30 per cent (Diop 2001; Sakho 2002).

In 2003, at a consultative seminar organized in Accra by Actionaid Ghana and ABANTU for Development various NGOs together with the District Assembly women representatives demanded that 15 to 30 per cent of the parliamentary seats be reserved for women (Benyin 2003). As of 2004, women made up only 7 per cent of the Ghanaian legislature.

Over the past decade, women's coalitions and alliances in many African countries – from South Africa to Sierra Leone, Mali, Uganda, Zambia, Botswana, Namibia and elsewhere – have begun adopting joint manifestos that outline their aspirations for political equality, including the need for electoral quotas.

In Mali, for example, women politicians summarized their political aspirations in a document called the 'Bamako Declaration', which outlined ways to advance women's political participation and improve the status of Malian women. It was translated into several local languages, widely broadcast on the national media and read at the official ceremony commemorating International Women's Day. This publicity raised the profile of women parliamentarians and the visibility of the causes they were advancing (National Democratic Institute n.d.).

What has become abundantly clear from the experience of the last few years is that without quotas, African countries will not achieve the desired target. Already in southern Africa observers have found that there is increasing consensus across political party lines that quotas are a necessary short-term way of ensuring that women get a foot in the door. A recent Gender Links study, *Ringing up the Changes: Gender in Southern African Politics* (Lowe-Morna 2004b) found that 76 per cent of the 172 decision-makers polled said they agreed with quotas. However, several participants qualified their answers, for example, by saying that they should be short-term. The study also found that with the exception of the Seychelles (where there is little support for quotas due to the island's long history of women's active participation in decision-making) there is much stronger support for quotas among women than among men.

Post-conflict factors

Many countries that came out of recent civil war or wars of liberation have tended to be more likely to adopt quotas and to find ways to increase women's political representation. After conflict, these countries generally drew up new constitutions and re-established their parliaments from scratch. Similarly, countries in Africa with higher representation of women due to quotas were more likely to be newly independent countries, hence they were also countries where women most recently obtained the right to vote and to run for office. Moreover, women were not contending with entrenched male incumbents as they sought political representation. These trends of post-conflict ascendance of women decision-makers have been identified worldwide (Jabre 2004).

Of the 12 African countries with the highest rates of female representation in parliament, eight (Angola, Mozambique, South Africa, Uganda, Rwanda, Eritrea, Burundi, and Namibia) have undergone liberation wars or civil conflict in recent years. Upheavals of this kind shake up existing social and cultural norms, even if only for a short time, opening a space for women to play non-traditional roles.

Mozambique, for example, has undergone three upheavals in its recent history: the struggle for independence from Portuguese colonial rule; the civil war fuelled by apartheid South Africa post-independence; and then the switch from a one-party to a multi-party system. Struggle has played an important part in attitudes towards the liberation of women, at a personal and a political level. For example, Mozambique National Resistance Movement (Renamo) MP Hirondina Herculano recalled that she has done the same tasks as men from the age of 16 when she started fighting for Renamo. She trained to use weapons and to parachute. 'In the bush, I shared the same problems and conditions as the men'.

Like the South West African People's Organization (SWAPO) and the African National Congress (ANC), the early philosophy of the ruling Front for the Liberation of Mozambique (Frelimo) party opened the door to debate on gender issues. Although sometimes from a rather 'male' perspective, Frelimo concerned itself with women's empowerment as far back as the struggle for independence in the 1970s.

At independence from Portugal in 1975, President Machel prioritized women's literacy and eliminating discrimination against women in this traditionally patriarchal society. The constitution at independence enshrined equality of women and men. Since then, a series of progressive laws have been passed to advance the status of women. Frelimo put women into decision-making positions in the so-called 'dynamizing groups', tribunals and local councils. In the 1977 elections, the percentage of women elected ranged from 28 per cent in local councils to 12 per cent in the National People's Assembly. This was the highest percentage of any African country reporting to the Second World Conference on Women in Copenhagen in 1980. A 16-year civil war took over most of the countryside and undid much of the progress. Women from both Frelimo and Renamo took to the battlefield. The civilian population in the rural areas, mostly women and children, suffered horrific brutalities, including mutilations and rape. Women and children comprised most of the hundreds of thousands of people who had to flee to neighbouring countries and made up most of the millions displaced within the country. The women often headed households, albeit dependent on foreign aid for their survival.

The peace accord of October 1992 enabled people to return to their lands. The war had disrupted education and literacy campaigns and thwarted efforts to improve the delivery of social services. During the war and after, Mozambique has also suffered devastating droughts and floods. Many of the disruptions may have made it easier to start afresh in terms of implementing new gender policies. Mozambique subsequently has made notable progress in advancing the status of women. The new constitution adopted in 1990 paved the way for the transition to multi-party democracy and an emphasis on women's equal rights. Mozambique held its first multi-party elections in 1994, narrowly won by Frelimo, which had fielded a relatively large number of women candidates. The party also adopted a quota for women's representation in 1994.

In Mozambique, women's roles during the turmoil shaped their interest in politics in the post-conflict period as was the case in many other countries coming out of wars of liberation and civil conflict. In some of these countries, their left leaning political tendencies reinforced an interest in advancing women's status. But perhaps most important was the fact that they were wiping the slate clean and starting afresh in creating new political configurations. They did not have to contend with replacing entrenched male incumbents with women and therefore were better positioned to craft more equitable political systems.

State objectives

The adoption of quotas can also be explained by changing domestic agendas, which may go beyond the aforementioned concerns having to do with the advancement of women, adhering to international and regional norms, responding to pressures from women's movements, and at times implicit pressures from donors. Here it is instructive to separate the agendas of women's movements from those of the state.

States have sometimes adopted quotas in an effort to create a modern image for themselves in order to challenge more conservative societal forces, including Islamist movements in predominantly Muslim countries (Morocco and Tunisia, for example). In the Ugandan case, many of the women who have been elected to the reserved seats are seen as having been given these seats in exchange for their loyalty to the president. These same women have been used to promote some very anti-democratic and anti-women legislation.

Similarly, in Rwanda there are those in the opposition who are concerned that a political calculus by the ruling Front Patriotique Rwandais (RPF) may be driving much of their interest in promoting women legislators. The number of female legislators jumped from 26 per cent in 1994 to 49 per cent after the 2003 elections. Rwanda's demographic changes may explain some of the emphasis on female representation. The 1994 genocide left women heading up to half of all households (Mutume 2004). Gender relations were dramatically transformed after the genocide, as women took up leading roles in the community, household, and as income providers. Women buried the dead, rebuilt shelters, located homes for nearly 500,000 orphans, and took over non-traditional business such as brickmaking, construction and mechanics (Powley 2003: 14–16). Rwandan women's efforts to rebuild the country and overcome the ethnic divisions embedded in Rwanda's social fabric forced them to think of themselves differently and develop skills they otherwise would not have acquired. Women activists become involved in the peace process at the grassroots level and became an important force for conflict resolution through various women's organizations. This explains, in part, the dramatic change in female representation but it does not explain everything.

Rwanda adopted a new constitution in 2003, calling for a minimum of one-third of women in all decision-making positions and setting aside 24 (30 per cent) of all seats for women in legislative elections. In addition to these reserved seats, another 15 women were elected into non-reserved seats in the 2003 election, bringing the total number of women elected to 39 out of 80 seats in the lower house. Like the District Councils in Uganda that serve as an electoral college, the Women's Councils in Rwanda elect the women to the reserved seats in the parliament. Women's Councils at the grassroots level elect women representatives to successive higher administrative levels from the cell level to the sector and district levels, skipping the provincial level, and then to the senate through what becomes an electoral college. Reminiscent of the late 1980s/early 1990s position of women in Uganda vis-à-vis President Museveni, women and women's organizations in Rwanda have supported President Paul Kagame's anti-sectarian and pro-women approach and are very much driven by an overwhelming desire to build peace and promote forgiveness (Powley 2003: 16). After the genocide, the RPF leadership emphasized women's role in the reconciliation and reconstruction processes and encouraged women to enter public office. This won them considerable support among the female population. The government can in turn count on a loyal cadre of supporters who will not challenge RPF authority, even though many of the Women's Councils that voted the women in are made up of genocide survivors who have not always seen eye to eye with Kagame. The RPF ensured that in the 2003 elections no serious political opposition groups were allowed to participate freely or run for office. The RPF has effectively silenced any criticism or challenge to its authority (Human Rights Watch 2003). Given that 26 per cent of the seats are not held by the RPF, the RPF is guaranteed an additional loyal constituency through reserved seats for women. To better understand this dynamic it is important to note that the top leadership posts held by women have primarily gone to pro-RPF Anglophone Rwandans who earlier had lived in Uganda or elsewhere (Powley 2003: 34).

Much the same quid pro quo existed between the state and women in Uganda (although the ethnic equation is not the same), but 20 years later it was being strained as the women's movement was facing considerable disillusionment with the limits of Museveni's pro-women policies and openness to political reform. It is important to pay attention to these other potentially undemocratic uses of women's quotas because they determine the extent to which women can effectively use their positions in parliament to advance a pro-woman agenda.

Democratizing influences

Another factor facilitating the introduction of quotas has been the movement towards democratization and political liberalization throughout Africa, albeit the trends have been uneven with considerable stalling, backsliding, and resistance to breaking with authoritarian tendencies in many countries. Africa is nevertheless in the throes of major political transformation. Over the last three decades, the remaining vestiges of colonialism have been removed. During the last two decades, several countries have experienced 'second generation' revolutions, namely the shift from one party to multiparty rule and from military to civilian rule. The more democratic forms of government that emerged in many parts of Africa led to an increase in the number and voice of opposition parties; a new lease on life for the often outspoken if perilous independent media; and a mushrooming of civil society. These trends broke the stranglehold of the single-party and its related mass organizations that had dominated women's mobilization up until the late 1980s. It allowed for the creation of new independent women's organizations and resulted in the creation of new lines of patronage no longer tied to the state or single party. For women, this has meant new possibilities for political engagement although there are important exceptions and setbacks.

In some countries, multipartyism resulted in co-operation between women's organizations that cut across party lines. Saran Diabaté, a member of the Guinean People's Union Party (RPG), recounts how she and a delegation of Guinean women politicians had been inspired by the unity of women's organizations that cut across party lines during a visit to Senegal. They returned home and created the Women's Political Party Organization (FPP), the first inter-party political organization of women in Guinea with the aim of fundraising, training for women in leadership and negotiation skills; and building stronger synergies between women's NGOs and women politicians and working to lessen rivalries and strengthen co-operation between women's organizations (USAID 2002).

In contrast, in Namibia, many of the fissures within the women's movement today fall along party lines. Efforts to unite the women's movement before and after independence proved elusive. These eventually dissipated along party lines between the Democratic Turnhalle Alliance (DTA)-led Federation of Namibia Women that never got off the ground, and the Namibia National Women's Organization that has remained close to the SWAPO party (Becker 2000). Relations between SWAPO and a number of women's organizations in Namibia are tense.

About 25 of Africa's sub-Saharan states would fall into 'partly free' category used by Freedom House and of these nine had some form of legal quota for women and three had representation of women that exceeded 20 per cent of parliamentary seats. Of the nine African countries that would be considered democratic, three have quotas. Finally, of the ten 'not free' regimes, four have quotas. In other words, quotas are adopted by countries regardless of regime type. Democratic countries tend to favour party-based quotas rather than reserved seats or constitutionally mandated quotas.

African debates around quotas

Needless to say, there are many critics of quotas, even among feminists in Africa, many of whom believe the practice leads to tokenism and can become yet another mechanism in the service of patronage politics. Arguments critical of quotas in Africa are varied. Opponents of the quota policy may focus on the political motivations of the measure, arguing that it is simply a political manoeuvre by those in power to win women's votes and ensure a solid block of female supporters in parliament. As Aminata Cisse Diaw, Katy Cisse and Aminata Kasse have observed in the case of Senegal: 'The implementation of a voluntarist policy of taking into account quotas or parity has largely been based on calculations related to electoral concerns' (Diaw *et al.* 1999). These concerns have often been raised in countries adopting reserved seats such as Uganda, Tanzania, and most recently in Rwanda.

One of the major concerns has to do with the worry that women elected will not be qualified and will simply serve as tokens, who are unable to work the system. This has especially been an issue where there simply have not been enough qualified women willing to run for office to reach the set quotas.

In South Africa, Democratic Alliance (DA) Chief Whip Douglas Gibson argued that quotas are 'hopelessly wrong. Would you then say that 10 per cent of the cricket team should be white and the rest black because that is the make up of the nation? You would not, because not everyone wants to play cricket. We should aim for a situation where people with merit get there and there are many meritorious women. Merit is not what keeps them out. It should get them in'. Yet when asked if the ANC quota had influenced the DA, Gibson said: 'I suppose so. One's conscious of the fact that they have done so. We are aware of the need for everyone to have an equal opportunity to be here, and if they don't have an equal opportunity we will help to create it'.

Others are concerned that quotas will devalue the status of women who win without the help of quotas. Winstone Hamadulu, councillor for Chakunkula ward in Lusaka, Zambia, noted:

> I do not think that the quota business is fair or useful. Everyone should get where they are by merit. For example if we have women in parliament that are there to fulfill quotas, they cannot be respected. The challenge is to win an election on your own merit, not by grace.

Other women who win fair and square will also be disadvantaged because they will be perceived as having got to their position by a quota, instead of sheer hard work.

(Lowe-Morna 2004a)

Yet the whole idea of merit is challenged by Thenjiwe Mtinso, South Africa's Ambassador to Cuba and chair of Gender Links:

In conditions of inequality and disadvantage it is folly to talk of merit. The 'meritocrats' use 'Merit' as a gender smokescreen to keep doors to decision-making firmly shut on women. They know very well that the disadvantaged groups need equity measures to facilitate their movement from the periphery to the centre of decision-making. Quotas are not a permanent feature of democracy but rather a mechanism in the transition to it.

(Mtintso 2003)

There has been little research in Africa on the extent to which quotas actually lower the quality of legislators. The evidence from our research is that quotas have not led to tokenism in the proportional representation (PR) system at national level, but have raised concerns at local level. Quotas have also raised some concerns in plurality-majority systems where seats are reserved for women and in the mixed system where there is already a sense of 'some are more equal than others'. However, quotas have been acknowledged in these instances as a learning opportunity for women to be able to compete on equal terms with men in the future. In South Africa, there has been a sharp learning curve for new women parliamentarians, but they have conscientiously met the challenges of their new position.

In 1998 Lydia Kompe, an activist with the Rural Women's Movement (RWM), reflected on how her views had changed since she first came into office as a parliamentarian:

When I came here I felt out of place, isolated, with no education and I was just bombarded by everything. I could not participate. I was completely powerless despite the fact that I was in a powerful institution. I only started to grasp most of the things in 1996. I had also chosen committees where I was at least comfortable and which were not that technical. Now I can stand up and challenge any one and especially the opposition with confidence. I realize that the lack of confidence had shackled me for a long time, made me withdraw and made me bitter against those who were privileged with the know-how. All that resentment that built up has now disappeared with the confidence that I have.

(Mtintso 1999)

New women parliamentarians in South Africa as well as elsewhere in Africa generally came into parliament and found that previous norms still prevail. Women often felt marginalized because they had a hard time penetrating the informal old boys' networks and clubs where so many important decisions are debated and agreed upon.

However, many ANC women parliamentarians in South Africa improved their position on the ANC list between the 1994 and 1999 elections as evidence that once in parliament, women have gained acceptance and credibility in their own right (Mtintso 1999). Some of these changes are dramatic. For example, former Minister of Health, now Minister of Foreign Affairs Nkosozana Zuma moved from position 51 to three on the list, and there is frequent speculation that she could be the first woman vice president of South Africa.

In addition to the debate on tokenism, quotas have also been said to be problematic when other measures have not been taken to improve the position of women. Some women's organizations have gone to great lengths to train women parliamentarians and potential candidates. However, most parties have simply argued that women did not have the requisite skills or there were not enough women willing to run and were unwilling to initiate training programs to enhance women's political skills (Diop 2002).

Yet another concern is that by introducing quotas that others will be encouraged to make claims for special seats based on ethnic and regional claims, which, given Africa's enormous cultural diversity, might open a Pandora's box of claims and counterclaims (Diop 2002).

Some debates have to do with the mechanisms used to implement quotas. In Uganda, many in the women's movement have not rejected quotas but, rather, are critical of various biases inherent in the electoral college that selects women to the parliamentary women's seats.

Proponents of gender-based electoral quotas argue that discrimination against women will not reverse itself on its own, necessitating special interventions. An implicit quota has already been in place advancing only men and therefore quotas are needed to turn this situation around. The Chair of South Africa's Agriculture and Land Affairs Portfolio Committee Neo Masithela explained that he had initially opposed quotas – 'I saw them as a barrier'. He changed his mind after attending a youth conference in Mauritius where young women comprised only about 5 per cent of the participants. 'We need to assist those who do not understand quotas to understand them. One thing is to argue that quotas will deprive men. But what have we been depriving women of all these years?' (Lowe-Morna 2004a: 17).

Some advocates of quotas argue that capable women often lack the resources, political experience, education and political connections to run for office. They are frequently outside of the old boys' networks and don't have the connections to build support. Popular perceptions may still suggest that a woman's 'proper' place is in the home rather than in politics. Prohibitive cultural attitudes against women's involvement persist among both men and women. Women themselves may be reticent to run for office because politics itself is sometimes considered 'dirty', 'divisive', 'leading to sectarian hostilities', and even 'the cause of violence' (Ondego 1997). Women also may avoid politics because of cultural norms against women speaking in public. Campaigning and being a leader often involves travel, spending nights away from home, going to bars to meet people, and meeting men, all of which puts women politicians at risk of being thought of as 'loose women' or 'unfit mothers'. Not only may they find themselves and their families under attack or the subject of malicious gossip, but husbands sometimes will forbid their wives to enter into politics. Some husbands are threatened by the possibility that their wives will interact with other men. Other husbands fear the social stigma directed against their wives, or they worry that their wife's political preoccupations will divert her attention away from the home.

There are also practical considerations that constrain women that are related to gender inequalities in the division of labour. Women leaders complain that men often schedule political meetings in the evenings and then come late to them, making it difficult for women who have to cook dinner and put children to sleep. Women often lack the time to aspire for office, because unlike men, they shoulder not only the demands of bringing in an income, but also the heavy responsibilities of caring for the home and children. Women, more often than men, are also limited by the lack of financial resources. And if they get campaign funds from a man, this may raise questions about the nature of their relationship. All these constraints are used as arguments to justify special measures like quotas to help level the playing field between the genders.

For many it is a matter of justice that women be integrated into all key societal institutions and have parity with men (Diop 2002: 3). As the SWAPO Women's Council leader Eunice Iipinge explained:

> We really want to have half of it, that's why we are calling for the zebra [party] list. To us that constitutes justice . . . it constitutes legitimacy . . . women are the majority in the country so if women are not involved in decision making then the question of legitimacy comes up . . . so we really want to see the zebra list [zipper list] introduced.
>
> (Bauer 2004)

Others argue that women parliamentarians are required to fight for women's interests and that female parliamentarians are likely to take up issues relating to women. Women bring their own perspectives to political life and have particular interest-specific forms of legislation. A corollary argument is that legislatures should be representative of the broader society of which women constitute over half the population.

Some argue that quotas can also make people realize the implications of gender inequalities in social institutions. As ANC MP Mapetjane Kgaogelo Lekgoro explained: 'quotas are a constant reminder that no matter which area of governance you are working in, you need to ask the question: where are women? Quotas are not scientific, but they are a way to achieve a particular level of awareness'. Thus the issue of quotas has been a way of educating people about gender equality.

ANC MP Maureen Malumise noted that in the first parliament in 1994, some men resented the quota and it showed. But by the second term, 'they were friendlier, they did not feel threatened, they were beginning to understand gender issues and to articulate them very well' (Lowe-Morna 2004a: 16).

Impact of quotas on representation

In Africa there are no legislative laws requiring all parties to adhere to a quota at the national level. There are primarily two kinds of quotas in Africa: constitutionally mandated quotas and party mandated ones. There are constitutionally mandated: (1) executive appointments (Kenya, Swaziland); (2) reserved seats that only women can vie for regardless of party (Rwanda, Uganda, Eritrea); and (3) in the case of Tanzania, there are special seats reserved for women, which are allocated to political parties based on their proportional number of parliamentary seats won in an election. Outside of those cases, individual parties set their own quotas on a voluntary basis, which can be quite unreliable. The more democratic leaning countries in Africa (Botswana, Mali, Mozambique, Namibia, Senegal and South Africa) have tended to prefer quotas set by parties themselves rather than adopting legal quotas such as reserved seats or candidate quotas mandated by constitutions or law.

African countries with quotas have had on average 22 per cent of legislative seats held by women compared with 14 per cent of seats held by women in countries without quotas. Countries with constitutionally mandated reserved seats have on average 30 per cent of their parliamentary seats occupied by women, while countries with party quotas average 17 per cent held by women.

Party quotas require voluntary compliance. Where parties have quotas they do not always abide by them. The ruling Cameroon People's Democratic Movement (CPDM), for example, introduced a 30 per cent quota for female candidates in 1996. The major opposition party, the Social Democratic Front (SDF), followed suit with a 25 per cent quota. But neither party has stuck to their quota targets. Moreover, women's names appear generally at the bottom of party lists (Adams 2003).

Similarly, the Senegalese Parti Socialiste (PS), in line with the Socialist International, has set a 25 per cent quota for female nominations. During the nominations for the 1998 elections, two-thirds of the co-ordinating committees applied the quota, and some rural committees even went beyond it and achieved parity. But others did not even nominate a single woman.

Some parties have not placed women favourably on the party list. As is well known, location on the party list makes an enormous difference and quotas can only make a difference where women are placed prominently on the candidate lists, are alternated with men 'zebra style' (as they say in southern Africa), or where they are listed in alphabetical order.

While relying on the voluntarism of party-based quotas may be unreliable, the reserved seat quotas raise another set of dilemmas. The fear is that the reserved seat quotas may become a ceiling. Women who want to run for office are told to run only for the reserved seats rather than for open seats as well, as has been well documented in the Ugandan case (Tripp 2000). Once the quota is met, there is a sense that all has been accomplished and that there is little need to pursue full equal representation.

One of the main benefits of introducing electoral quotas has been the way an influx of women has helped influence popular perceptions of the acceptability of women being active in politics. In Uganda, for example, in a span of less than a decade, the reserved seats for women had the effect of making what had been almost unheard of and culturally unacceptable – namely women serving as legislators – into something that is virtually taken for granted today by both men and women. One of the most important consequences of the reserved seats in Uganda was to give women the exposure, political experience and confidence to run on their own in open electoral races. With each election in Uganda, increasing numbers of women have run for the open seats against men. In 1989, two women won open constituency seats. By 2001, 32 ran for constituency seats and 13 won. The biggest change, however, was in the overall numbers of women running for office. In 1996 the total number of women running for parliamentary seats was 135, while in 2001, 203 women ran in the parliamentary elections.

Impact of electoral systems

There are four main types of electoral systems in Africa: 14 countries have party list proportional systems (List PR); 12 have first-past-the-post plurality system (FPP); seven have two rounds majority systems, and four have mixed systems. A handful have various other systems, including a block vote majority system in Mauritius; different types of party block vote plurality-majority in Cameroon, Chad and Côte d'Ivoire; FPP and List PR plurality-majority system in Madagascar. Many of these systems have been inherited from previous colonial rulers. Thus, almost all the FPP plurality systems are in countries that were once under British or Belgian rule;

Table 5.2 Female representation in legislatures in Africa by electoral system

Electoral system	Median percentage of seats held by women	Number of countries with system
Proportional (List PR)	16.4[a]	14
Mixed (Parallel and MMP)	19.3	4
Plurality (FPP)	10.4	12
Majority (Two Rounds)	8.0[b]	7

For sources and definitions, see Table 5.1.

Notes
a Figures for Guinea Bissau not available.
b Figures for Central African Republic not available.

almost all the List PR proportional systems were once Portuguese or French colonies with a few exceptions. All the two-round majority systems are former French colonies as are all the mixed systems.

On balance the proportional representation systems yield greater levels of female representation than do the plurality-majority electoral systems with the mixed member proportional system resulting in the highest rates of female representation.

Reserved seats and the plurality-based systems

The Tanzanian case shows how increases in numbers in plurality-based systems can be achieved through constitutionally mandated reserved seats. Of the 61 (22.3 per cent) women in the Tanzanian parliament after the 2000 elections, 47 women (20 per cent) owe their presence to the constitutional quota, which reserves one-fifth of the seats in parliament for women. While the elections are contested on a constituency basis, the seats reserved for women are allocated between parties on the basis of the proportion of votes that they garnered in parliamentary elections. Each party determines its own mechanism for filling the seats, with some nominating the women and others allowing women party members to elect their candidates.

Women in the parties thus compete among themselves for a place on their party list, but not with men. Women are, of course, free to contest the constituency seats. The additional 2.3 per cent of women in the Tanzanian parliament consist of 12 who contested the election as candidates and two appointed by the president.

In March 2005, Tanzania increased the number of seats reserved for women from 20 to 30 per cent, to bring it in line with the targets set in the 1997 SADC Declaration on Gender and Development. Activists, however, fear that these reserved seats may have unintended negative consequences, because of the relative disadvantage that women who come in on reserved seats face.

According to Tanzania Gender Networking Programme (TGNP) board member Aggripina Mosha, activists are concerned that in the long term, the affirmative action measure could have a 'crippling effect because women can become scared to stand on their own in constituencies. We are pushing for the parties to have a policy that requires that at least 30 per cent women should be nominated by the party to stand for constituency seats. If the parties throw their support behind women in constituencies as they do for men, the women will win'. Mosha notes that in the 2000 elections, of the 13 women nominated by the ruling Chama Cha Mapinduzi (CCM) party to stand in constituencies, 12 went through. She says this shows that women can succeed in the majority system if their parties are genuinely committed to increasing the representation of women (Lowe-Morna 2004a: 22).

The dilemmas of voluntary party quotas in a PR system

Sitting high in the regional and global ranking lists for women in parliament, South Africa and Mozambique have both achieved their successes through the voluntary party quotas of the ruling ANC and Frelimo parties respectively. Both countries have a PR electoral system.

In South Africa's first post-apartheid elections in 1994, the ANC had to make some amendments to its election list to ensure that women constituted at least one-third of the top half of the list (reckoning that it would win at least 50 per cent of the vote). But by the second elections in 1994, a sufficient proportion of women had made their way onto the list through the branch nomination system for the party not to have to 'engineer' the list.[2]

In both countries, the ruling parties have now exceeded the 30 per cent quota they set for themselves, with women claiming 33 of the seats in South Africa and 35 per cent of the seats in Mozambique. In Mozambique, of the 160 Frelimo MPs, 71 (or 44 per cent) are women. The opposition party Renamo, does not have a policy of quotas, and only 16 out of its 90 representatives or 17.7 per cent of its parliamentarians are women. If Frelimo had not exceeded its quota, Mozambique would not have made the 30 per cent target. Still, there are now three times as many female Renamo MPs than after the 1994 elections that ushered in multiparty democracy in Mozambique. This is an illustration of the snowball effect of voluntary quotas adopted by ruling parties. Similarly in South Africa, women constitute 35.7 per cent of the ANC seats and 20.8 per cent of opposition seats, giving an overall average of 32.8 per cent women in parliament (Lowe-Morna 2004a: 22).

Table 5.3 shows that while the representation of women in the ANC increased by 1.5 percentage points to 37.2 per cent of the ANC members of parliament, the representation of women in all opposition parties increased between 1994 and the third elections in 2004. Overall, the

Table 5.3 Changes in women's representation in South Africa

Party	1994			2004		
	Total	Women	Women %	Total	Women	Women %
African National Congress	252	90	35.7	279	104	37.2
Democratic Alliance	7	1	14.2	50	13	26.0
Inkatha Freedom Party	43	10	23.2	28	5	17.8
New National Party	82	9	10.9	7	0	0
United Democratic Movement				9	4	44.4
Independent Democrats				7	3	42.8
African Christian Democratic Party	2	0	0	6	2	33.3
Freedom Front Plus				4	0	0
United Christian Democratic Party				3	0	0
Pan Africanist Congress	5	1	20.0	3	0	0
Other				4	0	0
Total	400	111	27.8	400	131	32.7

Source: Parliament of South Africa.

representation of women in the national assembly rose by 5.05 percentage points between 1994 and 2004, as a consequence of diffusion.

While opposition parties publicly oppose quotas, many of the women in these parties said they supported them. They looked to the ANC to help move the gender agendas in their parties, and acknowledged that quotas have had a snowball effect.

As a woman from the opposition Democratic Alliance (DA) put it:

> I'm all for quotas but my party is not. Tory parties traditionally don't go for quotas wherever they are in the world, but I have had meetings with women in such parties wherever they are in the world and secretly we know that the only thing that works is quotas but we have not been able to persuade our colleagues. Quotas are important to get over the first barrier, because after that you have the tipping factor. Otherwise you have a perpetual tiny minority of women. However, the fact that quotas are around has focused the minds of men in whatever party they are in.
>
> (Lowe-Morna 2004a: 23)

This has given rise to two lines of argument in South Africa. While accepting that the ANC quota has jolted them into action, opposition parties argue that as the level of women's representation is increasing in their parties without resorting to quotas, there is no need for them.

Gender activists, on the other hand, have argued that the danger of voluntary party quotas where only one party adopts such a quota is that if the support of that party declines, the representation of women will also drop. There is also the more fundamental question about the responsibility of *all* parties for ensuring women's equal participation in politics.

The 50–50 campaign in South Africa points out that if the country adopted a legislated quota that would require all political parties to have a quota of 50 per cent while retaining the proportional system, it would become the first country in the world to achieve gender parity in its national assembly.[3]

The campaign won an important first victory when it lobbied against the changing of the PR system for national elections in South Africa to a mixed system in the 2004 elections. The ANC has argued that the PR system is not necessarily in its interests because as the party with the greatest support among the majority black population it could arguably win more seats through the 'winner takes all' system. But it has supported the retention of the PR system because it is more inclusive (an important factor in a country with as divisive a history as South Africa) and because it has been an important factor in boosting women's participation from 2.7 per cent during the apartheid era to the present 30 per cent level.[4]

The ANC has also stated its support for a 30 per cent legislated quota but has fallen shy of the 50 per cent being called for by gender activists. While the ANC Women's League raised the issue of a 50 per cent legislated quota at the ANC congress in December 2002, it did not get much support.

Still, the quota has been critical in South Africa in ensuring a virtual overnight boost to the numbers of women in decision-making. The internal struggles within the ANC to secure even the 30 per cent quota has also been a key mobilizing tool for women, and a critical component of transforming the attitudes of men within the party.

Legislated quotas in a PR system

As South Africa dithers over the issue of a legislated quota, local government in Namibia provides an example of the powerful combination of the PR system, a legislated quota, and voluntary measures by a political party for achieving a rapid and guaranteed increase in the representation of women in politics. But the inconsistency between this achievement and the representation of women in other areas of politics in Namibia raises concerns about the coherence of government strategy and – underpinning this – its commitment to achieving the 30 per cent target in all areas of decision-making.

Anna Philander, chairperson of the Tses Village Council in Southern Namibia, points out that there is an inconsistency between Namibia having a high level of women in local government, yet only 3 per cent women in regional councils and 26 per cent women in the national assembly. 'We have to start at the highest level to put more women there. Currently at our regional level, there are no women', she said (Lowe-Morna 2004a: 25).

Local and national assembly elections in Namibia are run on a PR basis, while regional elections are based on a majority system. The issue of what electoral system should apply at local government level has been a contentious one in both Namibia and South Africa because of the legacy of apartheid in these two countries, leaving geographical landscapes that are heavily divided along racial lines.

Although at a theoretical level there are strong arguments for plurality-majority system at local level because voters need to be able to access their representatives, SWAPO in Namibia has argued (against much pressure from the opposition) for the retention of the PR system to ensure that the interests of all racial groups at local level are addressed.

The retention of the PR system, provisions in the Local Authority Act for certain minimum numbers of women in local structures that have been strengthened over time, and SWAPO's decision in the second local government elections to adopt a 'zebra' or one woman, one man system in its lists delivered the impressive 42 per cent women in this sphere of government (Hubbard 2001).

On the other hand, Namibia does not have a legislated quota nor has SWAPO applied a voluntary quota to elections for the national assembly. Some argue that the steady increase in women's representation in the national assembly to its current level of 26 per cent obviates the need for 'special measures'. But, as in South Africa, the 50–50 campaign in Namibia is making the case that to ensure equal representation of women at national and local level, legislation should be passed requiring all parties to have a 'zebra' list system for these elections.[5]

Short of changing the electoral system at regional level, the 50–50 campaign has put forward options for requiring that parties field equal numbers of male and female candidates, or that each constituency have a male and female candidate for regional elections. The inconsistency between the representation of women at local, regional and national level in Namibia casts doubt on the extent to which the government there has mapped out a clear strategy for achieving the 30 per cent target in all areas of decision-making.

A particular concern expressed by gender activists in Namibia during the focus group meeting is why the ruling party has been more amenable to special measures for women's representation in local but not in other spheres of government. The interpretation of this in Namibia is that rather than this being a positive recognition of the role women play at community level, it is a cynical reflection of women's unwaged work.

Conclusions

The African cases point to both some of the peculiarities of African experiences when it comes to electoral quotas as well as some of the commonalities with other world regions. The influence of civil conflict has perhaps, more than in other regions, served as an impetus to introduce legal quotas. Women in these instances were not contending with male incumbents and found it easier to make inroads. Quotas were often introduced into a situation where new constitutions were being rewritten and new governance structures were being crafted, making it easier to put questions of gender representation on the table.

More than other world regions, there has perhaps been greater reliance on constitutionally mandated reserved seats in Africa, in countries like Uganda, Tanzania, Rwanda, Eritrea, Djibouti, Sudan, Somalia's transitional government, and Morocco. Historically, Ghana and Egypt would have also been in this category. This perhaps reflects in these instances a greater concern for guaranteed outcomes in terms of female representation and a lack of confidence in party compliance or initiative.

Regional influences have also been especially important as an impetus for the adoption of quotas in Africa. SADC, in particular, has played an important role in pushing its member countries to take measures to increase the representation of women in national and local governing bodies. Regional women's organizations and networks, have similarly, been very important in pushing for these changes.

Africa leads numerically in countries around the globe that have adopted 50–50 campaigns for gender parity in political representation. How successful these movements will be remains to be seen, but for the time being, increasing numbers of countries are finding themselves faced with pressures for radical change in female representation.

In other respects, Africa shares many of the same dilemmas that other regions confront. The debate over quotas in Africa and elsewhere has gone hand in hand with discussions about how to make women's representation matter. Where a significant presence of women is combined with a range of enabling factors including a background and history of struggle, a democratic dispensation, dynamic links with women's movements and ways to enhance the personal agency of decision-makers, there is a marked impact on institutional culture, attitudes, laws, policies, and service delivery.

Already there are some indications that women parliamentarians are making a difference in the way politics is conducted in Africa. There are, for example, differences between the style, procedures, norms and discourse in political institutions in the countries that have a high representation of women compared to those that do not.

Where women parliamentarians are found in larger numbers, there has been greater awareness of the importance of gender equality and the representation of women in key public bodies. More attention has been paid to reforms affecting women, including legislation pertaining to women's land rights, property rights, family relations, rape, and women's citizenship rights. There has been greater attention given to innovative approaches like the gender budgeting initiatives that have captured the imagination of the region and provide a potentially powerful tool for gender mainstreaming through tracking resource allocations. These are just a few of the ways in which increased representation of women as a result of quotas are beginning to make a difference. At the same time, Uganda and more recently Rwanda, serve as cautionary tales of the limits of such quotas within undemocratic regimes. As long as civil and political liberties are curtailed, women's potential to make a genuine difference remains restricted.

Notes

1 Extensive portions of this chapter make use of previous research carried out by the authors, including *Ringing Up the Changes: Gender in Southern African Politics* authored by Colleen Lowe-Morna (2004b) and 'Electoral Gender Quotas: A Key to Equality? Southern African Input' also by Colleen Lowe-Morna (2004a).
2 Interview, South African Minister in the Presidency Essop Pahad.
3 Led by the Gender Advocacy Project (GAP), campaign members include the Commission on Gender Equality (CGE), Gender Links (GL), Women's Net and the Institute for Democratic Alternatives in South Africa (IDASA).
4 Interview, Essop Pahad, South African Minister in the Office of the Presidency.
5 Led by the organization Sister Namibia, the campaign includes over 20 Namibian NGOs, which have organized workshops and events around the country calling for the equal representation of women in all areas of decision-making.

Bibliography

Adams, M. (2003) 'Cameroon', in A.M. Tripp (ed.) *The Greenwood Encyclopedia of Women's Issues Worldwide: Sub-Saharan Africa*, Westport, Connecticut: Greenwood Press, pp. 82–107.
Bauer, G. (2004) '"The Hand That Stirs the Pot Can Also Run the Country": Electing More Women to Parliament in Namibia', *Journal of Modern African Studies*, 42, 4: 479–509.
Becker, H. (2000) 'Striving for change: The struggle for gender equality in Namibia', in E. Iipinge and M. Williams (eds) *Gender and Development*, Windhoek: University of Namibia and UNDP, pp. 30–47.
Benyin, C. (2003) 'Women on War: Give Us 30 Per cent of Parliamentary Seats', *Public Agenda* (Accra), 5 September.
Diaw, A.K. *et al.* (1999) *Campagnes législative de 1998: Démocratie où-es-tu?* Dakar: Senegalese Women's Council (COSEF).
Diop, A.D. (2002) 'Les quotas en Africa francophone: Des débuts modestes', in J. Ballington and M. Protais (eds) *Les Femmes au parlement: Au Delà du Nombre*, Stockholm: International IDEA, pp. 133–42. Online. Available at: http://www.idea.int (accessed 24 January 2005)
Diop, A.S. (2001) 'Senegalese Women Want To Be Elected Not Electors', *Panafrican News Agency (PANA)*, newswire 12 February.
Freedom House, Online. Available at: http://www.freedomhouse.org.
Hubbard, D. '50/50 Options for Namibia', prepared by Legal Assistance Southern African Politics' Centre for the Namibian Women's Manifesto Network, June 2001.

'Rwanda: RPF Seeks to Eliminate Opposition: Elections Set to Solidify Power', (press release), *Human Rights Watch*, New York, 8 May 2003. Online. Available at: http://hrw.org/backgrounder/africa/rwanda0503bck.htm (accessed 10 February 2005).

Inter-Parliamentary Union (IPU) Online. Available at: http://www.ipu.org>.

International IDEA and Stockholm University, 'Global Database of Quotas for Women', Online. Available at: http://www.quotaproject.org.

Jabre, K. 'Enhancing the Role of Women in Electoral Processes in Post-conflict Countries', Inter-Parliamentary Union, paper prepared for Expert Group Meeting on 'Enhancing Women's Participation in Electoral Processes in Post-Conflict Countries', Glen Cove, New York, January 2004.

Lowe-Morna, C. (2004a) 'Electoral Gender Quotas: A Key to Equality? Southern African Input', unpublished, Johannesburg: Gender Links.

Lowe-Morna, C. (ed.) (2004b) *Ringing Up the Changes: Gender in Southern African Politics*, Johannesburg: Gender Links.

Mtintso, T. (1999) 'The Contribution of Women Parliamentarians to Gender Equality', unpublished thesis of a Masters degree in Public and Development Management, Johannesburg: University of Witwatersrand.

—— (2003) 'The quota debate rages on', *Amalungelo: A Bi-Monthly Journal for Gender Justice in Southern Africa*, 2: 39–40. Online. Available at: http://www.genderlinks.org.za/amalungelo/toc.asp?eid=2 (accessed 10 February 2005).

Mutume, G. (2004) 'Women break into African politics: Quota Systems Allow More Women to Gain Elected Office', *Africa Recovery*, 18, 1: 4.

National Democratic Institute (n.d.) 'Women in Malian Politics'. Online. Available at: http://www.ndi.org/globalp/women/onepagers/mali_tif.pdf (accessed 24 January 2005).

Ondego, O. (1997) 'Obstacles to women's political empowerment', *GENDEReview – Kenya's Women and Development Quarterly*, 4, 2: 5–6.

Powley, E. 'Strengthening Governance: The Role of Women in Rwanda's Transition', paper presented at the Women Waging Peace Policy Commission, September 2003.

Sakho, A. (2002) 'Les femmes représenteront 30 pour cent des candidates de 13 partis aux elections locales', *Interpress Service News Agency*, 14 April.

United States Agency for International Development (USAID) (2002) 'Mission to Senegal Shows Women Solidarity is Essential'. Online. Available at: http://www.usaid.gov/gn/democracy/news/011108_senegalstudytrip/ (accessed 27 January 2005).

Tripp, A.M. (2000) *Women & Politics in Uganda*, Madison: University of Wisconsin Press; Oxford: James Currey and Kampala: Fountain Publishers.

6   The Balkans

From total rejection to gradual acceptance of gender quotas

Milica G. Antić and Sonja Lokar

Introduction

This chapter tells the story about exclusion as well as inclusion of women in post-conflict restoration and democratization processes in the Balkans. The term Balkan covers countries and territories from geographical West to East: Slovenia, Croatia, Bosnia and Herzegovina, Serbia and Montenegro, Kosovo, Albania and the Republic of Macedonia. All of them except Albania were parts of the former Socialist Federal Republic of Yugoslavia. All of these countries were countries which after the Second World War had been developing softer or stronger communist or socialist regimes and countries which in the end of 1980s and/or in the beginning of 1990s started the processes of transition – which again differ a great deal – from one-party rule to the political pluralism.

In the last decade the Balkan region experienced a total collapse of the socialist or communist regime, which in many parts of ex-Yugoslavia was followed by traumatic conflicts and wars and is now in a period of restoration. In analysing women's exclusion and inclusion in post-conflict Balkan region, we will particularly focus upon the role of women's organizations and international agents, but seen in the broader context of the social and political structures in the region as well as in the context of the changing discourses on equality in the post-conflict restoration and democratization process. We argue that the post-conflict situation in the Balkans has made it extremely difficult for women in the political parties and for women's NGOs to be heard. However, this total restoration of the political systems has opened windows of opportunity, which some in women's organizations have skilfully been able to use.

When discussing Yugoslavia (and its socialist past) one should know that due to its specific geopolitical position, a special type of socialism had been developed in comparison with the Eastern socialist block. Three main contributing factors can be delineated. First, Tito's break-up with Stalin's Informbiro, which directed Yugoslavia on a separate route of non-alignment movement. Second, a turn toward more liberal social and economic policies initiated by the concept of 'self-management' (Schopflin

2002). Third, the proximity of federational borders with the West. All three aspects reflected in the politics and conduct of people's and especially women's daily lives, but it was the third factor which had the most direct impact. This did not apply for Albania, where the socialist-communist regime maintained its prominent position to the very end.

The context

There were many common developments and features as well as many differences in the region in socialist times. The understanding of the so-called women's question, among the common features, is one of our interests in this chapter. It was widely understood, and in accordance with Marxist theory and ideology, that the women's question is a part of the class question.[1] Separating the issue from the class question would have endangered the attainability of the valuable solution and taken away its general social character (Dojčinović-Nešić 2000: 619–23). This question was going to be solved by the activity of communist party and self-organized workers and citizens (in former Yugoslavia) or by communist state and its agencies. No independent organization of women was therefore needed, that is why some of our feminist's writers would say that this was a period of the state feminism or feminism from above (Jalušič 1999). One can indeed witness big changes in the position of women during the socialist (communist) period: state feminists succeeded to ensure the prohibition of gender based discrimination, introduce the formal equality of women and women's right to vote, right to abortion based on the Constitution or law, paid maternity leave for employed women, equal access to schooling and paid work, declaration of equal salary for equal job, publicly subsidized network of child care facilities etc., to list only the most important.[2]

Different countries experienced the transition period differently: in terms of duration, intensity, form and results. Apart from the distinct levels of economic development, there are big differences in GDP, political systems, national, religious and cultural structures of societies, etc. While Slovenia's development was the quickest and the country has recently become the fully-fledged member of the European Union, the progress of other countries has been modest with wars in the Balkans being the most important reason behind that. Slovenia, on the contrary, got away with only ten-day confrontation between Slovene Territorial defence, Slovene police forces and Yugoslav National Army forces. Other parts of the former Yugoslav Federal State were damaged by continuous and exhausting war years that witnessed dreadful activities of ethnic cleansing that are now culminating with the trials of war criminals at the International Hague Tribunal.

During the first years of the major political changes and especially during the wars, the big issues of the establishment of independent national states, privatization, market economy, political and religious pluralism, state and institution building, to name only the most important, reshaped the concept of the woman/worker. Mainstream politics reduced women to a reproductive part of the national body – a part carrying an important role in such periods.[3] The forms of these misconceptions varied in different countries. They covered a wide range of issues: from the expectations that women would prefer to leave their paid jobs, stay at home and take care of children and family, attempts to legalize the sanctity of life from the very conception in order to forfeit women's rights to abortion (Slovenia), to the attempts of legal prohibition of abortion (Croatia). Moreover, the rapes of women of other nationalities in the war (Bosnia, Croatia, Serbia, Kosovo), and the move to make women call for the military protection of the army (Kosovo), etc.[4]

Mainstream politics, during the transitional or war period, did not allow questions regarding gender equality and political participation of women to be raised in any of the respective countries. Moreover, the majority of women, disillusioned by the transitional period or war, considered mainstream politics a dirty business, which is a time-consuming and highly corrupted activity (see also Jalušič and Antić 2001). Up to the mid-1990s, women's NGOs in these countries – if present – were weak, powerless and without sufficient external support (know-how, moral and financial means), unable to serve as a pressure group for increasing female presence in public life and politics.[5] Until the end of the war in Bosnia and Herzegovina (B&H) in 1995, women's NGOs in this region were mostly absorbed into the struggle for peace and human rights of women in war inside the regionally and globally connected women's pacifist's movement. The positive outcome of this engagement was that rape in wartime was finally defined as a crime against humanity by the international law (UN Beijing Conference on Women in 1995). Most of the women's NGOs groups of the Balkans in this period dealt also with the so-called social or security issues such as SOS help lines, support to the victims of rape, safe-houses for women victims of violence, economic self-support, etc. Only in Slovenia and Croatia were the so-called equality issues raised – it consisted of the effort to protect the right for safe and legal abortions, removal of gender discrimination from the language used in laws and professions, increase of women's presence in politics, etc. The argument that women are not interested in politics did not hold true. Women took an active interest as they were politically informed and quite numerous members of political parties, but they remained powerless and invisible. However, step by step the situation started to change. In the early 1990s, women started to get organized within political parties, trade unions and other spheres of life. Slovenia was the first country to legally introduce the changes. In 1991, the ad-hoc coalition successfully protected the right of free and safe abortion in the new Slovenian Constitution (Jalušič 1994: 135–57).

The discourse

The perception of three wider concepts: democracy, representation and citizenship, create an important framework in which the debate about gender equality has been discussed. Namely, in the 1990s when quotas started to be discussed in the political arena, at least in the northern part of the region, 'democracy' and 'democratization' served almost as magic words. Democracy was understood as a representative democracy with the strong emphasis on the representation of ideas and interest groups; in some cases its limits were discussed as well (see Gaber 1999: 57–84). Party pluralism, through which citizens exercise their political rights, was seen as an essential element of the new understanding of a democratic regime. Various analytical works of that time observed that the strong civil society that reached its peak at the end of 1980s had started to weaken.[6] The human potential active in the organizations of civil society moved to the newly built party politics. It was believed that parties are the only agents of these representative democracies and that the civil society had already completed its task. Social group representation was not considered as a problem until recently.[7] When the concept of representation was taken into account, ideological differences were perceived as the ones that have to be represented through the political parties. Apart from that, all geographical regions should be represented in the politics, more precisely in the parliament (this is accomplished through the electoral systems and works for example in 'Županijski dom' in Croatia). Only in Slovenia ethnical groups were taken into account, but only the autochthon groups such as Italians and Hungarians who have lived for centuries in the territory of Slovenia. No special attention was paid to the representation of other ethnic minorities that arrived during the 1960s and 1970s from the less developed regions of the federal state. Similar situations evolved in the other parts of the Balkan region – among other factors this proved to be a potent reason that led to the wars. In addition, no special attention was paid to the social strata representation, only recently women's representation received some attention in the public and political discourse. Citizenship as a concept is more or less understood in terms of passive citizenship.[8] A citizen has rights and duties but these notions had been mixed and misunderstood: in many cases the rights were taken as duties and the lack of real political rights was overlooked. For example, the right to vote in the whole region was taken as almost obligatory, like a duty. That is why Yugoslavia had almost 100 per cent participation in the elections during the socialist period. Yet now, when voting is taken as a right and not a duty, the turnout is sometimes very low (for example, only 28.35 per cent in the first election to the European Parliament in Slovenia). Citizens' freedom of choice was the magic formula everywhere, especially the freedom to participate in politics. The question of the unequal starting point of different social groups (women included) had never been seriously discussed.

In this context we cannot overlook the importance of the influence of liberal political and feminist discourses that reached the region from Western European and Nordic countries either via personal contacts or via official co-operations of different women's organizations, groups, and leftist political parties, recently also state institutions like Governmental Office for Equal Opportunities in Slovenia.

When quotas started to be discussed in the region, they were treated in the context of equality and more specifically – gender equality. Due to the fact that gender equality in politics was not high on the political agenda and that feminism as a theory and practice had been neglected for quite a long time, one cannot speak about strong and widely organized women's movements. Since gender studies was in its beginning (see Bahovec 1993 and Jalušič 2002), it is not surprising that there were many distinct interpretations and misunderstandings of the concept of equality and gender equality.

Freedom versus equality

In order to understand the debate on women in politics we have to make a short excursion into the past socialist times. In socialist times people were considered to be first workers then citizens. According to the Constitution, they were equal regardless of nationality, race, sex, language, etc. The equality of working people was the core of the constitution and taken for granted. Women were equal, too, but equal as workers and protected only as working mothers. The discourse of equality prevailed in these times, but more or less as the social equality. In the field of politics, women's rights were limited to the right to vote and to the right (or sometimes almost duty) to be active in the Communist Party and in other Communist Party controlled socio-political organizations. Moreover, the discourse on women as a social group, as a collective, had been suppressed.[9] Namely, it was widely understood that women have no special needs and rights other than those of the working class. Gender equality was mainly understood as equality within a social class (see Tomšič 1978). There was a vague perception that de facto gender equality was still not properly established due to the heritage of the capitalist past or the influence of backward religious practices. The latter factors would be gradually changed with special measures supporting equality of working mothers and increased participation of women in politics by using quotas. Seeking equality in other fields like asking for women's freedom of political organization, social innovation and sexual orientation was perceived as a bourgeois deviance and/or radical feminist demand for which there was no room under socialism. In conclusion, one can state that the equality discourse inside the social class (working people) prevailed, but attempts to introduce the topic of freedom in the political discourse were immediately suppressed.[10]

After the collapse of the socialist regimes, the rhetoric of social equality had been quickly forgotten and the rhetoric of freedom installed and quickly prevailed. 'Freedom' was a kind of magic formula. Above all, the freedom of choice was highly promoted in the field of consumption and transferred to other fields as well – among them politics. Now we are free to choose among different political options, parties are the agents of these options and we – the citizens – free to choose among them. It seems that this is all we need. The question of unequal positions, which in the field of politics means unequal starting positions for women, seems to be unimportant. It is usually ignored, that unequal starting positions are limiting women's freedom of choice to a large extent.

Formal versus substantial equality

In the end of 1980s and in the beginning of 1990s, minor women's groups were established that started to tackle the questions which were not discussed before: violence against women (SOS help lines), lesbian rights (Lilith), women in politics (Group Women for Politics), etc.[11] Now and again they take a part in public discussions on some important issue such as women in politics in the first multi-party elections, abortion rights, violence against women and children).[12] There is an ongoing process of construction of women as political subjects with their political interests formed and presented. These interests, needs and demands were publicly presented by different women's/feminist organizations and/or groups, but the realization of them did not receive appropriate attention. That was mostly due to the fact that 'big issues' subsumed all the others, including women's issues. For example, it was widely believed that it was not a proper time for the issues of gender equality, making them wait for more 'peaceful' times (see also Antić 1991).

In politics the principle that women's right to vote makes them legally and politically equal to men prevailed. It was the question of free choice of any individual how she or he would choose to exercise that right. This principle stresses the importance of formal equality of women and neglects the importance of social inequalities which decisively influence their politically unequal position (Pateman 1989: 214). Having said that we do not want to undervalue the formal or legal equality, it is still obvious that not enough has been done. The process has not led to equal opportunities and, consequently, to equal results. Feminist circles have often posed the question whether a democracy, which disregards the political equality of women, is democracy in the true sense of the word. It is referred to as 'unfinished democracy', while more radical feminists use the term 'male democracy'.[13] In the last few years (after important goals like joining the EU and NATO have been reached in Slovenia, and wars ended upon the termination of Milošević's regime) the readiness to do more to achieve substantial gender equality increased and possibilities to accept special measures to assure a larger women's presence in politics widened.

Different understandings of the concept of gender equality

Five different understandings of the concept of equality can be identified in the post-socialist period of this region: forced emancipation, product of radical feminism, sameness, equality of opportunity (more rarely) and/or equality of results (outcomes). When the concept of gender equality was publicly and politically discussed, it was often misunderstood and interpreted in a way that can threaten 'real equality', especially in the beginning of 1990s.

The understanding that gender equality is a kind of forced emancipation can be found among traditional and ideologically right of the centre, strongly Catholic oriented individuals, political parties as well as anticommunists. They argue that gender equality was the product of a communist or socialist past when ordinary people had not been consulted on anything but forced to do everything. In this sense women were not consulted as to whether they wanted to work or not, whether they wanted the abortion right or not, whether they wanted to be comrades or not, etc. Now, in democracy, we all have the right of choice and, according to the groups mentioned above, women do not want to be a part of a paid work force which they were once pushed into.[14] They think that abortion is a crime, that women want to be ladies rather than comrades, etc.[15] The second understanding of gender equality is that it is something inborn/ authentic – a product of radical feminism – and imported from the West. In a way it has brought forward issues that were not considered problematic here. We are all equal according to our Constitution and the law and that is sufficient.[16] If somebody wants more than this, the answer is that it is only a problem of application of these laws in everyday life, not more. Women have the same rights as men; if they do not want to exercise these rights, it is their own choice.[17] A part of the general public misunderstood the quest for equality as an attempt to impose a sameness which they would dislike. They would say that women and men are unequal and different and it should stay like this. Men would often support this perception stating that their wives are quite happy being women and staying at home. Furthermore, that they do not need to be publicly or politically active, they take care of their children and stay at home to tend them, etc.[18] The concept of gender equality as the equality of opportunity is not widely spread among the public. It is promoted among feminist and liberally oriented individuals and groups. They defend the standpoint that what people need is something more than formal equality according to the law, but genuine equality of opportunity or equality of the position of both genders. Sometimes special treatment or special measures are needed to acquire this equality – equality of results.[19]

Three steps from rejection to enactment of the quotas

The comparison of trends in the percentage of women in parliaments in the most developed European democracies with the ones of the Balkan countries from mid-1980s to 1999 shows a striking polarity. While formal and de facto political power of women in the developed European countries was steadily growing from the mid-1980s, then women in the Balkan countries, in the beginning of the 1990s, were literally robbed of the possibility to influence important historical changes of their societies from the inside through the means of their newly created political institutions – parties, parliaments and governments. It took them ten years to start to reverse the trend.

Electoral quotas have three distinct mainstream ideological backgrounds in all the Balkan countries, though the time frame slightly differs from country to country:

1 Since 1990, after the first free elections, until Beijing UN 4th World Conference on Women in 1995, there was an open conservative setback. Electoral gender quotas are openly rejected.
2 1995–9: a period of unwilling acceptance of the ideological concepts of the Beijing Platform for Action, and gradual acceptance of electoral gender quotas within the parties. This process was initiated mostly by the influence of the Socialist International Women, CEE Network for Gender Issues and the struggle of the women organizations within Social Democratic Parties.
3 1999–2004: a period, within the framework of the Stability Pact for the South Eastern Europe (SP), when women became a distinct, novel political subject – proclaiming themselves as key factors and agents of democratic change in the Balkan region. Also the time of enactment of the quotas rules and the start of the parity movement. OSCE Missions in B&H and Kosovo combined with the bottom up pressure of women NGOs on the one hand and the SP Gender Task Force (SP GTF) complex activities in all other Balkan countries on the other hand as main international/regional/national promoters of the enactment of the quotas in all other Balkan countries.

The window of opportunity for the women of the Balkans – to effectively reject the role of victims and objects of mainly male, conservative, nationalistic politics – opened with the inauguration of the Stability Pact for South Eastern Europe in Sarajevo in July 1999. A loose network of donor and beneficiary states and international organizations came together in order to ensure peace, democracy, human rights and economic prosperity in this war-torn region. SP Gender Task Force (SP GTF)[20] was established upon the appeal of more than 150 women's organizations and activists from 13 South Eastern European countries asking women to achieve a formal position at all three SP Working Tables and to be treated as important agents of the democratic change. The main focus of the SP GTF was the political empowerment of women. In 1999, when SP GTF started to work in the Balkans, there were only few female councillors and even fewer female mayors. The average of women MPs was 7 per cent. 30 per cent quotas rule was enacted only in one country – in Bosnia and Herzegovina (B&H). Slovenia[21] and Montenegro did not have any female ministers. Weak governmental gender equality mechanisms on national level were established only in Slovenia,[22] Macedonia, Croatia and Albania. Not a single Equal Opportunity Act was enacted. No country had gender equality ombudsman installed by the law or already in place. The main tools used for political empowerment of women were as follows: training/capacity building, organizing, campaigning. Massive training included more than 16,000 existing and future women NGOs, Trade Union and political party activists. They were trained in the topics of gender equality and women's human rights. Besides that, strong and broad coalitions were created to tackle cross-cutting issues. In addition, capacity building was immediately transformed into political initiatives based on networking, campaigning and lobbying for the establishment of quotas, change of electoral legislation, and effective state mechanisms of gender equality.

Major changes have occurred in the four years of systematic work by many political figures coming from inside and outside of the respective countries: women's party clubs and sections, women's NGOs and national machineries for gender equality. Active were also international organizations like SP GTF (Woodward 2001), OSCE Missions,[23] Council of Europe, UNDP, UNIFEM, some large international NGOs – CEE Network for Gender Issues,[24] Star Network, Kvinna till Kvinna, National Democratic Institute, Norwegian People's Aid and many different Western political foundations. As Table 6.1 shows equal opportunity act or anti-discrimination law have or are going to be enacted in all countries/territories in the region. National gender equality mechanisms have been established at all levels (governmental, parliamentary and local) in almost all countries.[25] Specialized ombudsmen for gender equality have been installed in B&H, Croatia and Vojvodina in 2003 and in Slovenia in 2004. All of the Balkan countries are members of the CEDAW convention and all of them (except Serbia and Montenegro) have submitted at least one CEDAW report.

The changes described above took place in the majority of countries in the region in accordance with the 'sandwich strategy' as SP GTF coined the term. A 'sandwich strategy' consists of the planned combination of the top down pressure coming from the international agents (such as UN, OSCE/ODIHR, SP, Council of Europe, European Commission and Parliament) and their support in the form of funding and know-how. Pressure from below is created by the SP GTF, which helps to build up regionally connected and extensive coalitional movements of cross-cutting gender

Table 6.1 Regional overview of the state of affairs in gender equality mechanisms in the Balkan region

Country/territory	Equal Opportunity Act or Anti-Discrimination Law	Quotas at national (N) local (L) regional (R) European Parliament (EP) level	Women councillors at local level %	Women MPs %	Electoral system
Albania	Yes (2004)	No quotas	n/a	5.7 (2004)	MMP
Bosnia & Herzegovina	Yes (2003)	N, L	7.9[a] (2000)	16.7 (2004)	List PR
Croatia	Yes (2003)	No quotas	15.0 (2004)	21.7 (2004)	List PR
Macedonia	In preparation	N, L	8.4 (2004)	18.3 (2004)	List PR
Serbia & Montenegro (Montenegro)	In preparation	No quotas	8.9 (2004)	10.6 (2004)	List PR
Serbia & Montenegro (Serbia)	In preparation	N, L	6.2[a] (2000)	11.3 (2004)	List PR
(Serbia Vojvodina[b])	Yes (2003)	R, L	24.6[c] (2004)		List PR
Slovenia[d]	Yes (2002)	Only for EP[e]	13.0 (2004)	11.1 (2004)	List PR
UNMIK/Kosovo	Yes (2004)	N, L	28.0 (2004)	29.0 (2004)	List PR

Source: The data is based on the official databases of the Electoral Commissions of respective countries/territories, gender equality governmental mechanisms or official data about the elections, published electronically by the OSCE Missions in respective countries/territories.

Notes

a Bosnia & Herzegovina and Serbia held local elections in the autumn of 2004. Preliminary results in Serbia show that the 30 per cent quota provision in the law had a great impact. 15 to 25 per cent of the elected councillors in the new local councils are women.

b Serbia Vojvodina – Autonomous Province within Serbia.

c The figure does not include the results of the city of Novi Sad where elections are to be repeated for the second time.

d Slovenia had an independent Parliamentary Commission for gender equality from 1990–2000, when it was included into the Commission for Home Affairs. Such a development is not an isolated case. However, all newly established gender equality mechanisms are extremely fragile.

e Only Slovenia is a current member of the EU.

Key electoral systems: Proportional Representation: List PR. Mixed: MMP = Mixed Member Proportiona equality issues. These two pressures were deliberately used to have an effect upon national governments and leaders of political parties in order to make them focus more on gender equality in the legislation, institutional build-up and practice.

Introduction of the voluntary party quotas

In the Balkans, voluntary party quotas were first installed mostly by the left wing parties. Formal establishment of the women organizations and introduction of the party quotas in the political parties' statutes were set as the conditions, created by the Social International Women, to attain the full membership among the new social democratic parties in the Socialist International. CEE Network for Gender Issues was used as a regional support for the dispersion of the voluntary party quotas in all new social democratic parties in transition countries. In most of the cases these party quotas were neither fully applied nor effective. From 1994 women activists from left and centre-left parties started to advocate for the legal quotas, and from 2001 for 50 per cent legal quota (parity). The struggle for legal quotas gained momentum when OSCE Missions came to B&H and Kosovo, and when SP GTF started its activities in the region. In a parallel move, laws introducing legal quotas for all parties were proposed in many of the countries, in the beginning without success.

Party by party approach

In the Balkans, before 1998, the introduction of the voluntary party quotas was everywhere based on the development of the organized women's groups within the parties and their close connections with their sister parties and their international organizations abroad. The support of the Socialist International Women, the Party of European Socialists and its regional NGO named CEE Network for Gender Issues was the most valuable. Social democratic parties and the Liberal Democracy of Slovenia were the forerunners of this process in the region.

The introduction of firm party quota rules in *Slovenia*,[26] in 1996, for the candidate lists in the United List of Social Democrats (ULSD central-left party, the third biggest parliamentary party in 1992–6) started out successfully but ended up in a major defeat. Resisting to the majority of male party leaders at the party congress before the general elections in 1996, the Women's Forum of the ULSD managed to introduce the firm 33 per cent minimum quota for men and women on all party lists for all elections, see Table 6.2. The party's parliamentary group was also tasked with the mission to pass the 40 per cent quota for all parties in the parliament. However, no cross-party coalitions were formed in this issue in the parliament. This happened partly because the Women's Forum of the ULSD wanted to use the issue only to increase the visibility and attractiveness of

Table 6.2 Party electoral quota provisions in the Balkan region

Country and parties	Quota (year of introduction)	Rules about ranking	Women or neutral	Sanctions (sanctions used)	Implementing body	Women MP of the party %
Albania						
SP	25% (2003)	Yes	Women	No	n/a	5.7 (2004)
BIH						
SDP	30% (2001)	No	Women	No	Presidency	0.0 (2002)[a]
Croatia						
SDP	40% (1996)	No	Neutral	Yes (yes)	Supervision Board	35.0 (2004)
Macedonia						
SDUM	30% (2002)	No	Neutral	Yes (no)	Presidency	25.2 (2002)
Montenegro						
SDP	20% (1999)	Yes	Women	No	Party Presidency	0.0 (2003)[a]
Serbia						
SDP	30% (2000)	Yes	Neutral	No	Women's Forum	33.0 (2003)
Slovenia						
ULSD	33% (1992)[b]	No	Neutral	Yes (yes)	Party Presidency	20.0 (2004)
LDS	40% (1998)	No	Neutral	Yes (no)	Party Council	4.0 (1996)
	33% (2000)	No	Neutral	Yes (no)		14.7 (2000)
	25% (2003)	Yes	Women	No (n/a)		13.0 (2004)

Source: The data in the table is based on the official databases of the Electoral Commissions of the respective countries/territories, gender equality governmental mechanisms or official data about the elections, published electronically by the OSCE Missions in respective countries/territories.

Notes
a 0 per cent means that the party has certain number of MPs, but that they are all men!
b In 1997 firm quota was transformed in a soft quota – the Party Presidency has discretion not to implement it to the full.

the ULSD for the women voters. Second, the failure to form coalitions stemmed from the activity of male party leaders in all other parties. To be more precise, they cunningly made use of their most prominent female MPs to mount an open resistance against the enactment of the quotas. Hence, the enactment of the quota rule failed in the parliament.[27] Because of the party's own quota rule, ULSD for the first time ever had 42 per cent of women on its lists. However, the Women's Forum was not strong enough to secure any of the female candidates a really 'safe seat'[28] and not a single woman from the ULSD was elected.[29] In the elections in 1996 the voters had shifted slightly towards the right and the ULSD lost a third of its voters. The parties who were against the enactment of the quotas did not give a real chance to their female candidates either, and consequently Slovenia got the lowest representation of women after the introduction of the women's voting right in 1945 – only 7.8 per cent of female MPs. It was the first government to be formed after 1945 that lacked female ministers for three years. After this defeat, the ULSD leaders blamed the firm quotas for the defeat, whereupon the party congress in 1997 transformed the firm 40 per cent quota into just a morally obliging 40 per cent target. It also became clear that the impact of the electoral system on gender balance in politics is crucial: the quota rule, even if applied, could not work if the electoral system did not change. Single mandate voting units should be cancelled and replaced by the party lists in the districts where the strict placing rules can be followed.[30]

Liberal Democracy of Slovenia (LDS) and its predecessor, League of Socialist Youth, enlisting some influential female members – who also formulated the demand for a Ministry for Women at that time – started to discuss quotas as early as in 1989. In practice, these were more pursued targets than firm quotas (Antić 1998: 213). The party programme from 1990 agreed to have 30 per cent quotas for the next election but did not act accordingly. This is the reason why, in 1994, it was obligatory to follow the rule only until the last stage of the nomination process (party council's nomination stage) for the candidate list for the national election, and consequently, less than 30 per cent women were presented on the party's candidate list presented for the election. In 1998, the party's Women's Network made a gender neutral proposal of quotas according to which neither sex could have less than one-third of the candidates on the party candidate list for the national election (Antić 1998: 214). This share was lowered to 25 per cent for the election of 2000 by the rule to increase it in each subsequent election for three percentage points, with the 40 per cent share of men and women set as the final objective. This quota provision is obligatory, which has been respected in both elections – 2000 and 2004. In 2000, five women from the party made it to the parliament (out of 34 MPs). In 2004, after the party dramatically lost 11 seats, it still maintained three women in their parliamentary group; all three possess parliamentary experience which is important in their work.[31]

The general elections in 2000 in *Croatia*[32] revealed the crucial import-ance of the combined engagement of the strong women's NGO national network and a strong left wing party when installing party quotas. This NGO network, (called Ad Hoc Women's Coalition[33]) active already since 1996, was strong enough to bring the issue of the serious women's under-representation in politics into the mainstream political discussion before the elections in 2000. Ad Hoc Coalition proposed the enactment of the 40 per cent legal quota for men and women on all party lists with the use of the zipper system for the first eight places on the lists, without success. But during the electoral campaign all parties were forced to publicly speak on the issue and, consequently, most of them gave verbal support for the increased female presence in decision-making bodies. However, the Social Democratic Party (SDP – former reformed League of Communists in Croatia, the strongest opposition party before the elections in 2000, and the first party in the winning coalition after these elections) had, as the major party, introduced voluntary party quotas (40 per cent) in its statute from 1996 as it was applying for the full member-ship in the Socialist International, although without ranking rules, see Table 6.2. In 2000, the party indeed respected 40 per cent minimum quota for men and women on all its electoral lists but not the zipper system in the ranking. The SDP promoted its serious approach to women's rights as one of its specific electoral offers. The SDP in Croatia rejected the law on quotas, proposed by a small party with the argument that every party was free to use the quotas if it wanted to do so. Even if the proposal to introduce 40 per cent quota in parliament failed, the number of women in the Croatian parliament nearly tripled – 21.8 per cent of female MPs.[34]

In the national elections of 2004, a combination of the public pressure of the women's NGOs Coalition on all political parties, a media campaign led by the SP GTF partners, and a firm resolution of the ruling SDP to again implement its electoral quota of 40 per cent, forced the biggest opposition party to allow its female candidates to have some real chances on its lists. Croatia, therefore, became the first country in the region which did not diminish the percentage of women in the parliament even when it did not have electoral quotas in the law. For the SDP, the election was disastrous. It was the only party which had implemented and respected 40 per cent quota and then lost the elections during the consid-erable shift of the general public towards the political right. The strength of the combination of the SDP's application of its voluntary party quotas and strong women's movement in making the issue important also for the biggest Croatian right-wing political party, could be measured by the fact that in the new government, formed by the Croatian Democratic Union (CDU, former Tudjman's party), again a woman became a vice Prime Minister with three additional women appointed as ministers. When the CDU's male MPs became ministers, they were replaced by female MPs after which the percentage of women in the parliament in February 2004 grew from the initial 17.8 per cent back to 21.7 per cent.

Gentlemen's Agreement approach

Until the last election in 2002, representation of women in Macedonia[35] was very low.[36] The awareness of the latter led gender equality activists to establish the SP GTF Macedonian Women's Lobby in March 2000, bringing together 400 women, leaders of all women's groups in civil society, politics and in the Department for Gender Equality within the Ministry of Labour. In July 2000, just before the local elections, this Lobby had prepared and lobbied strongly for the Gentlemen's Agreement. Each party leadership was asked to give a fair chance to at least one of its women to be elected as a mayor, place at least one woman candidate among every three candidates and not to include less than 30 per cent of women on their lists. Twelve party leaders from the strongest parliamentary parties signed this Gentlemen's Agreement but not a single party respected it to the full extent. Nevertheless, Macedonia elected its first three female mayors. The number of women councillors nearly doubled and reached 8.4 per cent. Regardless of this headway, Macedonian Women's Lobby reached the conclusion that only the legal quotas with strong penalties would be a warranty strong enough to secure real chances for female candidates. The Macedonian experience served as the best practical guideline for the establishment of similar cross-party agreements in the early stages of the struggle for the legal quotas in Serbia and Montenegro.

Lessons learnt from the use of the voluntary party quotas

In the transitional Balkan countries, mostly the left-wing parties, as in the Nordic countries, were the ones to start the process of implementing quota system. Nevertheless, women soon realized that parties did not willingly respect the rules of their own statutes. Political parties mostly exercised the verbal strategies – as Lovenduski called it – in supporting women's entrance into the politics (Lovenduski 1993: 1–15). Parties are still not clearly profiled and political consensus in fundamental national values of democracy still in the making (see Antić 2000: 127–40). The battle over the gender equality issue between the central and left-wing parties can easily lead to the loss of already gained improvements in all the parties. Slovenian experience taught the Balkan women that in this region the contagion theory of Matland and Studlar acts in a distorted way. Namely, the introduction of the firm and binding quota rule in the statute of a relatively strong party might not influence others to follow suit. They realized that the defeat of women in one parliamentary party will considerably weaken women's position in all other parties. The combination of the strong, genuine NGOs coalition from one side and a major party with firm

Table 6.3 Electoral quotas in the law in the Balkan region

Country/ territory	Year of introduction	Quota provision federal (F), national (N), local (L), European Parliament (EP)	Rules about ranking	Women or neutral	Sanctions (sanctions used?)	Implementing body	Women in parliament %
Bosnia & Herzegovina (B&H)	1998	30% (F, N, L)	Yes	Neutral	No	OSCE	*State level (2002)* Lower House: 16.7
	2000	30% (N, L)	Yes	Neutral	No	OSCE	Upper House: 0.0 *Federation of B&H (2002)*
	2002	33% (N, F)	Yes	Neutral	No	Electoral Commission	Lower House: 20.6 *Rep. Srpska (2002)* 16.9
Macedonia	(2002)[a]	30% (N)	No	Neutral	Yes (yes)	Electoral Commission	18.3 (2002)
	2004	30% (L)	Yes	Neutral	Yes (yes)		
Serbia	2002	30% (L)	Yes	Neutral	Yes	Electoral Commission	11.3 (2003)
	2004	30% (N)	No	Neutral	No		
Slovenia	2004	40% (EP)[b]	Yes	Neutral	Yes (yes)	Electoral Commission	11.1 (2004)
UNMIC/Kosovo	2000	30% (L)	Yes	Women	Yes (yes)	OSCE	29.0 (2004)
	2001	33% (Regional Assembly)	Yes	Women	Yes (yes)	Director for elections	

Source: The data in the table is based on the official databases of the Electoral Commissions of respective countries/territories, gender equality governmental mechanisms or official data about the elections, published electronically by the OSCE Missions in respective countries/territories.

Notes
a In a 'Gentlemen's Agreement' of 2000, which preceded the first enactment of the quota, twelve political parties promised to include at least 30 per cent women on their lists. However, the promise was not kept.
b The quota for the EU parliament brought 42.9 per cent of women MEPs from Slovenia. In 2005 the quota of 20 per cent with the ranking rules was enacted also for the local elections

principles in the use of its electoral quotas from the other is a strong guarantee that the equal political representation of women prevails even during the rule of right-wing parties. Unfortunately, Croatia was the only one in the region to fulfil this condition.

The approach of the cross-party 'Gentlemen's Agreement' revealed serious lack of gentlemen among the male political party leaders in the Balkans. Nevertheless, it triggered the process and doubled the inadequate percentage of elected women in Macedonia, Serbia and Montenegro. First and foremost, this approach clarified to the women in the parties as well as to the general public that in the Balkans women need concrete laws to secure their proper representation in parliaments.

Electoral quotas established by law[37]

In this section the introduction of legal quotas applying to all political parties in a country are analyzed. It began with Bosnia and Herzegovina in 1998, but after the turn of the century also Macedonia, Serbia, and Kosovo introduced gender quotas by law. In Slovenia legal quotas were introduced in 2004 for the election to the European Parliament, see Table 6.3 for an overview.

Bosnia and Herzegovina[38]

From the very beginning, the strategy of the SP Gender Task Force (GTF) for political empowerment of women had two lessons taught in hundreds of *Women Can Do It I* seminars in all Balkan countries. First, the lesson learnt from the defeat in Slovenia in 1996 and second, the lesson learnt from the great process of the enactment of the first quota rule in the region – in B&H in 1998. In fact, women of Bosnia and Herzegovina were to discover the so-called sandwich strategy.

In B&H, after the Dayton Peace Accord in 1995, women in numerous NGOs were much better organized and the awareness of gender equality issues stronger than that among women activists in most of the political parties. Only the Social Democratic Party (SDP – reformed League of Communists of B&H) had an organized women's group and 30 per cent quota in its statute but in reality largely not practiced. Strong support and close co-operation among the OSCE Mission, an informal network of women NGOs and some individual woman politicians in 1998, led to the consensus between the international authorities and national political leaders on the enactment of the 30 per cent quota rule in the provisional electoral legislation, see Table 6.3. A female candidate had to be placed on at least every third place of each party's list for the elections in both state entities. The party lists were closed. In one single step in 1998, the percentages of women MPs in the parliaments of the two state entities – the Federation of B&H and in Republika Srpska – grew from 2 per cent to

26 per cent. Most of the newly elected female MPs were newcomers and acted mostly in the background. They only had two years to rise into prominence, for the new general elections were held in 2000, and most of them did not succeed in this task.

During the next general elections, the international authorities in B&H decided to give the voters the preferential vote (open lists). It was immediately clear that open lists are harmful for the anonymous candidates. The share of elected women in both entities dropped from 26 per cent to 20.6 per cent in B&H and 16.9 per cent in Republika Srpska. Parties of B&H and international supporters did not invest enough into the promotion of women politicians. Even worse, when female MPs started to demonstrate leadership capacities, party leaders in several cases tried to push them to the bottom or even out of the lists. Women mostly became losers of the open lists. Nevertheless, in cases of successful and respected female politicians positioned on the bottom of lists, the voters could still push them up the lists and preferential votes helped them to be elected.

UNMIK/Kosovo[39]

When UNMIK took military and political protectorate over Kosovo, many international organizations with a gender equality mandate came into the country with their different ideas on how to empower women in Kosovo. The problem was that they did not take much account of the existing experiences of women's NGOs in Kosovo at the grassroots level.[40] They had little knowledge of what should be done within political parties occupied only by ethnic-related concerns. Female politicians had poor knowledge on why and how gender equality should become an integral part in the overall solution of Kosovo's status and democratic development. Consequently, the first enactment of the 30 per cent quota rule in the local elections in November 2000, see Table 6.3, was perceived as something imposed by the foreigners. This understanding was even held by many women in political parties. The voters had a preferential vote. The parties had a problem finding sufficient number of women who would also be accomplished politicians. Many women were placed on the lists just to fill in the quota rule. Many of them resigned immediately after the elections and were replaced by men, with no regulation to prevent such a development. The result of the first local elections, therefore, with the 30 per cent quota in the law was meagre: only 8 per cent of the councillors were women. The lists for the first elections for Kosovo's Assembly – Kosovo Provisional Institution of Self-Government in 2001, were closed, quota provisions were strengthened: at least one-third of the candidates should be women, and one-third of them men. One candidate from each gender should be included at least once among three candidates, counting from the first candidate on the list. Penalties[41] were introduced for non-compliance – the list had to be changed in accordance with the law or decertified. Closed lists and the same quota rules as for the Assembly elections were applied for the local elections of 2002. As a result of these legal regulations, the percentage of elected female MPs and councillors in Kosovo grew to the highest level in the Balkans – 29 per cent (2004).

The mandate of international factors in all other Balkan countries was much smaller. In Serbia in 2000, the OSCE Mission had not been established yet, in Macedonia the OSCE Mission did not see gender equality issue as its priority, the same applied for the OSCE Missions in Albania and in Montenegro. Before the start of the SP GTF activities in the region in 2000, there was nobody to help organizing women NGOs and women in political parties to come together in order to form their national strategies for political empowerment of women. From the start, women had the bitter experience that parties did not respect their own statutes and were not punished for it by their members or electorate. The situation began to change when the SP GTF summoned national gender equality coalitions, which started to lobby for the enactment of the quota regulations.

Republic of Macedonia[42]

After the initial success and lessons learnt from their Gentlemen's Agreement for the local elections in 2000, the SP GTF Macedonian Women's Lobby in 2002, supported by the Minister of Labour, Department for Gender Equality, training of *Women Can Do It II* in all Macedonian parliamentary and some non-parliamentary parties, a huge media campaign and lobbying action, the parliament passed the following quota rule for the forthcoming national elections: 'In the proposed lists of candidates, each sex has to be represented by at least 30 per cent of the candidates'.[43] The lists which do not respect this quota rule have to be adjusted or they are going to be rejected by the Electoral Commission.

All attempts to follow the examples from Bosnia and Herzegovina and Kosovo in order to pass the quota amendment with clear ranking rules failed. Large-scale lobbying action and public campaigning were necessary to persuade the parties to offer to their female candidates at least some eligible positions. The campaign was successful and the percentage of female MPs went up from 7.8 to 18.3 per cent, also due to the introduction of the pure proportional representation as mentioned before.

For the local elections in 2004, Macedonian Women's Lobby united the pressure coming from the biggest women's NGO, which publicly launched its request for the enactment of the 40 per cent quota for men and women, the use of the zipper system in the ranking, and savvy lobbying of the most prominent female parliamentarians from different parties to reach the compromise. As a result of this strategy, Macedonian Sobranie enacted the 30 per cent minimal quota and a loose ranking rule in May 2004: at least 30 per cent of the candidates of the less represented sex should be placed in the first half of all lists for the local elections.

Serbia

Milosević's regime managed always to secure the victory of the Serbian
minority in the local governmental elections in three Southern Serbian
local communities that had a remarkable presence of Albanian and Roma
populations. Albanians, therefore, boycotted the elections in October
2000. Ethnic tensions were mounting with occasional armed conflicts in
1999 and 2000. Only new and democratic Serbian leaders from Belgrade,
as well as much diplomatic effort and work could restore peace and start to
restore trust between the three ethnic groups. In 2002, Serbian government convinced Albanians, Serbs and Roma inhabitants of those three
localities, that the elections would be really free and fair, whereupon they
agreed to come to vote. It seemed to be a wise idea to bring more women
into the local governance in the climate where male inhabitants of different ethnic groups used recently to shoot at each other. This made the task
of some influential members from the Political Women's Network easier to
persuade the late Prime Minister Zoran Djinjić, his government and the
majority in the parliament to vote for the strong quota rule that secured
every third position on every list for the female candidate. The lists were
closed. The elections were carried out smoothly. In Bujanovac, an Albanian
man became a mayor for the first time ever and nearly 18 per cent of councillors in those three local communities today are women.

After the assassination of the Prime Minster Djindjić, Serbian women's
movement lost the impetus. There was almost no campaign for the
improvement of the women's representation prior to the last Serbian election in 2003. These elections were held in the depressive mood that had
captured the voters of the former Democratic Opposition of Serbia (DOS
– coalition of 18 parties' opponents to Milošević), disappointed with the
transition and the way the DOS leaders handled the difficult situation.
The Radicals (their leader Šešelj is currently on trial in The Hague)
became the biggest single party in the country; remains of the former
democratic opposition block were able to put together the government
only by gaining Milosević's party support. The new parliament decided to
include special measures for the parties of national minorities in the Electoral Law. Some influential female parliamentarians, members of the Political Women's Network, grasped this opportunity to propose the
amendment of 30 per cent quota for women. Paradoxically, a number of
the MPs from the former democratic opposition block voted against this
amendment, while all the MPs from the Radical Party voted in favour of it
and the amendment was passed.

Slovenia

As mentioned above, the Slovenian experience with the party quotas was
not very successful in a sense that it did not evoke the break-through in

the representation of women in politics. Dissatisfaction with the situation among women and men who were active supporters of women in politics led to the establishment of a nation-wide network, named Coalition for Parity, in 2001. Nearly 200 well-known women from different political backgrounds and some influential male allies set a common goal to achieve the 'equal representation' in all political decisions-making bodies. In 2001, this coalition began to act by using the accession process to the EU as a pressure factor. Moreover, it worked closely with some female MPs and some prominent male political leaders to introduce changes into the Slovenian legislation to improve the situation of women in politics. These activities culminated in the signing of the proposal by more than two-thirds of all the MPs requesting for the constitutional change that would allow the enactment of the positive measures in politics. The amendment was enacted in the parliament in July 2004.[44]

In the autumn of 2003, all political parties nominated only men as their delegates for the European Parliament (EP) after Slovenia, as the only Balkan country so far, had joined the European Union. Feminist activists of all major party groups in the European Parliament urged their party leaders to send letters to the party leaders of the Slovene parliamentary parties with the request to enable 30 to 50 per cent of their women candidates to become MEPs. In December 2003, the Coalition for Parity initiated the amendment of the Law on European Parliament Elections. Women parliamentarians from the governing coalition with the support of some male colleagues persuaded the parliament to enact a binding 40 per cent quota for men and women and obligatory positioning of at least one person from each sex among the first three candidates on each list.[45] All but one parliamentary party placed their first female candidates on the second place of their lists. It was proven once again that voters mostly trust their party choice and ranking of candidates. The pressure from the EP party groups, the enactment of the 40 per cent quota and ranking rules, the pressure from the Coalition for Parity to enable female candidates to have at least the second position on the lists and the fact that European Parliament is for the majority of politicians less attractive than the national one, were decisive factors in bringing 42.9 per cent of women (three out of seven) MEPs from Slovenia into the European Parliament.

Crucial impact

The Balkan region does not have a country that could be followed as a model or used as a driving force. Slovenia was always the one to start the new initiatives for the political empowerment of women but was not always the most successful in implementing them. One can agree that the impetus and the progress derived mostly from the international and regional exchange of experiences and useful practices. Internal changes of electoral laws from plurality-majority to mixed and proportional

representation, as mentioned before, had an impact, as well as empowerment of women from within their political parties.

Regional and European know-how, best practice exchange and the
approach of the CEE Network for Gender Issues helped social democratic women to raise the awareness of national politics and public
opinion necessary for the process of change. Adaptation and innovation
of the Norwegian *Women Can Do It* manual and training modules were
decisive for the encouragement and capacity building of women politicians in the region.[46] Essential was international support from the UN,
OSCE, UNIFEM, UNDP, Stability Pact, Council of Europe and few big
international NGOs who were willing to move their initial focus from the
NGOs towards the gender issue in political parties. The establishment of
the wide national cross-cutting issue coalitions was also important for the
development of large capacity building, success of the quotas or campaigns of parity advocacy. Establishment of the Balkan women's inven-
tion of the new international institution – SP GTF, systematic application
of the 'sandwich strategy', continuation of the regional and cross-
European experience and know-how, exchange of approaches, conscious
development of the strategic planning, national and regional networking
in cross-cutting issues, advocating and lobbying for the political empowerment of women – all these processes bestowed upon the political
empowerment of women clear priorities and necessary support from
international donors.

Conclusion: empowerment of women in politics through gender quotas

Women in the Balkans lost the first window of opportunity during the collapse of the socialist political systems in the start of the transition in
1990/1. However, they refused to take up the role of the victims of
conservative and aggressive male politics. Women became the survivors
of the transition and Balkan wars in the 1990s. After 2000, active women
of the Balkans successfully became the agents of democratic renewal and
gradual integration of the Balkans into the European Union.

Researches done in this field proved that there were several obstacles
on women's way to political power: strong patriarchal political culture,
weak women's movement, poor or non-existing national machineries for
gender equality, unfavourable electoral systems, unstable party systems,
and male-dominated political élites (Jaquette and Wolchik 1998; Jalušič
and Antić 2001; Matland and Montgomery 2003). Moving from election to
election made it more obvious that the strongest obstacles are parties and
party gatekeepers (Siemienska, Illonszki, Antić in Jalušič and Antić 2001)
which, even when parties had accepted quotas, did not respect the rule.
Women's strive for quotas in parties were often stigmatized and marginalized (Antić and Illonszki 2004). It was therefore obvious that women

cannot achieve more political power only through voluntary party quotas but quotas have to be established by the national legislation.

However, in the long run, besides temporary defeats, public discussion and collective actions to introduce quotas in the party statutes or in the laws have nevertheless empowered women. Gender equality in politics in the Balkans definitely became an important political issue. This was confirmed in Macedonian elections in 2002 and 2004, Croatian and Serbian elections in 2003, Serbian presidential elections in 2004 – here Bogoljub Karić, the moral winner of the first round of the Serbian presidential elections in 2004, was the only candidate who had particularly targeted female voters – and finally the first EP elections in Slovenia in 2004.

Women politicians and the general public need much deeper knowledge about the modern concept of gender equality as well as electoral systems, influence of different electoral systems on women's eligibility, influence of the so called open lists and different sorts of preferential voting, the best practices regarding quotas and/or parity regulations in political parties, state constitutions, electoral or party legislation, and new possibilities for the financing of electoral campaigns (Antić and Gortnar 2004). There are many crucial roles played by different factors such as regional women's networks, CEE Network for Gender Issues, creation of a new regional institution – SP GTF – and wide cross-cutting coalitions of women's movements and issues on European, regional and national levels. We have not seen a single successful enactment of the quotas or parity rules without a strong, internationally linked and supported coalition of women's movements or issues in the Balkan region.

The case of Slovenia, which did not get much financial support from abroad, shows the value of this support: the progress without it was organic but utterly slow. Albania is the proof that no matter how big the support is from abroad, it cannot replace stamina, determination and organizational abilities of nationwide coalitions on women's issues. It remains to be seen how sustainable the gains are in this process. The Balkan countries have experienced a strong international impact on the concepts, funding and know-how but have rather weak women's nationwide movements. We do not rule out a reversal of the positive developments that have taken place so far.

While stressing the importance of international support, we still want to underline that the most crucial task is to be done inside each particular country. It is difficult to measure the difference that the increased presence of elected women is having upon politics and in the political culture of their parties and countries. Most of the evidence we have concerns the women in parliaments. Their number is still below 30 per cent everywhere, many of them are newcomers and back-benchers. There is still little research conducted on their work in the parliaments. The research done in the last Slovene parliament proves that even a small minority of female MPs can make some changes (Antić 2004: 81–117). What one can learn about the process is that at least a number of the selected women did not seem to forget that they were elected because of the strong pressure from women's organizations. Many of the women politicians feel the responsibility to continue to work hand-in-hand with civil society's women's movement, even if this priority does not remain for all of them. Once elected, some female MPs had started to work on the establishment of gender equality state mechanisms and Equal Opportunity Acts, improving the legislation crucially important for gender equality: electoral legislation (Macedonia, Serbia), penal codes (Slovenia, Croatia, Serbia, B&H), family laws (Serbia, B&H), Labour laws (Serbia), laws on privatization of the state or company-owned flats (B&H). Party discipline and the need to increase women's personal power and visibility within their own parties often make it difficult for female MPs to openly continue the co-operation with women from the competing or opposition parties. It takes a great political talent and very earnest commitment to maintain one's political career while balancing between the loyalty to a party and to the women's cause. In the Balkans, like elsewhere, the balance is not commonplace among politicians of both sexes.

In the last ten years, women of the Balkan region have made a big leap in their struggle for the equality in decision-making bodies. For more than a decade this region was known only for the worst. There seems to be a paradoxical rule: the worse the overall situation, the more active and persistent women activists. Women in the Balkan countries, amidst difficult political and social circumstances, were more tough and consistent than the ones closer to the EU integration. In the field of the political empowerment of women, Slovenia is lacking behind all other countries but Albania in the Balkan region. In the Appeal for the establishment of the SP GTF, in 1999, women activists from the Balkans stated:

> Women organized in civil society and in politics, we demand an equal and active role in the development and implementation of the Stability Pact. We demand and accept the responsibility to work together with representatives of our governments and of international community towards the lasting peace, good neighborly relations and stability for our individual countries as well as for the South Eastern Europe, as conditions for further European integration. Women are the stakeholders and have a vital interest in peace, prosperity and sustainable human development of this region, which cannot be achieved without the active participation of more than a half of its population.
>
> (Internal documentation of GTF Center for Gender Equality in Zagreb)

In four years, active and organized women from civil society and political parties have succeeded in transforming the mainstream political discourse on gender equality from a discourse typical for the conservative backlash to a discourse of the acceptance of the highest European standards of gender equality in the legislation and institutional building; from the rejection of the quotas altogether, through the experience that party voluntary quotas are not effective enough, to the acceptance of quotas in legislation and the aspirations for parity in the future.

Notes

1 More about the class nature of gender politics in the region see: Čalovska and Jančić (1975); Tomšič (1978).
2 More about women's lives in socialist period see: Tomšič (1978), Jogan (1986), Papić (1989), Sklevicky and Rihtman (1996), Ramet (1999), Hrženjak (2002).
3 Marina Blagojević even writes that women's body acquired the status of an ethnical territory (Blagojević 2000).
4 Further on the transition period and women see: Antić (1992), Ule and Rener (1997), Blagojević (2000).
5 Story about women's NGOs in Slovenia, for example, through the eyes of the actors can be found in the book *Kako smo hodile v feministično gimnazjo (How Did We Attend Feminist Gymnasium)* (Jalušič 2002).
6 For example, see Mastnak (1992), Štrajn (1995), Rizman (1997).
7 See papers from symposium Ženske, politika, demokracija: Za večjo prisotnost žensk v politiki (Women, politics, democracy: For improved presence of women in politics) (Antić and Jeram 1999).
8 There are some recent researches done on the citizenship issue, available online at the Centre for Educational Policy Studies (2004), Mirovni inštitut (Peace Institute) (2004) and Znanstveno raziskovalni center pri SAZU (The Scientific Research Centre SASA) (2004).
9 Such as the unfortunate fate of Angela Vode (1892–1985), who was publicly excluded and her works published only in the end of 1990s, recently by the publishing house Krtina. See Vode (1998, 1999, 2000).
10 There were few serious attempts to introduce some liberalism in economy and politics in Croatia, Serbia and in Slovenia in 1970s, yet they were all quickly politically trammeled by Yugoslav Communist Party (for example Stane Kavčič, Savka Dapčevič Kučar, Mika Tripalo and others).
11 More about these groups see Jalušič (2002).
12 See contemporary issues of weekly Mladina, for example, and special issues of Časopis za kritiko znanost on abortion or women and family, etc.
13 The concept of 'unfinished democracy' can be found in the works of Scandinavian feminist authors (see e.g. Haavio-Mannila *et al.* 1985). Also the term 'male democracy' is quite wide-spread and debated by many female authors from the so-called socialist camp (see the proceedings Gender, Politics and Postcommunism (Funk and Mueller 1993)).
14 Maca Jogan writes that the most common statement pictured socialism pushing women into factories, and that women did not gain anything from the socialist emancipation, only lost (Jogan 2001: 211).
15 Examples can be found in the political speeches of some right-wing MPs in the Parliament (Ervin A. Schrazbartl, Marcel Štefančič) in the beginning of 1990s (Ivančič *et al.* 1992) and in the articles and statements of the Catholic Church high officials discussing the issues of maternity and abortion right (see also Bahovec 1991).

16 For example, see the official standpoint of the Government in the debate on quotas in Slovenian Parliament. It stated that the introduction of special measures (quotas) into the law on political parties is not necessary as gender equality had already been regulated by the Constitution (Antić and Gortnar 2004: 73–81).

17 Such perception of gender equality can be found in general public as well as among those high state officials who, from time to time, deal with the issue.

18 This is usually a common sense argument maintained by those who are not familiar with the issue. However, when these persons are in the position to speak about it, they consider this understanding as the valid counter argument.

19 This notion can be found in the politics of some women's groups on the left of the political centre (ULSD and LDS parties), official standpoints of Governmental Office for Equal Opportunities, and in the papers and books of some feminist activists or authors (Jogan, Lokar, Jalušič, Antić, Mencin, Rener, etc.).

20 For more information on the SP GTF see Woodward (2001) and Lokar (2002).

21 From 1996 till the end of 1999 Slovenian government did not have any female minister.

22 Important steps were made in Slovenia in the first half of 1990s under the government of LDS: in 1990 Committee for Women's Politics (later for Equal Opportunities), in 1992 Governmental Office for Women's Politics (later for Equal Opportunities). For more see Jalušič and Antić (2001: 24).

23 For more on the impact of the OSCE and SP GTF see: Taarup (2003: 28–9).

24 For more information about CEE Network for Gender Issues see online source Gender Network at European Forum for Democracy and Solidarity (2004).

25 In Albania and Serbia & Montenegro there have been national gender equality mechanisms at governmental and parliamentary level and in Slovenia at governmental level.

26 Slovenia had five free general elections during which 18.7 per cent of women MPs were elected in 1990, 13.3 per cent in 1992, 7.8 per cent in 1996, 13.3 per cent in 2000 and 12.2 per cent in 2004 (Statistical Office of the Republic of Slovenia 2004).

27 For more about history of failures of gender quotas in Slovenian Parliament see Antić and Gortnar (2004: 73–81).

28 Slovenia has rather complicated electoral system: eight districts with 11 single mandate electoral units. Hence, in most of the cases, women candidates in less safe units have to run against their strongest male colleagues in 'safe' units. If the party gets less than two seats per district, not one of its female candidates will be elected. It was proven that even with a respected quota of 40 per cent, female candidates would lose if their party was in decline and win if it was on the rise. ULSD had 40 per cent gender quota in 1996 elections and lost 3.6 percentage points with not a single woman from its eight lists elected. In 2000 ULSD exercised the same quota rule yet raised its share in parliamentary seats from nine to 12.1 per cent. Three out of its eleven elected candidates in 2000 were women – 27.2 per cent. In 2004, ULSD respected the quota of 40 per cent but lost one seat in the parliament – thereby cutting its share of female MPs to two or 20 per cent.

29 See the analysis of the election in Antić (1998: 155–218).

30 This proposal was developed by Milica G. Antić in her paper 'Slabosti obstoječe variante sistema sorazmernega predstavništva z vidika izvolitvenih možnosti žensk' (Antić 1999: 171–91).

31 See the analysis of the work of Slovenian MPs in Antić and Ilonszki (2004: 81–117).

32 Croatia held five free general elections and elected the following percentage of female MPs: 4.7 per cent (1990), 5.4 per cent (1992), 7.1 per cent (1995), 21.8

per cent (2000), 17.8 per cent (2003) (Muslin 2000: 44 and IPU 2004 – http://www.ipu.org/wmn-e/world.htm).

33 This is a network of 44 local and some national female NGOs, such as Autonomous Women's House Zagreb, CESI, Center for Women Studies, Women's Infotheque, working for women human rights and political empowerment of women from 1996.

34 According to Glauduric one has to be aware of the effect of the elimination of single member district, SMD, seats for that election and the fact that women were selected and nominated in order they could improve their intra-party positions (Glaurdić 2003: 267–84).

35 Macedonia held four free general elections and elected the following percentage of female MPs: 4.2 per cent (1990), 3.3 per cent (1994), 7.5 per cent (1998), 18.8 per cent (2002) (Ristova 2003: 197 and IPU 2004 – http://www.ipu.org/wmn-e/world.htm).

36 One of the influential factors that supports higher representation of women in the Parliament (Sobranie) after the last election (female share almost tripled) is, according to Karolina Ristova, the change of electoral system from plurality-majority (1990, 1994) to combined (1998) and 'pure' representation system (2002) with the elimination of all single member district, SMD, seats (Ristova 2003: 213).

37 In all Balkan countries/territories, different types of proportional electoral systems are used. This makes the enactment of quota rules more efficient. But in Slovenia with specific type of proportional electoral system it was proved in the general elections in 1996 and 2000 that quota rules did not even work in this system from the reason that had a single mandate voting units. See also note 31.

38 Bosnia and Herzegovina held five free general elections and elected the following percentage of female MPs: no data available for 1990, 1996, 1998, and 2000, in 2002 it was 16.7 per cent (IPU 2004 – http://www.ipu.org/wmn-e/world.htm).

39 Kosovo became an UN protectorate after the peace agreement following the NATO bombing of Serbia and Montenegro in 1999.

40 Before the end of Milošević terror in Kosovo, female NGOs comprised mostly of Albanian women. The establishment of Serbian, Roma and other female NGOs followed after 1999.

41 In all the cases described above, the candidate lists which do not apply quota provisions are decertified by Electoral Commissions.

42 The Republic of Macedonia was born as an independent state in the process of the dissolution of the Socialist Federative Republic of Yugoslavija in 1991. Due to the dispute with Greece it was established under internationally accepted name of Former Yugloslav Republic of Macedonia (FYROM).

43 Law of Election of Members of Parliament, article 37, accepted, 25 June 2002

44 Article 43 of the Slovenian Constitution says: 'The law determines measures for stimulation of equal opportunities of women and men for the candidacy into the state and local representative bodies' (Slovene parliament 2004b).

45 See online source Slovene Parliament (2004a).

46 In 1998 CEE Network for Gender Issues translated Norwegian Labour Party Women Manual into all languages of the region and undertook the training of 125 social democratic female leaders of the Balkans. During the three different modules of the *Women Can Do It* training in 13 countries/territories of the CEE from 2000 on, only SP GTF trained more than 15,000 women from different political parties, trade unions and NGOs. Since 2001, Norwegian People's Aid organized similar types of training in most of the Balkan countries for another group of thousands of women.

Bibliography

Antić, M.G. (1991) 'Yugoslavia: Democracy between Tyranny and Liberty: The Situation of Women in the Post-"socialist" Nation State', *Feminist Review*, Special Issue: *Shifting Territories: Feminism, Socialism, Europe*, 39: 148.

—— (1992) 'Yugoslavia', in C. Corrin (ed.) *Superwomen and Double Burden: Women's Experience of Change in Central and Eastern Europe and Former Soviet Union*, London: Scarlet Press, pp. 155–79.

—— (1998) *Ženske v parlamentu*, Ljubljana: Znanstveno in publicistično središče.

—— (1999) 'Slabosti obstoječe variante sistema sorazmernega predstavništva z vidika izvolitvenih možnosti žensk', in M.G. Antić and J. Jeram (eds) *Ženske, politika, demokracija: Za večjo prisotnost žensk v politiki*, Ljubljana: Urad za žensko politiko, pp. 171–91.

—— (2000) 'Ne-srečno razmerje: strankarska politika in ženske v državah vzhodne srednje Evrope', *Družboslovne razprave*, 34–5: 127–40.

—— (2004) 'Women in Slovene Parliament: Below the Critical Mass', in M.G. Antić and G. Ilonszki (eds) *Women in Parliamentary Politics, Hungarian and Slovene experiences compared*, Ljubljana: Peace Institute, pp. 81–116.

Antić, M.G. and Gortnar, M. (2004) 'Gender Quotas in Slovenia: A short analysis of failures and hopes', *European political science*, 3, 3: 73–81.

Antić, M.G. and Ilonszki, G. (2004) *Women in Parliamentary Politics, Hungarian and Slovene Experiences Compared*, Ljubljana: Peace Institute.

Antić, M.G. and Jeram, J. (eds) (1999) *ženske, politika, demokracija: Za večjo prisotnost žensk v politiki*, Ljubljana: Urad za žensko politiko.

Bahovec, E.D. (ed.) (1991) *Abortus – pravica do izbire?!*, Ljubljana: Skupina Ženske za politiko.

Bahovec, E.D. (ed.) (1993) *Časopis za kritiko znanosti, domišljijo in novo antropologijo*, Special Edition: *Od ženskih študij k feministični teoriji*, Ljubljana: Študentska organizacija Univerze v Ljubljani.

Blagojević, M. (ed.) (2000) *Mapiranje misoginije u Srbiji, diskurzi i prakse*, Beograd: ANŽIN – Asociacija za žensku iniciativu.

Centre for Educational Policy Studies (CEPS) (2004) Online. Available at: http://ceps.pef.uni-lj.si/ (accessed 20 November 2004).

Čalovska, L. and Jančić-Starc, J. (eds) (1975) *Socializem in osvoboditev žensk*, Ljubljana: Komunist.

Dojčinović-Nešić, B. (2000) 'Feminizam: Predrasude, stereotipi i negativni stavovi', in M. Blagojević (ed.) *Mapiranje misoginije u Srbiji, diskurzi i prakse*, Beograd: ANŽIN – Asociacija za žensku iniciativu, pp. 619–32.

Funk, A. and Mueller, M. (eds) (1993) *Gender Politics and Postcommunism*, New York: Routledge.

Gaber, S. (1999) 'Reprezentativnost kot problem sodobnih demokracij', in M.G. Antić and J. Jeram (eds) *Ženske, politika, demokracija: za večjo prisotnost žensk v politiki*, Ljubljana: Urad za žensko politiko, pp. 85–100.

Gender Network at European Forum for Democracy and Solidarity (2004) Online. Available at: http://www.europeanforum.net/gendernw_home.php (accessed 7 November 2004).

Glaurdić, J. (2003) 'Croatia's Leap towards Political Equality: Rules and Players', in R. Matland and K. Montgomery (eds) *Women's Access to Power in Post Communist Europe*, Oxford: Oxford University Press, pp. 285–303.

Haavio-Mannila, E. *et al.* (eds) (1985) *Unfinished Democracy: Women in Nordic Politics*, Oxford: Pergamon Press.

Hrženjak, M. (ed.) (2002) *Making Her Up: Women's Magazines in Slovenia*, Ljubljana: Peace Institute.

Inter-Parliamentary Union (IPU) (2004) 'Women in National Parliaments', Online. Available at: http://www.ipu.org/wmn-e/world.htm (accessed 21 November 2004).

Ivančič, I., Jančić, P. and Zupanič, J. (1992) 'Matere in ostale ne-enakovredne ženske?', *Daily Večer*, Maribor, 6 March, p. 2.

Jalušič, V. (1994) 'Troubles with Democracy: Women and Slovene Independence', in J. Benderl and E. Kraft (eds) *Independent Slovenia: Origins, Movements, Prospects*, New York: St. Martin's Press, pp. 135–58.

—— (1999) 'Women in Post-Socialist Slovenia: Socially Adapted, Politically Marginalised', in S.P. Ramet (ed.) *Gender Politics in the western Balkans: Women, Society and Politics in Yugoslavia and the Yugoslav successor States*, Pennsylvania: Pennsylvania State University Press, pp. 51–66.

Jalušič, V. (ed.) (2002) *Kako smo hodile v feministično gimnazijo*, Ljubljana: Založba/*cf.

Jalušič, V. and Antić, M.G. (2001) *Women – Politics – Equal Opportunities: Prospects for Gender Equality Politics in Central and Eastern Europe*, Ljubljana: Peace Institute.

Jaquette, J.S. and Wolchik, S.L. (1998) *Women and democracy: Latin America and Central and Eastern Europe*, Baltimore: Johns Hopkins University Press.

Jogan, M. (1986) *Ženske in diskriminacija*, Ljubljana: Delavska enotnost.

—— (2001) *Seksizem v vsakdanjem življenju*, Ljubljana: Fakulteta za družbene vede.

Lokar, S. (2002) 'Introduction', in *Women Can Do It II, Integration of gender equality issues in parliamentary parties work in South East Europe*, Project Report, Novi sad: Stability Pact Gender Task Force, pp. 5–11.

Lovenduski, J. (1993) 'Introduction: the Dynamics of Gender and Party', in J. Lovenduski and P. Norris (eds) *Gender and Party Politics*, London: Sage, pp. 1–15.

Mastnak, T. (1992) *Vzhodno od raja*, Ljubljana: Državna založba Slovenije.

Matland, R. and Montgomery K. (eds) (2003) *Women's Access to Power in Post Communist Europe*, Oxford: Oxford University Press.

Mirovni inštitut (2004) Online. Available at: http://www.mirovni-institut.si (accessed 21 November 2004).

Muslin, M. (ed.) (2000) *Žene Hrvatske u brojkama*, Zagreb: Povjerenstvo Vlade Republike Hrvatske za pitanje jednakosti spolova.

Papić, Ž. (1989) *Sociologija i Feminizam*, Beograd: Istraživačko-izdavački centar SSO Srbije.

Pateman, C. (1989) *The Disorder of Women*, Cambridge: Polity Press.

Ramet, P.S. (ed.) (1999) *Gender Politics in the western Balkans: Women, Society and Politics in Yugoslavia and the Yugoslav Successor States*, Pennsylvania: Pennsylvania State University Press.

Ristova, K. (2003) 'Establishing a Machocracy: Women and Elections in Macedonia (1990–8)', in R. Matland and K. Montgomery (eds) *Women's Access to Power in Post Communist Europe*, Oxford: Oxford University Press, pp. 196–216.

Rizman, R. (1997) *Izzivi odprte družbe*, Ljubljana: Liberalna akdemija.

Schopflin, G. (2002) *Nations, Identity, Power*, London: Hurst.

Sklevicky, L. and Rihtman D.A. (ed.) (1996) *Konji, žene i ratovi*, Zagreb: Ženska infoteka.

Slovene Parliament (2004a) Passed Laws. Online. Available at: http://www. dz-rs.si/si/aktualno/spremljanje_zakonodaje/sprejeti_zakoni/sprejeti_zakoni. html (accessed 21 November 2004).

Slovene Parliament (2004b) Slovene Constitution. Online. Available at: http://www.dz-rs.si/si/aktualno/spremljanje_zakonodaje/ustava/ustava.html (accessed 20 November 2004).

Statistical Office of the Republic of Slovenia (2004) Elections. Online. Available at: http://www.stat.si/tema_splosno_volitve.asp (accessed 22 November 2004).

Štrajn, D. (ed.) (1995) *Meje demokracije*, Ljubljana: Liberalna akdemija.

Taarup, N.A. (2003) 'International Implementation of Electoral Gender Quotas in the Balkans: A Fact-Finding Report', The Research Program on Gender Quotas. Working Paper Series 2003: 1. Stockholm University: Department of Political Science.

Tomšič, V. (1978) *Ženska, delo, družina, družba*, Ljubljana: Komunist.

Ule, M. and Rener, T. (1997) 'Nationalism and Gender in Postsocialist Societies: is Nationalism Female?', in T. Renne (ed.) *Ana's Land: Sisterhood in Eastern Europe*, Oxford: Westview Press, pp. 220–33.

Vode, A. (1998) *Spol in upor*, Ljubljana: Krtina.

—— (1999) *Značaj in usoda*, Ljubljana: Krtina.

—— (2000) *Spomin in pozaba*, Ljubljana: Krtina.

Woodward, A. (2001) 'Women are Doing It' – building a Gender Balanced Democracy using Sticks, Carrots and Kisses', in M.A. Rukavina (ed.) *Building national gender equality mechanisms in South East Europe: Women's use of the state: 1999–2001*, Ljubljana: Stability Pact Gender Task Force, pp. 42–6.

Znanstveno raziskovalni center pri SAZU (2004) Online. Available at: http://odmev. zrc-sazu.si/zrc/ (accessed 20 November 2004).

7 The Arab region

Women's access to the decision-making process across the Arab Nation

Gihan Abou-Zeid

This chapter will focus on the implementation of quotas in the Arab Nation. Initially, it is worth noting that various Arab states have introduced quotas despite the generally pessimistic atmosphere regarding women's capabilities or place in the public sphere. The chapter explores the factors that made such a development possible. Moreover, we will demonstrate that reserved seats, with or without election, are the most frequently utilized form of gender quotas, which is to be expected given that methods of seat allocation from above are prevalent in the Arab region. Despite challenges, gender balance is now an added consideration to the long-standing tradition of seat allocation based upon tribal, religious or ethnic lines. Finally, we will examine whether gender quotas can propel the process of empowering Arab women and help change pessimistic perceptions about women in the political world.[1]

The Arab context

The Arab region is affected by an array of influences which shape its political, economic and social reality. At the political level, most of these countries have been subjected to oppressive foreign occupation by British, French and Italian forces.

Some countries still suffer under foreign occupation: Israel continues to occupy Palestine and Syria's Golan Heights. In 2003, Iraq succumbed to American-British occupation after 13 years of economic sanctions. Likewise, the region has endured a series of interstate and intrastate armed conflict. Libya and Iraq have been exposed to a variety of economic, political and military pressures. Iraq has been omitted from the Arab region chapter, since a later chapter will examine the unique situation in occupied Iraq.

A total of 4.1 million Palestinian refugees – who constitute the world's largest refugee population – are forced into refugee camps in Jordan, Lebanon, Syria, the West Bank and Gaza Strip, where they suffer from poverty, a lack of services, home demolitions, and alienation. Even outside the refugee camps, Palestinians who live in the occupied territories share most of these same problems. Women make up half of all Palestinian refugees in these camps.

With a stalled and uncertain peace process, the economies of Arab countries have had to bear a new and sustained burden, resulting in a reprioritization of expenditures, placing military spending on top. Moreover, the decline in oil prices over many years has contributed to the weakening of Arab nations' GNP annual growth rate.

In a context of privatization policies and poor spending, public education in the Arab region – with the exception of the Gulf States – barely meets the development and labour market needs. In an environment where the traditional role of women is sanctified, the dropout rate among poor girls is very high.

Arab societies use all possible means to entrench their value-based heritage, by promoting customs and traditions that curb women's activities and confine their existence to the framework of the family. The prevalence of customs and traditions varies in rural and urban communities. In the former, women are largely constrained, whereas in the latter they enjoy broader opportunities, which allow them to take on roles other than reproduction and farm labour.

Within the framework of Arab society, which displays an extremely limited margin of democracy, the political will of the people fails to produce any effect. Political regimes in the Arab region take on one of two forms – monarchy or republic. Jordan, Morocco and Gulf States such as Oman, Kuwait, Qatar, Saudi Arabia and Bahrain all have a hereditary monarchy, albeit with diverse political systems. The United Arab Emirates (UAE) is a federation of seven states. While Bahrain and Kuwait have political parties, Oman, Saudi Arabia and the UAE do not. All republican regimes, with the exception of Libya, have political parties, although often with some restrictions.

Political rights of women in the Arab nation

The above factors constitute an integral part of the reality of women's political participation. Historically, women in all Arab states effectively participated in the liberation movements during the age of colonialism. Driven by patriotism and without prior planning, they were heavily involved in the anti-colonialism struggle. After independence, however, they were confined to their homes only to start another struggle to obtain their rights. When the state regime actively began to control the public space, women tended to become passive and inactive, Suad Joseph argues (2001).

The constitutions of most Arab states provide that citizens are equal with respect to political rights, and they grant women the right to vote and run for elections. Even the Gulf States are starting to move. In Kuwait, the feminist and progressive movement finally gained the right to vote and stand for election for women, while in Saudi Arabia, women were still banned from voting or standing for election in the Kingdom's first municipal elections in more than 40 years because of cultural and political barriers (Abou-Alsamh 2004).

Of the 22 members of the League of Arab States, 15 are State Parties to the Convention on the Elimination of All Forms of Discrimination Against Women (CEDAW). Although Arab women who marry foreigners do not lose their own nationality, almost all 15 make reservations to Article 9, section 2, which mandates that states 'grant women equal rights with men with respect to the nationality of their children' (UN 1979). While some of these states merely claim that they are not bound by Article 9, section 2 of CEDAW, others creatively attempt to explain why the child's nationality will mirror that of the father. It is from this basic right to a nationality that the domestic rights and duties of citizenship flow. For example, privileges like the right to vote, hold a passport for international travel and access to certain social welfare plans, are usually reserved for citizens.

Only personal status laws and family laws are guided by strict and rigid interpretations of *Sharia*. Women's status is remarkably similar in Arab countries. All Arab constitutions expressly stipulate gender equality with respect to all rights; however, personal status laws have constituted a barrier to women in all Arab states. With the exception of Tunisia, most laws in the Arab world make a woman's right to work subject to her husband's approval. He may either grant or deny his wife this most basic and fundamental right.

After independence, Arab states did not take any measures to stimulate the political participation of women, although they heeded women's calls for education and the improved health services.

Factors influencing the adoption of gender quotas in Arab countries

There are very few women in Arab politics. Few Arab states have passed positive/affirmative action measures like quotas. However, new demands are being heard. Women in Arab states occupy an average of 6.4 per cent of the parliamentary seats – 6 per cent in the lower house and 7.5 per cent in the upper house. The highest percentage of women in parliament is in Tunisia where women occupy 22.8 per cent of the 182 seats. Some countries such as Kuwait, Bahrain and Saudi Arabia have no women in their respective legislatures, as Table 7.1 shows.

While it may be argued that a multitude of factors affect decisions by Arab governments to adopt quotas focused on increasing the presence of women in parliament, this chapter identifies the following three as the most influential:

1   International and regional influence.
2   The relation between structural adjustment programmes and quotas.
3   The Arab women's movement.

Table 7.1 Women in Arab politics

Country	Right to vote recognized (year)	Party competition in elections	Women in parliament %	Electoral system
Algeria	Yes (1962)	Yes	6.2 (2002)	List PR
Bahrain	Yes (1973)	No	0.0 (2002)	Two Rounds
Comoros	Yes (1956)	n/a	3.0 (2004)	Two Rounds
Djibouti	Yes (1946)	Yes	10.8 (2003)	PBV
Egypt	Yes (1956)	Yes	2.4 (2000)	Two Rounds
Iraq	Yes (1980)	Yes	n/a (2005)	List PR
Jordan	Yes (1974)	Yes	5.5 (2003)	SNTV
Kuwait	Yes (2005)	No	1.5 (2003)[a]	Block Vote
Lebanon	Yes (1952)	Yes	2.3 (2000)	Block Vote
Libya	Yes (1964)	No	n/a (1997)	N
Mauritania	Yes (1961)	Yes	3.7 (2001)	Two Rounds
Morocco	Yes (1963)	Yes	10.8 (2002)	List PR
Oman	Yes (1997)	No	2.4 (2000)	FPP
Palestine	Yes (1946)	Yes	5.6 (1996)	Block Vote
Qatar	Yes (1999)	No	0.0 (1999)	N
Saudi Arabia	No (neither gender)	No	0.0 (2001)	N
Somalia	Yes (1956)	No	8.4 (2004)	T
Sudan	Yes (1964)	Yes	9.7 (2000)	FPP
Syria	Yes (1949)	Yes	12.0 (2003)	Block Vote
Tunisia	Yes (1957)	Yes	22.8 (2004)	Parallel[b]
United Arab Emirates	No (neither gender)	No	0.0 (1997)	N
Yemen	Yes (1967)	Yes	0.3 (2003)	FPP

Sources: Hawthorne (2002), El Sawy (2004), Ottaway (2004),
http://www.ipu.org
http://www.electionworld.org
http://www.pna.gov.ps/Government/gov/palestinian_legislative_council.asp
http://news.bbc.co.uk/1/hi/world/middle_east/293171.stm
http://womenshistory.about.com/library/weekly/aa091600a.htm
http://www.miami.com/mld/miamiherald/2004/11/10/news/opinion/10141353.htm?1c
http://www.washprofile.org/english/15%20(March%2023)/ottaway.asp
http://www.tunisiaonline.com/elections2004/partis/index.html
http://www.cidcm.umd.edu/inscr/polity/report.htm#naf
http://www.irinnews.org/report.asp?ReportID=43143&SelectRegion=Horn_of_Africa&SelectCountry=SOMALIA

Notes
a According to Kuwait law, all ministers become members of parliament and, consequently, the first woman minister, Maasoma Mubarek, is an appointed member of parliament.
b Tunisia has a PBV and List PR mixed system.
Key electoral systems: *Plurality-Majority:* FPP = First-Past-the-Post, Two Rounds System, Block Vote, PBV = Party Block Vote. *Proportional Representation:* List PR. *Mixed:* MMP = Mixed Member Proportional, Parallel. *Other:* SNTV = Single Non-Transferable Vote. N = No provisions for direct elections. T = Transitional (countries that in November 2004 did not have any electoral law).

International and regional influence

International conferences, which highlight specific issues, are often vital in encouraging states to protect civil rights at the domestic level. Many of these conferences also result in the drafting of international conventions and declarations, and two such documents have been important for women's rights: The Convention for the Elimination of All Forms of Discrimination Against Women (CEDAW) and the Beijing Platform for Action (PFA), both drafted under the auspices of the United Nations (UN). It was not until after the UN's 4th World Conference in Beijing in 1995 that states started to embrace the concept of quotas for women on a large scale.

NGOs that attended the conference played a large role in the proliferation of the quota idea. The conference served as a cross-border information sharing and brainstorming centre. Activists could then adopt and improvise on reform strategies they encountered at the conference based upon the specific needs in their home countries. According to estimates, there are thousands of NGOs in the Arab countries that take on women's issues as one of their primary concerns (Karam 1999: 14).

International conferences themselves do not trigger reforms, but rather add international affirmation to national efforts. International conferences are held, and declarations are made, to bring human rights concerns into the mainstream discourse. UN entities as well as UN-sponsored conferences that promote human rights implementation in general, and women's rights and development in particular, lend international prestige to those who work for these issues at the grassroots level (Karam 1999: 26). Their support validates the work of these local NGOs. UN-backed conferences have a galvanizing effect on issues that are discussed at these international meetings.

If we take the case of Morocco, we will notice that two negative Amnesty International reports as well as the World Bank Structural Adjustment Program played a role in the revision of the Moroccan constitution. The start of the women's movement in the 1970s and the international focus on women's rights during the 1980s and 1990s paved the way for the Moroccan quota initiative. It should also be noted that since 1999, Morocco has tried to gain international approval by implementing a series of liberalization efforts. Looking 'modern' comes with many economic incentives such as access to the Euro-Mediterranean market and World Bank initiatives (Hall 2003: 51).

The regional influence might be just as, if not even more important as the international for the diffusion of quotas for women. Implementation of the Moroccan quota served as a point of reference for other Arab states as far as when to pressure their governments for change. One event became especially important. In November 2002, representatives from 18 Arab states attended the Women's Summit in Jordan, which put special focus on quotas as a method to give disempowered Arab women a political voice. The Director of the United Nations Development Program Regional Bureau for Arab States, Rima Khalaf Hunaidi called for an action plan to jumpstart the integration of women into politically prominent positions. The conference recommended that Arab countries follow the Moroccan example (Pelham 2002).

The relation between structural adjustment programmes and quotas

Adoption of structural adjustment policies in Arab countries has aggravated the distribution of resources and income. The high levels of unemployment and low rates of income and savings have left about 60 per cent of Arab nationals, over 50 per cent of which are women, poor. Meanwhile, 10 per cent of the population is steadily increasing their wealth, whereas the middle class, which comprises 30 per cent of the population, struggles to maintain the minimum standard of living, which is declining year after year (El Baz 2003: 8).

These globalization policies with privatization and cuts in social welfare have had a tremendous effect on the global south, causing many of these governments to change laws which have had a disproportionate impact on the disempowered masses, most of which are women. Women activists, particularly from the left, have come to this realization and are now demanding that women have a say in the decision-making process. Quotas are so far the only open door into this male-dominated world, according to the Center for Legislative Development (2004).

Countries, particularly in the developing world, often make superficial changes in order to appease the United States and Western Europe. In the Arab world, initiating minimal human rights reforms, providing strategic military bases and 'US-friendly governments' are sufficient to secure loan guarantees from the US and EU. What is certain, however, is that the changes Arab developing countries make are usually negligible.

The Arab women's movement

The Arab women's movement started as a political movement, which dates back to the inception of Arab nationalism in the twentieth century (Abou-Zeid 2002: 2). The women's struggle was part and parcel of the struggle against colonialism and occupation. The women who participated in the resistance came from all social and economic classes. Even uneducated, poor, village women participated.

Initially these women's groups had not yet organized under our modern notions of a movement. In large measure, this was due to their precarious situation in the midst of the resistance, which focused on self-determination and sovereignty.

The resistance harboured various ideological camps, each with its own resistance tools. Nationalists, Socialists, and some Islamists accepted the idea that women should have a more visible place in society and play different roles.

After independence, men started to situate themselves in decision-making posts while pushing back women into the private sphere. The role of mutual respect and co-operation that often existed during the struggle for liberation began to crumble. However, activist women resisted male attempts to exclude them from the public sphere and started to demand equal rights using various methods. They established NGOs and feminist journals, and organized and attended Arab women's conferences. These conferences not only focused on women's issues, but equated them with wider political problems as well. Even films and movies of the time started to break traditional stereotypes of women.

Later the Arab women's movements joined the global women's movement, and their participation in international conferences was apparent, especially UN conferences. Pan-Arab women networks increased and by the end of 2003, all Arab women's organizations were established, including Arab women institutions.

Usually the world community works along with local women's groups and NGOs. However, national leaders are sometimes pressured into adopting quotas despite the lack of initiation by internal women's groups. This is most likely to occur in previously war-torn nations. International pressure that forcibly imposes a quota upon any population is sometimes seen as an infringement on national sovereignty and interference in domestic affairs (Krook 2004: 15–17), and this can breed hostility towards universal ideas cloaked in 'Western' garb.

The quota system in the Arab nation

Since the dawn of independence, the quota system was applied in the interest of various groups, on a religious (Lebanon), ethnic (Jordan) or categorical basis (Egypt). It is only recently that Arab states have begun to apply gender quota, and always according to the following two systems: Voluntary political party quotas for electoral candidates and reserved seats.

Voluntary political party quotas for electoral candidates

As the only Arab countries, Tunisia and Algeria utilize the political party quota system (see types of quota systems in Table 7.2). While both Algeria and Tunisia are almost exclusively Muslim societies, Tunisia stands as a unique model in addressing women's issues from both the Arab and Islamic contexts. Tunisia has promulgated laws that are particularly fairer to women in the fields of personal status, employment and political participation compared to her sister state, Algeria, largely because of the

Table 7.2 Quota types in Arab politics

Country	Quota type (year of introduction)	Quota provision
Algeria	*Party Quotas*	
	National Liberation Front (2002)	2 women candidates for every 5
	Peace Movement (2002)	2 women candidates for every 5
Djibouti	*Legal Quotas (2002)*	10%
	Reserved Seats	
Egypt	*Legal Quotas (1979–84)*	30 of 360 (8.3%)
	Reserved Seats	
Iraq	*Legal Quotas (2004)*	n/a
	Candidate Quotas (2004)	
Jordan	*Legal Quotas (2003)*	6 of 110 (5.5%)
	Reserved Seats	
Morocco	*Gentleman's agreement (2002)*	30 of 325 (9.2%)
	Reserved Seats	
Somalia	*Legal Quotas (2004)*	25 of 245 (10.2%)
	Reserved Seats (appointed)	
Sudan	*Legal Quotas (since 1978 with variations)* Reserved Seats	35 of 360 (9.7%)
Tunisia	*Party Quotas*	
	Democratic Constitutional Rally (2004)	25%

Source: See Table 7.1.

government's enlightened interpretations of Islam. While Algerian President Boutflika has taken steps to bolster women's participation, he remains cognizant of Algeria's sensitive political atmosphere, where the conservative Islamic tide is still relatively strong. Many who identify with Algeria's Islamic movement are women, who despite their contributions are convinced that politics is the men's domain, and men should take up the plight of women through the lenses of Islamic jurisprudence.

There are exceptions like Algeria's Louisa Hanoun, who was nominated Secretary General of the Worker's Party, which won 21 of 389 seats in the National People's Assembly in the 2002 elections. In April 2004, Hanoun became the first Algerian woman to run for the presidency. Other notable exceptions in Algeria include appointment of the first woman *wali* (mayor) as well as two women chief justices. The number of female judges in Algeria also increased over a period to 137 out of 404 in 2001.

In Tunisia, the ruling Democratic Constitutional Rally Party (DCRP) has set up ad-hoc structures devoted to increasing the political role of women. It is the only party to do so, but the DCRP controls 80 per cent of the parliamentary seats, while opposition parties hold only 20 per cent. The DCRP allocates 25 per cent of its seats to women. (Bouchkouj 2004). The party also appointed a female secretary and entrusted her with women's affairs. She became an assistant to the secretary general at the national level. However, the role of women in opposition parties remains marginal.

In both Tunisia and Algeria the quota has been of immense assistance to women. In 2004, women in Tunisia won 43 of the 189 seats making up 22.8 per cent of the parliament's composition, the highest percentage in the region. In the House of Representatives, the post of Second Assistant to the Head of the House was allocated to a woman.

Similarly in Algeria, parliamentary seats were allocated to women of the ruling National Liberation Front, who had two female candidates out of five for each of Algeria's 48 districts. Also the peace movement has designated a woman among its five nominees for each district. Yet, in densely populated areas, the party's slate nominates a woman from among three candidates. With the application of the party quota system in Algeria, women gained 24 of the 389 seats (or 6.2 per cent) in the 2002 elections.

Reserved seats

Morocco, Tunisia, Jordan, Somalia, Sudan and Djibouti currently employ a system of reserved seats, while Egypt has done so in the past. As Table 7.2 shows, reserved seats are the most widespread type of quotas for women in the Arab region. While Morocco, Jordan and Egypt have dealt with conservative Islamic movements, the pressures of traditional tribal ideology and loyalty have been added in the case of Jordan, Morocco, Somalia, Sudan and Djibouti. Islamic political parties, which are tolerated, but kept under close scrutiny in Morocco and Jordan and completely banned in Egypt, defend women's rights from an Islamic law paradigm that calls for the establishment of justice, equality and solidarity in accordance with Islamic jurisprudence. Reluctance to rattle the conservative Islamic segments of society as well as the patriarchal hierarchy is responsible for Morocco, Jordan and Egypt's decisions to become State Parties to CEDAW with reservations: reservations were made to provisions in the Convention, which under their interpretation of Islam, are contrary to Islamic law. It should be noted that Djibouti acceded to CEDAW in December 1998 without reservations or declarations. Sudan and Somalia, like the United States, are not State Parties to CEDAW. As a failed state, currently run by warlords, Somalia appears to be excused considering that any potential international obligations have been de facto suspended for the time being. Due to the shared geographical location, historical experiences, and current political realities of North African and Middle Eastern Arab States compared to Sub-Saharan Arab States, the discussion below of reserved seat systems has been divided along these lines.

North African and Middle Eastern Arab States

Morocco and Jordan have introduced reserved seats for women, although with different models. Before the 2002 Moroccan national election, the government introduced a reform bill to the election law. The situation seemed ripe for discussing women's representation, and such discussions took place within political parties, civil society organizations, and media institutions, in addition to parliament. The lobbying led to the adoption of a women's national list, and the success was the result of the following steps:

Step one: Under the leadership of the National Coordination Committee of Party Women, nine parties and 20 women's organizations accepted a memo with specific proposals to guarantee women's representation in elected council. Their proposal focused on:

- Adoption of a quota system.
- Adoption of a fair election system.
- Reservation of a definite number of parliamentary seats for women.
- Financial measures to motivate political parties to introduce women as candidates for election; and to prevent accumulation of responsibility in order to give women and youth an opportunity to participate.

Step two: The proposal was introduced to parliament, which approved changing the electoral systems to a list system.

However, the provision of equality in the Moroccan Constitution prevented the adoption of quota and reserved seats like in the case of France. In response to the pressure by women's organizations, political parties instead made a 'gentlemens's agreement' to set aside for the next election all 30 slots on the so-called national list for female candidates. In Morocco, most members of parliament are elected in 92 multimember districts, whereas 30 seats are elected in one national constituency.

This obligation was successful in helping 30 women get elected. Five women were also elected outside of the national list. The 35 women represent 10.8 per cent of the 325 seats. At the same time, one of Morocco's political parties, the Socialist Union for Popular Forces (or USFP) has a voluntary party quota for women, with 20 per cent of their party list reserved for women candidates. Two of the five women elected without reserved seats came from the USFP. One woman from the Constitutional Union (UC) and two women from the Independence Party (I) won the other three freely elected seats (Abdul Aziz 2004: 4).

Even if it is too early to evaluate the performance of the elected women MPs, their activity seems to reflect the sincerity of political parties to involve qualified and strong women candidates (Bilmodin 2004). Moroccan MP Meluda Hazib feels that the 'consensus reached among the parties is a step in the right direction, and we are currently working towards moving from an agreement to the adoption of a party quota through law'.

In Morocco, it was grassroots activism assisted by a socialist oriented government that helped bring quotas to the surface. As a result, the first Human Rights Ministry in an Arab state was established, two women in the Ministry's advisory council were appointed, and women's involvement in the judicial field increased, with nine women reaching the post of chief justice. This coincided with the decision to appoint an adviser on women's affairs to the Monarch and three women among the 37 ministers.

Like Morocco, Jordan too was concerned about a hostile response from both Islamists and tribal constituencies, and consequently all pleas to implement a quota for women were ignored. In 2002, Jordan's largest party, the Islamic Action Front (IAF), referred to quotas for women as state interference with fair and free elections (Pelham 2002).

Nevertheless, during the 2002 Women's Summit in Jordan, calls were made to follow the Moroccan example (Pelham 2002). In the 2003 elections, the government did just that and reserved six of the 110 (or 5.5 per cent) of the seats in the House of Representatives for women as per the law. In this manner, Jordan differs from Morocco, since the system of reserved seats is legally codified and not dependent on the will of political parties to honour their word. Jordan's women parliamentarians were selected depending on the percentage of votes they received in their respective constituencies, rather than the number of votes they received. These seats are not limited by geography or constituency, but the six women winners are those who obtained the highest percentages in any of the constituencies (Abu-Ruman 2004). This is the reason that only women from the countryside were elected, and none from Amman. Although Jordan introduced 54 women candidates in the 2003 general elections, none won outside of the framework of reserved seats. Previously in 2001, King Abdullah II had appointed three women – among the 40 appointed members – to the House of Notables, making up 7.5 per cent of the membership.

Unlike Morocco's party slate system, Jordan's House of Representatives candidates are selected on a single vote for a single candidate basis (SNTV). This electoral system is widely criticized by political groups due to the clan-based nature of the Jordanian society. The single vote for a single candidate style does not give the voter the chance to select the most qualified candidate, let alone a woman candidate, but rather plays into clan politics. Loyalty is foremost to the clan, and the clansman's ability to represent the interests of Jordanian society is questionable. For this reason, Jordan's political parties advocate a party slate system.

However, Jordanian tribes are learning to use the reserved seat system to their advantage as demonstrated in the 2003 elections. When larger tribes could guarantee their male candidate's parliamentary seat, based upon the custom of tribe block voting, having a women candidate run under the six seat quota allowed for the possibility of securing two parliamentary seats. On the other hand, smaller tribes could use the quota system to introduce a woman candidate and increase their chances of securing a parliamentary seat. The tribes' use of the quota system reflects the malleability of tribal ideology, which traditionally sees politics as the theatre of men, in circumstances were tribal power is at stake (Dunne 2003: 3).

Although no longer applicable, we briefly examine Egypt as the first example of the reserved seats system in the Arab world and as a yardstick of both the Moroccan and Jordanian experiences. In 1979, a presidential decree was passed regarding the application of the quota system (law 21/1979), defining a formula reserving 30 seats (out of 360 seats) for women in parliament. Thirty of the electoral districts had a requirement that at least one woman be elected, and there were reserved seats for farmers and workers (Abou-Zeid 2003: 2). In 1979, 35 women (9 per cent) became members; in 1984, 36 women became members (Abou-Zeid 2003: 3). The quota system was applied in both instances. Women, by virtue of the law, were allowed to compete with men for other seats, whereas men were not permitted to contest seats assigned to women. Also, the president has the right to appoint ten members of parliament, including at least two women. When the Constitutional Court granted a petitioner's plea to abolish the list-based voting system in accordance with Egyptian Law No. 114/1983, the women's quota was eliminated as well (Al-Sharbini 2004). The court found this law unconstitutional because it only allowed party-affiliated MPs to present themselves on the election lists, thereby excluding independents (Al-Sharbini 2004). At the subsequent election in 1987, women won only 2.2 per cent of the seats. The Egyptian example is discussed later.

Sub-Saharan Arab states

Sudan, Djibouti and Somalia all utilize some version of reserved seats as a method to boost women's participation in the political process. These three sub-Saharan African states are situated between Arab and African culture. All three suffer unmatched poverty, starvation, a flood of refugees either into or out of the country and, in the case of Somalia and Sudan, continue to suffer from political turmoil and civil strife. Because of the devastation internal armed conflict has brought to countries like Sudan and Somalia, domestic women's groups have directed their focus on relief and humanitarian efforts to serve their communities.

While the constitutions of Sudan, Djibouti, and Northern Somalia (known as the Republic of the Land of Somalia) guarantee gender equality, tribal tradition has been a barrier to women's empowerment and political participation.

In *Somalia*, as in Jordan, where tribal politics is the strongest, the tribe has integrated its first loyalty into the quota. The Somali Interim People's Council, comprising 245 members, was appointed by clan chiefs. Twenty seats were designated to be appointed by the President, five seats for minorities and 25 for women. The division ensured equal representation of all clans. There is no official or unofficial estimate of the number of Somali clans, so the equal representation of clans is questionable (Aden Dire 2000). However, the clans generally agreed upon to be most prominent consist of the Darod, Dir, Hawiye and Issak clans, collectively referred to as Samale, and the Digile and Mrifle clans referred to as Sab. Women's seats were allocated in a manner so that each of the major clans is represented by five women. The remaining women seats were allocated to small clans. Women are therefore entering politics as clan representatives in the parliamentary council, and some might say that this is in reality a system of reserved seats for tribal representation. The strong loyalty to the clan has undermined the religious opposition, which tried to curb women's public participation, and has left the government inept to deal with Somali tribes. Currently about 12 of Somalia's clans are involved in armed struggles.

Somali women nevertheless continue to preserve and maintain a presence in the Interim Council, attempting to transcend any clan differences and divisions for the sake of healing their war-torn nation. The civil war has brought Somali women closer together in an attempt to set a good example in co-operation.

In 1953, *Sudan's* Constitution gave women the right to vote and stand for election (see Table 7.1). In 1978, Sudan established a gender quota for women parliamentarians. (Kuku 2004). Women used this right during the first general parliamentary elections held in 1954. During the 1986 to 1989 elections, women MPs won 7 per cent of parliamentary seats by free election. In 1989, 25 (or 8.3 per cent) were appointed MPs. In addition, a number of women were appointed to the local legislature (Isa 2001: 125). Today, Sudanese women serve in senior posts, such as ambassadors. The President has also appointed advisers to women's affairs ministerial portfolios. Women have been allowed to serve in the judiciary since 1946, and there are currently five female judges.

Sudan's unicameral legislature, or National Assembly, consists of 360 members, 270 of which are popularly elected. A supra-national council known as the National Convention elects the other 90 members. The most recent legislative elections were held in 2000 when the government allocated 35 parliamentary seats to women, accounting for 9.7 per cent of the legislature. In today's political arena, the Democratic Feminist Alliance has become the government's main opposition party (Kuku 2004). In effect, Sudanese women have been very politically active. They have the political experience necessary to be effective, which has forced the government to think of ways to attract the women's vote.

Djibouti was the last of these three countries to institute a quota for women. In October 2002, the cabinet approved the allocation of 10 per cent of House of Representative seats to women. 14 women stood for elections, of whom six won seats out of a total of 65 parliamentary seats, making up 10.8 per cent. Khadiga Abeeb was appointed as chief of the Supreme Court, a post which entitles her to temporarily assume the presidency of the republic when the post is vacant. The government also established the Ministry of Women, Family and Social Affairs, where the first woman minister took the helm.

Political participation beyond the quota system

In the following section, women's political representation in Arab countries that do not apply gender quotas is discussed. The majority of Arab countries belong in this category, as Table 7.1 shows. Even if several of these countries apply some kind of quotas based on religion or clan, quotas for women are not accepted.

Syria

Although no quota is applied, women representation in the Syrian parliament is the second highest of all Arab states. In the recent Peoples' Council election, held in 2003, women won 30 seats (or 12 per cent) of the 250 available seats. All 30 women who secured legislative seats came from the National Democratic Front, which is a coalition of nine parties and led by the ruling Ba'ath Party. None of the women who ran as independents won in their campaign bid (UNDP 2004). These circumstances seem to indicate that this high percentage was a result of governmental sponsorship. The hope is that this visibility will eventually translate into a more significant role for women in the decision-making process.

The ruling Ba'ath Party has a long history of implementing active policies towards women. The Ba'ath Party's philosophy encourages women to be active politically, and the party depends upon women for its composition. The Ba'ath Party has welcomed women into the military, government, university and all areas of public life. Women are active through the General Union of Syrian Women, which was founded in 1967 and operates across the different governorates (districts) with the aim of providing girls and women with skills and to train and build their capabilities.

Lebanon

In 1989, after Lebanon's almost 16-year civil war ended, the State established a quota for Lebanon's various religious sects. The president was designated to be a Maronite Christian, the prime minister a Sunni Muslim, and the chairman of the House of Representatives a Shi'ite Muslim. This quota system also applies to the parliamentary representation. Seats are equally divided among Muslims and Christians, i.e. each sect has 64 seats. Muslim seats are divided among the Muslim sects with 27 for Sunnis and 27 for Shi'a. The remaining ten seats are divided among Druze and Alawites. Likewise, the Christians' seats are divided: 34 for Maronites and 30 for other Christian sects. Each voter may vote for more than one candidate and may simultaneous vote for parliamentarians of different sects.

A major reason for not having quotas for women concerns the sectarian division of the ruling powers. In competing for control, the different religious sects do not want to risk having women represent them. Despite the absence of a women's quota for the House of Representatives, three women were elected in 2000, making up 2.3 per cent of the total seats.

Yemen

In Yemen, women make up an extremely small percentage of the political parties' membership. No single party has nominated a woman to stand for elections, but 37 women ran as independent candidates, and only one of them won a seat (0.3 per cent of the total seats) in the House of Representatives. However, both traditional and well-educated men and women have rejected the idea of women running without party affiliation on the grounds that it deprives them of the democratic experience. Women's groups are currently very active, and there is discussion in political circles of implementing a quota for women.

One important factor that distinguishes Yemen's power structures from those of other Gulf States is the degree to which tribal culture dominates. All sources of power, whether political power or economic, are rooted in tribal dynamics. It is this preservation of tribal culture and tradition that has stunted the women's movement and prevented Yemen from, among other things, building a modern state infrastructure. Moreover, Yemen has the least apt tools needed to confront tribal culture. Today Yemen stands as one of the poorest, weakest and least developed states in the Arab world. Historically, however, Yemen has one of the oldest and richest civilizations dating back almost 4000 years.

Mauritania

Women obtained the right to vote and be nominated for office in 1961. The illiteracy rate among women is estimated at 68.1 per cent. Consequently, their political participation is limited, and only three women have a seat in the National Assembly, which equals 3.7 per cent of the total seats. Likewise, there are three women in the House of Senates, amounting to 5.4 per cent of the total membership.

Comoros Islands

Women in the Comoros Islands still have not obtained many of their rights, and their illiteracy rate estimated at 50.7 per cent. Besides, there are no universities, and training opportunities are limited. Women suffer extreme poverty and harsh economic conditions. The legislative power is represented in the 30-member Union Assembly, which was dissolved in 1999, but new elections were held in 2004 and resulted in the election of one woman (equalling 3 per cent).

Palestine

In the first presidential elections held in 1996, Palestinian women set a precedent when Samiha Khalil was nominated for the presidency, winning 11 per cent of the votes. During the 9 January 2005 elections, there were no women among the seven presidential candidates. The election law does not provide for allocation of any of the National Palestinian Legislative Assembly's 88 seats to women. However, six seats have been allocated to the Christian minority and one to the Samiris. Nevertheless, five women won parliamentary seats in 1996, constituting 5.6 per cent of the Palestinian National Authority's legislature. But there is a 20 per cent gender quota for representation in every local council under the Palestine National Council's election law (Andersson 2004). Given all the hardships of the occupation, Palestinian women continue to be active and are trying to implement a women's quota under the current Palestinian Reform Plan.

Libya

Libya is divided into 30 municipalities, each with its own municipal congress. Inhabitants of each municipality nominate five persons to represent them in the main municipal congress of their respective municipality. The congress is like a mini-legislative assembly, and there are no women represented among the five candidates. Statistics indicate that the total percentage of female representation in the municipal congresses is 35 per cent, all by appointment.

Libyan economic laws also state that women should obtain a minimum of 20 per cent of the economic activity licenses – which is deemed a quota in the economic sphere – with the aim of stimulating women's economic role.

Gulf States

Except for Kuwait and Bahrain, the Gulf States do not have elected legislative councils. Meanwhile an advisory council, which plays the role of parliament, has been elected in Oman since 1997. Qatar had its first elections in 1999 for the municipal council, which plays an advisory role. In Kuwait, a 60 per cent majority of the conservative Islamist-controlled parliament recently voted to grant women the right to vote (next election 2007).

Although there were eight women candidates in Bahrain's 2002 parliamentary elections, none of them won. Women activists note that a system of reserving one or two seats for women is needed to guarantee that women are not denied access to the decision-making process. Since the 2002 elections, Bahraini women have started to call on the kingdom to enact a system of reserved seats for women. The monarch has made a partial compromise and appointed six women to the 40-member advisory council (or 15 per cent), which shares the legislative duties with the elected House of Representatives. This percentage has not been fixed as a permanent quota allocation, but Bahraini women activists are working hard for it.

Women's status is largely similar in Qatar and Oman, as those in power in each country enjoy a political will that spurs women to expand their presence in all public fields. Qatar is the first Gulf State to appoint a female minister (Ministry of Education), and Oman appointed two female ministers and one ambassador. Moreover, two women won in the parliamentary elections (the Advisory Council). Meanwhile 2.3 per cent of the State's Council members are women, appointed by the government which also appointed women in the leadership posts. Five women were appointed to undersecretary posts. Qatar has no legislative council, but rather a 30-member advisory council without a single female.

Although Saudi Arabia's feminist movement is in its preliminary stages, progress has been made. In 2003, women were appointed to the National Human Rights Commission, and in 2004 a women was appointed to the board of the Journalist Syndicate (Ambah 2004; Amnesty International 2004). The kingdom has also appointed some women to the 120-member appointed advisory council. The Minister of Interior later clarified that women would not be participating in the country's first municipal elections in 40 years, whether as voters or candidates (CNN 2004), even though Saudi Arabia's election law does not prevent women from voting or standing for election. Elections to fill half of the 178 municipal council seats – half of the seats are filled by appointment – were held at the beginning of 2005 (Abou-Alsamh 2004). Although they do not participate in the elections, Saudi women remain optimistic that they will enter municipal councils through appointment (Abou-Alsamh 2004).

In the United Arab Emirates, the Federal National Union – an advisory body – is composed of 40 members. There are no women members, although there are promises from the government to this effect.

In the Gulf States, the human rights development process has started out in reverse. The countries quickly accumulated wealth through petroleum revenues and could have decided to skip the human rights development stage, so to speak. This has not been the case, however, and the Gulf region is actively involved in improving the respective countries by engaging all segments of civil society. More and more NGOs are being established within the Gulf region. Bahrain is, however, the only Gulf State with a substantive human rights movement, which is starting to take on a political dimension.

In general, the ruling regimes of the respective Gulf countries are trying to build modern state infrastructures and institutions in all respects. The quality of education, educational budget and training in the Gulf, surpasses other Arab States and is on a par with that found in the US and Europe. Both girls and boys receive equal education despite the sex segregation in schools. In Oman, there is even a quota for women wishing to enter the engineering colleges to be involved in fields in which they are under-represented.

Change can also be seen in the political and economic realms. Until recently, everything in Gulf nations was by appointment and a result of nepotism. Today, advisory councils have been established which are symbolic of political development. With respect to economics, all Gulf States have a commercial chamber with elected members. The electoral process that started in the commercial chambers may spread to broader political life. However, women's participation in governing bodies is extremely restricted in the Gulf States.

Obstacles facing Arab women

The impediments to women's political participation are significant, particularly for Arab women. The dire economic situation in the majority of Arab countries (except the Gulf States) results in many different daily problems. Important factors such as the role of the tribe and the cultural stereotypes will be highlighted here.

The role of the tribe

While many experts on the Arab world highlight religion as the most important ideology affecting the formation of culture, an equally, if not more important factor often ignored is the role of the tribe. In Arab societies, such as in Jordan, Upper Egypt, Somalia, Sudan, Djibouti, Yemen, the Gulf, the Arab Maghrib, and others, where the bond of tribal allegiance is strong, Islam is used to further tribal dogma rather than the other way around. Tribal bonds take precedence over all other loyalties (Charrad 2001).

The power of tribal affiliations can be traced to early Islamic times and was only rattled when the West invaded Arab land and installed foreign systems of governance and administration. However, the tribes remained resilient and learned to adapt to the changing political environment (Fandy 1994: 1–4), as was seen by the examples of Somalia and Jordan. One of the main differences between the role of the tribe in the three Sub-Saharan African States of Sudan, Somalia, and Djibouti and the rest of the Arab world is that in the former, tribal rivalry has literally ripped these nations apart. Arab people usually look to their MPs for help, focusing their attention on someone they can trust – someone with contacts, power and authority to solve problems and provide services. While it is acceptable for women to ask men for assistance, it is unconventional for the community to ask women.

The role of cultural stereotypes

According to cultural stereotypes, women are seen as pure, saintly, feeble-minded, irrational and just simply weak. The Arab women's movement is currently working to change these cultural biases. Studies presented by Arab women at the Beijing Conference focused on two types of empowerment – to empower women MPs and to change community attitudes towards the capabilities of women. Those women who do persevere inside the vestibules of the world's parliaments are seen as having shed their femininity and mutated into some kind of she-man.

Women politicians are often criticized for being 'ineffective'. These women are seen as not on a par with their male colleagues simply because they are women, regardless of the fact that these women might be brilliant orators, highly educated, and charismatic. Wherever there are women, society is staring, waiting for them to falter, and ready to judge.

Because women's issues are viewed as soft topics for discussion, women parliamentarians who use their position to advocate gender rights are sometimes putting their political career on the line. In Egypt, most women MPs went to the extreme to demonstrate that they were objective when it came to gender issues by arguing against women's rights. MP Dr Fawziya Abdul-Sattar was elected outside of the quota system, and nevertheless was one of the strongest voices against Egypt's Nationality Law to transfer the woman's nationality to her children. In general, it is important to realize that many effective and active women politicians stay out of parliament because they refuse to be puppets of a 'joker' party.

The method of entering parliament through the quota only buttresses the notion that women are not real parliamentarians. Rather they are viewed as second-rate politicians, who are clients of the State patron that installed them into office. This was most clearly demonstrated in Egypt. Morocco is not expected to suffer the same fate, since the multi-party representation of women parliamentarians supports their respective parties' ideology. Even those who do not feel compelled to honour this client-patron relationship choose to toe the government line, because they either have no constituency or political base (International IDEA 2003: 67).

The quota discourse in the Arab nation

According to Azza Karam, there are two related effects of globalization. The first is when foreign concepts and values are integrated into domestic culture. The second is when a society fears that its culture will be absorbed into the hegemonic culture and lose its identity. It is here that a society becomes defensive in the perceived face of extinction and resorts to the most extreme ideologies of its history in order to stress its originality (Karam 1999: 6–7). This fear of losing cultural identity is one of the main reasons why resistance to gender quotas and women in politics, generally, is prevalent in Arab political culture.

Proponents of the quota system make the following arguments: (1) Quotas will give women the opportunity to be represented in parliament and give them a say in the decision-making process. (2) Politics will make women more confident and build their character. (3) Women are half of the society, and it is only fair that they occupy half of the parliamentary seats since only women can truly understand and advocate on behalf of other women. (4) Quotas are mere examples of the expanding ideas of equality and proportional representation needed to reach an optimal democratic political system. (5) Jumpstarting the integration of women into politically prominent positions will help change the cultural constraints which have thus far prevented women from accessing the political realm. (6) Women parliamentarians will not alienate male constituents since historically men have represented the male perspective and adequately continue to do so. Also many issues are universal human concerns and therefore gender neutral, and therefore either gender can advocate the issue. (7) Quotas are a provisional measure to ensure equity since women have a history of discrimination. Quotas therefore constitute an indispensable method of positive/affirmative action. (8) The visibility of women in parliament can serve as a role model for other women and help change the patriarchal constructions of women. (9) Early Islamic history acknowledges the politically active roles women played, thereby proving to conservative Islamic parties that women are politically competent. (10) The argument that the quota will result in many unqualified women getting elected is not convincing because under free elections, legislative halls are crowded with many unqualified men who have not made positive contributions to epidemics like war, starvation, and disease. Some might even say that these 'freely elected' men have instigated and aggravated already intense situations. (11) Women will bring forward women's issues and concerns, which they alone have firsthand knowledge of and experience with.

Opponents argue: (1) One third of all Arab women are illiterate and therefore do not have the capability to discuss complex issues such as state policy and budgets. In essence, uneducated women will be elected in a simple bid to meet the quota. (2) Women in the Arab world have limited resources. Both Arab women who work inside and outside of the home usually depend on their husbands for monetary support, since it is the man who controls the household finances. (3) The fact that Arab women are entrusted with all the child-rearing duties brings up the question of who is going to raise the children. A mother who has no time for her children serves as an example of a society falling apart. (4) Broad democratic reform is under discussion throughout the Arab world, and women should not be singled out for differential treatment. (5) Arab culture is not currently ready to accept politically active women. Assertive women are looked upon as abnormal, not as potential decision makers. (6) Arab women are without a strong political history, and parliamentarians need a strong political record to stand behind to give them credibility. (7) Singling out women for special treatment will be held unconstitutional since the constitutions of Arab countries assert the equality of their citizens under the law. (8) Arab governments use the quota to gain female puppet parliamentarians who will be politically loyal to them. (9) Conservative Islamic groups, which have a strong presence in the parliaments of the Arab world, will refuse to accept women in decision-making positions. (10) It is undemocratic because one should not forcibly install women into government via quotas, without which they might have not been elected. Finally, (11) quotas may serve as a glass ceiling for women rather than as a steppingstone.

As the long list of arguments from opponents shows, the resistance to quotas comes from traditional forces, using what in the introduction was called the '*politics-is-a-men's-business discourse*' as well as from circles who are positive towards the inclusion of women, but sceptical as to the use of quotas in contemporary Arab society.

Conclusion

The various forms of the gender quota in Morocco, Tunisia, Algeria, Jordan, Sudan, Somalia and Djibouti have set a precedent for the rest of the Arab world. In the legislative halls of Yemen and Palestine, designing a quota is being discussed. Nevertheless, Arab women have a long road to travel before establishing any significant presence in the legislature. Women continue to face many hurdles to parliamentary integration.

Stepwise integration

The adoption of the quota in the Arab world cannot be an overnight phenomenon. Women cannot spontaneously appear in the corridors of parliament without: (1) getting society accustomed to seeing women in decision-making roles; and (2) building a women's record of public participation. For example, women need to make a sizeable showing in labour unions, syndicates, the judiciary, university politics, and other decision-making aspects of life. Early exposure to the political world is perhaps the single most valuable tutorial. This can be achieved by a form of state-sponsored positive/affirmative action plan in all areas where women are underrepresented. The Egypt experience, see later, highlights the necessity of empowering women to enter the political world. Women can be empowered by networks with activists, parliamentarians, academics and others across the world to discuss not just quota initiatives, but all issues of special concern to women. Building a network was one of the tools used in Morocco to lobby for reserved seats for women.

Implementation of quotas in Arab countries, which only recently permitted women into the political process, is best carried out as part of broad political and economic reform plans (International IDEA 2003: 69). Currently Arab countries from Morocco to Egypt, and from Jordan to the Gulf, are discussing major state reform initiatives. Voices in the Arab women's movement are getting louder. In countries without measures, women are pushing for gender quotas. In countries with gender quotas, activists are calling for a more significant percentage.

Empowerment of weak groups is a long process, which needs time, a strong strategy, and political will. Currently we have the political will, which may help quota adoption, but we still must build strong alliances using various measures. From the experience of Arab countries, gender quotas as a measure of positive/affirmative action will be more effective when gender quotas: (1) are embedded in national law and political party regulations; (2) empower women politicians by seeing other women permeating other decision-making arenas; and (3) raise community awareness about gender while simultaneously implementing quotas to boost the visibility of women in the political fora, which may even change stereotypes about women.

An example for good and bad: the Egyptian experience

Although Egypt's trial with a gender quota was short-lived, it can serve as an example for other Arab States who are thinking of implementing measures to promote women's participation in the political world. Before exploring the specifics of the Egyptian case, three general points of reference need to be established. First, it is not enough that women are elected or appointed to office; they must be qualified and well prepared. Second, the use of quota itself as a measure to empower women is very effective, but needs to exist in a supportive atmosphere of societal engagement. Third, the gains of quota implementation will depend on a combination of political and cultural factors. These three principles will be examined in turn below.

When any state sets out to apply a new governmental measure, appropriate planning is required. Egypt's quota implementation was rushed without adequate planning or preparation of the political theatre. Women needed the right tools and training in how to be active MPs.

During the five years of Egypt's quota implementation, which lasted through 1984, there were 36 women MPs – 30 via the reserved seat system and six elected outside of the quota system. In five years, these 36 women managed to present and discuss only five issues. Three years prior to the quota in 1976, six women MPs presented and discussed eight issues before parliament. Therefore, the participation of Egyptian women MPs elected outside of the quota was greater than the participation of women elected with the assistance of the quota. This provided fuel for the anti-quota tide, which made statements to the effect that Egypt did not need a lot of 'dresses', but rather people to discuss vital issues (PARC 2000: 209).

Second, there was no support from effective and influential institutions like the media, which was there merely to evaluate and judge women MPs daily. Because of the media's influence, the masses were not supportive. Only members of the informed public and intelligentsia lent their support to women MPs.

Prior to implementing the quota, the government did not campaign, lobby, or consult any influential groups. Because these groups felt ignored, they were antagonistic to the government's quota policy.

The Egyptian government learned a lot from its previous experience because in the coming years it launched broad campaigns to gain the support of influential institutions prior to implementing a new policy. This was the case with the government's implementation of *Kanun al Khola* (a law which gives women the right to seek divorce) and prohibition of female genital mutilation (FGM). With respect to both these laws, the government learned to speak with religious authorities and even went to *Al-Azhar* to ask for religious re-interpretation.

Egypt was the first Arab country to introduce quotas for women. However, this happened in a period of political and social changes, and the conclusion is that Egyptian society, and that includes the women's movement, was not well prepared to accept gender quotas, especially not when introduced by higher authorities. Nevertheless, the experience bore fruit and became a springboard for a dialogue about women's parliamentary participation (Abou-Zeid: 2003).

Arguments raised by opponents of gender quotas stress that quotas contribute to the stigmatization of women. This argument, while it may be true, is disingenuous. First, women, like all disempowered and historically discriminated categories face some kind of stigmatization. Therefore, the discourse surrounding gender quotas for women politicians should focus on quotas as one tool to remove this stigmatization. The stigmatization comes from past discrimination against women, not from reform efforts aimed at addressing and repairing the damage done by discrimination.

What is needed to make quotas work?

Quotas can help change the patriarchal attitudes that prejudice women politicians and women generally, but only if certain conditions are met. First, women must establish a prior record of visibility in the public sphere throughout their lifecycle starting from primary school. Women cannot simply appear unexpectedly into the public realm. They need to pre-exist in substantial numbers in all of life's decision-making bodies. Second, women must be supported by influential and effective institutions such as the media, the educational system, religious authorities, and prominent political parties. Third, women must be present in the body of political parties to gain experience, confidence, and the skills necessary to be effective parliamentarians. Most importantly women need to be active in the formation and/or change of party policies. Fourth, religious institutions must be fairer to women both in practice and ideology. Religious establishments need to re-examine the ethics that govern them. Fifth, women MPs need to be strategically prepared and serve as mentors for one another. Sixth, quotas cannot be introduced roughly without preparing society. Quota implementation should be consistent, yet gradual. Any spontaneous initiation will be met with antagonistic resistance. Seventh, cultural norms need to develop in parallel with law, policies, and systems in order to be more inclusive of women. Eighth, there should be a quota in the executive body of political parties, something that was effective in the German experience. Ninth, Arab women need to receive essential empowerment through education, employment, training and be legally supported at many levels.

Despite the long hard road that lies ahead of women in their struggle to become participants in the male-dominated political world, progress is being made. Gender quotas for women jumpstart women's integration in the political process by making them visible in the political arena. Without quotas, women may not have even obtained their now-limited political voice. Quotas may also assist more traditional sectors of Arab society see women in a new light – as strong, assertive decision makers with skills, knowledge and experiences that are specific to their gender and may contribute to the development of a better tomorrow, not just for women but for their respective communities as a whole.

Note

1 Many thanks to Amany Khalel and Dina Obied for their assistance with this chapter.

Bibliography

Abdul Aziz, M. (2004) 'Morocco Experience', in *Al-Mara al-Maghribiya wa al-Barlaman*, Cairo: Alliance for Arab Women.

Abou-Alsamh, R. (2004) 'Saudi women cast a long shadow', *Al Ahram Weekly*, 2–8 December, 719. Online. Available at: http://weekly.ahram.org.eg/2004/719/re12.htm (accessed 13 February 2005).

Abou-Zeid, G. (2002) 'In Search of Political Power-Women in Parliament in Egypt, Jordan and Lebanon', in A. Karam (ed.) *Women in Parliament: Beyond Numbers*, Stockholm: International IDEA.

—— 'Introducing Quotes in Africa: Discourse in Egypt', paper presented at The Implementation of Quotas: African Experiences, Pretoria, November 2003.

Abu-Ruman, H. 'Gender Quota in Jordan', paper presented at the Enhancing Women's Political Participation through Special Measures in the Arab

Region Conference, UNDP/International IDEA Conference, Cairo, December 2004.

Aden Dire, N. (2000) 'A Lame Duck Parliament', *Somalia Watch*. Online. Available at: http://www.somaliawatch.org/archivejuly/000817201.htm (accessed February 13, 2005).

Al-Sharbini, M. 'Women's Political Participation: Between Equality and Equal Opportunity', paper presented at Enhancing Women's Political Participation through Special Measures in the Arab Region Conference, UNDP/International IDEA Conference, Cairo, December 2004.

Ambah, F.S. (2004) 'A Women Runs for Office in Saudi Arabia', *The Christian Science Monitor*, 16 September. Online. Available at: http://www.csmonitor.com/2004/0916/pols04-wome.html (accessed 13 February 2005).

Amnesty International (2004) 'Saudi Arabia: Women's Exclusion from Elections Undermines Progress', 17 November. Online. Available at: http://news.amnesty.org/index/ENGMDE230/52004 (accessed 13 February 2005).

Andersson, A.C. (2004) 'Report: The Palestinian Elections-A Real Chance of Involving Palestinian Women in Politics?', Jerusalem: The Ecumenical Accompaniment Programme in Palestine and Israel (EAPPI). Online. Available at: http://www.eappi.org/eappi.nsf/index/rep-aa-04121703.html (accessed 13 February 2005).

Bilmodin, F. 'Moroccan Women MPs', paper presented at joint Arab Women's Alliance and the European Commission Conference, Cairo, January 2004.

Bouchkouj, N. Secretary General of the Arab Parliamentary Union (interview), Cairo, Egypt (6 December 2004).

Center for Legislative Development (2004). Online. Available at: http://www.cld.org (accessed 13 February 2005).

Charrad, M.M. (2001) *States and Women's Rights: The Making of Postcolonial Tunisia, Algeria, and Morocco*, Berkeley: University of California Press.

CNN.COM (2004) 'Saudi Women Denied Vote, Candidacy'. Online. Available at: http://www.cnn.com/ (accessed 11 October 2004).

Dunne, S. (2003) 'Hashemite Kingdom of Jordan: Electoral Report Needs Assessment Mission'.

El Baz, S. (2003) 'Globalization, Gender, and Equality in the Arab World', in *Nur for Studies and Research*, Cairo: Women and Globalization.

El Sawy, Nada (2004) 'Gulf Women Pushing Ahead on Education, Vote', *Women's eNews*, 13 June, Online. Available at: http://www.womenenews.org/article.cfm/dyn/aid/1869/context/archive (accessed February 8, 2005)

Electionworld, Online. Available at: http://www.electionworld.com/

Fandy, M. (1994) 'Tribe vs. Islam: The Post-colonial Arab State and the Democratic Imperative', *Middle East Policy Council Journal*, 3, 48: 8.

Hall, E.C. 'Quotas and Transnational Networks Answering the Challenge of Moroccan Women's Access to Political Space', paper presented at the 960 Political Science Seminar, 2003.

Hawthorne, A. (2002) 'Do Elections in the Arab World Matter?', Elections Today Summer/Fall, Online. Avaliable at: http://216.239.59.104/search?q=cache:45kb5Xn49kAJ:www.ciaonet.org/olj/et/et_sumfal02/et_sumfal02b.pdf+competitive+party+elections+in+Arab+countries&hl=en (accessed February 8, 2005).

Inter-Parliamentary Union (IPU) Online. Available at: http://www.ipu.org

International IDEA (2003) *The Implementation of Quotas: Asian Experiences*, Quota Workshop Report Series no. 1, Stockholm: International IDEA.

Isa, F. (2001) 'Al-Mashakalat al-Lati Tawajaha al-Mara al-Sudaniya fi al-Masharaka al-Siyasia', in H. Abdul Rahman (ed.) *Political Participation of Women in North Africa*, Cairo: Center of Future African Studies, p. 6.

Joseph, S. (2001) 'Women and Politics in the Middle East', in S. Joseph and S. Slymovics (eds) *Women and Power in the Middle East*, Philadelphia: University of Pennsylvania Press, pp. 34–40.

Karam, A. (1999) 'Strengthening the Role of Women Parliamentarians in the Arab Region: Challenges and Options', New York: UNDP-POGAR.

Krook, M.L. 'Reforming Representation: The Diffusion of Candidate Gender Quotas Worldwide', paper presented at the International Studies Association Annual International Convention, Montreal, March 2004.

Kuku, N. Research Coordinator of the Gender Center for Research and Training in Khartoum, Sudan, (interview) Cairo, Egypt (5 December 2004).

Ottaway, M. (2004) 'Women's Rights and Democracy in the Arab World', Carnegie Papers 42, Washington DC: Carnegie Endowment for International Peace, Online Available at: http://www.ceip.org/files/pdf/CarnegiePaper42.pdf (accessed February 8, 2005).

Pelham, N. (2002) 'Arab Women Demand Quotas', *The Christian Science Monitor*, 6 November. Online. Available at: http://www.csmonitor.com/2002/1106/p07s01-wome.html (accessed 13 February 2005).

Public Administration Research & Consultation Center (PARC) (2000) *Tamthel al-Mara fi al-Majalis al-Mantakhaba*, Cairo: PARC.

United Nations Development Programme (UNDP) (2004) 'Syria: Elections', Programme on Governance in the Arab Region. Online. Available at: http://www.pogar.org/countries/syria/elections.html (accessed 13 October 2004).

United Nations (UN) (1979) 'Convention on the Elimination of All Forms of Discrimination Against Women', *UN Treaty Series*, 1249: 13.

8 Western Europe, North America, Australia and New Zealand

Gender quotas in the context of citizenship models

Mona Lena Krook, Joni Lovenduski and Judith Squires

Gender quotas remain controversial. The specific controversies surrounding gender quotas vary across countries and regions. The type of controversy influences not only the likelihood of gender quotas being adopted, but also the form that these quotas take and the effectiveness of their implementation. The region discussed in this chapter comprises 17 countries – Australia, Austria, Belgium, Canada, France, Germany, Greece, Ireland, Italy, Luxembourg, New Zealand, the Netherlands, Portugal, Spain, Switzerland, the United Kingdom, and the United States – that are part of what is sometimes, paradoxically, termed the 'West'.[1] Unlike the other regions discussed in this book, it is a political rather than a geographical region: although located on three different continents, the countries share important commonalities as stable representative democracies in which the socio-economic position of women is relatively high. Democratic institutions, nonetheless, vary widely across these countries and include majoritarian and proportional electoral systems, conflict- and consensus-based party systems, and parliamentary and presidential governments, organized according to unitary and federal principles. Further, despite important gains in women's social and economic status in recent years, individual countries differ dramatically with regard to the percentage of women in parliament, ranging from 11.5 per cent in Italy to 36.7 per cent in the Netherlands.

Increasingly aware of gender imbalances in political representation, political parties and national legislatures across the region have taken steps over the last 20 years to promote women's access to political office through party quotas, legal quotas, and 'soft' quotas. These policies thus have a much longer history than similar policies in other regions of the world, with many being adopted 10 or 15 years prior to the United Nations Fourth World Conference on Women. As such, international and transnational influences have played a much smaller role than in other areas of the world, although social democratic parties have engaged in some sharing of strategies across national borders (Short 1996; Wisler 1999). Consequently, the region has only two countries with legal quotas –

Table 8.1 Women's representation in single or lower House of Parliament, 1984–2004 (%).

Country	1984	1994	2004	Electoral system
Australia	5.4	10.2	25.3	AV
Austria	9.3	21.3	33.3	List PR
Belgium	5.6	9.4	35.3	List PR
Canada	9.6	18.0	20.6	FPP
France	5.3	6.1	12.3	Two Rounds
Germany	9.8	26.3	32.2	MMP
Greece	n/a	n/a	14.0	List PR
Ireland	8.0	12.0	13.0	STV
Italy	7.9	15.1	11.2	MMP
Luxembourg	n/a	n/a	17.0	List PR
Netherlands	14.0	20.0	37.0	List PR
New Zealand[a]	13.0	21.0	28.0	MMP
Portugal	7.2	13.9	19.1	List PR
Spain	6.3	15.7	36.0	List PR
Switzerland	11.0[b]	21.5[c]	23.0	List PR
United Kingdom	3.5	9.2	17.9	FPP
United States	5.0	11.0	14.0	FPP

Source: Centre for Advancement of Women in Politics (2004), Library of Parliament (2004), Ministry of Social Development (2004), Parliament of Australia (2004), Lovenduski (2005), official statistics from Swiss Parliament.

Notes
a Prior to the 1996 elections, the electoral system in New Zealand was first-past-the-post plurality.
b This figure is from 1983.
c This figure is from 1995.
Key electoral systems: *Plurality-Majority:* FPP = First-Past-the-Post, Two-Rounds System, Alternative Vote. *Proportional Representation:* List PR, STV = Single Transferable Vote. *Mixed:* MMP = Mixed Member Proportional.

a strategy that became popular only in the 1990s and spread primarily through international contacts – and is instead characterized by the widespread use of party and soft quotas. In all countries, these policies originated with women in civil society and inside the political parties, who presented gender quotas as a way to win support among female voters. Despite their relatively long history, as well as their roots in civil society, these measures nonetheless remain controversial as a strategy across most of the region.

In this chapter, we survey the adoption and implementation of party quotas, legal quotas, and soft quotas in the 'West'. Following the definitions outlined in Chapter 1, we employ the term 'party quota' to refer to policies adopted by individual political parties and the term 'legal quota' to refer to laws passed by national legislatures to regulate the selection of female candidates. In a new contribution, we introduce the term 'soft quota' to capture a third ambiguous but pervasive category of measures that seek to increase women's representation, either indirectly through

internal party quotas or more directly through informal targets and recommendations. Comparing quota campaigns around the region, we discover striking differences with regard to the content of quota debates, the
types of policies adopted, and the broader impact of quotas on women's
parliamentary representation. These variations, we argue, stem from distinct models of political citizenship that frame gender quotas as means to
fulfil or undermine existing beliefs about equality, representation, and
gender. To explore these dynamics, we examine seven cases of quota
reform that we select according to three criteria: citizenship model, quota
type and geographical region. We conclude that models of political citizenship play a crucial role in determining the shape, and ultimately the
success, of gender quota campaigns.

Framing quota debates

Ideas about the nature of citizenship pervade and frame quota debates at
both the party and the national levels. In contrast to scholars who have
developed numerous citizenship typologies based on social and economic
factors (Schmitter 1979; Esping-Andersen 1990), we identify three broad
models of *political citizenship* – liberal, republican, and consociational/
corporatist – that, we assert, influence attitudes and approaches towards
gender quotas. *Liberal citizenship models* are characterized by a philosophical commitment to individualism and often have majoritarian electoral
systems that yield two-party systems, one-party cabinets, and executive
dominance (Lijphart 2002). *Republican citizenship models* embody a philosophical commitment to universalism and typically involve a politically
centralized form of democracy in which popular sovereignty is expressed
at the level of the nation (Jennings 2000). Finally, while often treated as
distinct,[2] *consociational and corporatist citizenship models* share a philosophical
commitment to social partnership and consensus and thus are generally
governed by proportional representation (Lijphart 2002).

These three models, we argue, generate distinct political logics that
influence the prospects and outcomes of quota campaigns. Building on
research which finds that quota campaigns are successful to the extent
that quotas mesh with pre-existing political dynamics (Sgier 2003), we theorize that different models of political citizenship create distinct
opportunities and constraints in efforts to institute gender quotas: quota
debates that take place within liberal models will focus on definitions of
equality, those within republican models will centre on the nature of political representation, and those within consociational/corporatist models
will raise questions about gender as a political identity. These varied focal
points of contention, in turn, appear to be related to the types of gender
quotas that are eventually pursued: liberal polities prefer soft quotas but
sometimes adopt party quotas, republican polities pass legal quotas, and
consociational and corporatist polities accept party quotas and sometimes

turn to legal quotas. To specify the role of citizenship models in gender quota campaigns, we briefly outline the various conceptions of equality, representation, and gender inherent in the three models to pinpoint their part in shaping views on the legitimacy of special measures to increase women's access to political office.

Equality

Political parties and national political cultures embrace various notions of equality, with the main point of controversy being whether the goal of public policy is equality of opportunity or equality of results. Because gender quotas seek to promote equal results, this distinction has crucial implications for quota campaigns. Generally speaking, the liberal citizenship model favours equal opportunities, attributes responsibility for unequal outcomes to individuals themselves, and views prospects for change in terms of individual initiative. In contrast, the consociational and corporatist models seek to foster equal results, place the onus for unequal outcomes on broader social structures, and understand the potential for change in terms of collective responsibility. The republican model occupies a space in between these two extremes: it promotes equal opportunities but enjoins citizens to transcend their individual identities to assume the position of the universal citizen. These patterns suggest that quota policies are more congruent with consociational and corporatist models, or more specifically, that these models are the least likely to challenge quotas on the grounds that these violate existing norms of equality. Political parties, however, sometimes develop distinct submodels of citizenship in line with certain elements of their party ideologies: social democratic parties favour equal results even in liberal and republican polities, while liberal parties support equal opportunities even in consociational and corporatist polities (Inhetveen 1999; Davidson-Schmich 2002).

Political representation

Democratic systems reflect and embody various concepts of political representation, with the basic divide distinguishing between a principal-agent notion of representation, when one person acts on behalf of another in that person's interests, and descriptive representation, when one person acts on behalf of another by reflecting their physical, social or other ascribed characteristics. Gender quotas do not necessarily promote one or the other concept of representation, but these notions strongly shape the kinds of normative arguments made for and against quotas. The liberal model stresses principal-agent representation and views quotas simply as a means to provide fair access for qualified individuals. The consociational and corporatist models, in contrast, emphasize descriptive representation and see quotas as a means to acknowledge and promote group-based identities and interests. The republican model again falls between these two poles: it envisions principal-agent representation that reflects the qualities and interests of the universal citizen and accepts quotas only if they further this universal dimension. These dynamics reveal that quota policies are most consistent with consociational and corporatist models, as these models are the least likely to challenge quotas on the grounds that these violate the principal-agent notion of political representation.

Gender

State and party policies of all types, finally, incorporate and reflect different ideas about gender, with the central issue of contention concerning the unity of the category 'women', and as a subset of this question, the relationship between equality for women and for members of other marginalized groups. Gender quotas necessarily employ the category of 'women' as a single entity, overlooking the fact that women as a group are invariably stratified by a host of other identities. The liberal model simply brackets the issue of gender by focusing on individuals rather than groups. The consociational and corporatist models, in contrast, often engage in complex negotiations of claims made by women and by minority groups. Efforts to institute gender quotas sometimes meld, but frequently clash with attempts to promote equality for other marginalized groups (Jenkins 1999; Meier 2000). The republican model, similar to the liberal model, recognizes only the universal citizen, separate from and above all concrete identities. These patterns indicate, once again, that consociational and corporatist models provide the best match for gender quota policies. Nonetheless, competing demands from other groups may play a crucial role in thwarting claims for women as a group, if opponents raise doubts about gender as a category on a par with other identities.

Political citizenship and gender quotas

Integrating these theoretical elements, we anticipate that countries with similar models of political citizenship will experience similar quota debates, will adopt similar types of quota policies, and will achieve similar outcomes in terms of the percentage of women elected to parliament. A quick survey shows that these expectations are largely confirmed across the countries in our sample. Those with consociational and corporatist models have all adopted party quotas, while two have also pursued legal quotas, with the result that women's representation in these countries tends to be relatively high. In contrast, those characterized by liberal models of citizenship have all opted for soft quotas, while two have also implemented party quotas, leading to a mixed record of low to medium levels of female representation. The one country with a republican model, finally, has tried party and legal quotas with little success, with one of the lowest proportions of women in the entire region.

To explore the complex interplay of these ideas in the context of specific cases, we now examine more closely seven instances of quota reform, selecting countries according to three criteria: citizenship model, quota type, and geographical region. Consequently, we analyze campaigns for party quotas in Germany, the United Kingdom, and Australia, which span corporatist and liberal citizenship models and medium and high levels of representation; legal quotas in Belgium and France, which cover consociational and republican citizenship models and low and high levels of representation; and soft quotas in New Zealand and the United States, which incorporate liberal citizenship models and low and high levels of representation. To facilitate comparison across the seven countries, we consider political contexts, policy details, decision-making procedures, processes of implementation, and broader measures of impact that shape the origins and outcomes of gender quota policies.

Table 8.2 Models of citizenship, quota types, and quota outcomes (lower house)

Country	Citizenship model	Quota Type	Women in parliament (year of election)[a]
Austria	Corporatist	Party	33.3 (2002)
Belgium	Consociational	Legal and Party	35.3 (2003)
Germany	Corporatist	Party	32.2 (2002)
Greece	Corporatist	Party	14.0 (2004)
Italy	Corporatist	Party (ex-legal)	11.2 (2001)
Luxembourg[b]	Corporatist	Party	17.0 (2003)
Netherlands	Consociational	Party	36.7 (2003)
Portugal	Corporatist	Party	19.1 (2003)
Spain	Corporatist	Party	36.0 (2004)
Switzerland	Consociational	Party	23.0 (2003)
Australia	Liberal	Party and Soft	25.3 (2001)
Canada	Liberal	Soft	21.1 (2000)
Ireland	Liberal	Party	13.3 (2002)
New Zealand	Liberal	Soft	29.0 (2002)
United Kingdom	Liberal	Party and Soft	17.9 (2001)
United States	Liberal	Soft	14.0 (2003)
France	Republican	Party and Legal	12.3 (2002)

Source: UNDP (2003), Lovenduski *et al.* (2005).

Note

a UK, 2005 election: 19.7 per cent women; Germany, 2005 election: 31.8 per cent women.

b The only party to have a quota in Luxembourg is the small Green Party.

Countries with party quotas

Party quotas are the most common type of formal quotas in the 'West', as they are found in 14 of the 17 countries in this region and span all three citizenship models. Examining the cases of Germany, the United Kingdom, and Australia in greater detail, we find that debates in Germany focus on gender as a political identity, while those in the UK and Australia revolve around competing definitions of equality. Across all three cases, we discover that quota proposals originate with women's groups inside the political parties, but that their efforts generally culminate in quota adoption only when elites perceive these policies as an effective way to compete favourably with other parties for the support of female voters (cf. Matland and Studlar 1996), either because they are a new party seeking to establish an initial basis of support or an existing party aiming to overcome a string of electoral losses. We also find that in all three cases left-wing parties are the first to pursue gender quotas, but that despite an emphasis on electoral benefits, quotas generally remain controversial due to unresolved debates over the relevance of gender and the meaning of equality.

Germany

Germany has a mixed proportional and majority electoral system. Until the 1990s political scientists characterized the West German political competition between the left wing Social Democratic Party (SPD) the right wing Christian Democratic Union (CDU) – Christian Social Union electoral alliance and the centre Free Democrat Party as a two and one-half party system. With the rise of the greens in the 1980s the characterization became a two and two-half party system, signifying the presence of third parties and the continuing dominance of the traditional left and right. After reunification in 1990 six parties took most of the votes as the traditional parties were joined by the Party of Democratic Socialism (PDS). In light of the electoral system, which combines first-past-the-post plurality and list proportional representation, party quotas have applied only in list-based elections. The first quotas for electoral lists were applied in 1983, when the Green Party adopted a 50 per cent quota and required that all lists alternate between women and men (Meyer 2003). Seeking to avert an erosion in electoral support, the SPD quickly responded by adopting its own 25 per cent quota policy for party lists in 1990 – subsequently raised to 33 per cent in 1994 and 40 per cent in 1998 – which led its main rival, the CDU, to adopt its own 33 per cent soft quota, or *quorum*,[3] for party lists in 1996. In the wake of reunification, the PDS also adopted a 50 per cent quota, although this decision was embedded within a separate set of political dynamics and thus took place largely in isolation from developments in the former West Germany.

In line with its corporatist model of citizenship, debates over quotas in

Germany have revolved primarily around 'gender' as criteria for candidate selection. Initially, women inside the parties did not support gender quotas: women in the SPD had voted against instituting quotas for women when the issue was first raised in the 1970s, while women in the CDU expressed ambivalence when party leader Helmut Kohl placed quotas on the party agenda in the 1990s (Meyer 2003). Although they initially believed that quotas were unnecessary or simply demeaning to qualified women who wished to pursue political office, they soon linked the recognition of 'gender' to electoral success, pointing to the example of their rivals (the Greens for the SPD and the SPD for the CDU) to press for the adoption of special measures to promote women's political representation. While opponents voiced concerns that quotas would undermine 'merit' as a key consideration in candidate selection, advocates in the former West Germany justified quotas on the grounds that women were equal citizens whose increased participation would enhance the overall 'quality' of politics (Inhetveen 1999; Kamenitsa and Geissel 2005), while those in the former East Germany noted the high price of reunification and its especially strong impact on women (Brzinski 2003). These arguments, however, generally made little progress until women's groups succeeded in convincing influential male allies to throw their support behind gender quotas, most often by casting women's representation as an issue that would enable their parties to win crucial votes among women.

As a result of these strategies, all but two parties – the Christian Social Union (CSU) and the Free Democratic Party (FDP) – apply gender quotas in their candidate selection procedures. Compliance with these regulations, nonetheless, varies by seat and by party, mainly because national parties establish recruitment policies but regional parties are responsible for implementing them. Among seats decided by proportional lists, where quota policies govern the selection of candidates, most parties approximate their quota goals, nominating between 34 per cent and 49 per cent women. In constituency elections, however, parties generally do not match their quotas for list elections, nominating between 21 per cent and 37 per cent women (McKay 2003). The lack of quotas for constituency seats, therefore, appears to contribute to a much lower proportion of women selected to contest these particular elections. All the same, the presence of quotas for party lists, combined with the relative balance between parties with and without quotas, resulted in the election of 32.8 per cent women in 2002 (Table 8.2).

In light of their limited scope, party quotas have thus been incredibly successful in increasing the number of women elected to the lower house of parliament. Nonetheless, gender quotas still generate a great deal of resistance across all political parties in Germany. On the one hand, opponents protest quota policies during each new election cycle, forcing advocates continually to justify and defend quotas for women. On the other hand, women who benefit from these policies report being stigmatized by their male colleagues, both as women and as quota beneficiaries. Consonant with the German corporatist model of citizenship, therefore, quota debates have focused mainly on the question of gender as a criteria for candidate selection. At the same time, the notion of group representation implicit in this model explains why quotas have diffused rapidly across the political spectrum, while enduring controversies over the issue of equality – a question that divides political parties – suggest why proponents have focused on party and soft quotas, rather than legal quotas.

United Kingdom

The United Kingdom has a first-past-the-post (FPP) electoral system and, until recently, was a two-party system dominated by the Labour and the Conservative Parties. Third parties, although normally present in the House of Commons, were not able to challenge the dominance of the two major parties. However, the seat and vote share of the centre Liberal Democrat Party increased steadily during the 1990s. Given the nature of the electoral system, party quotas have addressed not party lists but party shortlists, or the slate of possible candidates in each single-member district. The first quotas for shortlists appeared in 1981, when the Social Democratic Party (SDP) approved a resolution requiring that at least one woman be included on every candidate shortlist. It increased this commitment to at least two women on every shortlist before the 1983 elections, and when the SDP merged with the Liberal Party in 1988, the newly formed Liberal Democrats agreed to retain this shortlisting policy. Under pressure from women members who, inter alia, drew attention to its weakness among women voters, the Labour Party reacted in 1987 by mandating that in districts where a woman had been nominated, at least one woman had to be included on the shortlist for constituency selection. In 1990, the party conference agreed to a 40 per cent quota for women in all positions inside the party and a target of 50 per cent women in the party's delegation to parliament within ten years or three general elections. After the latter policy failed to have much impact on women's representation in the following elections, the party strengthened the policy in 1993 to require that all-women shortlists be used to select candidates in half of all vacant seats that the party was likely to win, including those seats where a Labour MP was retiring. In contrast, the Conservative Party did not pursue any attempts to nominate or select more female candidates during this period, although in the early 1980s, party selectors generally sought to include at least 10 per cent women on the party's list of approved candidates (Vallance 1984).

Reflecting these distinct policy approaches, debates over quotas in the UK have varied across the three political parties. Given the broader liberal model of citizenship, however, almost all of these controversies have centred around competing notions of 'equality' in candidate selection. The Liberal Democrats focused primarily on links between equality and candidate qualifications, with advocates arguing that women deserved representation and would be no worse than men as political representatives, and opponents expressing concerns about the possible stigmatization of 'quota women' and the need to preserve 'merit' as a consideration in candidate selection. Discussions inside the Labour Party were slightly more diverse, as proponents claimed alternatively that increasing the proportion of women would achieve greater equality among women and men, would have a positive impact on the policy-making process by involving greater numbers of women, or would help the party win new electoral support, particularly among female voters (Lovenduski 2005). The Conservatives, for their part, remained firmly opposed to positive action of any kind on the grounds that quotas were demeaning to women and undermined 'merit' as a central criterion of candidate selection (Squires 1996).

Lingering ambivalence over the legitimacy of gender quotas within the liberal model – manifested partly in the choice to pursue shortlist quotas in a framework of regional quotas (Short 1996; Lovenduski 2005) – also exposed these measures to legal challenge. Indeed, soon after all-women shortlists were introduced for the selection of parliamentary candidates in the Labour Party, two male members challenged the policy in an industrial tribunal, arguing that allowing only women to run as candidates in certain constituencies was a violation of the Sex Discrimination Act. The court declared all-women shortlists illegal in 1996, although some argued that this judgment was based on an erroneous interpretation of the law (Russell 2000). During debates on devolution in 1998, therefore, several members of parliament proposed reforming the Sex Discrimination Act to allow explicitly for the use of positive action in the selection of candidates for political office. Although these reforms did not pass, several political parties in Scotland and Wales adopted measures to promote women's representation in the new Scottish Parliament and National Assembly for Wales – despite the atmosphere of legal uncertainty – and adjusted these policies to the aspects of the new mixed electoral system where they anticipated gaining most of their seats. Anticipating that they would win mainly in single-member districts, the Scottish and Welsh Labour Parties decided to apply a 'twinning' strategy to ensure that equal numbers of women and men would be elected to constituency seats.[4] The second largest parties in both regions, the Scottish National Party (SNP) and Plaid Cymru, recognized that they would instead win most of their seats from party lists. Plaid Cymru thus required that the first and third positions on these lists be occupied by women, while the SNP simply encouraged local parties to place women near the top of all party lists, after a 'zipping' proposal was rejected by the party conference (Russell *et al.* 2002). These developments, and a drop in the number of women elected to the House of Commons in 2001, sparked renewed debate on the issue of positive action. They culminated in reform of the Sex Discrimination Act in 2002 to allow – but not require – parties to pursue quotas to increase women's selection as candidates for political office (Childs 2002).

These concerns and solutions regarding conflicts between quotas and equality are reflected in patterns of implementation across parties and across elections. Although all-women shortlists were declared illegal in 1996, the Labour Party did not overturn candidate selections that had already been made, and as a result, the proportion of women in parliament doubled after elections in 1997 to 18.4 per cent, due almost exclusively to the use of all-women shortlists. No parties applied quotas in the next elections in 2001 – although the Labour Party mandated gender-balanced shortlists and the Liberal Democrats required the inclusion of women on all shortlists – and women's representation dropped slightly to 17.9 per cent. In Scotland and Wales, in contrast, elections in 1999 brought 37 per cent women to the Scottish Parliament, with Labour sending 50 per cent women and the SNP 43 per cent, and 40 per cent women to the National Assembly for Wales, with Labour electing 57.1 per cent and Plaid Cymru 35.3 per cent. Elections in 2003 largely built on these gains, as women's representation increased to 39 per cent in Scotland and to 50 per cent in Wales, due again largely to the policies of the Labour and the nationalist parties (Squires 2004).

The multiple arenas and levels of debate thus complicate the story of the adoption and implementation of gender quotas in the UK. Across all parties, quotas for shortlists have proven extremely contentious, provoking a great deal of resistance and even leading to the repeal of measures aimed at promoting female candidates. Further, despite the opportunities afforded by reform of the Sex Discrimination Act, only the Labour Party re-instituted quotas for women. The Liberal Democrats rejected a proposal for all-women shortlists in favour of a target of 40 per cent female candidates in winnable districts in 2001 and dropped their previously successful policy of 'zipping' in European Parliament elections in 2002. The Conservatives, meanwhile, continued to oppose quotas in favour of a policy of persuading constituencies to select women to winnable seats. The Labour Party, however, changed course in light of the reform and decided in 2002 to apply all-women shortlists in at least half of all seats where incumbent Labour MP's were retiring, with the goal of electing at least 35 per cent women (Childs 2004). Consistent with the British liberal model of citizenship, therefore, quota debates have revolved mainly around the tension between quotas and existing norms of equality. A stronger sense of group representation and equality of results within the Labour and nationalist parties – common among many social democratic parties across Europe – accounts for why this party has been more willing than other parties to adopt quota policies. The system-level focus on principal-agent representation, equal opportunities, and candidates as individuals, nonetheless, has constrained the specific types of quotas adopted, leading parties to pursue party and soft quotas that regulate shortlist, but not candidate, selections.

Australia

Australia has an alternative-vote majority electoral system and a party system dominated by two large political groupings, the Australian Labor Party (ALP) on one side and the Liberal Party (LPA) and the National Party (NP) on the other. Despite the winner-take-all aspect of the electoral system, candidate selection does not involve shortlists but instead 'pre-selection' to single-member districts. The first quotas for pre-selection emerged in 1994, when the ALP agreed to pre-select women in 35 per cent of winnable seats at the federal and state levels by the year 2002. The roots of this policy, however, extend back as far as the 1970s, when the party began to recognize the need to promote women in politics – following a defeat in elections in 1977 – and adopted a policy in 1981 that aimed at matching the representation of women at all levels of the party to their proportion among party members, between 25 per cent and 30 per cent (Simms 1993). The two major right-wing parties dismissed the use of quotas and targets as counter-productive, but in response to the ALP policy, the LPA announced that it would nominate as many women without the need for quotas, while the leader of the NP called on local parties to pre-select more women (Whip 2003). When the ALP policy expired in 2002, the party revisited the question of women's representation and increased its goal to 40 per cent female office-holders and 40 per cent female candidates in winning seats by 2012.

Consistent with its liberal model of citizenship, debates over quotas in Australia have centred around concerns to promote fairness and equality, although discussions within and across the three parties have taken up the issue from two opposing angles. Inside the ALP, women mobilized for the 35 per cent quota by arguing that women constituted 50 per cent of the population and thus should occupy 50 per cent of all political offices, while male leaders focused on the benefits to society of drawing on the talents and resources of a wide variety of people (Van Acker 1999; Sawer 2002). Many men within the party, however, argued against this measure – as well as the earlier affirmative action policy – on the grounds that it interfered with selection on the basis of merit. Men and women inside the LPA and the NP echoed these arguments about merit, but Liberals added that quotas were unnecessary, as well as patronizing to capable women who, they claimed, would be selected anyway (Johnson 2000). Feminists within these organizations, nonetheless, continued to encourage their parties to adopt non-quota measures to facilitate women's participation (Chappell 2002).

As in Germany proposals for quotas in the ALP originated in

discussions within the party about how to regain voter support, especially in the wake of a disastrous electoral defeat in 1977 (Sawer 1994). Taking advantage of this situation, women inside the party initially focused on gaining access to positions within the party, hoping that these changes might in turn influence candidate selection outcomes. When this approach did not produce these changes, women launched a new campaign ten years later to extend affirmative action to the electoral arena. These efforts intersected with a recommendation by a parliamentary committee in 1992 that all parties examine their candidate selection procedures to identify patterns of discrimination and develop appropriate affirmative action policies (Sawer 1997). Drawing on these national debates, women lobbied various groups within the party, and between 1992 and 1994 gained the support of the trade unions, all female Labor parliamentarians, the national secretary, most state secretaries, and the prime minister (Kirner 1994). As a result of this internal pressure, the party conference agreed to a target of 35 per cent women by 2002. Eight years later, as the policy was on the verge of expiring, women pressed for an increase in the quota to 50 per cent across all areas of the party, but managed only to secure a commitment of 40 per cent by 2012 (Tuohy 2002; Whip 2003).

The outcomes of the first three elections following the adoption of the 35 per cent quota suggest that this policy has produced mixed results. Despite passage of the ALP quota in 1994, elections in 1996 witnessed a drop in the percentage of women among Labor MPs, at the same time that the overall proportion of women increased to 14.3 per cent, due to a jump in the number of LPA women elected (Sawer 1997). While many inside the LPA pointed out that this result was achieved without the use of a quota system, the ALP policy had not been passed in time to affect selections for these elections. Further, both parties had in fact nominated approximately the same number of female candidates, but more women were elected with the LPA as a result of the large swing in favour of the LPA-NP coalition. When the ALP quota policy took effect in the next elections in 1998, these patterns began to change as the percentage of women in parliament increased to 22 per cent, with the ALP electing almost twice as many women as the LPA-NP coalition. These trends continued in 2001, when women's parliamentary representation increased to 25.3 per cent: while the number of LPA-NP women elected remained stagnant, the ALP again nominated almost twice as many female candidates and brought four more women into the House of Representatives (Whip 2003; Inter-Parliamentary Union 2004).

Quotas inside the ALP have thus led to a notable increase in the proportion of women elected to parliament. Nonetheless, the party has struggled over the details of quota implementation. In 1996, these disagreements inspired a group of women to establish an organization, modelled on EMILY's List in the United States,[5] to provide financial and moral support to female candidates who achieved pre-selection to a winnable ALP seat and who demonstrated commitment to feminist principles (Chappell 2002; Sawer 2002). Although the goal of the group was to support female candidates endorsed by the ALP, it had no formal links to the party and met with fierce resistance (Carney 1996). While the party leadership has grown more willing over time to intervene to place women in winnable spots, many feminists continue to criticize the quota for facilitating the election of women loyal to male-controlled party factions, at the same time that many men continue to express their opposition to the policy (Chappell 2002). Young women inside the party, however, argue that the quota has enabled women to break through in Australian politics by encouraging skilled women to come forward as candidates (Tuohy 2002). While the Labor Party has somewhat successfully negotiated the tension between quotas and equality that serves as a focal point of debate in countries with liberal models of citizenship, the other two major parties have increasingly emphasized the importance of equal opportunities and candidates as individuals: the LPA has now largely abandoned its efforts to promote women, while the NP recently voted down a proposal to place more women in federal and state government (Whip 2003). These divisions, in turn, explain the party-specific nature of quota solutions and thus the preference for party and soft quotas as a solution to women's under-representation.

Countries with legal quotas

Legal quotas are much less common in the 'West', as they exist for the national legislature in only two of the 17 countries in this region.[6] Because they appear in countries with two distinct models of citizenship, we observe that debates in Belgium centre on gender as a political identity, while those in France question the means and ends of political representation. Similar to countries with party quotas, we find that quota proposals issue from women's groups inside and outside the political parties, but distinct from those countries, we note that quota laws were adopted largely with the consensus of all parties in parliament, most of whom were concerned not to appear 'out of touch' on the issue of women and politics. Further, while rates of implementation vary across political parties, we find that left-wing parties are not always better than right-wing parties in conforming to quota requirements, even when left-wing parties are initially more amenable to quota reform, because of on-going concerns about the relevance of gender and the purposes of political representation.

Belgium

Belgium has a list proportional representation electoral system and, as a result of linguistic divisions within the country, has a party system characterized by ten effective parties, five associated with each language group, that cover the spectrum of far-left to far-right, including the Flemish Liberal Party (VLD), the Flemish Social Democratic Party (SP), the Flemish Christian Democratic Party (CD&V), the Flemish Block (VB), the Flemish Separatist Party (N-VA), the French Socialist Party (PS), the French Liberal Party (MR), the French Christian Democratic Party (CDH), the French Green Party (Ecolo), and the French Separatist Party (FN). Given the list-based electoral system, legal quotas – as well as party quotas – have been aimed at increasing the proportion of women on each party's candidate list. The first party quotas appeared as early as 1985, when the VLD adopted a 20 per cent quota. It was soon followed by the Movement of Citizens for Change (MCC), now part of the MR, with a 33.3 per cent quota in 1986; the Flemish Green Party (Agalev), with a 50 per cent quota in 1991; the SP with a 25 per cent quota in 1992; Ecolo with a 50 per cent quota in 2000; and the PS with a 50 per cent quota in 2000. The first legal quotas were mandated by the Belgian parliament – on the initiative of the government – in 1994 through the Smet-Tobback law, which specified that women would comprise at least 25 per cent of all electoral lists until 1999, after which the quota requirement would be raised to 33.3 per cent. Following the passage of a new law on equality between women and men, parliament revisited the quota requirement and raised it to 50 per cent in 2002 (Meier 2004).

In light of its consociational model of citizenship, debates over gender quotas have tapped into the long-standing tradition of descriptive representation in Belgium, which guarantees the participation of a range of different groups based on linguistic, religious, and class cleavages (Meier 2000).[7] In the case of language, for example, a certain number of seats are reserved for members of these groups – Flemish, French, and German – to ensure their presence in all elected political bodies. The major point of contention in these debates, however, has been whether gender is a category of representation on a par with these other identities (Marques-Pereira 2000). Aware that even those opposed to quotas for women accepted the idea of proportionality, advocates of gender stressed that the balanced representation of key social groups was an essential legitimizing feature of the political system and mobilized on the basis of this norm to justify the adoption of quotas for women, both inside the parties and at the national level (Mateo-Diaz 2002; Murray 2003).

These disagreements soon fed into extensive bargaining over the form that the gender quota law would eventually take. At the most basic level, the governing parties agreed that gender quotas would apply to electoral lists, and thus only to potential candidates for political office, rather than to the total number of seats available, as was the case with linguistic groups, who were guaranteed a specific share of the seats regardless of election outcomes (Meier 2004). In terms of more specific details, however, the parties could not agree on whether or not to regulate the placement of female candidates. The initial form of the bill suggested a maximum of two-thirds of candidates of the same sex in list positions that a party was likely to win, but the final version of the bill dropped this second requirement in favour of simply applying the quota to the party list as a whole, on the grounds that mandating candidate placement would interfere too much in parties' right to compose their own lists. To ensure that parties nominated the minimum proportion of women, however, the law required them to leave any positions open that should have been occupied by a woman, if the party could not find a sufficient number of female candidates (Marques-Pereira 2000).

These provisions led to a dramatic increase in the number of women nominated as candidates, but only a marginal rise in the number of women actually elected to the national parliament, as parties tended to place their female candidates in list positions where they were unlikely to win election (Carton 2001). Because parties generally followed the letter, but not the spirit, of the law, women's representation increased to 23.3 per cent in 1999, far short of the 33.3 per cent quota requirement, with notable differences across the parties in terms of the number of women elected. In light of these shortcomings, parliamentary debate over the new quota law in 2002 added a stipulation that the first three – and eventually the first two – candidates on a party list not be members of the same sex. This provision helped increase women's parliamentary representation to 35.3 per cent the following year, although this outcome remained far below the 50 per cent requirement, due to the combined influence of two factors. On the one hand, the new 'zipper-principle' applies only to the top positions on a party list, leaving the rest of the list positions open and thus permitting parties to place their other female candidates near the bottom of their lists (Murray 2003). On the other hand, a new electoral reform reduced the number of electoral districts from 20 to 11, thus increasing the number of seats available in each district. This reform, paradoxically, reduced the number of seats subject to regulation and thus the broader effectiveness of the new quota law (Meier 2004). The consociational model of citizenship, therefore, has created opportunities to argue for improved descriptive representation, but claims about gender as a political identity have not meshed seamlessly with existing guarantees for other groups. Indeed, provisions for women differ fundamentally from those for linguistic groups: women receive quotas, while language groups get reserved seats (cf. Htun 2004). The general ethos of proportionality, nonetheless, has facilitated the adoption of both legal and party quotas, which have each mutually influenced increases in the other (Meier 2004).

France

France has a two-round majoritarian electoral system[8] and, as a result of the two-round system, has a party system characterized by a range of parties that contest the first round of elections but that typically form coalitions amongst each other to contest the second round. These parties include the centre-right Union for a Presidential Majority (UMP, a new party formed primarily by the former Rally for the Republic, RPR), the centre-left Socialist Party (PS), the centrist Union for French Democracy (UDF), the far-right National Front (FN), and the far-left Green Party (Verts). Due to the majoritarian nature of the electoral system for national elections, early quota regulations addressed only elections governed by proportional representation, like local, regional, and European Parliament elections. The first party quotas emerged in 1974, when the PS introduced a 10 per cent quota for women in these elections. The party subsequently increased this policy to a 15 per cent quota in 1977 and a 30 per cent quota in 1990 – which it extended to parliamentary elections in 1996 – but rarely implemented any of these policies to their fullest extent (Opello 2002). Around the same time that these debates got underway in the PS, several women in parliament sought to establish legal quotas for local elections. They succeeded in gaining a 25 per cent quota in 1982, but the courts almost immediately overturned the law on the grounds that it was unconstitutional. Devising a new set of strategies, advocates launched a new campaign for quotas in the 1990s and eventually secured constitutional reform in 1999 and electoral reform in 2000 to mandate a 50 per cent quota – or 'parity' – for women in local, regional, national, and European Parliament elections.

In light of their failures, earlier attempts to institute and implement quotas fundamentally shaped later debates over parity, leading to an extended discussion of the meaning of representation in the republican model of citizenship. The court decision declared law-based quotas unconstitutional on the grounds that quotas violated the principle of equality before the law, which precluded all types of division of voters and candidates into categories for political voting (Mossuz-Lavau 1998). This verdict defended a notion of representation that did not recognize social differences and forced advocates to develop a more fundamental critique of existing political principles. Inspired by discussions inside the Council of Europe over the concept of 'parity democracy', they argued that existing understandings of equality and representation – as well as their subject, the universal citizen – were originally deemed to apply only to men. Instead of abandoning these concepts, they proposed reforming the constitution to provide for the equal representation of women and men in political life, on the grounds that this was the only way to recognize explicitly the two sexes of the abstract universal citizen. This policy differed fundamentally from quotas, they claimed, because quotas implied special representation rights for minorities, while parity simply called for the equitable sharing of power between women and men, the two halves of the human race (Gaspard *et al.* 1992; Agacinski 2001). Opponents responded that parity reified sexual differences and threatened to spur claims by other groups for similar concessions, with fatal consequences for the secular and universal republic. In their view, any shortcomings in founding principles were simply a legacy of their historical implementation and would evolve naturally over time (Ozouf 1995; Badinter 1996).

Leaders of the two main political parties made their first public commitments to pursue a parity law after elections in 1997. Within days of coming to office, the new PS prime minister announced that he would pursue an amendment to incorporate parity into the constitution, which was soon followed by a pledge by the RPR president that he too would support constitutional reform if nothing else could be done to ensure women's access to political office. The following year, negotiations between the two leaders revolved around the phrasing of the provision and its exact placement in the constitution, with the two eventually agreeing to replace the term 'parity' with 'equal access' and to amend the section on national sovereignty. Conservatives in the Senate later insisted on substituting the verb 'guarantees' with 'favours' equal access, thus reducing the claim for equal representation of women and men to the milder goal of increasing the number of female candidates (Sineau 2001). The bill was then adopted unanimously by the National Assembly and by an overwhelming majority in the Senate in 1999. This set in motion a second round of debates regarding reform of the electoral law to specify and enforce equal access. To the disappointment of many parity advocates, the bill passed in 2000 focused on the nomination of female candidates, rather than on the proportion of women elected, and made weak provisions for elections to the National Assembly, whose low percentage of women had inspired the parity campaign in the first place (Giraud and Jenson 2001).

As a result, patterns of implementation vary across levels of government and across political parties. In local elections in 2001, where parties were required to present lists with equal numbers of women and men, the percentage of women in local councils increased to 47.5 per cent (Sineau 2002: 3). In contrast, in national elections in 2002, where parties were required to present equal numbers of male and female candidates across all electoral districts, the percentage of women increased only marginally to 12.2 per cent. While regulations for local elections made specific placement requirements on the penalty of having the list rejected, regulations for national elections made no mention of placement and imposed relatively mild financial penalties for those parties that did not comply, equal to half the difference in their percentages of male and female candidates. This penalty, however, only applied to the first round of elections and thus parties likely to stand in the second round could earn back some of their lost funding by winning a high number of seats. This penalty structure thus created distinct incentives for smaller and larger parties to comply with the quota law: smaller parties were less likely to win seats in the second round, so they were under pressure to maximize the amount of state subsidy they could claim in the first round, while larger parties could afford not to sacrifice male incumbents and to recoup some of their losses in the second round (Green 2003; Murray 2003; Baudino 2005).

Given its limited scope for national elections, the parity law has effected little change in the number of women elected to the lower house of parliament. Its remarkable success at the local level, where implementation provisions were relatively strict, nonetheless, is constrained by the fact that the law does not apply to towns with fewer than 3500 inhabitants, which comprise 93 per cent of all municipalities and 85 per cent of all local councillors in France.[9] Even without parity, however, women's representation increased in these towns as well to 30.1 per cent, bringing the total percentage of women in local government to 33 per cent (Sineau 2002: 3). Indeed, parity sometimes served as a convenient pretext for leaders to eliminate male councillors that they did not like (Bird 2003). Prospects for further change are mixed. After national elections in 2002, the new right-wing government initiated discussions on a number of electoral reforms that would, in essence, undo several of the most effective aspects of the parity law, including the system of electing representatives in regional and European elections (Green 2003). Both houses of parliament, however, passed a new law in 2003 to require strict alternation between women and men for regional elections. These on-going discussions reflect the systemic nature of the parity reforms, which combined with the many voting systems in France, require attention to the details of implementation at various levels of election. They are thus deeply influenced by the republican model of citizenship, which has compelled advocates to redefine equal representation in order to gain the nearly unanimous consent of both houses of parliament for constitutional and electoral reform. These demands, shaped by earlier legal setbacks and the experience of ineffective party quotas, explain the turn to legal quotas, but also reveal the limits of focusing more on theoretical justifications than on more practical issues of implementation.

Countries with soft quotas

Although several political parties and two countries in the 'West' have adopted formal quotas to regulate the selection of female candidates to parliament, most parties and countries in the region reject or resist quotas as an option in efforts to bring more women into political office. All the same, many of these parties and countries have sought to promote women in politics through a third category of measures that we label 'soft quotas', which aim to increase women's representation indirectly through internal party quotas or more directly through informal targets and recommendations. This approach prevails among parties and countries that embrace liberal models of citizenship because it facilitates access but does not necessarily mandate outcomes. Taking a closer look at the cases of New

Zealand and the United States, we discover remarkable resistance to the notion of gender quotas for political office but find that political parties in each country pursued various types of 'softer' strategies to promote women's representation, a compromise made necessary by a continuing emphasis on equal opportunities.

New Zealand

New Zealand had a first-past-the-post plurality electoral system until 1993, when it adopted a mixed PR-majority system. As a result, the party system has evolved from a largely two-party system to a multi-party system dominated by one left-wing party, the New Zealand Labour Party (NZLP), and one right-wing party, the National Party (NP), who are joined by a number of other smaller parties with seats in parliament, including the nationalist New Zealand First Party (NZFP), the libertarian ACT New Zealand party (ACT), the left-wing Green Party (GPA), the centrist United Future New Zealand (UF), and the left-wing Progressive Coalition (PC). While the earlier electoral system simply ran on a winner-take-all principle, the new electoral system combines list proportional representation and first-past-the-post plurality elections. Although women's representation had registered strong increases under the earlier electoral system, the government argued that one of the advantages of adopting a new system was its anticipated effect on the proportion of women in parliament (Ministry of Women's Affairs 1998). With the change in the electoral system, the NZLP leader proposed party quotas, but this was rejected in favour of a change in the party constitution to include a principle of gender balance for all selection procedures (Drage 2001). Thus, at each candidate selection conference, the party 'pauses for thought' after each bloc of five candidates to consider the balance of gender, ethnicity, age and experience. The GPA also embraces the principle of parity in its nominations, but the party has never adopted specific quotas or applied strict alternation on its lists, as is the case with Green parties elsewhere in the world. The NP, for its part, has not adopted quotas, but similarly talks of the need to take 'balance' into account (Catt 2003).

Consistent with its liberal citizenship model, debates over gender quotas in New Zealand have focused on issues of equality, particularly with regard to the need to take conscious steps to promote equality between women and men. Despite the tendency to treat citizens as individuals rather than groups, the country nonetheless has a strong national discourse concerning the rights of Maoris, the indigenous people of New Zealand, for whom a certain number of seats have always been reserved in parliament (Cody 2003). Indeed, during its official interventions in the electoral system debate, even the Women's Electoral Lobby said more about Maori representation than women's representation. Similarly, debates within the NZLP on quotas for women reflected a widespread belief that change could occur without the need for formal rules, with many claiming that the party had evolved beyond the need for quotas and thus was already predisposed towards selecting a balanced list (Catt 2003). These views stem from the fact that the party had applied soft quotas since the 1970s, when the NZLP experienced a disastrous electoral defeat and women used the opportunity to campaign for more women in parliament and in decision-making positions within the party. Their demands resonated within the party, not least because the party had lost crucial electoral support to the new left-wing New Zealand Values Party, which presented 25 per cent female candidates in 1975 (Hill and Roberts 1990; McLeay 1993).

During the first two elections under the new electoral system, all parties increased the number of female candidates in winnable seats, mainly through the use of soft quotas for list elections. As a result, the overwhelming majority of female MP's won seats decided by list proportional representation, bringing the total proportion of women in parliament to 29 per cent (Ministry of Women's Affairs 1998). Two elections later, however, the parties placed fewer women in winnable positions, leading to an overall decline in the proportion of women in parliament, from 31 per cent in 1999 to 28 per cent in 2002 (Cody 2003: 41). While most of this decline was due to the victory of right-wing parties with relatively few women on their lists, even the NZLP had placed fewer women in spots where they were likely to be elected, because the policy of 'pausing for thought' had become less effective with each successive election (Catt 2003).

Informal quota measures have thus led to significant increases in the proportion of women elected to parliament. Although the policy of 'pausing for thought' constituted a novel solution to the widespread resistance to gender quotas, its success – paradoxically – has led to complacency among all parties that these trends will continue upward. At the same time, the large influx of female leaders in recent years has provoked an apparent backlash against women in politics, who no longer need 'special treatment', according to detractors, because they occupy many top political positions. The liberal citizenship model, therefore, continues to exert a strong effect on quota debates in New Zealand, reinforcing existing preferences for equal opportunities rather than equal results. Despite a historical tradition of group representation for the Maoris, proponents have thus made little headway in campaigns for party and legal quotas, leading them to advocate softer measures to promote women's political representation.

United States

The United States has a first-past-the-post electoral system and a two-party system dominated by the centre-left Democratic Party and the centre-right

Republican Party. Among all the countries surveyed in this chapter, the US stands out as the one in which proposals for gender quotas for elected positions have made virtually no mark in political debates, in part because the system of primary elections means that voters select candidates and thus that party control over candidate nomination is relatively weak. Despite their lack of attention to candidate quotas, however, both parties have devoted a significant amount of time discussing quotas for internal party positions. Soon after women were granted the right to vote in 1920, the Democrats mandated that the Democratic National Committee (DNC) be composed of one man and one woman from each state and territory, while the Republicans adopted a similar measure, which they abandoned in 1952 but replaced in 1960 with a rule calling for 50–50 representation in all convention committees (Baer 2003). Following protests at its party convention in 1968, the DNC later ratified guidelines requiring state parties to select women as national convention delegates in proportion to their presence in the state population (Harvey 1998). These reforms came under attack in 1972, however, and the party rewrote delegate selection rules to ban 'quotas' in favour of affirmative action. The Republicans, in contrast, chose not to regulate the state parties, although some states mandated 50–50 representation on their state central committees (Baer 2003).

As in other countries with liberal citizenship models, debates on gender quotas in the US have centred around the issue of equality, fluctuating between a desire to combat discrimination and concerns to preserve merit as a criteria of delegate selection. Most notably, the quotas established for the Democratic convention in 1972 were a response to a series of events in 1964 and 1968 that highlighted the exclusion of certain groups within the party, especially African-Americans (Baer 2003). The overturning of 'quotas' in favour of 'affirmative action' that year, however, shifted this discourse to one that promoted qualified individuals – not ascriptive groups – as convention delegates (Carroll 1994). Nonetheless, decisions to pursue internal party quotas clearly stemmed from electoral incentives to appear more inclusive: the parties established their first 50–50 rules in an attempt to demonstrate to female voters that they were willing to represent women's interests, and they reviewed their delegate selection procedures in response to criticisms that they discriminated against women, African-Americans, and people under 30 (Harvey 1998; Costain 1999; Baer 2003).

All the same, both parties implemented these new regulations in different ways and to varying degrees. In terms of delegate selection, the Democratic quotas in 1972 had an immediate impact, raising the proportion of women at the convention from 13 per cent to 40 per cent (Harvey 1998: 220). When the party replaced quotas with affirmative action, the party allowed states that filed affirmative action plans to be exempt from any scrutiny of their selection practices. Without external intervention, women's recruitment was again subject to local party traditions, and the proportion of women at the national party convention dropped to 34 per cent. The Republican Party regarded the selection of convention delegates as a state matter, so when the reform commission considered party reform in the early 1970s, no specific regulations were adopted. Following the dramatic upsurge in the number of female delegates to the Democratic party convention, however, Republicans began to select more women. Without clear requirements, however, the proportion of women has wavered between 20 per cent and 40 per cent (Baer 2003: 131–2).

Quotas for internal party positions have thus enabled women to participate to a greater degree in party matters and, indeed, women originally pursued equal representation on party committees out of the belief that these positions would provide an important wedge for gaining broader influence as a group within the party. Early experiences on these committees, however, revealed to women that these committees were actually relatively powerless and, when real issues arose, decisions were often taken not by the committee but by the chairman acting alone, by small groups of men meeting privately. As a result, women soon became disenchanted with the 50–50 rule, especially because men often seemed to choose those women who were most willing to go along with them (Freedman 2000). Even more obviously, the presence of soft quotas has not translated into any great gains in legislative representation, as women won only 14.3 per cent of the seats in the House of Representatives and 14 per cent of the seats in the Senate in 2002 (Inter-Parliamentary Union 2004). In circumscribing debates over the meaning of equality, the liberal model of citizenship has thus tightly restricted the range of options available to quota campaigners. Although measures exist to guarantee the descriptive representation of ethnic minorities, most notably African-Americans and Hispanics, legal and party quotas for women have simply been rejected out of hand (Klausen and Maier 2001), allowing only the adoption of soft quotas far removed from the sphere of electoral politics.

Conclusions

Campaigns for gender quotas are inevitably framed by existing beliefs about equality, representation, and gender, which come together in various ways to form three distinct models of political citizenship. Tracing seven particular cases of quota reform, we find that citizenship models not only given rise to specific controversies surrounding gender quotas, but also influence decisions to adopt specific types of gender quotas, as well as their broader impact on the proportion of women elected to parliament. A particular model of citizenship, however, does not automatically guarantee a certain outcome, either positive or negative. Rather, awareness of these models sheds light on the opportunities and constraints for quota campaigns in specific contexts, providing advocates – and opponents –

with crucial insights into the normative arguments that facilitate and undermine quota reform.

Notes

1 The Nordic countries, with their exceptional records of women's political representation, are treated in Chapter 3.
2 This is because consociationalism is often used to signify political arrangements, while corporatism is typically used to refer to relations of social and economic bargaining (Royo 2002). Following Lijphart (2002), we stress the basic similarities of these two models.
3 Aware of the negative connotation of the word 'quota' in conservative circles, the party adopted the less objectionable term 'quorum' to refer to its requirement of one woman for every two men. See Wiliarty (2001).
4 'Twinning' involved pairing constituencies according to geography and winnability and then selecting a woman as the candidate for one of the constituencies and a man as the candidate for the other. This system, advocates argued, would produce the same results as all-women shortlists but would be more difficult to challenge legally, since men would not be excluded from selection contests.
5 EMILY's List was founded in 1985 to provide financial support to elect pro-choice Democratic women to the Senate and House of Representatives in the United States. See http://www.emilyslist.org.
6 Italy instituted legal quotas specifying a minima of one-third candidates of either sex for the 2004 elections to the European Parliament. These were backed by financial sanctions whereby parties that did not comply forfeited a proportion of their state reimbursement of electoral expenses. (Guadagnini 2005).
7 Quotas have also been considered in Belgium on the grounds of age and ethnicity.
8 This system applies only to elections to the National Assembly. Other levels of government in France apply a range of other electoral systems, including list proportional representation.
9 Parity does not apply in these towns because they are governed by a different type of electoral system, which allows voters to strike candidates' names, change the order of candidates, and add new names to the list.

Bibliography

Agacinski, S. (2001) *Parity of the Sexes*, trans. L. Walsh, New York: Columbia University Press.
Badinter, E. (1996) 'Non aux quotas de femmes', *Le Monde*, 12 June.
Baer, D.L. (2003) 'Women, Women's Organizations, and Political Parties', in S.J. Carroll (ed.) *Women and American Politics: New Questions, New Directions*, New York: Oxford University Press, pp. 111–45.
Baudino, C. (2005) 'Gendering the Republican System: Debates on Women's Political Representation in France', in J. Lovenduski (ed.) *et al. State Feminism and Political Representation*, Cambridge UK: Cambridge University Press.
Bird, K. (2003) 'Who are the Women, Where are the Women, and What Difference Can They Make? Effect of Gender Parity in the French Municipal Elections', *French Politics*, 1, 1: 5–38.

Brzinski, J.B. (2003) 'Women's Representation in Germany: A Comparison of East and West', in R.E. Matland and K.A. Montgomery (eds) *Women's Access to Political Power in Post-Communist Europe*, New York: Oxford University Press, pp. 63–80.

Carney, S. (1996) 'Labor Women are still doing it for themselves', *The Age*, 16 November.

Carroll, S.J. (1994) *Women as Candidates in American Politics*, 2nd edn, Indianapolis: Indiana University Press.

Carton, A. (2001) 'The General Elections in Belgium in June 1999: A Real Breakthrough for Women Politicians?', *European Journal of Women's Studies*, 8, 1: 127–35.

Catt, H. 'Frail Success: The New Zealand Experience of Electing Women', paper presented at the European Consortium of Politics Research, Joint Sessions of Workshops, Edinburgh, March–April 2003.

Centre for Advancement of Women in Politics (2004) 'Dáil Éireann general election results by gender, 1918–2002'. Online. Available at: http://www.qub.ac.uk/camp/Irishhtmls/TD2.htm (accessed 12 December 2004).

Chappell, L.A. (2002) *Gendering Government: Feminist Engagement with the State in Australia and Canada*, Toronto: UBC Press.

Childs, S. (2002) 'Concepts of Representation and the Passage of the Sex Discrimination (Election Candidates) Bill', *Journal of Legislative Studies*, 8, 3: 90–108.

—— (2004) *New Labour's Women MP's: Women Representing Women*, London: Taylor & Francis.

Cody, H. (2003) 'Early Lessons from Mixed-Member Proportionality in New Zealand's Westminster Politics', *The New England Journal of Political Science*, 1, 1: 34–51.

Costain, A.N. (1999) 'Quotas in American Politics', *Swiss Political Science Review*, 5, 1: 106–10.

Davidson-Schmich, L.K. 'Voluntary Gender Quotas and Women's Representation: Evidence from German State Legislatures', paper presented at the Annual Conference of the Southern Political Science Association, Savannah, GA, November 2002.

Drage, J. (2001) *Report on the State of Women in Urban Local Government: New Zealand*. Online. Available at: http://www.capwip.org/readingroom/new_zealand.pdf (accessed 24 January 2005).

Esping-Andersen, G. (1990) *The Three Worlds of Welfare Capitalism*, Princeton NJ: Princeton University Press.

Freedman, J. (2000) *A Room at a Time: How Women Entered Party Politics*, New York: Rowman & Littlefield.

Gaspard, F., Servan-Schreiber, C. and Le Gall, A. (1992) *Au pouvoir, citoyennes!: liberté, égalité, parité*, Paris: Éditions du Seuil.

Giraud, I. and Jenson, J. (2001) 'Constitutionalising Equal Access: High Hopes, Dashed Hopes?', in J. Klausen and C.S. Maier (eds) *Has Liberalism Failed Women? Assuring Equal Representation in Europe and the United States*, New York: Palgrave, pp. 69–88.

Green, M. 'La Parité – To Be or Not to Be?', paper presented and the European Consortium of Politics Research, Joint Sessions of Workshops, Edinburgh, March–April 2003.

Guadagnini, M. (2005) 'Gendering the debate on political representation in Italy: a difficult challenge', in J. Lovenduski (ed.) *et al. State Feminism and Political Representation*, Cambridge UK: Cambridge University Press.

Harvey, A.L. (1998) *Votes Without Leverage: Women in American Electoral Politics, 1920–1970*, New York: Cambridge University Press.

Hill, R. and Roberts, N.S. (1990) 'Success, Swing and Gender: The Performance of Women Candidates for Parliament in New Zealand, 1946–1987', *Politics*, 25, 1: 62–80.

Htun, M. (2004) 'Is Gender Like Ethnicity? The Political Representation of Identity Groups', *Perspectives on Politics*, 2, 3: 439–58.

Inhetveen, K. (1999) 'Can Gender Equality be Institutionalised? The Role of Launching Values in Institutional Innovation', *International Sociology*, 14, 4: 403–42.

Inter-Parliamentary Union (2004) 'Women in National Parliaments: Situation as of 31 August 2004'. Online. Available at: http://www.ipu.org/wmn-e/classif.htm (accessed 12 December 2004).

Jenkins, L.D. (1999) 'Competing Inequalities: The Struggle Over Reserved Seats for Women in India', *International Review of Social History*, 44: 53–75.

Jennings, J. (2000) 'Citizenship, Republicanism and Multiculturalism in Contemporary France', *British Journal of Political Science*, 30: 575–98.

Johnson, C. (2000) 'The Fragility of Democratic Reform: New Challenges to Australian Women's Citizenship', in S.M. Rai (ed.) *International Perspectives on Gender and Democratisation*, New York: St. Martin's Press, pp. 182–201.

Kamenitsa, L. and Geissel, B. (2005) 'WPAs and Political Representation in Germany', in J. Lovenduski (ed.) *et al. State Feminism and Political Representation*, Cambridge UK: Cambridge University Press.

Kirner, J. (1994) 'Half by 2000'. Online. Available at: http://labor.net.au/emilyslist/news/speeches/941001kirner.html (accessed 10 May 2004).

Klausen, J. and Maier, C.S. (eds) (2001) *Has Liberalism Failed Women? Assuring Equal Representation in Europe and the United States*, New York: Palgrave.

Library of Parliament (2004) 'Women Candidates in General Elections – 1921 to Date'. Online. Available at: http://www.parl.gc.ca/information/about/process/House/asp/WomenElect.asp?lang=E&source=hoc (accessed 13 October 2004).

Lijphart, A. (2002) 'The Evolution of Consociational Theory and Consociational Practices 1965–2000', *Acta Politica*, 37: 11–22.

Lovenduski, J. (2005) *Feminizing Politics*, Cambridge UK: Polity Press.

Lovenduski, J. (ed.) *et al.* (2005) *State Feminism and Political Representation*, Cambridge UK: Cambridge University Press.

Marques-Pereira, B. 'Quotas and parity in Belgium within a European framework', paper presented at the International Political Science Association World Congress, Quebec, Canada, August 2000.

Mateo Diaz, M. (2002) 'Do Quotas Matter? Positive Actions in the Belgian Parliament', *Res Publica*, 44, 1: 49–72.

Matland, R.E. and Studlar, D.T. (1996) 'The Contagion of Women Candidates in Single-Member Districts and Proportional representation Electoral Systems: Canada and Norway', *The Journal of Politics*, 58, 3: 707–33.

McKay, J. (2003) 'Women in German Politics: Still Jobs for the Boys?', *German Politics*, 13, 1: 56–80.

McLeay, E. (1993) 'Women and the Problem of Parliamentary Representation: A Comparative Perspective', in H. Catt and E. McLeay (eds) *Women and Politics in New Zealand*, Wellington: Victoria University Press, pp. 40–62.

Meier, P. (2000) 'The Evidence of Being Present: Guarantees of Representation and the Belgian Example', *Acta Politica: International Journal of Political Science*, 35, 1: 64–85.

—— (2004) 'The Mutual Contagion Effect of Legal and Party Quotas: A Belgian Perspective', *Party Politics*, 10, 5: 583–600.

Meyer, B. (2003) 'Much Ado about Nothing? Political Representation Policies and the Influence of Women Parliamentarians in Germany', *Review of Policy Research*, 20, 3: 401–21.

Ministry of Social Development (2004) 'Representation of Women in Government'. Online. Available at: http://socialreport.msd.govt.nz/civil-political-rights/representation-women-government.html (accessed 3 February 2005).

Ministry of Women's Affairs (1998) *Status of Women in New Zealand 1998*. Online. Available at: http://www.mwa.govt.nz/women/status/cedaw007.html (accessed 3 February 2005).

Mossuz-Lavau, J. (1998) *Femmes/homes pour la parité*, Paris: Presses de Sciences Po.

Murray, R. (2003) *Was the low number of women elected to France's National Assembly in 2002 indicative of the failure of parity as a policy?*, MRes Dissertation, London: Birkbeck College.

Opello, K.A.R. (2002) *Ideas and Elections: Explaining the Timing and Nature of the French Socialist Party's Gender-Based Quota*, doctoral thesis, New York University.

Ozouf, M. (1995) *Les mots des femmes: Essai sur la singularité française*, Paris: Fayard.

Parliament of Australia (2004) 'The Number of Women in Parliament'. Online. Available at: http://www.aph.gov.au/library/parl/hist/noswomen.htm (accessed 3 February 2005).

Royo, S. (2002) *A New Century of Corporatism?: Corporatism in Southern Europe*, Westport: Praeger.

Russell, M. (2000) *Women's Representation in UK Politics: What can be done with the Law?*, London: The Constitution Unit.

Russell, M., Mackay, F. and McAllister, L. (2002) 'Women's Representation in the Scottish Parliament and National Assembly for Wales: Party Dynamics for Achieving Critical Mass', *Journal of Legislative Studies*, 8, 2: 49–76.

Sawer, M. (1994) 'Locked Out or Locked In? Women and Politics in Australia', in B.J. Nelson and N. Chowdhury (eds) *Women and Politics Worldwide*, New Haven: Yale University Press, pp. 73–91.

—— (1997) 'Women are People Too!', speech to Women into Politics Lecture Series, Sydney, Australia, 10 June. Online. Available at: http://www.womensconv.dynamite.com.au/moswip.htm (accessed 5 June 2000).

—— (2002) 'The Representation of Women in Australia: Meaning and Make-Believe', in K. Ross (ed.) *Women, Politics, and Change*, New York: Oxford University Press, pp. 5–18.

Schmitter, P. (1979) 'Still the century of corporatism?', in P. Schmitter and G. Lembruch (eds) *Trends towards corporatist intermediation*, London: Sage.

Sgier, L. 'Political Representation and Gender Quotas', paper presented at the European Consortium of Politics Research, Joint Sessions of Workshops, Edinburgh, March–April 2003.

Short, C. (1996) 'Women and the Labour Party', *Parliamentary Affairs*, 49, 1: 17–25.

Simms, M. (1993) 'Two Steps Forward, One Step Back: Women and the Australian Party System', in J. Lovenduski and P. Norris (eds) *Gender and Party Politics*, Thousand Oaks: Sage, pp. 16–34.

Sineau, M. (2001) *Profession: femme politique. Sexe et pouvoir sous la Cinquième République*, Paris: Presses de Sciences Po.

—— (2002) 'Institutionalizing Parity: The French Experience', in J. Ballington and M.J. Protais (eds) *Les femmes au parlement: Au-dela du nombre*, Stockholm: International IDEA, pp. 121–32.

Squires, J. (1996) 'Quotas for Women: Fair Representation?' in J. Lovenduski and P. Norris (eds) *Women in Politics*, New York: Oxford University Press, pp. 73–90.

—— (2004) 'Gender Quotas in Britain: A Fast Track to Equality?', The Research Program on Gender Quotas. Working Paper Series 2004: 1. Stockholm University, Department of Political Science.

Tuohy, W. (2002) 'Labor's young women ready to rumble', *The Age*, 12 October.

United Nations Development Programme (UNDP) (2003) *Human Development Report*. Online. Available at: http://www.undp.org/hdr2003 (accessed 12 December 2004).

Vallance, E. (1984) 'Women Candidates in the 1983 General Election', *Parliamentary Affairs*, 37, 3: 301–9.

Van Acker, E. (1999) *Different Voices: Gender and Politics in Australia*, South Yarra: Macmillan.

Whip, R. (2003) 'The 1996 Australian Federal Election and its Aftermath: a Case for Equal Gender Representation', *Australian Feminist Studies*, 18, 40: 73–97.

Wiliarty, S.E. (2001) *Bringing Women to the Party: The Christian Democratic Union (CDU) as a Corporatist Catch-All Party*, doctoral thesis, University of California, Berkeley.

Wisler, D. (1999) 'Parité politique: la diffusion d'un principe', *Swiss Political Science Review*, 5, 1: 110–14.

9   South Asia

Gender quotas and the politics of empowerment – a comparative study

Shirin M. Rai, Farzana Bari, Nazmunessa Mahtab and Bidyut Mohanty[1]

Introduction

South Asia has seen the world's first woman prime minister – Srimavo Bandaranayake – come to power in Sri Lanka, one of the longest serving prime ministers anywhere in the world – Indira Gandhi – in India and the youngest woman prime minister – Benazir Bhutto – in Pakistan. In Bangladesh, two women have held the position of Prime Minister since 1991 – Begums Zia and Sheikh. And yet, women's representation in politics in the region has been very limited and continues to be so at the national level. In this chapter we review the quota debates and provisions in three countries of South Asia – Bangladesh, India and Pakistan (see Table 9.1). While there has been some empirical work done on the process by which quotas for women were introduced and implemented and on the outcome of the quota for both women representatives and local government institutions in each of the three countries (Bari 1997; Buch 2000a; Mahtab 2003), this is the first comparative study on the issue.

Unlike the other chapters in this book, we concentrate on quotas for women in local government, even though national level debates are becoming increasingly prominent in the region. We do this because there is now sufficient data available to assess the impact of quotas in these three countries. The presumptions, which are not unproblematic or even accurate that have focused legislation on local institutions as sites for women's participation and empowerment have been the following: (a) women are more comfortable participating in local politics than in politics further away from home; (b) that 'the local' is closer to the needs of the people than national politics; and (c) that given the high levels of illiteracy among women local politics is more within the grasp of women participating in local government institutions than the 'high politics' of parliaments (Rai, forthcoming). The debates on quotas in all three countries have also centrally taken into account issues of differences among women. Of particular concern has been the elite nature of representative politics in terms of both class and caste, and of women in political life in particular (Rai 1997, 2002).

Table 9.1 Quota types in South Asia

Country	Women in parliament: % and number of seats (year of election)[a]	Quota type	Year of introduction		Quota provision		Electoral system
			National	Local	National	Local	
Bangladesh	2.0, 6 of 300 (2001)	Legal quotas(C)	2004[b]	1996	45 of 345 seats (13%)	At least three women (25%)	FPP
India	LH: 8.3, 45 of 541 (2004)	Legal quotas (C) (local level) Party quotas (national level)	n/a	1992	Indian National Congress Party (15%) Assa People's Council (35%)	Not less than 33%	FPP
	UH: 11.6, 28 of 242 (2004)						
Nepal	LH: 5.9, 12 of 205 (1999)	Legal quota (C)	1990	1990	LH: 5% of contesting candidates	20%	FPP
	UH: 8.3, 5 of 60 (2001)	LH: Candidate quota UH: Reserved seats			UH: 3 of 60 seats (5%)		
Pakistan	LH: 21.6, 74 of 342 (2002)	Legal quota (L) (national level)	2000	2000	Senate 17% National Assembly 17% Provincial Assemblies 17%	33%	FPP
	UH: 17.0, 17 of 100 (2003)	Legal quota (Devolution of Power Plan) (local level)				29–33%	
Sri Lanka	4.9, 11 of 225 (2004)	No quota					List PR

Source: Chowdhury (2003), Mahtab (2003), Raman (2003), Reyes (2003), International IDEA and Stockholm University (2004), IPU (2004).

Notes
a LH = Lower House, UH = Upper House.
b No election has been held yet.
Key Quota Type: Legal Quotas: Constitutional (C) or Law (L).
Key Electoral Systems: *Plurality-Majority*: FPP = First-Past-the-Post. *Proportional Representation*: List PR.

After reviewing the historical and socio-economic context in which quotas have been introduced in South Asia, and the evidence from the various studies on the implementation of quotas in local governance, we conclude that quotas form part of a long history of constructing post-colonial citizenship, but that they are also part of current governmental strategy for addressing a complex set of issues relating to the status of the nation within the international community. The quotas in South Asia are thus incremental as well as 'fast track' (see the introduction) in an historical context that is complex. We suggest that while quotas are important in addressing the exclusion of women from the public political sphere they can only form one part of a multi-faceted strategy for empowering women, which must together with increased political participation also involve a redistribution of socio-economic resources within societies.

The context

The legacy of the British rule, which led to the partition of India into two (India and Pakistan[2]) coloured the first debates on quotas in South Asia. The first quotas were part of the British administrative regime in South Asia. The official stand of the Indian National Congress under the leadership of Mahatma Gandhi was to oppose quotas – particularly quotas based on caste and religion. However, the British Government introduced quotas for a range of minorities under the Government of India Act of 1935. Independence came with the partition of India in August 1947. In both Pakistan and India, the tradition of quotas continued. In India, the Dalit leader Ambedkar articulated the need for quotas for the lowest castes and tribes (Baxi 1995), and this was enshrined in the Constitution. In India the women's movement came out strongly against quotas on the grounds of equal citizenship rights (Rai and Sharma 2000). Pakistan instituted quota of 5 per cent for women under its first constitution, which was rather arbitrary and based on colonial legislation rather than on percentage of population (which would have given a parity position to women).

The mediation by the post-colonial state between discourses of modernity and nationhood and nation and culture informed the debates on the 'woman question' (Chatterjee 1993; Rai 2002). In India, Sarkar has argued that, it was 'cultural' and not 'political' nationalism that enabled middle class modern women to enter into the public sphere by 'domesticating' the nationalist project within the home (Sarkar 1983; John 2000: 3822). Chatterjee's insight into 'presence without empowerment' helps in explaining what may have motivated those supporting the emergence of reservations in India. While the constitution provided women with important rights – equality for women within the legal processes, rescinding of obviously discriminatory practices, right to the vote, to education and in most cases to property, and laws against violence against women – the implementation of these rights was patchy and lacked state commitment

(Rai 2002). Further, the state's insistence upon its secular character was mediated by its need to reassure Muslim minorities, which led to the recognition of 'personal law'[3] for religious groups. This created a context where the Indian constitution reflects the dominant (unequal) gender relations on the one hand, while the state rhetoric on citizenship continues to insist upon the equality between men and women on the other (Pathak and Sudarajan 1992).

In Pakistan, the state negotiated its identity between what it means to be Islamic on the one hand and to be a modern nation-state that treats all its citizens (including women) equally and therefore provides them with a political framework within which they can all be represented. In India, however, we find that tensions emerge early in these negotiated identities, which have repercussions for women's rights. The same tensions emerge in Bangladesh but in a very different context of civil war/war of independence. As Kabeer has pointed out, the tension is between religious and national identities where language, dress and the culture of day-to-day living of Bengalis of East Pakistan rubs against the grain of the Islamic framework that they share with west Pakistan (1988).

While the historical legacy of colonialism provided challenges for the post colonial state in terms of its own identity – which led to the positioning of women in the political systems in particular ways – the economic legacy of colonialism and the continued struggle of the post-colonial states to address issues of modernization and development were also critical in framing the problem of women's empowerment. The levels of poverty for all the countries of South Asia were high, but women were particularly marginalized within the political economy. The vast majority of South Asian women is illiterate, in poor health, invisible in the system of national accounts, and suffers legal, political, economic and social discrimination in all walks of life. Women in South Asia (including figures for Nepal and Sri Lanka) continue to have low rates of participation in the governance institutions where quotas do not apply. They occupy only 7 per cent of the parliamentary seats, 9 per cent of the cabinet seats, 6 per cent of the positions in the judiciary and 9 per cent in the civil service (UNDP 2000).

The post-colonial state in South Asia has different political systems. India is a hybrid of centralized economic management of the country accompanied by a federal, multi-party, first-past-the-post electoral and political system which allowed for political competition at both the national and the provincial (state) levels. In Pakistan, after a brief interlude, the military became a dominant force in political life, though it was challenged in different periods by democratic forces. In Bangladesh too, this pattern of rule was seen until recently, when a fragile but growing stabilization of democratic government is visible.

226 *Shirin M. Rai* et al.

Quota discourses in South Asia

We can identify three distinct phases in the unfolding of quota discourses that led to provisions of special measures for women in the region. Phase one was that of constitution making after the achievement of independence in 1947. Here, debates on citizenship and the position of the state in society marked the period.

In India, the Congress Party's general commitment to addressing caste-based inequalities was translated by Ambedkar into specific measures, called 'reservations' or quotas, under the 9th Schedule [Articles 330 and 331[4]]. There were also certain re-distributive strategies introduced in tandem with the quotas: the quotas that were put in place were comprehensive – in education at all levels, in state employment, including the judiciary, as well as in political institutions. They were in the first instance provided for 50 years, but from 1989 extended for another 40 years, pointing to the political sensitivity of removal of quotas once they have been established. As noted above, while there was discussion of quotas for women in the Constituent Assembly, this was rejected by women members representing the All-India Women's Congress, as demeaning for women struggling for equality with men in all spheres of life. However, the precedence had been set for using quotas as a means of recognizing historical exclusion.[5] In Pakistan, the recognition of women's exclusion and the symbolic importance of their inclusion for an Islam Republic led to quotas for women but was not accompanied by a comprehensive approach to provisioning for the basis of women's wider socio-economic needs. Reservation of seats for women in the national and provincial assemblies, senate and local government was agreed in the first constitution of 1956 at a minimal level of 3 per cent. Women were always elected on reserved seats through indirect election. The revised Constitutions of 1962 and 1973 also provided reservation of seats for women at similarly low levels of 2.75 per cent and 5 per cent respectively in the national and provincial assemblies. The insignificant number of reserved seats combined with indirect mode of election on women's reserved seats together with a failure to address the socio-economic and religious basis of women's exclusion proved a failure in terms of mainstreaming women in politics and providing opportunity to play an effective role in politics. In Bangladesh the first constitution of the country, promulgated in 1972, provided for 15 indirectly elected reserved seats for women in the national parliament for a period of ten years. This gave women a minimum representation of 4.7 per cent. Members elected to the general seats constituted the Electoral College for electing candidates for the reserved seats (Chowdhury 2003).

The second phase of quota politics for women begins in the 1970s and 1980s. This, of course, is also the time when international organizations such as the UN were beginning to recognize the importance of women in public life. The UN Conference on Women held in Mexico on the status of women world-wide and the declaration of the Decade for Women in 1975. Women's groups in South Asia were affected by these developments. Diffusion of ideas on women's participation in public life however had to be mediated within the nationalist context. Women's groups did not wish to be seen as 'westernized' and cut off from their own culture. To negotiate the boundaries of tradition and citizenship was a challenge to the women's movements and groups in the South Asian region.

The state in India responded to UN exhortations and some unease about women's status within Indian society among women's groups by establishing the first Commission on the Status of Women in India (CSWI) in 1972. This once again debated the reservation issue. A majority of the CSWI members rejected the step as a retrograde one from the equality conferred by the constitution. The CSWI recommended the constitution of statutory all women panchayats at the village level to look after the welfare of women, though this was not implemented by most state governments. The National Perspective Plan for Women (1988–2000) recommended a reservation of at least 30 per cent of the total seats for women in the local government institutions. These developments towards a quota system for women's representation reflect some wider political processes in the country. As Gopal Jayal has argued, there was a growing concern over the 'failure of development programmes, and the perception that these would be able to perform better with local participation which would help to identify local needs...' (forthcoming). By the 1990s the women's movement in India had begun to engage with the state at both the local and the national level, and women's groups were being consulted by the government on issues of women's welfare culminating in the establishment of the Women's National Commission in 1992.[6] Attention towards the mobilization of women's vote came in the context of the collapse for the Congress dominated political system and the beginning of coalition governments in India. Women were regarded as a new constituency by Rajiv Gandhi, the leader of the Congress Party, who addressed the issue of India's modernity by focusing on the position of women in the country. The 1992 provision of reservation of seats in local government for women under the 73rd and 74th Amendments to the Indian constitution was a key intervention by his government.[7]

In 1985, the number of reserved seats for women in the Pakistan national assembly was raised to 20 (10 per cent) for the period of ten years or three general elections, whichever came earlier. Women's mobilization came in the context of the enactment of the Hudood Ordinances in 1979 by the military dictator General Zia-ul-Haq. These Ordinances were a set of six laws, which were used to 'Islamize' criminal law.[8] Ali has sketched out the struggles of Pakistani women to find a voice that allowed them to be both secular citizens as well as Muslims (2000). A mature women's movement responded by organizing rallies against the legislation and by demanding equal representation. Women only police stations, pressures on political parties to have more women on their lists and a lobbying of the media to report atrocities against women made for the background for arguments for higher representation of women in political institutions. Efforts to 'fulfil commitments in international treaties and conventions to promote women's free, equal and full political participation' are summed up in the Report of the Commission of Inquiry for Women (August 1997), the National Plan for Action (NPA) (September 1998) and the National Policy for Development and Empowerment of Women (March 2002) (Ali 2000: 54).

In Bangladesh, the international donor agencies, working with/in the UN framework of Women in Development (WID) were instrumental in pushing forward the discourse of gender equality (Kabeer 1994, 1995; Goetz 1996, 1997). A major part of the development budget is underwritten by external funding, which makes donor pressure an overwhelming source for change. International pressure also comes from the UN and other international NGOs that support particular forms of initiatives – quotas for women being one – to address issues of gender inequality. The role of NGOs in Bangladesh in addressing the quota issues is also important. While many NGOs are involved in providing micro-credit (Kabeer 1995) others focus on political empowerment issues, particularly women's representation in political institutions (Kabeer 1999). They also mobilize women at the local level, provide them with support and training, which is largely funded by international donor agencies and institutions. The1986 Constitution did not provide for quotas but with regard to local government institutions, Article 9 of the Constitution stated that, 'The state shall encourage local government institutions composed of representatives of the areas concerned and in such institutions special representations shall be given as far as possible to peasants, workers and women'. Reservation of seats was re-incorporated into the constitution in 1990, valid for ten years. This provision lapsed in 2001, which means that the present parliament does not have reserved seats for women (Chowdhury 2003), though it was reintroduced in 2004 at 13 per cent of seats in the next parliament.

The third, or the current, phase can be characterized by several key elements. Economic liberalization has led to the further erosion of the welfare state in India and Pakistan. The latter has also felt the crushing burden of refugees on its Afghan border as well as expenditure on security. At the international level, the 'third wave' of democratization has led to pressures on military regimes to democratize on the one hand, and the 'war on terror' has led to Musharraf being courted by the US on the other. Discourses of constructed modernity (democratic and liberalizing regimes) and fundamentalism (Taliban, al-Qaida, jihad) have formed the backdrop of the region's most recent engagements with the changing international system. We have also seen a world-wide consensus emerging about the relevance of state feminism, especially after the Beijing Conference, 1995, and the emergence of an international discourse on the importance of women's empowerment through participation in political institutions of the state as well as supra-state institutions (Bystendinzky 1992; Parpart *et al.* 2002). This phase has seen the debate on the extension of quotas for women to the national parliament in India and the extension of quota provisions in Pakistan and Bangladesh, where in the wake of the Beijing Conference the government 'announced a National Policy for the Advancement of Women in 1997. The Policy called for a larger number of reserved seats in the legislature for women through direct elections' (Chowdhury 2003). At the national level in Pakistan – the Senate, National and Provincial Assemblies – 17 per cent of the seats are reserved for women.

Quota provisions in local government: a comparative perspective

In this section we examine the provisions of the local government quotas for women. We will argue that variations in the actual quota systems in the three countries influence the opportunity of women to participate fully once elected.

The new local level quotas introduced during the 1990s were directly elected reserved seats in all three countries.[9] The percentage of reserved seats was raised in India and Pakistan to 33 per cent and to 25 per cent in Bangladesh. These changes have been described by Raman for example as 'historic and one of the most significant attempts at transforming the Indian polity in the direction of greater democratization and decentralization of powers' (Raman 2003: 24). In Pakistan, Reyes claims that it has 'opened up not only an enormous political space but a strategic opportunity for women to make a difference in setting and implementing the agenda of local governments' (Reyes 2003: 44). In Bangladesh, Chowdhury argues that the direct election to local bodies in Bangladesh 'has brought about a qualitative change in their role perception. On the whole they have claimed a space within the local bodies and have raised spirited calls to have their terms of reference and spheres of activity defined' (Chowdhury 2003: 55).

How do the new local quota systems work?

Even though the countries have a common political history the local political systems vary slightly from each other.

In India, the 1992 73rd and 74th Constitutional Amendment Acts addressed the questions of strengthening the role of the local government and made provision for reserving not less than 33 per cent of the total seats in the local government for women (Mohanty 2003). As Table 9.2 shows, Gram Panchayat is the lowest level and is meant to consist of eight to ten villages, though since the population is the criteria it can also serve

Table 9.2 The local systems in Bangladesh, India and Pakistan

Country	Level	Name	Number of councils	Elected
Bangladesh[a]	District	Zila Parishad	60	n/a[b]
	Sub-district	Upazila/Thana Parishad	450	n/a[b]
	Union level	Union Parishad	4,500	Directly
	Village level	Gram Sarkar	68,000	n/a[b]
India[c]	District	Zila Panchayat	530	Directly
	Sub-district	Panchayat Samities	5,910	Directly
	Village level	Gram Panchayat	231,630	Directly
Pakistan[d]	District	Zila councils	100	Indirectly
	Sub-district	Tehsil/Town council	330	Indirectly
	Union level	Union councils	6,000	Directly

Sources: Siddiqui (2002), Graff (2003).

Notes
a The urban local system consists of City Corporations and Pourshavas (municipal bodies) (Mahtab 2003).
b According to the Local Government Reform Commission Report 1996, Bangladesh has a four-tier local government structure. However, until now nothing has been determined regarding the three-tier Zila, Upazial/Thana and Gram. No consensus has been reached regarding their composition, function or mode of election including the number of seats reserved for women, and no elections have been held at any of these levels.
c The urban local system is a three-tier system: Municipal corporation (mega cities), Municipal Council (small cities) and Nagar Panchayat (transitional areas) (Sharma 2003).
d The Tehsil Council is called Town Councils in the urban areas (Graff 2003).

just one village. The Gram Panchayat has about 12,000 to 15,000 inhabitants, though the Acts do not specify any such number leading to variations across the country. The number of members in Gram Panchayat is not fixed but varies from five to 30 members including a Pradhan (chairperson) and vice chairman depending on the size of the population in the district. The Panchayati Raj system is a party political system and the members are elected as candidates from a party list on a first-past-the-post basis and serve a mandatory term of five years in single-member districts. There is also one-third reservation for women among the positions of the chairpersons of these bodies (Baviskar 2003). There is a rotating system of reservations for women, which means that if you have a Panchayat with nine villages and nine members, in three of these villages only women candidates can stand for election. In the next election women will stand in three other villages (Baviskar 2003).

In Bangladesh, the local system in Bangladesh consists of four tiers, but until now continuous elections have been held only to Union Parishad (see Table 9.2). The reservation of seats for women in local government institutions in Bangladesh is stipulated under Article 9 of the Fundamental Principles of State Policy of the Constitution of Bangladesh. Direct election of women representatives to the rural local government Union Parishad as well as the urban local government was provided for in order

to implement the constitutional provision. This also conformed to the recommendations of the Study on the Institutional Review of the WID Capability of the Government of Bangladesh 1996 and the Local Government
Commissions Report 1997.

The number of members in Union Parishad is fixed and does not
depend on the population size of the union unlike the system in India. A
union covers five to 15 villages with an average population of 24,500
people (Nathan 1998: 110; Thörlind 2003: 61–2). Union Parishad consists
of one chairperson, nine general members and three women members in
reserved seats, totally 13 persons. This means that the percentage of
women will be at least 23 per cent and not 25 per cent, as there are no
quotas allocated for the post of chairperson. All the positions are directly
elected including the chairperson on a first-past-the-post basis in non-
party based elections (Siddiqui 2002). The chairperson is elected from the
whole Union Parishad and the post is open for both men and women to
contest. The nine general members are directly elected from one of the
nine wards the union is divided into and also open for both men and
women. The women in the reserved seats don't have any special ward of
their own but are elected from three of the general wards (Aminuzzaman
2003). In these wards (open for women only) women candidates contest
against each other but are elected by votes from both men and women.

As Pakistan is a federal republic the local government has been viewed
as a provincial decision area. Therefore the reservation of seats for women
to the local government has varied between the different provinces (Graff
2003). Women's right organizations and activists have demanded the
restoration of the provision of reserved seats for women together with a
demand for a substantial increase of 33 per cent reserved seats for women
to be filled through constituency-based direct election by joint electorate.
The successive governments of Banazir Bhutto and Nawaz Sharif failed to
respond positively to women's demand on the issue. In 1999 a military
coup removed the civilian government and as a part of a democratization
process the military regime of Musharraf adopted the Devolution of
Power Plan in 2000 to establish an identical set up of local government
bodies in all four provinces of Pakistan. As Table 9.2 shows this guaranteed 33 per cent quota for women at all three levels of the local government; Zila council (district level), Tehsil council (sub-district level) and
Union Councils (union level). The members of the Union Councils are
elected directly but the Tehsil and Zila councils the members are elected
indirectly by an electoral college formed by the elected councillors in the
Union Councils. The Union Council consists of eight to ten villages. It is
composed of 21 members – one Nazim (chairman), one Naib Nazim (vice
chairman), eight general Muslim seats, four women Muslim seats, four
Muslim peasant/worker seats, two women peasant/worker seats and one
religious minority seat. This means that six out of 21 seats are reserved for
women, and that the actual quota percentage is 29 per cent and not

33 per cent, which is the figure that is usually quoted. This is due to the fact that there were no quotas allocated for the Nazims' or the minority seats (Graff 2003). The elections to Union Council are on a first-past-the-post and non-party based as in Bangladesh but contrary to both India and Bangladesh the union serves as a multi-member ward for election of the council members. The women for the reserved seats are elected by votes from both men and women as in the other two countries (Graff 2003).

This comparison shows that the quota systems in the three countries are slightly different. In both Pakistan and Bangladesh quotas have been introduced at both national and local levels, while in India the quotas were introduced at the local level and the Bill to introduced quotas at the national level still languishes in the system (Rai 2000). In India there is a system of ward rotation for the reserved seats, which is not present in Pakistan and Bangladesh. In Bangladesh the wards for the reserved seats for women are three times bigger than the 'general seats'. This is not the case in the other two countries. In Pakistan the union is not divided into different wards – as in India and Bangladesh – but serve as a single constituency for all the candidates. In Pakistan and Bangladesh the local elections are non-party-based in opposition to the system in India. In India the seat of the chairman is included in the quota system, which means that one-third of the members are women. That is not the case in Bangladesh and Pakistan. However, there are also some similarities in these different quota regimes. All three electoral systems have constitutional histories bound up with the British colonial past, are plurality-majority political systems and the women are directly elected by both male and female votes.

Further, the analysis of quota provisions in different countries shows some level of diffusion of ideas. Various elements can be evaluated here. All three states are signatories to CEDAW (though with certain opt outs) and therefore have to report to the Commission on the Status of Women (CSW) regularly. This, together with the Beijing and post-Beijing UN initiatives prioritizing women's participation in political institutions have provided the impetus to examine quotas as a strategy for women's empowerment. A second element of diffusion is the role that women's movements and NGOs have played in demanding that women's exclusion from political institutions be addressed. Some of these demands have been the result of responses to state law, as the anti-Hudood law movement in Pakistan. The women's movements in all three countries have been influenced by the shift in the international women's movements from scepticism towards to engagement with state institutions. Finally, donor agencies are a source of diffusion of ideas on quotas. Familiarity with the Indian quota system, for example, makes donors suggest this pattern in Bangladesh though this might or might not be suitable in the country's political context. However, there is also some evidence that diffusion between these countries is limited. For example, critics in India have pointed out that seat reservations by rotation hinders the emergence of real leaders because for first time participants, a five-year tenure is too short to nurture a constituency which reverts to being a 'general' constituency at the end of that period. However, in Bangladesh, critics of fixed constituencies for women have pointed out the benefits of the rotational system. Formal acknowledgement of 'best practice' exchange is absent in the context of the poor state-to-state relations.

Quotas in practice: do they make a difference?

Measuring the impact that the introduction of quotas might or might not have had is difficult. One clear measurement would be the increase in the number of women in local government after the introduction of quotas. However, this can only be a quantitative assessment of the impact that quotas have made. A more complex issue might be whether the increased representation of women in local government has increased their active participation in local government bodies. Here we would need indicators such as attendance data, data about the number of times women speak in local government meetings, whether or not women have introduced and succeeded in getting through specific policy initiatives, and even empowerment indicators (training, travel and meeting with other women involved in local government, mentoring, etc.) would have to be examined. A further level of complexity might arise when we examine the context of women's participation – levels of education, health and cultural and economic position of women, which has crucial effect on their access to both state and community resources needed for performing their roles as representatives in local government. Finally, of course, we need to factor in availability, reliability and coherence of data available, which in many cases are scarce.

Given the complexity of measuring impact, our conclusions are that issues of process and outcome, individual experience and systemic issues have influenced the implementation of the quotas.

Women's numerical representation

Women's representation in local government has increased in all the three countries and we suggest that this is because of the introduction of quotas in one or other form. In India, after approval of the constitutional amendments, two elections (in 1995 and 2000) have been held in almost all states and today one million women occupy positions as members or heads in the rural and urban local government bodies (Baviskar 2003). It has been estimated that within a span of ten years about six million women have participated in the political process as candidates or elected members (Buch 2000b) While there are variations among the states in the magnitude of women's representation, most of the states have managed to meet the constitutional target of 33 per cent seats for women and in some states this proportion has exceeded. For example in Karnataka women occupy 43.6 per cent in local bodies. This means that a large number of women have managed to win general (unreserved) seats, defeating rival male and female candidates (Baviskar 2003). Bangladesh has held two elections under the new quota probation – in 1997 and 2003. In each of these elections over 40,000 women contested over the almost 13,000 reserved seats which all were filled. In Pakistan however only 36,000 of the over 40,000 seats were filled despite the fact that almost 49,000 women contested in the elections that were held during 2000 and 2001. Most of the problems were reported from districts in the North West Frontier Province (NWFP) where many women were neither allowed to contest nor to cast their votes.(Bari and Khan 2001: xii).

Challenges to participation

Have the new systems with a higher percentage of reserved seats as well as direct election not only increased the number of women but also improved the quality of their participation – in contrast to the previous often criticized systems of indirect election? One of the indicators of the success of the quota strategy would be to demonstrate that women's increased presence within local government is resulting in the improved functioning of local government institutions in these countries. Our conclusion is that gender and class regimes mediate political participation in all the three countries. State provision, formal and informal networks and customary laws prevent women from participating fully in local government. There is also a lack of education, training and resources for women representatives. Finally, their dependence on male members of household and inability to access economic resources (there are no salaries for local government representatives) are also inhibiting their performance. At the same time it seems like the new systems of reserved seats have created a social mobilization of rural women and changed their status both in the family as well as in the society, and have empowered them.

There is no consensus among the researchers here, which reflects different definitions of, for example, empowerment. In India it is often reported that the reserved seats for women have been filled with 'proxies' – the housewives of the male politicians without any real power (Nanivadekar 1997b). It is estimated that over 90 per cent of elected women are first timers. Even if the policy of reservation has helped some politically active women to be elected, these women have a lower political awareness and as such their participation in politics does not disturb patriarchal family systems. No gender differences were found between the men and women representatives with respect to their priority issues (Nanivadekar 1997a, b). Sharma is also critical and argues that women are expected to adjust to the imperatives of party structures for their political survival

(Sharma 2004). Some micro-studies show that the elected women have not addressed any specific gender issues (Ekatra 2003; Ghosh 2003). At the same time other studies suggest that elected women in Gram Panchayats are making a difference in shifting the focus of development policy by highlighting basic needs issues like water, food security, education and livelihood and become effective supporters of women's interests (Datta 1998; Mohanty 1999; Jayal and Nussbaum 2003). see Table 9.3.

In Pakistan the impact of the new quota system is yet to be seen. Initial research shows that there are frequent complaints by women councillors that they do not receive invitations to the council meetings. They are not consulted in development planning at the district and Union Council levels. At the same time a study showed that female councillors have a strong community contact (Pattan Development Organization 2004). A case study about the urban local government in Bangladesh shows that the elected women members can act as motivators, supervisors, and can be engaged in project planning, implementing, monitoring and evaluation processes. However, the participation of the ward commissioners in the activities of the city corporations is low (Mahtab 2003).

The problems for the elected women can be explained by several

Table 9.3 Women's representation in local government

Country	Issues introduced by women
Bangladesh	–Lack of good communication – damage of roads due to incessant rain during the rainy season, lack of maintenance of these roads and no plans to repair the roads or construct new roads –Proliferation of urban slums, rise in urban population due to rural–urban migration; increase in urban poverty –Lack of women's education – their limited participation in development activities, increase in violence against women, demand for dowry, lack of implementation of laws protecting the rights of women, child abuse, and denial of justice
India	–Speedy disbursement of rice and wheat through Public Distribution System (PDS) –Widow pensions –Low cost shelters –Encouraging girl child to join the schools –Construction of bathing *ghats*
Pakistan	–Education for girls –Access to drinking water –Price increase –Access to health centres and trained health workers in communities, particularly for delivery of babies –A say in spending the development funds assigned to local bodies –Violence against women

Source: Interview with Shaheen Sardar Ali (first chair of Pakistan Women's National Commission) 29 November 2004; Mahtab (2003), Mohanty and Mahajan (2003).

factors. According to Kabeer, the northern plains of the Indian sub-continent and Bangladesh belong to a belt of 'classic patriarchy' characterized by the institutionalization of extremely restrictive codes of behaviour for women. They stand in contrast to societies of South India and much of Southeast Asia whose institutions and practices permit a more egalitarian system of gender relations. At the heart of this system of social arrangements is the institution of *purdah* or female seclusion which defines and limits the personal and economic autonomy and social power of women and confines women into the private sphere of the home (Kabeer 1988). These patriarchal social relations are limiting women's ability to participate fully in the political life of the local community. In India the issue of caste-based discrimination forms an added layer of exclusion for women.

Further, in most states in India the role of panchayats is still principally confined to implementing centrally conceived schemes. The lack of administrative and financial autonomy prevents these institutions from fulfilling their role as institutions of self-government and the elected women have been addressing gender issues within very narrow parameters set by the panchayats (Mathew 2002; Mohanty and Mahajan 2003; Raman 2004). A similar situation is reported from Bangladesh where the lack of resources and authority is also a problem of the local government (Frankl 2004).

A third issue is the nature of representation by women within the reserved seats. In Bangladesh, the reserved seats have no ward of their own. Instead one reserved seat covers three wards of the general seats, which creates problems when it comes to who the elected women represent, access to development funds and campaigning as they must cover a much bigger area (Frankl 2004). Mahtab's study showed that the women commissioners in the local government were undermined as they were deprived of their responsibilities and financial allocations for development of their constituencies (Frankl 2004). In Pakistan, all members are elected from multi-member constituencies but despite this, women are not given equal share of the development fund as they are not perceived to have any direct constituency or ward. In India, the elected women have their own ward as they practice a system of rotation. This system has the advantage that the elected women have their own ward and a clear mandate. At the same time it also works against women's interest. Women that have been elected from a reserved ward in the first election have to compete with men as well as women in the next election. And when the ward is 'open' no party wants to nominate a female candidate. An option is to contest in one of the other three wards that have been reserved but then she will have no benefit from the work that she might have done before (Baviskar 2003).

Another issue is low or no special honorarium. In India, a Panchayat member gets between Rs. 10–50 as 'sitting fee' for attending a meeting. In many cases, if she is an agriculture labourer she will lose Rs. 50 as her daily wage and she cannot feed her family (Baviskar 2002). In other studies (Rai forthcoming; Sharma 2003) several women pointed out that without a salary the Panchayat is more open to corrupt practices and to being dominated by upper class individuals who can afford not to be paid. The issue of payment is also a particular one for women as being paid brings them status – 'maan' – within the family.[10] In Pakistan, councillors who come on reserved seats are not offered any honorarium, which makes it difficult for women councillors to fund transportation costs out of their own pocket, as most of them are economically dependent on the male members of their families. In Bangladesh, the members are supposed to get some honorarium to cover transportation costs and so on but not all members are able to get their money (Frankl 2004). The study made by Mahtab 2003 showed that the women commissioners do not have proper facilities, such as specific office space, transport and other facilities.

As noted before, the local elections in India are party-based as opposed to Bangladesh and Pakistan where the elections are non-party based. More research is needed to examine the role of the political parties and how women's membership of these institutions might affect their work within the panchayats (Parpart *et al.* 2002). In the Indian local elections there is always a high number of candidates not affiliated to any political party (Nanivadekar 1997a), and a study by the NGO Ekatra suggested that 70 per cent of women have succeeded in raising issues at various levels even without the backing of political parties. In Bangladesh, elections are supposed to be on a non-party base but according to Ahmed the parties control and decide who will represent the party in the elections even at the local level. By doing so they play an important role in shaping women's representation in formal politics (2003). In Pakistan, Bari and Khan argue that party-less local government has provided the space to the poor to nominate their own candidates as well as forced the local elite to involve disadvantaged groups in the process of nominating candidates (Bari and Khan 2001).

The age, education, socio-economic status and political background of the elected women seem to have a crucial effect on their access to both state and community resources needed for performing their roles as representatives in local government. In India, studies conducted in several parts of India show that a majority of the women belong to the lower socio-economic strata both in terms of education and class (Buch, 2000b, 2001). In India, a majority of the elected women are from 'non-political' families with no previous political experience. The seats reserved for the Scheduled castes and Scheduled Tribes means that the rich and politically dominant families are not able to grab the positions (Baviskar 2003). At the same time it seems like the percentage of women from lower incomes is lower at the leadership levels (Mohanty and Seldon 2003). When it comes to age, studies have shown that, in the first election, most of the women were 40 years old or older (Datta 1998; Ghosh 2003). In the second election however studies have shown that relatively younger groups have been elected (Panchayati Rai Update 2003). Similar findings from the survey done in Pakistan by Pattan Development Organization in 2001 show that more than half of the women were illiterate, very few own land and a majority of them had never contested elections before and neither had their families. And as in India, the percentage of women from the lower strata of the society decline among the higher positions and levels in the local government. Almost 60 per cent of the elected women are 45 years old or younger. In Bangladesh, however, a study done by World Food Programme in 1999 showed that the elected women had a better socio-economic status than the average rural women. Over 40 per cent were between 30 and 38 years of age and even though a majority of the elected women were housewives, most of them had at least a secondary education (86 per cent). Most of the elected women came from landowning families and 53 per cent owned more than five acres of land – a substantial amount in a country were half of the rural people are landless. The study also showed that both the elected member and her family were very active in the village, where they were known for considerable social involvement even before the election (World Food Programme 1999). More research needs to be done to explain the differences between India and Pakistan on one hand and Bangladesh on the other. According to Mohanty the high average of women from lower social economic strata must be regarded as a success when it comes to decentralization since women from all classes of society have been represented (Mohanty 2003).

The lack of previous political experience as well as low level of education and socio-economic status underlines the need for training and capacity-building among the elected women. In Bangladesh training is offered by both the government and NGOs. A 2002 study (Democracywatch 2002) showed that the elected members had received at lot of training from different NGOs but also that they wanted and needed more training. The study also showed that effective training would mean including both men and women. In India evaluations have shown that the women want education and training continuously. So far most of the training programmes have focused on rules and regulations of local government but according to Raman the training also has to focus on problem-solving methodologies. People have to be trained for self-government (Raman 2004).

Despite the problems, however, the reservation for women in local government have, together with other movements like for example the micro-credit movement, created a massive social mobilization in the rural area (Mohanty 2003). In India the women's participation in the public sphere of Panchayats has also enhanced their status in their families, castes and villages (Baviskar 2003; Sharma 2003). In Bangladesh too, women's participation in local politics has led to a measure of increased freedom, reduced inequality and oppression (Frankl 2004). As elected members of Union Parishad, some women have been able to introduce some change in the traditional village court. This, as well as the membership in the Union Parishad, has made them well known in the village and given them a larger social network than before.

Conclusions

A comparative study of quotas for women in the South Asian region addresses several important issues of the gendered nature of political participation and representation. Our study suggests that quotas for women in representative bodies at the local level came about as a result of many different factors – an internal debate about the ways in which marginalized groups can be compensated for historical exclusions from public life; external pressures from global social institutions such as the UN and the women's movements and the interaction of national women's groups with these; the changes in the nature of state politics as well as the shifting position of party and factional groups within national politics.

Here, we raise some theoretical issues about quotas. In terms of the politics of representation, quotas address the historical inequality, which kept women out the public sphere. Both participation and representation have historically been hotly contested concepts. The politics of representation has reflected a wide variety of views towards quotas. From the justice argument to the empowerment argument, quotas have been seen as important elements of addressing women's historical exclusion from political institutions and processes. As it is clear from the case study of South Asia presented here, the outcome of quota regimes is equally complex. On the one hand, we see quota-based representation in local government reflecting the gender regimes of inequality and worry about the co-option of women into state machinery without any significant shifts in their status or indeed the status of local government institutions. On the other, however, we do see some clear indications that participation made available through quotas does impact upon familial and institutional relations even though this impact is rather fragile and will need further nurturing in order to be consolidated. Quotas in this sense are a start, which have the potential to kick-start other processes of empowerment of women.

Quota politics is also the politics of citizenship. As we have seen above, the constitutional debates in the three countries reflected the nature of particular citizenships which meant that women's citizenship was formalized through equality provisions without necessarily the providing the entitlements that were critical to operationalizing these. Women's movements had to struggle for making political rights real and these struggles point to the dynamic and unfolding nature of citizenship debates and rights. While the early struggles demanded universal political rights, current movements have insisted upon mainstreaming a gendered perspective in political institutions, as well as upon the importance of entitlements for citizenship which include both socio-economic justice, as well as a discursive shift from the earlier national citizenship rights to the demands for universal human rights. The introduction of quotas is the result of these struggles and a response to the limitations of the equality discourse when not backed up by social and political commitment to its implementation.

Through a multi-layered analysis of the quota debate in South Asia, we become conscious of several issues. First, as economic restructuring of national economies under pressures from international economic institutions bites along lines of class, gender and race, debates about the socio-economic entitlements to citizenship are increasing in importance (Fraser 1995; Coole 1996; Hoskyns and Rai 1998). In particular we find feminist theorists and policy analysts pointing out the importance of distinguishing between socio-economic and political bases of citizenship (Lister 1997; Yuval-Davis and Pnina 1999). It is in these debates on citizenship that feminists have also encountered yet again the issue of differences among women – the realization that if socio-economic contexts are important for women's citizenship to be actualized, then there needs to be an acknowledgement that not all women shared the same economic and social space. Citizenship debates are important if we are to assess whether quotas open up the space for the recognition of women's under-representation in politics, but also whether by making possible women's participation in politics they empower women. Local government quotas can work to empower women only when this wider context is taken into account. Second, empowerment is not the possession but the exercise of power – not simply power over, but power to. In the context of local governance in South Asia, 'individual empowerment, whether it be gaining skills, developing consciousness, or making decisions, takes place within the structural constraints of institutions and discursive practices' (Parpart *et al.* 2002: x). Third, measuring empowerment can be a problematic. How will we measure the empowering effect of being elected the 'sarpanch', or meeting other women in an institutional setting? It is the issue of keeping in view both the process and outcome of policies that Nancy Fraser has addressed in her work on 'politics of recognition' vs 'politics of redistribution' (1995).

Fraser suggests that identity politics allows for recognition of inequalities within society but not necessarily to a 'politics of redistribution'. Redistribution of resources, which underpin exclusion of presence and of voice cannot she argues be addressed simply through the politics of recognition. As we have seen above, issues of caste, class and religion continue to divide women and are reflected in the nature of local politics. Iris Marion Young, however, takes issue with this interpretation of identity-based recognition. She argues that in the very process of arguing for the recognition of hitherto excluded or marginalized groups, there takes place a redistribution of discursive power (1997). The politics of recognition and redistribution therefore unfold simultaneously. However, as Anne Phillips has argued in the context of political systems, the shift from the politics of 'ideas' (by which she means ideas organized within the structures of political parties) to the politics of presence (by which she means representation of identities in politics) is problematic. She argues instead that, it is 'in the relationship between ideas and presence that we can best hope to find a fairer system of representation, not in a false opposition between one or the other' (1995: 25). In this sense, quotas have the potential to bring together the politics of ideas and that of presence. However, where both Young and Phillips fail to address the point made by Fraser is the relationship between structural inequalities of a socio-economic system and its impact on the politics of recognition as well as representation. Hoskyns and Rai have argued that '[the] feminist challenge is limited by a current lack of focus on the importance of redistributive policies that are rooted in the structural inequalities of capitalist production and exchange' (1998: 362). It is our conclusion, that if quotas are to fulfil their potential for addressing women's exclusion from political life, women's struggles need to focus on the issue of redistribution of resources if power relations in society are to be fundamentally changed.

Notes

1 Emma Frankl has worked as a research assistant on this chapter. The authors are grateful for the effort and energy she has put into helping with the chapter.
2 Pakistan was further divided in 1971, when Bangladesh came into existence after a civil war.
3 This allows people of different religions to follow their own religious rather than secular state law in the area of marriage, divorce, custody, etc.
4 Article 331 stipulated a reservation of seats for the Anglo-Indian community for two years if the President thought it to be under-represented in parliament.
5 However, class-based exclusion was not taken on board the quota regime. Rather, this was to be addressed through equal opportunity provisions on grounds that class mobility allows a way out of the poverty trap, which the caste structure does not allow. This approach to reservation has led to the charge that the 9th Schedule creates sub-elites within the scheduled castes and tribes, limiting the redistributive role of quotas.
6 Rai's interviews with women activists suggest that quotas were largely the result of government initiative. The 'seven sisters' (important women's NGOs) were consulted at the stage when the decision to introduce quotas had been taken, but it was largely femocrats within the government that formulated the policy. In India, said Dr. Vina Mazumdar (Centre for Women's Development Studies), 'reservations have generated a debate, not a movement'. (Interview with Dr Vina Mazumdar, 22nd April 2004. New Dehli.)
7 There have been discussions about introducing the same type of legislation at the national level called the 84th Amendment Bill but it has not yet passed (Rai 2000; Raman 2003).
8 'The Hudood Ordinances disregard the testimony of women for inflicting *hadd* or punishment ... evidence of four, adult male Muslims is required of the

actual act of penetration as proof of adultery or rape ... Women also stand discriminated against because these laws fix a lower age of criminal responsibility for girls than for boys' (Ali 2000: 47).

9 As outlined in the introduction, it is important to make a distinction between 'reserved seats with indirect election' and 'reserved seats with direct election'. Systems with indirect elections have a certain number of seats that are reserved for women but they are nominated and elected by, for example the direct elected representatives at a lower level. In systems with direct election there are certain seats reserved for women to whom only women are allowed to contest.

10 'Maan' is an important word here. It can translate in many different ways but essentially denotes respect, though this might be underpinned by pride. A place for the woman within the family might be enhanced if she is bringing in some income, together with the recognition she gets for the 'job' which can be characterized as 'public service'. This also supports Amartya Sen's contention that paid work outside the home is a prerequisite for women's improved status within the family.

Bibliography

Ahmed, K.U. 'Women and Politics in Bangladesh', paper prepared for the International Conference on Women and Politics in Asia, Halmstad, June 2003.

Ali, S. (2000) 'Law, Islam and the Women's Movement in Pakistan', in S.M. Rai (ed.) *International Perspectives on Gender and Democratisation*, Basingstoke: Macmillan, pp. 41–63.

Aminuzzaman, S.M. 'Strengthening the UP: Problems and Prospects', paper presented in a workshop on Local Government and Reforms: Issues and Prospects, Dhaka, April 2003.

Bari, F. (1997) 'Discovering Female Representatives in Local Government', unpublished report.

Bari, S. and Khan, B.H. (2001) *Local Government Elections 2001. Phase III, IV & V*, Islamabad: Pattan Development Organization.

Baviskar, B.S. (2002) 'Including the Excluded, Empowering the Powerless', *Sociological bulletin*, 51, 2: 168–74.

—— 'Impact of Women's Participation in Local Governance in Rural India', paper presented at the Rural Network Conference, Inverness, June 2003. Online. Avaliable at: http://action.web.ca/home/sap/india_resources.shtml?x=69013&AA_EX_Session=633056f178b041549c8b010d037a076b (accessed February 9 2005).

Baxi, U. (1995) 'Emancipation as Justice: Babasaheb Ambedkar's Legacy and Vision', in U. Baxi and B. Parekh (eds) *Crisis and Change in Contemporary India*, London: Sage, pp. 122–47.

Buch, N. (2000a) 'Women's Experience in New Panchayats: The emerging leadership of rural women', Occasional Paper 35, Delhi: Centre for Women's Development Studies.

—— (2000b) 'Panchayats and Women', in G. Mathew (ed.) *Status of Panchayati Rai in the States and Union Territories of India*, New Delhi: Concept.

—— (2001) 'The 73rd Constitution Amendment and the Experience of Women in the New Panchayati Rai Institutions (PRIs): A Critical Evaluation', in A. Pinto and H. Reifeld (eds) *Women in Panchayati Raj*, New Delhi: Indian Social Institute.

Bystendinzky, J.M. (ed.) (1992) *Women Transforming Politics: Worldwide Strategies for Empowerment*, Bloomington and Indianapolis: Indiana University Press.

Chatterjee, P. (1993) 'The Nationalist Resolution of the Women's Question', in K. Sangari and S. Vaid (eds) *Recasting Women, Essays in Colonial History*, New Dehli: Kali for Women.

Chowdhury, N. (2003) 'Bangladesh's Experience – Dependence and Marginality in Politics', in International IDEA *The Implementation of Quotas: Asian Experiences* Quota Workshop Report Series no. 1, Stockholm: International IDEA, pp. 50–8.

Coole, D. (1996) 'Is class a difference that makes a difference?', *Radical Philosophy*, issue 77, May/June.

Datta, B. (ed.) (1998) *And Who Will Make the Chapatis? A Study of All-Women Panchayats in Maharashtra*, Calcutta: Stree.

Democracywatch (2002) *Assessing Training Program for the Female Members of the UP*, Dhaka: Democracywatch.

Ekatra (2003) *Women and Governance Reimagining the State*, New Delhi: Ekatra.

Frankl, E. (2004) 'Quota as Empowerment. The Use of Reserved Seats in Union Parishad as an Instrument for Women's Political Empowerment in Bangladesh', The Research Program on Gender Quotas. Working Paper Series 2004: 3, Stockholm University: Department of Political Science.

Fraser, N. (1995) 'From Redistribution to Recognition? Dilemmas of Justice in a "Poststructuralist" Age', *New Left Review*, 212: 68–93.

Goetz, A. (1996) 'Dis/organizing gender: women development agents in the state and NGO poverty – reduction programmes in Bangladesh', in S.M. Rai (ed.) *Women and the State: International Perspectives*, London: Taylor and Francis, pp. 118–42.

—— (1997) *Getting Institutions Right for Women in Development*, London: Zed Books.

Gopal Jayal, N. (forthcoming) 'Development or Empowerment? Women's Participation in Pachayati Raj Institutions', *Democratization*.

Ghosh, A. (2003) 'Women's Reservation in Urban Local Bodies: A Perspective from Chennai Municipal Corporation Election, 2001', *Indian Journal of Gender Studies*, 10, 1: 117–41.

Graff, I. 'Women's Representation in Pakistani Politics – the Quota Systems under the Musharraf Regime', paper presented at the International Conference on Women and Politics in Asia, Halmstad, June 2003.

Hoskyns, C. and Rai, S.M. (1998) 'Gender, Class and Representation: India and the European Union', *European Journal of Women's Studies*, 5, 3–4: 345–65.

Inter-Parliamentary Union (IPU) (2004) Online. Available at: http://www.ipu.org/ (accessed 10 March 2005).

International IDEA and Stockholm University (2004) 'Global Database of Quotas for Women', Online. Available at: http://www.quotaproject.org (accessed 10 March 2005).

Jayal, N. and Nussbaum, M. (2003) *Gender and Governance An Introduction*, Human Development Resource Centre, New Delhi: UNDP.

John, M.E. (2000) 'Alternate Modernities? Reservations and Women's movement in 20th Century', *India Economic and Political Weekly*, 35, 43, 44: 3822

Kabeer, N. (1988) 'Subordination and struggle: Women in Bangladesh', *New Left Review*, 168: 95–121.

—— (1994) *Reversed Realities: Gender Hierarchies in Development Thought*, London: Verso.

—— (1995) 'Targeting women or transforming institutions? Policy lessons from NGO anti-poverty efforts', *Development and Practice*, 5, 2: 108–16.

—— (1999) 'Resources, Agency, Achievements: Reflections on the Measurement of Women's Empowerment', *Development and Change*, 30: 435–64.

Lister, R. (1997) *Citizenship: Feminist Perspectives*, London: Palgrave.

Mahtab, N. 'Women in Urban Local Governance: A Bangladesh Case Study', paper presented at the International conference on Women's Quotas in Urban Local Governance: A Cross-national Comparison. New Delhi, February 2003.

Mathew, G. (2002) 'Ten Years on', *The Hindu*, 27 December.

Mohanty, B. (1999) 'Panchayat Raj Institutions and Women', in B. Ray and A. Basu (eds) *From Independence Towards Freedom, Indian Women since 1947*, New Delhi: Oxford University Press.

—— 'Women's Presence in Panchayats (Village Councils) in India: A New Challenge to Patriarchy', paper presented at the International Conference on Women and Politics in Asia, Halmstad, June 2003.

Mohanty, B. and Mahajan, V. 'Women's Empowerment in the Context of Seventy-third and Seventy-fourth Constitutional Amendment Acts', paper presented at the conference: A Decade of Women's Empowerment through Local Government in India, New Delhi, October 2003. Online. Available at: http://action.web.ca/home/sap/india_resources.shtml?x=69009 (Accessed February 9, 2005).

Mohanty, M. and Seldon, M. (2003) 'Reconceptualising Local Democracy Preliminary reflections on democracy, power and Resistence', Panchayati Raj Update, 10(4), New Delhi: Institute of Social Sciences.

Nanivadekar, M. (1997a) *Electoral Process in Corporation Elections: A Gender Study*, Mumbai: Bharatiya Stree Shakti.

—— (1997b) *Empowering Women. Assessing the Policy of Reservation in Local Bodies. A Report*, Mumbai: Rambhau Mhalagi Prabodhini.

Nathan, I. (1998) *When Poor People Participate. A Case Study of a Local Government election in a Locality of Rural Bangladesh*, Aarhus: Politica.

Panchayati Raj Update (2003) 'Fact File Bihar Panchayat Election 2001', 10(2) New Delhi: Institute of Social Sciences.

Parpart, J.L., Rai, S.M. and Staudt, K.A. (eds) (2002) *Rethinking Empowerment Gender and Development in a Global/Local World*, London: Routledge.

Pathak, Z. and Sudarajan, R. (1992) 'Shahbano' in J. Butler and J.W. Scott (eds) *Feminists Theorize the Political*, London: Routledge.

Pattan Development Organisation (2004) *Voices of Women Councilors*, Islamabad: Pattan Development Organisation.

Phillips, A. (1995) *The Politics of Presence*, Oxford: Oxford University Press.

Rai, S.M. (1997) 'Gender and Representation: Women MPs in the Indian Parliament', in A. Goetz (ed.) *Getting Institutions Right for Women in Development*, London: Zed.

—— (ed.) (2000) *International Perspectives on Gender and Democratisation*, Basingstoke: Macmillan.

—— (2002) *Gender and the Political Economy of Development*, Cambridge: Polity Press.

—— (forthcoming) 'Panchayats, Women's Representation and Deliberative Politics'.

Rai, S.M. and Sharma, K. (2000) 'Democratising the Indian Parliament: the "Reservation for Women" Debate', in S.M. Rai (ed.) *International Perspectives on Gender and Democratisation*, Basingstoke: Macmillan, pp. 149–65.

Raman, V. (2003) 'The implementation of Quotas for Women: The Indian Experience', in International IDEA *The Implementation of Quotas: Asian Experiences*, Quota Workshop Report Series no. 1, Stockholm: International IDEA, pp. 22–32.

—— (2004) *Globalisation, Sustainable Development and Local Self-Government. Challenges of the 21st Century: The India Experience*, New Delhi: Center for Women's Development Studies.

Reyes, S.L. (2003) 'Quotas in Pakistan: A Case Study', in International IDEA *The Implementation of Quotas: Asian Experiences*. Quota Workshop Report Series no. 1, Stockholm: International IDEA, pp. 42–7.

Sarkar, S. (1983) *Modern India, 1885–1947*, Delhi: Macmillan India Ltd.

Sharma, A. 'Women's Political Participation and Leadership in the Governance of Municipal Institutions in an Indian State', paper presented at the International Conference on Women and Politics in Asia, Halmstad, June 2003.

Sharma, K. (2004) 'From Representation to Presence: the paradox of power and powerlessness of women In PRIs', in D. Bandyopadhyay and A. Mukherjee (ed.) *New Issues in Panchayati Raj*, New Delhi: Concept Publishing Company, pp. 48–66.

Siddiqui, T. 'Effective Participation of Women and Strengthening of Local Government in Bangladesh', paper presented at the seminar: Good Governance and Local Government: Changes and Challenges, Dhaka, December 2002.

Thörlind, R. (2003) *Development, Decentralization and Democracy. Exploring Social Capital and Politicization in the Bengal Region*, Dhaka: Pathak Shamabesh Book.

United Nations Development Programme (UNDP) (2000) *Human Development Report*, Oxford: Oxford University Press.

Young, M.I. (1997) 'Unruly Categories: A Critique of Nancy Fraser's Dual Systems Theory', *New Left Review*, 222: 147–60.

Yuval-Davis, N. and Pnina, W. (1999) *Women, Citizenship and Difference*, London: Zed Books.

World Food Programme (1999) *Elected Woman Members of UP. A Socio-Economic Study*, Dhaka: World Food Programme.

Part III

Short case studies

10 Gender quotas in post-conflict states

East Timor, Afghanistan and Iraq

Julie Ballington and Drude Dahlerup

The last two decades have witnessed a widespread trend towards democratization in many parts of the world, with old regimes crumbling under domestic and international pressure. This has brought the role of the international community in brokering peace deals and assisting in state building under the spotlight. Must democracy grow from below or can democracy be 'installed' from the outside? The international community faces enormous challenges when establishing governance and legal frameworks underpinning any successful transition to democracy. While all state building efforts are necessarily determined by the local historical and political context, an underlying commitment to a liberal rights-based approach to democracy, including the promotion of values such as a secular and democratic government, constitutionalism, competitive elections, the rule of law and respect for human rights, has tended to prevail in United Nations state building interventions (Samuels and Einsiedel 2003: 3).

With growing pressure from the international community, and finding expression in international conventions and treaties, a commitment to gender equality is now prevalent in discourses on post-conflict state building. This short chapter briefly traces the recent developments regarding the application of gender quotas in selected post-conflict states. Recent developments in countries like East Timor, Afghanistan and Iraq raise questions as to whether the political empowerment of women is possible through the introduction of quotas, and what roles can be played by the international community. It is also important to consider the role of domestic women's movements. In this context, it is necessary to question if the international community has demonstrated any real commitment to include women in post-conflict reconstruction efforts, and if so, whether empowerment can come from 'above'.

Electoral system design and quota rules

A key component of any post-conflict state building agenda is the design of electoral systems and governing institutions.

Table 10.1 Quota provisions in East Timor, Afghanistan and Iraq

Country	Year of election	Electoral system	Quota
Afghanistan	2005	SNTV	Yes. Constitutional of at least two women per province, or 27% of seats in the lower house. Electoral law to be determined
East Timor	2001	Parallel (List PR and FPP)	No. Quotas were forcefully lobbied for by women's groups, but rejected by the transitional authority.
Iraq	2005	List PR	Yes. According to Section 4(3) of the electoral law, political parties must place women in every third position on political party lists – 'no fewer than one out of the first three candidates on the list must be a woman, no fewer than two out of the first six candidates until the end of the list'.

Source: International IDEA and Stockholm University (2005).
Key Electoral Systems: *Plurality-Majority:* FPP = First-Past-the-Post. *Proportional Representation:* List PR. *Mixed:* Parallel. *Other:* SNTV = Single Non-transferable Vote.

In post-conflict countries, competitive elections are seen as central in promoting democracy and conferring legitimacy upon the new political order. Over the past decade, the international community has become involved in a wide range of activities, from providing technical assistance on constitutional and legal reforms including electoral systems, to advising on legislative structures and political party strengthening (Reilly 2003: 9–13).

Among other legal and constitutional issues, electoral arrangements are a key institutional variable in a political system with the potential to influence the extent to which excluded groups can gain access to elected bodies. The uneven political playing field on which women and men compete in elections has increasingly led to a number of reforms to safeguard women's presence in parliament, mainly in the form of quotas or other positive action strategies. They have taken varying forms, ranging from voluntary party quotas adopted by the ruling (liberation) parties in Mozambique and South Africa, to constitutionally guaranteed quotas in Rwanda, Afghanistan and Iraq, where the international community has been influential in their adoption.

From 1994, *South Africa* and *Mozambique* are early examples of countries where the introduction of quotas secured women positions in the newly elected decision-making bodies. In both countries, a homegrown and organized women's movement consisting of political women and women in civil society lobbied the ruling parties to adopt gender quotas with positive results. Quotas were voluntarily adopted by political parties rather than legislated as part of the electoral rules. While many women within the liberation struggle had developed networks with the international women's movement, these quotas were adopted by the political elite in response to homegrown pressure rather than as a result of pressure exerted by the international community.

In other cases, the introduction of gender quotas has been influenced to a great extent by recommendations from international and regional organizations, and supported by actors working at the country level. The recommendations of the 1995 Beijing Platform for Action, which called on governments to take steps to ensure women's equal access to, and full participation in, power structures and decision-making fora has provided a central lobbying platform. In establishing new electoral rules and processes in East Timor, Afghanistan and Iraq, legislated quotas have been proposed, and in all but one country adopted (see Table 10.1). Women's groups were key to the discussion about implementing gender quotas, and new coalitions were formed based on the demand for women's inclusion in the reconstruction processes. Yet the role of the international community, primarily through the Coalitional Provisional Authorities in Iraq, the Transitional Afghan government with UNAMA in Afghanistan and UNTAET in East Timor, together with domestic women's groups, has been influential.

East Timor

The United Nations Transitional Administration in East Timor (UNTAET) was charged with overseeing national reconstruction and preparing for the transfer of administrative power to the East Timorese at independence. It also oversaw the first national election in 2001. In exercising its functions, UNTAET was charged with observing internationally recognized human rights standards, including those of the Convention on the Elimination of All Forms of Discrimination Against Women (CEDAW), thereby incorporating the goal of gender equality into its legal framework.

In March 2001, the East Timorese network of 16 women's organizations, REDE, submitted a proposal to the National Council requesting that the electoral regulations for the Constitutional Assembly include a 30 per cent quota for women. It was proposed that at least 30 per cent of candidates on party lists should be women and placed in winnable positions (in every third position on the list). Quotas were defined by REDE as a temporary measure to open the door to women's participation in the Constitution making process (Pires 2002). The 30 per cent quota had previously been applied by UNTAET for the formation of the civil service and to the National Council.

The National Council and the UN Department of Political Affairs (DPA) however, rejected the inclusion of mandatory quotas in the electoral regulation in 2001. The UN was split in opinions over the introduction of mandatory quotas in East Timor: while UNIFEM, the High Commissioner for Human Rights and the UN's Division for the Advancement of Women supported such measures, the Electoral Assistance Division (EAD) of the DPA rejected it on the grounds that it contravened the UN definition of a free and fair election, stating that:

> UNTAET has exclusive responsibility for holding free and fair elections in East Timor ... (and) ... while some countries do have quotas for women (and for other groups) other democracies vehemently oppose the practice. This would include some members of the Security Council. Electoral quotas for women (and any other group) do not constitute international best practice for elections.
>
> (Quoted in Pires 2002: 2)

The exclusion of a quota provision in the electoral regulations met with strong reaction from the women's groups who protested, but who continued to lobby for a high representation of women. Political parties were encouraged through other special measures, such as allocating political parties extra broadcast time to include women candidates in winnable positions on party lists. Additionally, several training workshops for potential women candidates were held by the Gender Affairs Unit in partnership with UNIFEM (Whittington 2004: 4). Even though no legislated quota was introduced, women were elected to 27 per cent of the seats in the Constituent Assembly in August 2001. This body became the National Parliament on 20 May 2002, the date on which the country became independent, without any new elections.

The East Timor case demonstrates the importance of commitment by *all* bodies responsible for post-conflict state building. As Whittington notes '...as we are all aware, often the headquarters' policy-makers overlook or fail to grasp that the real value of any resolution lies not in the rhetoric but in its implementation' (Whittington 2004: 2). The rejection of the legislated electoral quota for women in East Timor by the United Nations was potentially an obstructive precedent.

However, renewed pressure for women's participation in involvement in post-conflict state building found expression in UN Security Council resolution 1325 on *Women, Peace and Security*, passed in October 2000. In the debate introducing 1325 in 2000, Kofi Annan stated that 'peace is inextricably linked to equality between women and men ... maintaining and promoting peace and security requires equal participation in decision-making' (Whittington 2004: 2). According to this new international discourse, all democracy-building policies are to ensure that a gender perspective is mainstreamed throughout applying to all decision-making, from peace accords through to constructing systems of governance. This discourse, together with the successful efforts to increase women's representation through quotas in Latin America and Africa, has contributed to bringing this issue of quotas for women to state-building efforts in Afghanistan and Iraq.

Afghanistan

The Afghan experience highlights the importance of women's inclusion in post-conflict settlements, as they provide for a provisional administration until such time as elections can be held and constitutional and legal frameworks can be established. Chinkin notes that peace agreements usually do not include quotas for women in political bodies, but they do so for other political groups. Rather, vague references about the importance of women's inclusion are made, such as the Provisions on the Interim Administration in Afghanistan in the Bonn Agreement which notes that due regard must be paid to the importance of the participation of women in all decision-making fora including the Emergency Loya Jirga (Chinkin 2003: 26).

While women only accounted for 5 per cent of delegates during the Bonn negotiations in 2001, 12 per cent of the nearly 2,000 delegates who attended the Emergency Loya Jirga in 2002 were women. It was convened to establish a transitional Afghan administration to govern the country until free and fair elections can be held. In the following Transitional Administration President Karzai appointed four women to key positions in his Cabinet.

Post-conflict transition periods provide an opportunity to rewrite the rules – from the constitution through to electoral laws and regulations. Three institutions were involved in making the new constitution in Afghanistan. First, the Constitutional Drafting Commission was made up of legal scholars and solicitors, and included two women out of nine. Second, the Constitutional Review Commission had seven women among its 30 members. As the third step, the Constitutional Loya Jirga was convened to revise and approve a draft of the Afghan Constitution submitted by the Constitutional Review Commission. Twenty per cent of the 502 *elected* representatives were women, 17 per cent of all delegates (Embassy of Afghanistan 2004; Nordlund 2004; OSAGI 2004: 4).

Article 83 of the Constitution adopted on 4 January 2004 guarantees a quota for women in the bicameral National Assembly. For the Meshrano Jirga, House of Elders or upper house, the President appoints one-third of the members, and 50 per cent of these shall be women (Embassy of Afghanistan 2004: article 83, chapter 5, art. 3). In the Wolesi Jirga, or lower house, women must hold at least 25 per cent of the seats elected for the first time in 2005. The Wolesi Jirga will consist of 249 parliamentarians, elected in the provinces according to the size of the population of each of the 34 provinces. At least two women are to be elected from each province, which raises the quota to at least 27 per cent for women. The

Joint Electoral Management Body (an independent institution comprised of national and international members with the mandate to conduct voter registration and hold elections), was responsible for drafting the electoral law which put the constitutional quota into effect. Different electoral rules have been proposed, ranging from a single-non-transferable vote system to proportional representation. In mid-2005, a SNTV electoral system was adopted.

Many actors were involved in the process leading to the constitutional quota, with the UN taking the lead. In February 2002, Kofi Annan called for 'temporary special measures, including targets and quotas, targeted at Afghan women' to accelerate the equality of women and men in decision-making (Annan 2002). The international community was active in having women's political representation placed on the agenda among the many other issues to be tackled.

However, women's groups in Afghanistan have been a key catalyst in the fight for gender quotas.[1] With many exiled Afghan women participating in the restructuring, the distinction between the international women's movement and national organizations and groups became less sharp (Dahlerup and Nordlund 2004). During the constitutional drafting process, different women's groups had called for 25 per cent female representation, and in September 2003 at a meeting on *Women and the Constitution* convened in Kandahar, an 'Afghan Women's Bill of Rights' was formulated. It consisted of 21 demands, one of which was 'equal representation of women in the Loya Jirga and Parliament'[2] (Afghan Women's Network 2004). Supporting the lobbying efforts were the Ministry for Women's Affairs, originally supported by the UN with funding provided by international agencies, and UNAMA, established to integrate all UN activities in coordination with the Afghan Administration including gender equality related issues. The developments in Afghanistan highlight the important role that the international community can play, when supported and working with the domestic women's movement and with the support of traditional institutions.

Iraq

The United States 'war on terror' initiated in 2001 and the subsequent military invasion of Iraq in 2003 has prompted new discourses on state-building interventions and the role of the international community. At least in theory, the Bush administration put women's rights as a central component of its policy to promote democracy in the Middle East, and is one of the four pillars of the Middle East Partnership Initiative (Ottaway 2004). This approach is in tune with UNDP's Arab Human Development Report from 2003, which views women's disempowerment as one of three main obstacles for human development in the region (UNDP 2003).

Since the fall of the Saddam Hussein regime, Iraq has been governed by the Coalition Provisional Authority (CPA) and the Iraqi Governing Council (IGC) established in July 2003. The IGC was handpicked by the CPA (US and UK occupying forces), where the inclusion of women therefore became dependent upon the willingness of the Authority to do so (Chinkin 2003: 26). This council was composed bearing in mind the ethnic composition of the Iraqi society, and consists of five different ethnic groups.[3] There are three women in this council, one of whom, Ms Akila al-hashemi,[4] was assassinated in September 2003, and later replaced by Ms Khufaji. The Council has the power to nominate and dismiss ministers, direct policies and it played an important part in drafting the interim constitution of Iraq.

The CPA was divided on the issue of quotas for women.[5] While the British government had proposed a 25 per cent mandatory quota for women in government, Iraqi politicians and the US government were not in favour (Khalil 2004). While there was clear rhetoric in support of women's rights, initially this was not to include implementing quotas. However, the three women represented in the IGC have all spoken in favour of quotas (except the newly appointed Ms Khufaji), as have women from around the country, including high profile female political leaders such as Nesreen Berwari, the only women minister out of a total of 25. Berwari has stated that 'to safeguard existing rights and to help the democratic process from being so easily usurped, Iraqi women urge that women hold no less than 40 per cent of representative position' (Berwari 2004). Others have demanded that women make up at least one-third of the committee drafting the constitution, and all political institutions, including the parliament and local councils.

Iraqi women's groups have also been outspoken on the pressing need for women to be included in reconstruction efforts and in governing bodies. One of the largest gatherings of Iraqi women took place in Hilla in October 2003 where 150 women participated. The conference discussed women's aspirations in the new Iraq, and developed proposals on a way forward, even if opinions were split on the issue of Sharia law. One of the recommendations of the conference, delivered to Paul Bremmer (then head of the CPA), was that the Iraqi constitution should assign a quota of no less than 30 per cent participation of women in political institutions (Women for a Free Iraq 2003). Other recommendations included that all laws that violate women's rights should be abolished and new laws enacted that protect the right of women. In addition to the local women's lobby, international women's organizations have been active in highlighting the importance of women's political representation in Iraq.

A constitutional commission, the Fundamental Law Committee (FLC), was appointed by the IGC in August 2003 to draft Iraq's interim constitution, or the Transitional Administrative Law (TAL). No women were appointed to the Committee. The TAL was approved by the IGC in March 2004 after many internal conflicts, mainly focusing on the subject of federalism and autonomy of Kurdistan, and also the issue of guaranteed female representation in the Transitional National Assembly. The TAL will serve as Iraq's interim constitution until a permanent constitution is adopted by 31 December 2005. It was perhaps somewhat surprising that the TAL recommended a target for women's representation, although weak in its enforcement, by requiring that 'The electoral law shall aim to achieve the goal of having women constitute no less than one-quarter of the members of the National Assembly and of having fair representation for all communities in Iraq, including Turcomans, ChaldoAssyrians, and others' (CPA 2004: Ch 4, Art. 30C).

However, the electoral law (Coalition Provisional Authority Order 96) approved by the IGC in 2004, provides for a proportional representation electoral system that includes a gender quota provision. The election of the Transitional National Assembly, which replaces the IGC, was held in January 2005. In the lists that were submitted to contest the 2005 election, at least one-third of the candidates had to be women (no fewer than one of the first three candidates on the list must be a woman, no fewer than two out of six, and so on until the end of the list). This provision surpassed the 25 per cent recommendation in the interim constitution. The reason for this, according to Carina Perelli, Director of the UN Electoral Assistance Division, is because the PR electoral system 'is so inclusive that it is expected that many lists will only have the first name of the list as a winner ... So it is a compensatory measure in order to ensure that 25 per cent of the seats are for women' (Pirelli 2004). As a result, 31.5 per cent of those elected were women.

Empowerment from above?

Despite the vast differences between East Timor, Afghanistan and Iraq, they share one commonality – the intersection between domestic women's movements and the international community has been pivotal for the adoption of special measures. However, there has been no uniformity regarding the interventions of international actors. On the one hand, UN recommendations provide a fundamental basis for the inclusion of women in state building, but on the other they need to be matched by political will from different actors at the national and international level to ensure implementation. In all three countries, however, national women's organizations have actively articulated their demands, being directly or indirectly influenced by the international discourse on the centrality of involving women in post-conflict state building processes.

Because of the active engagement of domestic women's groups, even if supported from the outside, the implementation of quotas has not entirely been empowerment from 'above'. Rather, empowerment in this instance needs to be measured by how international actors continue to place gender equality on the agenda in all reconstruction and state building efforts. The inclusion of women in the institutions of governance is critical, as gaining parliamentary seats is not an end, but a means for participating in authoritative decision-making that determines how a society functions. The attainment of gender justice in post-conflict states and in the consolidation of democracy in the long term depends on a host of factors including the development of a democratic political culture, the level of mobilization of women in civil society and the transparency and accountability of democratic institutions.

There is no doubt that the gender equality is on the international agenda in state building processes, even if the implementation of affirmative action measures like quotas are often surrounded by a cloud of controversy and debate, dividing the women's movement, political leaders and the international community on the issue. Can women be empowered by gaining parliamentary seats in highly clan-based and patriarchal societies? Perhaps the political elite has come to realize that women by their structural position in society may loyally represent clan or political interests, even if women politicians also represent a threat to the existing gender regime.

Notes

1 Local women's organizations include Women for Afghan Women, Afghan Women's Network, Afghans for Civil Society and the Revolutionary Association of the Women of Afghanistan.
2 See The Afghan Women's Network (2004) for more information at www.afghanwomensnetwork.org.
3 Shia Arab Muslims 13, Sunni Arab Muslims five, Kurds five, Turkmanis one, Assyrian one.
4 There are many different speculations as to why she was murdered, one being that she was a former member of the Ba'ath party and a firm supporter of Saddam Hussein before the invasion. She was also known to advocate women's rights.
5 In the co-called 'Government in Exile' of Iraq, chosen in London January 2003, gender quotas have been suggested by the high profile politician Ms Safia al-Souhil, but rejected by the leaders. The 'Government in Exile' consists of 65 members, three of these being women.

Bibliography

Afghan Women's Network (2004) 'Official Website'. Online. Available at: http://www.afghanwomensnetwork.org/ (accessed 28 January 2005).
Annan, K. (2002) 'Afghan Women May Still Suffer', *Associated Press.* Online. Available at: http://pz.rawa.org/rawa/annan-w.htm (accessed 29 January 2005).
Berwari, N. (2004) 'International Women's Day Speech', 8 March. Online. Available at: http://www.iraqcoalition.org/pressreleases/index.html (accessed 1 February 2005).
Chinkin, C. 'Peace Agreements as a Means for Promoting Gender Equality and Ensuring Participation of Women', paper presented at UN Expert Group

Meeting, Ottawa, November 2003. Online. Available at: http://www.un.org/womenwatch/osagi/ (accessed 27 January 2005).

Coalition Provisional Authority (CPA) (2004) 'Law of Administration for the State of Iraq for the Transitional Period'. Online. Available at: http://www.cpa-iraq.org/government/TAL.html (accessed 15 February 2005).

Dahlerup, D. and Nordlund, A. (2004) 'Gender Quotas: A key to Equality? A Case Study of Iraq and Afghanistan', *European Political Science*, 3, 3: 91–8.

Embassy of Afghanistan, Washington DC (2004) 'The Constitution of Afghanistan', January 3, Online. Available at: http://www.embassyofafghanistan.org/pdf%27s/Documents/adoptedConstitutionEnglish.pdf (accessed 16 February 2005).

International IDEA and Stockholm University (2005) 'Global Database of Quotas for Women'. Online. Available at: http://www.quotaproject.org (accessed 16 January 2005).

Khalil, A. (2004) 'Women Call for Equal Representation', *Women's E-News*, 2 June. Online. Available at: http://www.womensenews.org/article.cfm/dyn/aid/1703/context/archive (accessed 28 January 2005).

Nordlund, A. (2004) 'Demands for Electoral Gender Quotas in Afghanistan and Iraq', The Research Program on Gender Quotas, Working Paper Series 2004: 2, Stockholm University: Department of Political Science.

Office of the Special Adviser on Gender Issues and Advancement of Women (OSAGI) (2004) *Faces: Women as Partners in Peace and Security*, New York: OSAGI.

Ottaway, M. (2004) 'Women's Rights and Democracy in the Arab World', Carnegie Papers Middle East Series, no. 42, Washington: Carnegie Endowment for International Peace.

Pirelli, C. (2004) 'CPA Briefing on Electoral Preparations in Iraq', 4 June. Online. Available at: http://www.iraqcoalition.org/transcripts/20040604_Perelli_Prep.html (accessed 1 February 2005).

Pires, M. 'East Timor and the Debate on Quotas', paper prepared for workshop hosted by International IDEA, Jakarta, September 2002. Online. Available at: http://www.quotaproject.org/CS/CS_East_Timor.pdf (accessed 28 January 2005).

Reilly, B. (2003) 'International Electoral Assistance: A Review of Donor Activities and Lessons Learned', Working Paper 17, The Hague: Netherlands Institute of International Relations 'Clingendael'.

Samuels, K. and Einsiedel, S.v. (2003) 'The Future of UN State-Building: Strategic and Operational Challenges and the Legacy of Iraq', Policy Report, New York: International Peace Academy. Online. Available at: http://www.ipacademy.org/Publications/Publications.htm (accessed 28 January 2005).

United National Development Programme (UNDP) (2003) *Arab Human Development Report 2003*. Online. Available at: http://www.undp.org/rbas/ahdr/english2003.html (accessed 29 January 2005).

Whittington, S. 'UN Goals for Gender Mainstreaming', paper presented at the conference: Women and Post-War Reconstruction: Strategies for Implementation of Democracy Building Policies, Florida International University, Miami, March 2004.

Women for a Free Iraq (2003) 'The heartland of Iraq Womens Conference', Preliminary Report, Hilla: University of Babylon.

11 Indonesia

The struggle for gender quotas in the world's largest Muslim society

Cecilia Bylesjö and Francisia S.S.E. Seda

With excitement and exhaustion after months of hard lobby work the women activists marched into the parliament building in Jakarta, Indonesia February 18, 2003. The time was finally due for the House of Representatives (DPR-RI) to pass the General Election law 12/2003. The pleno session brought with it new hopes for the Indonesian public, and especially for those who were concerned about and had fought for an increased women's participation in the political system in the country.

(Seda 2003)

The parliament passed the General Election Law 12/2003 including Article 65(1) with recommendations that the political parties actively promote an increased number of women participating as political party candidates in the upcoming election. Even though the law was subject for limitations such as not being able to stipulate the exact number of women to be included as nominees and only including the national level as subject for the quota provision, the General Election Law was seen as a victory. The women's movement had suffered several set backs in 2002 and 2003 when their lobbying railed to secure these quotas in the Political Party Law 2002 as well as the State System Law 2003. The passing of the Article 65(1) was the ultimate proof that the movement's hard work, extended networking and co-operation between different groups on different levels had paid off. Even though it was a compromise between the major parties that had chosen to give the quota system their support, possibly because it was a recommendation of non-binding nature, it implied hope and impelled vigilance to continue to fight for the actual implementation of the quota by all political parties participating in the 2004 election.

Did the quota have an impact on the number of women nominated and elected in the April 2004 general election? What was the reaction by the political players towards the quota? What strategies were used to reach the goal of increasing the number of women in parliament? With the aim of enhancing the general understanding of the Indonesian political gender context the subject will be introduced by discussing the background to the law, the key actors and the different camps in the debate regarding the importance of introducing affirmative action in the form of a quota provision to the Indonesian political context.

Key actors and the growing movement for gender equality

The Indonesian civil society was under development and was constantly growing after the authoritarian regime had been replaced by a more democratic leadership and later by a democratically elected government in 1999. The so called 'reformasi era' had brought with it opportunities to mobilize and to gather support for democratic issues. As the democratic ideology became a 'natural' part of Indonesian politics the political patriarchal structure remained the same. Kofifah Indar Parawansa (2002) points out that in the regional parliaments no women were elected during the two first democratic elections. This political environment dominated by men gave rise to an increased criticism among the Civil Society Organizations (CSO) and led to an increased demand for women's access to politics.

The movement supporting the quota provision grew stronger as the General Election Laws were passed but there was some disagreement over the technical specifications. Issues regarding the numbers i.e. the preferred percentage of the quota varied between 20 and 30 per cent. The period in which the quotas were to be introduced differed with a timeframe varying between 2004 and 2009 election. The preferred type of electoral system as well as the type of list system differed among the quota supporters. As the passing of the General Election Law came closer the more coherent the women's movement became and resulted in joint demands for a 30 per cent obligatory electoral quota for women (as candidates on political party lists) to be introduced in the 2004 election and supported by the an open list system with the PR electoral system.

The key actors in the struggle for increased gender equality and later the gender quota consisted of members of CSOs, journalists, academic, political parties and parliamentarians. The involved CSOs did not constitute a separate women's movement within the Indonesian context, but included also CSOs that work with political, legal, electoral, and democratic reforms. The major Muslim women's organizations such as Muslimat, Fatayat, Aisyiah and others were all deeply involved with the work. Even though Indonesia is the largest Muslim country in the world the issue of a gender quota was not a religious issue with support divided among different religious groups. It was an issue that was supported or resisted along cross-party and cross-religious lines. The only exception was the small, more hard-line Muslim political parties (such as PBB and PDU) and the military fraction of the national parliament (DPR) who resisted the inclusion of the gender quota. However, the major Muslim political parties (such as PPP, PKB, and PKS) and non-Muslim (such as PDIP and Partai Golkar) did not follow a specific line. The dividing line was neither political nor religious but gender-related with almost all the women activists and women politicians working together to promote the gender quota, while the male members either reluctantly gave their support or did not support at all.

Pros and cons in the Indonesian quota debate

The main arguments presented in the quota debate in Indonesia did not differ from the general arguments usually used in the debate (Dahlerup 2003). The voices in favour of the gender quota saw the transitional period from an authoritarian to a more democratic political system as the prime time to stress for gender equality. The main argument was based on the just principles of equality; women constitute 50 per cent of the population and should therefore have 50 per cent of the power. This argument was based on the normative democratic concept where all citizens should have equal access and opportunity to participate actively (Mar'iyah 2003).

The group against the gender quotas saw no reasons for the affirmative actions to be introduced to Indonesian politics. Their arguments were based on meritocracy and advocated the prioritization of qualifications over that of gender within the selection process of candidates. Women were said to be lacking the right qualifications for participating as candidates, and they argued that there was not a sufficient number of women capable of competing in the next election. The principle of quota and affirmative action policies was considered to go against the principle of democracy where every citizen regardless of gender is equal in the eyes of the law and hence, the system considered should not contain any discriminatory elements (Seda 2003).

Implementing the recommended quota

After the passing of the law 12/2003, massive capacity building programmes for women were started in various parts of the country by major CSOs working in co-operation with various political parties both locally and nationally. Even though it was impossible to cover the whole country in such a short time (only one year) this problem was partly solved by the effort of the organizations to co-ordinate the activities according to theme and geography.

As one of the major criticisms against the quota had been the assumed lack of women qualified to participate as candidates the movement immediately worked towards rectifying this and made sure that women who were willing and capable of becoming candidates were listed and sufficiently trained. Targeted workshops for women candidates were held to empower and increase their understanding of the electoral system. Several organizations developed manuals and tools to prepare them for the task of becoming candidates as well as performing as elected MPs. This work also involved targeted activities with the aim of furthering awareness and socializing the quota and the election among the general public.

At the same time there was a constant lobby targeting political parties, emphasizing their responsibility in implementing the quota provision. The reaction from the parties' leadership varied and did not follow a political or religious pattern. Both the Muslim party PKB as well as the non-Muslim party Golkar were both shown to be more positive to the quota provision compared to the Muslim party PDU and as the non-Muslim ruling party PDIP. The lobby work generated an increased co-operation between both women outside and inside the political parties as well as women within the party body. A network of senior and junior women party members was established in which the senior women shared their experiences with the junior members with the aim of providing sufficient knowledge for becoming a candidate and later an elected MP. The co-operation with the international organizations also inspired the women by providing comparative knowledge and strategies to enhance the networking, both within and outside the country. This co-operation was questioned by the opponents of the quota provision system, who criticized the local movement for bringing 'foreign' ideas to the Indonesian political agenda. However, the movement continued its determined struggle and managed to build and improve its networks and skills.

The 2004 election

The Legislative General Election was held 5 July 2004 and included four different elections. The House of Representatives (DPR) at national level, the people's representative council (DPRD) at provincial and city level and the newly introduced regional representative council (DPD). The different elections used different electoral systems; at the DPR and DPRD level the PR-list system was applied, while the newly introduced DPD level applied a SNTV system with individual candidates. This meant that the candidates for the national and local levels had been selected by the political parties, while the candidates for the DPD level were individual without party affiliation.

The 2004 election resulted in a minor increase in the number of elected women, from 8.2 per cent in 1999 to 11 per cent in 2004 at DPR level. An increase of 2.8 per cent at the DPRD level. The new DPD level elected 21 per cent women.

For the House of Representatives (DPR) 7,756 legislative candidates from 69 electoral districts across Indonesia competed for the 550 seats. Of these 32.3 per cent were female and 67.6 per cent were male candidates. Twenty-four political parties competed in the 2004 legislative elections. Among the 24 political parties running in the election only eight did not fulfil the voluntary quota of 30 per cent women nominations. These eight political parties were mostly the old major political parties such as Partai Golkar, which only provided for 28.3 per cent of women on their nominations. But most parties did come close to the 30 per cent. The PDIP nominated 28.3 per cent, PPP 22.3 per cent, and PBB 23.8 per cent. The new political parties also came close to nominating 30 per cent women: PNI Marhaenisme (27.9 per cent), Partai Patriot Pancasila (28.3 per cent), Partai Demokrat (27.0 per cent), and Partai Nasionalis Banteng Kemerdekaan (29.6 per cent). Only the new hard-line Muslim political party of Partai Keadilan Sejahtera (PKS) exceeded the recommendations of 30 per cent and nominated 40.3 per cent women for national legislative candidates (Subiyantoro 2004).

So why did the electoral result turn out so disappointing with only 11 per cent women elected? Out of 2,507 women nominated for the National Parliament, only 242 (9.7 per cent) of the women candidates were ranked first on the list, and only 421 (16.8 per cent) were ranked as the second candidate on the party list. It was the old major political parties that were reluctant to rank their women candidates in the first and second slots of the nomination list. Partai Golkar only listed 17 women (5.9 per cent) out of their total candidates, PDIP also listed 17 women (7.0 per cent), PAN listed 21 women (6.6 per cent), PKB listed 24 women (9.4 per cent), PPP ranked 14 women (7.2 per cent), and PBB ranked 24 women (12.5 per cent). The relatively new party PKS, which nominated 40.3 per cent women, listed only 20 women (4.4 per cent) for the first and second slots in the nomination list (Subiyantoro 2004).

Thus the data shows that although there were breakthroughs for the nomination of women for the legislature, these breakthroughs were not really implemented by the major political parties competing in the 2004 legislative general elections. Both the largest party in parliament, Partai Golkar with its 43 per cent seats as well as the second largest party, PDI-P had a low percentage of women nominations. The women nominated had a lower percentage on top positions on the list with only 20.1 per cent women as opposed to 79.9 per cent men held first or second position on the party lists. (IFES 2004) A factor that has probably had one of the greatest impacts on the election result and the minor increase of elected women. An additional reason might be found in the voting pattern. Even though the voter turnout was relatively high (87 per cent) the lack of voters' familiarity with the new and more complicated procedures and mechanisms for voting could be an additional reason for the low percentage of women elected. Surveys have shown that only 21 per cent in a constituency would vote for a woman and only 33 per cent of a female part of the constituency would vote for a female candidate, which equals the recommended quota percentage. The low per cent increase must not be seen as a triumph for the opponents of the quota system, but instead should be seen as an indicator of the need not only for gender awareness raising work targeting the general public, but also for the need for that will ensure that candidate ranking is equally or more evenly distributed along gender lines for the top nomination spots.

The road ahead – towards increased gender equality

The 2004 legislative general election in Indonesia proved that the number of women is slowly increasing with the help of the quota provision. The voluntary quota did demonstrate that the number of women willing to participate as candidates were higher than expected. A result that stands as many of the political parties did nominate a higher number of women in the last election.

The extensive work provided by all actors involved in the process of enhancing women's political participation in Indonesia had a positive effect on the political agenda. Even if the actual number of women elected did not fulfil the quota provision of 30 per cent it must be emphasized that the outcome of previous gender work has resulted in an enhancement of the movement's ability to provide support to women candidates, proved its skilfulness in developing strategies to address gender issues and mobilize support regardless of political and religious affiliation. However, it is of great importance to stress the fact that the struggle for equality must continue and the networks established for the quota provision must be maintained. The awareness raising activities with the aim of increasing the general understanding of gender is essential for the future politics in Indonesia. Political parties are to remain gatekeepers for women's political access. It is therefore of great need to stress to the political parties their responsibility of taking the quota provision into account as they are nominating candidates in future elections. There is still a long road to travel until gender equality is reached, but more importantly, the gender quota must be considered as a great step toward increased gender equality as well as an indicator for the possibility of change within the Indonesian political context.

Bibliography

Dahlerup, D. (2003) 'Quota – A Jump to Equality', in International IDEA *The Implementation of Quotas: Asian Experiences*, Quota Workshop Report Series no. 1, Stockholm: International IDEA, pp. 10–18.

Mar'iyah, C. (2003) 'The Political Representation of Women in Indonesia: How can it be achieved?', in International IDEA *The Implementation of Quotas: Asian Experiences*, Quota Workshop Report Series no. 1, Stockholm: International IDEA, pp. 62–5.

Parawansa, K.I. (2002) 'Institution Building: An Effort to Improve Indonesian Women's Role and Status', in K. Robinsson and S. Nessell (eds) *Women. Gender, Equality and Development*, Singapore: Institute of Southeast Asian Studies, p. 68.

Seda, F.S.S.E. (2003) 'Political Parties and Women's Political Participation –

strategies to increase women's participation in politics through internal and structural organizational facilities', in International IDEA *Indonesia, Conference papers 2003,* Indonesia: International IDEA. Online. Available at: http://www.ideaindo.or.id/ (accessed 1 June 2004).

Subiyantoro, E.B. (2004) 'Keterwakilan Perempuan dalam Politik: Masih Menjadi Kabar Burung', *Jurnal Perempuan,* 34: 71.

The International Foundation for Electoral Systems (IFES) (2004) 'Results announced by KPU (DPR)'. Online. Available at: http://www.ifes.org/reg_activities/docs/DPR_Results_Announced_by_KPU_04-05-05_locked.xls (accessed 1 December 2004).

12 Affirmative action at the IPU

Kareen Jabre

On 1 January 2005, 15.7 per cent of all members of parliament and 14.3 per cent of ministers worldwide were women according to data collected by the Inter-Parliamentary Union (IPU). These figures represent an improvement, but the situation remains unsatisfactory. However, at the October 2004 IPU Assembly, women accounted for 29 per cent of delegates – twice the world average for parliaments and the result of affirmative action measures.

Quotas are central to the debate on women's participation in politics. But quotas are measures used by national entities – political parties, parliaments, or governments – and are seldom associated with international bodies. The importance of ensuring equal participation of women in international relations should not be underestimated. The case of the Inter-Parliamentary Union, one of the first – and perhaps the only – international organization to have taken affirmative action measures and set up its own internal quotas, is especially instructive.

Established in 1889, the IPU works for the enhancement and promotion of democracy through the strengthening of the institution of parliament. It brings together more than 140 national parliaments worldwide. The IPU defends democracy on the understanding that balanced participation by men and women in the management of public affairs is central to any democracy. In 1997, it consolidated these views in its *Universal Declaration on Democracy*, Article 4 of which explicitly endorsed the link between democracy and 'a genuine partnership between men and women' in the management of public affairs (IPU 1997: 4).

Over the past 30 years, the IPU has developed a comprehensive programme aimed at enhancing women's participation in parliaments. It also promotes the participation of women within its own structures, the ultimate aim being equality in participation, as stated in its statutes.

Women at the IPU – a story of slow but constant progress

The IPU has a complex structure. This chapter will be confined to describing participation by women in its three main decision-making bodies:

- The Assembly (formerly called the Conference), which is the principal statutory body that expresses the views of the IPU on political issues. It brings together parliamentarians to study international problems and make recommendations for action.
- The Governing Council (also known as the Inter-Parliamentary Council), which is the plenary policy-making body of the IPU. The Council establishes the annual programme and budget of the IPU and is responsible for the admission or suspension of Member Parliaments and associate Members.
- The Executive Committee, which is a 17-member body that oversees the administration of the IPU and provides advice to the Governing Council.

The history of women in national parliaments across the globe is one of difficult but gradual progress. At first glance, the same can be said for women's attendance at IPU meetings. At its inception, the IPU was a 'men's club'. In 1921, two women parliamentarians, from Germany and Denmark, were the first ever to participate in an IPU meeting, alongside

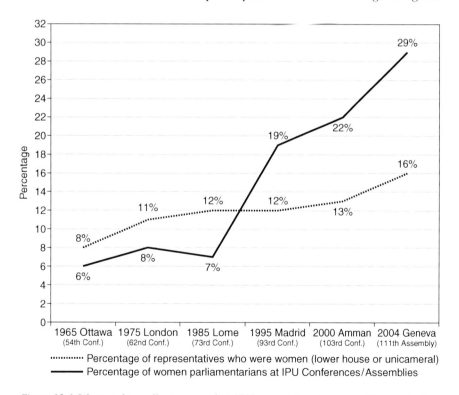

Figure 12.1 Women in parliaments and at IPU assemblies (sources: Women in Parliaments: IPU (2004b). Women at IPU Assemblies: IPU (unpublished statistics)).

108 male colleagues. From meagre beginnings in 1947, where women comprised only 1.2 per cent of all delegates, to slight progress in 1975, where they comprised 7.8 per cent of all delegates, the percentage skyrocketed to 29 per cent by the time the 111th Assembly was held in Geneva in 2004.

In the IPU's other decision-making bodies, the Executive Committee and the Governing Council, participation of women was extremely weak in the past and remains unsatisfactory. Symbolically enough, the first woman ever to be elected to the IPU Executive Committee was Mrs Molina Rubio of Guatemala, in October 1987, almost one century after the organization's creation. It was not until 1999 that a woman, Mrs Heptulla, then Speaker a.i. of the Indian Upper House of Parliament, was elected President of the Inter-Parliamentary Union.

What has driven the recent increase in women's participation at the IPU? Simply put, there has been a strong current of political will from within the Union, and a growing consciousness of the need for, and benefits of, gender equality within Member Parliaments.

Two periods stand out as major turning points in women's progress at the IPU: 1985 to 1990 and 1999 to 2004. In 1985 the IPU established a Meeting of Women Parliamentarians as an event to take place during IPU Conferences. The Meeting offered women parliamentarians a space of their own, and began to encourage Member Parliaments to send women to IPU Meetings. From 1985 to 1990, the increase in women's participation in IPU Conferences was exponential. However, despite the structures in place and a clear political will within the Union to see a greater presence of women parliamentarians, women's participation began to level off. Meeting the objective of equality would clearly require stronger measures – namely affirmative action and quotas.

The IPU's position regarding affirmative action measures and quotas

The IPU does not consider quotas as the prime solution to enhancing women's participation in politics. It prefers gradual change to mandatory measures. However, the organization recognizes that when change is slow in coming, quotas, as temporary special measures, are sometimes the only way forward. The use of affirmative action at the IPU was therefore not an easy choice. When the idea was raised in the early 1990s, it proved to be contentious. This was the case again in 1999. Affirmative action in any event can be a sensitive issue; in an international organization, it is particularly so.

Let us take a step back and look at the IPU's views regarding affirmative action measures. The organization's position was set out in its Plan of Action to correct imbalances in the participation of men and women in political life, adopted by the Inter-Parliamentary Council in 1994. The Plan of Action states that:

On a strictly interim basis, these measures may include affirmative action measures. Wherever the measure chosen is a quota system, it is proposed that the quota should not target women but that, in a spirit of equity, it may be established that neither sex may occupy a proportion of seats inferior to a given percentage.

(IPU 1994: C: II: 3)

In 1994, this was quite an important stand for a global organization to take. The statement clearly recognized the usefulness of affirmative action measures. The balanced approach to women's participation is also noteworthy, and is in line with the Union's promotion of gender partnership.

Since 1994, the IPU's position regarding quotas has not changed. It is not uncommon to find affirmative action measures mentioned in its resolutions, and even targets to help achieve gender equality in politics. In a resolution it adopted as recently as October 2004, the Union '*Strongly urges* parliamentarians to promote a stronger presence of women in political parties and at all levels of decision-making through the adoption, for example, of quota systems or other forms of affirmative action' (IPU 2004a: 16).

Clearly, the IPU has always considered quotas and affirmative action measures as a useful mechanism to improve upon a stagnant situation. However, using such mechanisms within the IPU required time, debate and careful argument.

What are the affirmative action measures in place at the IPU today?

Further to a three-year consultative process, in 2003 the IPU adopted a series of affirmative action measures and quotas intended to strengthen women's participation in its structures. These were:

- A straightforward quota system was introduced for elections to the Executive Committee: 20 per cent of its elected members now must be women.
- For the Governing Council, a gender-neutral target was adopted which, if strictly applied, would ensure that representatives of each sex would account for at least 30 per cent of its members: each delegation is entitled to three members (and therefore three votes), provided that both men and women are included in the delegation. Where this is not the case, the Member Parliament's voting rights and number of delegates on the Council are reduced by one (i.e. one-third of the total).
- Another gender-neutral target was adopted for the Assembly: where delegations attend IPU Assemblies without representatives of both

sexes three times in a row, their voting rights and officially registered numbers are reduced. This concerns all member parliaments of the IPU, including those that do not have any women MPs.

A politically supportive context and a participatory process

Several of the measures adopted in 2001 by the IPU bodies had already been proposed in one form or another some ten years earlier, mainly by women parliamentarians. At the time such proposals were deemed to be too forceful and were rejected. Ten years later, the context had evolved. By 2001, there was a general framework conducive to change at the IPU, which included:

– A strong women's movement

The growing influence of women in the IPU cannot be dissociated from the recent adoption of quota measures. The women's movement at the IPU has grown over the years and today holds an important place in the organization's decision-making. It began in 1985 with the creation of the Meeting of Women Parliamentarians. The Meeting became an official body of the IPU in 1999, occurring once a year on the occasion of the first annual IPU Assembly. It brings together women parliamentarians from around the world to discuss specific gender issues but also to influence the work of the IPU.

– Political support at the highest level

At its highest decision-making level, the IPU had to be politically supportive of greater participation by women within its own structures. Participation by women has been a priority for all the recent Presidents of the Union.

– Gender equality: the responsibility of both men and women

Many of the measures encouraging women's participation at the IPU were introduced as part of a broader package of reform. The question of gender equality was one among a number of elements proposed for the improvement of the functioning of the Union. It therefore was discussed by all, and was the responsibility of all.

With regard to the affirmative action measures relating to participation in the Assembly, these were spearheaded by the Gender Partnership Group, a body set up in 1997 comprising two men and two women from the IPU Executive Committee. Mandated to ensure that the Union took into account the needs of both men and women on an equal basis within its own structures, the Group started by looking at the participation by women in delegations to IPU meetings. Including men in this debate made it possible to avoid marginalizing the issue.

– A consultative process

The affirmative action measures were adopted as the result of a three-year consultation process with all Members of the IPU. The Gender Partnership Group's recommendations regarding the introduction of affirmative action measures and the possibility of sanctions for non-compliance were put to the IPU membership over the course of three Assemblies. Comments received were circulated widely.

The consultation revealed a wide range of opinions on how best to ensure women's participation and a gender balance in IPU events. Many IPU Members were opposed to imposing a specific gender composition on delegations to the Conference/Assembly, and preferred a voluntary system. Others felt that only a more rigid and mandatory system including sanctions could be effective. The IPU therefore devised a hybrid system, which would avoid imposing a mandatory quota on each delegation, but would involve sanctions if a delegation consistently ignored the need to ensure a gender balance.

The open consultative process was crucial to the adoption of the quota measures. These could hardly be contested, as they were the product of the IPU membership in its entirety, reflecting the variety of points of view, cultures and traditions within the Union's membership.

Preliminary assessment and conclusions

The affirmative action measures were adopted in 2003. Restrictions on voting rights at the Governing Council were implemented as early as October 2003 during an important political vote. The proportion of women in the Governing Council rose to 32 per cent. Sanctions on delegations to the Assembly were first implemented in October 2004, when five delegations had their voting rights and membership reduced.

It is still too early to assess the effects of these measures, although some preliminary conclusions can be drawn.

It is true that the presence of women at IPU Assemblies, the Governing Council and the Executive Committee has increased significantly in the past five years. For women at the Assembly, the 30 per cent mark was almost reached in 2004. Most notable, however, is the drop in the number of single-sex delegations, although some parliaments send delegations with a single woman member simply to avoid sanctions. The measures have yet to ensure a more balanced gender composition within delegations.

The progress cannot and should not be attributed exclusively to the quota system and the sanctions. It is also related to the way in which the entire issue figured publicly on the IPU's agenda, obliging the membership to address it. The Gender Partnership Group also helped to raise awareness and encourage change by monitoring progress (and publishing the names of single-sex delegations).

Quotas are not the only solution, and should be complemented by other measures to facilitate women's participation, both at the IPU and in national parliaments. To address the question of Parliaments in which there are no women, and that are therefore sanctioned at the IPU, the Gender Partnership Group has begun a series of hearings with delegations concerned, the aim being to establish a dialogue, monitor difficulties, encourage progress, assess needs and see if and how the IPU can assist their parliaments in opening their membership to women.

For many, quotas are not the first option but often a necessary and unavoidable step to break a stalemate. Quotas have an immediate effect on statistics, but quality counts as well as quantity. To achieve gender equality in politics, quotas must be accompanied by other initiatives, including awareness raising, training of women, and developing gender sensitive environments both in national parliaments and at the IPU. In the long run, only a shift in a country's political mores and culture will bring more women into the political arena.

Bibliography

Inter-Parliamentary Union (IPU) (1994) 'Plan of Action to Correct Present Imbalances in the Participation of Men and Women in Political Life'. Online. Available at: http://www.ipu.org/wmn-e/planactn.htm (accessed 15 February 2005).
—— (1997) 'Universal Declaration on Democracy'. Online. Available at: http://www.ipu.org/cnl-e/161-dem.htm (accessed 15 February 2005).
—— (2004a) 'Beijing + 10: An evaluation from a Parliamentary Perspective', Resolution, 1 October. Online. Available at: http://www.ipu.org/conf-e/111/111-3.htm (accessed 15 February 2005).
—— (2004b) 'Women in National Parliaments', Situation as of 30 November. Online. Available at: http://www.ipu.org/wmn-e/world.htm (accessed 18 February 2005).
The IPU's documents and statistics on the participation of women in parliaments throughout the world can be accessed at http://www.ipu.org.

Part IV
Concluding chapters

13 Electoral quotas

Frequency and effectiveness

Richard E. Matland

The chapters of this book provide a useful picture of the varied ways in which quotas function. This chapter steps back from the relatively detailed level of individual countries and regions to generalize on the global level about quotas. First, the chapter provides some general information on how the frequency of electoral quotas varies across country types distinguished on the basis of type of quota, the level of democracy within the country, and on electoral systems. Second, I distinguish between quota types by referring to the legislative recruitment process and how they are designed to affect different steps in the legislative recruitment process. In addition, a discussion is included of the effectiveness of various types of quotas. Getting quotas adopted is a crucial step, but there is also a need to consider their effectiveness.

Quota frequency

In Table 13.1, countries are divided on the basis of whether they are democratic, semi-democratic, or non-democratic based on Freedom House rankings. Countries are distinguished also on the basis of their electoral systems between those that are single member districts and those that are multimember districts.[1] Table 13.1 shows that among democratic countries only one of 27 (3.7 percent) countries with single member district electoral systems have legal quotas.[2] The percentage is still low, but noticeably higher for the multimember district electoral systems, where 18 percent of democratic states have adopted legal quotas. For semi-democratic countries, there is a substantially higher level of legal quota adoption, but again we see the pattern of quotas being more common among countries with multimember districts (36.4 percent vs 20 percent). Finally, in non-democratic countries, the pattern is reversed with a greater frequency of quota adoptions among countries with single member districts (18.5 percent vs 6.7 percent).

The distinct difference across levels of democracy in the frequency of legal quotas is partially explained by the power of political parties. In most stable democracies, political parties have established considerable

Table 13.1 Frequency of legal quotas[a]

	Democratic countries legal quota		Semi-democratic countries legal quota		Non-democratic countries legal quota	
	Yes	No	Yes	No	Yes	No
SMD[b]	1 (3.7%)	26 (96.3%)	4 (20.0%)	16 (80.0%)	5 (18.5%)	22 (81.5%)
MMD[c]	11 (18.0%)	50 (82.0%)	12 (36.4%)	21 (63.6%)	1 (6.7%)	14 (93.3%)

Notes
a To identify the level of democracy in countries data from Freedom House (2004) are used. Freedom House has two separate scales, which estimate the levels of political freedoms and civil liberties in 191 countries. For more information see: http://www.freedom house.org/
b SMD = Single Member District.
c MMD = Multimember District.

autonomy and power. The effect of legal quotas, especially in countries with single member districts, is to significantly limit the ability of parties' local affiliates to choose the candidates they desire. In established democracies, therefore, local parties are likely to fight to limit the ability of the government to propose meaningful legal quotas.

In the semi-democratic states, on the other hand, political parties tend to be more localized in the capital and often are indistinguishable from the parliamentary or governmental party. In addition, internal democracy standards often differ markedly. While party processes for choosing leaders and candidates may be highly democratic in the freest of countries, they are often anything but democratic in many semi-democratic countries. The power to select candidates often is still centralized in these partially democratic countries. Under these conditions there is likely to be less protest from the periphery, as they are not losing previously held powers. Furthermore, if there is a single member district system and the nominating procedures are made centrally for all districts, the party can see quotas as less of a burden because they can in effect think of themselves as creating a national slate on which to run.

Table 13.2 shows voluntary political party quotas are much more common across all levels of democracy where there are multimember rather than single member district electoral systems. There is a full 30 percent higher level of quotas in multimember district countries than single member district countries among both democratic and semi-democratic states. As political freedom increases, quotas become more common. A strikingly large proportion of the countries that are defined as free and have multimember electoral systems (59 percent) have at least some political parties that have adopted quotas.

When we compare across the two tables, there is considerable divergence concerning what kind of quota is likely to be found depending upon the level of democracy. Among the 88 democratic countries, there

Table 13.2 Frequency of political party quotas[a]

	Democratic countries political party quota		Semi-democratic countries political party quota		Non-democratic countries political party quota	
	Yes	No	Yes	No	Yes	No
SMD[b]	8 (29.6%)	19 (70.4%)	1 (5.0%)	19 (95.0%)	1 (3.7%)	26 (96.3%)
MMD[c]	36 (59.0%)	25 (41.0%)	12 (36.4%)	21 (63.6%)	3 (20.0%)	12 (80.0%)

Notes
a To identify the level of democracy in countries, data from Freedom House (2004) are used. Freedom House has two separate scales, which estimate the levels of political freedoms and civil liberties in 191 countries.
b SMD = Single Member District.
c MMD = Multimember District.

are only 13 with legal quotas (14.8 percent), while 44 (50 percent) have political parties with quotas. Among the 53 semi-democratic countries, on the other hand, quotas are more likely to be established at the level of the polity as a whole through a legal quota (30.2 percent) than at the level of individual parties (24.5 percent). Among the 42 non-democratic states, legal quotas show up in 14.3 percent of the countries, while party quotas show up in 9.5 percent. In short, the level of democracy affects both the frequency of quotas and their form. The greater popularity of legal quotas among semi-democratic states is consistent with the suggestion made by Tripp, Konate, and Lowe-Morna that these states find legal quotas attractive because they perceive them as conferring legitimacy. These states believe they will be seen as 'more democratic' if they adopt quotas. Not facing the considerable resistance from the political parties that is likely to occur in democratic states, it is relatively easy for the government to impose a legally mandated solution. Legal quotas, on the other hand, face a much tougher time in democratic states. There is likely to be resistance from the political parties and certainly in states with a liberal citizenship model the proposals will be met with arguments that imposing such a requirement is undemocratic, as discussed in Chapter 8.

Finally, the incentives in semi-democratic states for parties to adopt quotas are likely to be smaller than in democratic states. International surveys demonstrate a strong correlation between democracy status and gender values. Inglehart and Norris (2003) use the World Values Survey to show that semi-democratic states tend to be considerably more conservative in terms of their gender equality values than the democratic states (Inglehart and Norris 2003: 37, 44). While parties in states that score relatively high on gender equality values could reap political advantages among voters by promoting gender equality, for example by adopting quotas, the political advantages and therefore the incentives are likely to be smaller in the more traditional societies that dominate among the countries in the semi-democratic group.

Quota effectiveness: factors affecting quota success

While the existence of quotas is certainly of considerable importance, it is also important to consider whether they are effective and what factors determine their effectiveness. While a contagion effect may have occurred in the spread of quotas across countries, the adoption of quotas has not, on the whole, led to dramatic increases in women's representation. There are important exceptions where quotas have helped. Nevertheless, as the chapters in this book have shown, ineffectiveness comes in many different flavors. Legal mandates or party rules can be written in such a way that a party can comply with the letter of the law or party regulations without electing a significantly higher number of women. Ineffectiveness may occur when a law or party rule exists but the parties routinely ignore them and no significant sanctions are in place to penalize parties for failing to comply. Quotas may also fail, even if more women are elected, if women are treated as second-class legislators and when quotas become a ceiling rather than a floor for further growth of women's political power.

One case where there is good reason to be sceptical of the effectiveness of quotas is among non-democratic countries. In these states, quotas are unlikely to be meaningful in the sense of providing women with any real political input. While some of these polities may develop over time to where the legislature does have meaningful powers, at this time women in these legislatures are largely symbolic. There are, among the 42 countries that Freedom House defines as not free (non-democratic), ten that have either legal quotas or party quotas for women. There are a few intriguing cases but most are like North Korea where the quota is unsurprisingly met, i.e. there is a 20 percent quota and the parliament has precisely 20.1 percent women. The problem of course is that no real political power is wielded by the national assembly, and therefore levels of representation simply do not matter. While the regime may point to the significant level of women's representation as proof of how democratic they are, the reality is the meaningful decisions are made in other places.

Among these not free countries there are occasionally a couple of interesting cases. For example, Afghanistan is defined as not free, but is hopefully moving in the direction of greater democracy. As part of that process, it has written into its new constitution a quota insuring at least 27 percent of the new parliament will be female, with each province directly electing two women to parliament, see Chapter 10. When compared to the position of women in the most recent Afghani regime, even if there is only limited power in the parliament, simply holding these positions will represent an important symbolic victory for women. The other case that catches one's eye is Rwanda where 24 of 80 seats are reserved for women, but where women have also won a significant number of the seats on the closed list proportional representation ballots that make up most of the rest of parliament. Rwanda at 48.8 percent women is close to becoming the first national assembly that actually reaches parity. Again, it is worth remaining cautious, as there is still a serious question as to whether these legislatures will develop into meaningful bodies that set public policy. Nevertheless, as they move in the direction of greater democracy it appears there is every intention to insure women are significant participants in this process.

Legislative recruitment process and electoral quotas

For the remainder of this chapter I concentrate on democratic and semi-democratic countries. A useful step in analyzing the effectiveness of quotas is to consider the process of legislative recruitment and define how different types of quotas affect different steps of the legislative recruitment process. Figure 13.1 shows the process of legislative recruitment defined in three separate steps. At the outset, there is a pool of eligibles, those individuals who meet the formal requirements for serving in office. In the first step, individual citizens move from being eligibles to aspirants. Citizens effectively select themselves and signal an interest in political office. Studies in democratic countries have emphasized the role of ambition and resources as affecting the likelihood of an individual aspiring to political office. The second crucial step is moving from aspirant to being a candidate. At this stage, party gatekeepers select candidates to run for office. This process is affected by a number of factors, including existing

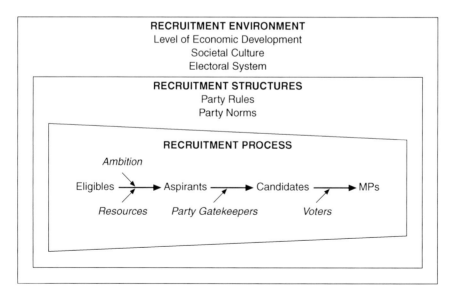

Figure 13.1 Legislative recruitment system (source: Matland and Montgomery (2003: 21)).

party rules and norms, but a primary concern throughout the process of selecting candidates is a party's beliefs as to what sort of candidates are likely to help them win votes. In the third step, an individual moves from being a candidate to being elected. This is the stage at which an individual must be chosen by the people, at least in democratic systems.

Quotas can be created to influence each of these three steps. Furthermore, as the analysis earlier in the chapter indicates, the type of quota adopted tends to vary systematically with the type of electoral system and degree of democracy. Quotas that attempt to guarantee greater equity at the first step from eligible to aspirants are most common among democratic states with single member district electoral systems. Quotas that attempt to guarantee greater equity at the second step from aspirants to candidates are most common among democratic states with proportional representation systems. Quotas that attempt to guarantee greater equity at the third step from candidate to member of parliament are most common among semi-democratic states and consist of a variety of reserved seats guarantees. Let us look at each of these steps and the quotas associated with them.

Aspirant quotas: quotas affecting the step from eligible to aspirant

Quotas affecting the step from eligible to aspirant have been applied to a limited degree and with limited effectiveness. These policies are meant to guarantee at least some women are among the candidates a party considers when it selects nominees. The most obvious shortcoming of such a quota from the perspective of effectiveness is that it only deals with the very first step of the recruitment process. Even if women make up a considerable number of the aspirants, there is no guarantee the party will choose in a manner that ensures women will also make up a large portion of candidates or voters will vote in a manner that insures a large number of women are elected.

Aspirant quotas are designed to influence an internal party process of choosing candidates. There are no cases of aspirant quotas being established at the legal level. Rather, these are quotas established by individual parties through party rules. Furthermore, they are exclusively the domain of single member district established democracies. In countries with multi-member district electoral systems, quotas ignore the step of choosing aspirants and instead aim at the stage of selecting actual candidates. Among partially free countries there has been both an emphasis on candidates and on actual MPs through reserved seats, but little on the stage of eligibles to aspirants.

Examples of these quotas can be found among several of the Anglo Democracies that have processes whereby local party members choose their candidates in a party caucus. The policies are most common among parties on the political left that have made an explicit policy commitment to increasing women's access. As noted in Krook, Lovenduski and Squires'

Chapter 8, Labour and the Liberal Democrats in the UK have a require-ment that the shortlist of candidates for open seats includes at least one female. The New Democratic Party in Canada has a similar requirement, and the pre-selection requirements in the Australian Labor Party function in a similar manner.

Aspirant quotas are adopted when a strong demand for greater equality arises in an institutional context where there is no easy way to accommo-date this demand. Aspirant quotas must be seen as an attempt to balance the desires of central parties to increase the number of female candidates against the adamant demands of local parties that the nominating process be controlled by the constituencies. The periphery and center struggle over the power to make important decisions concerning the candidate selection process.

The problem is especially acute in long-established democracies in single member district electoral systems, due to the power of local parties. These political systems tend to have developed extensive and powerful local level parties. After the power to select candidates has devolved down to the local level, it becomes difficult to take away. Local level party organizations will fight jealously to retain this power, across all political parties, regardless of their political persuasion.

The other factor that makes quotas so difficult to institute at this level is the single member district. Each local party only has one candidate to nominate, and so it is impossible to come up with a compromise where the national party selects a portion of the candidates and the local party chooses the rest. Therefore, some parties have settled for a system where the national party requires the local parties to at least 'consider' a woman as their nominee, i.e. aspirant quotas. Even this relatively weak form of quotas can be considered intrusive by the local party, and the success of the policy has been mixed.

Candidate quotas: quotas affecting the step from aspirant to candidate

The most common types of quotas are those designed to influence the step from aspirants to candidates. Candidate quotas require the party's list to include a certain proportion of women. The proportion can vary from a mere 5 to 10 percent all the way up to parity. These are almost exclus-ively the realm of multimember district electoral systems, usually propor-tional representation systems, but occasionally mixed systems. When used in mixed member proportional systems, the quotas apply only to the party list portion of the electoral system. Crucial to quotas leading to meaning-ful increases in representation under these conditions is that the propor-tion of the seats elected in the multimember districts is reasonably high.

Candidate quotas can be legal quotas as found in several Latin Amer-ican countries, or they can be party quotas as found among several Western European democracies, especially among parties on the left of the ideological spectrum. One obvious advantage in terms of effectiveness for legal quotas is that they apply to all parties. Voluntary party quotas apply only to those parties that have adopted them. It may be that those include only marginal parties, with few seats in the parliament, and therefore party quotas may have little effect on overall representation. Legal quotas, on the other hand, have the capability of dramatically and quickly increasing women's representation.

While there is a danger that voluntary party quotas may be of marginal influence, there is research showing the adoption of quotas is subject to contagion effects (Matland and Studlar 1996; Caul 2001). There are a number of countries where quotas were initially introduced by small parties often at the left margins of the political spectrum, but in reaction to these introductions more mainstream parties, with considerably larger parliamentary delegations, have then adopted quotas. Furthermore, party quotas have been aided by the promotion of quotas by international political party groups. In particular, as Antíc and Lokar noted in the Balkan chapter, the Socialist International has taken an active role in promoting quotas as a viable and important policy to help promote equal representation of women. New parties applying for membership to the Socialist International are required to have adopted candidate quotas.

Legal quotas exist in 23 countries that have multimember districts and are considered free or partially free by Freedom House. Twelve of these 23 cases are Latin American countries with either traditional proportional representation list systems, or in two cases, Mexico and Panama, a mixed member proportional system. Belgium, France, Bosnia and Herzegovenia, Serbia, Macedonia, and Armenia are the European cases of a candidate quota established by legal means. In the case of Armenia, the quota is set so low, 5 percent of party candidates, and only enforced for the proportionally elected portion of the parliament, that it is of limited effect.

Far more common in Europe, and in the world as a whole, are candidate quotas established by party rules. Out of the 94 countries that have multimember district electoral systems and are democratic or semi-democratic, 48 have party quotas. Most of the Western European democracies, at least in the Northern half of the continent, have significant numbers of parties that have adopted party quotas. In addition, many of the parties in Latin America that operate under systems where there are constitutional quotas, and increasingly social democratic parties in Eastern Europe, have taken it upon themselves to adopt internal party quotas. There are also a few cases in Africa. As noted by Tripp, Konate, and Lowe-Morna in Mozambique, 36 percent of the parliamentary seats are held by women, in large part due to a 30 percent quota adopted by FRELIMO along with a reasonably attractive electoral system where electoral thresholds and relatively few districts result in high party magnitudes. Still, the results in Mozambique are striking and along with South Africa present it as a true outlier in terms of overall representation on the African continent.

Htun and Jones (2002) studied carefully the effectiveness and application of legal candidate quotas in Latin America. As the Latin American chapter in this book describes, simply having a quota law is no guarantee the law will have any effect. Htun and Jones argue that for quotas to be effective, four conditions need to be met: the electoral system must have high district magnitude (the average number of seats elected per district), closed-list proportional representation, a placement requirement, and good-faith compliance from the political parties.[3]

Having a high district magnitude should ensure the party elects several MPs and thereby has the opportunity to elect a balanced slate. If district magnitude is low, the list of candidates may be quite well balanced, but if each list only elects the top one or two candidates, the outcome can be an overwhelmingly male parliament. Htun and Jones also recommend closed-list over open-list PR. Under open-list PR voters choose among the candidates the party has nominated. This allowance for preferential voting among party candidates opens up a danger that even if the parties presented lists that were evenly divided, the actions of voters could lead to men disproportionately being elected. By having systems that are closed, this places the responsibility of insuring equitable representation squarely onto the parties.

Htun and Jones also suggest an effective law must have a placement mandate, a point that Jones (2004) re-emphasizes in his analysis of various types of quotas used in Costa Rica. A placement mandate is a specification in the law requiring that women receive equitable representation throughout the whole list. Without a placement requirement there is a danger a party may place male party members in almost all of the top list positions, and include women primarily at the bottom of the list as filler. A party list could easily meet the requirement for having 30 percent women by having 50 percent of the spots which have no chance of getting elected being women and having only 10 percent of those list positions that have a realistic chance of actually getting elected being filled by women.

Finally, they note that good faith compliance with quotas by the political parties is needed for quotas to work. This may come about through the good will of the parties, but it is also helped significantly by effective sanctions that are applied if a party fails to promote women. Baldez (2004) notes a crucial factor in the effectiveness of quotas is support of other political institutions. In the Argentinean case, the court played a crucial role by establishing the legality of the quotas and by interpreting the law in such a manner that there was a placement mandate (Jones 1996). The Supreme Elections Tribunale (TSE) in Costa Rica also interpreted the law to require a placement mandate, significantly strengthening the Costa Rican quota law through judicial interpretation (Jones 2004).

When reviewing the Latin American cases using 2001 data, Htun and Jones found only two national assemblies met all the conditions they set, the Argentinean National Assembly where representation increased by more than 20 percent in two elections and the Paraguay Senate where the 20 percent quota written into law was met.[4] For these two bodies, the average increase in representation was 15.5 percent. In the other 13 cases where quotas existed, the average increase in representation was only 3.9 percent. As Table 4.3 demonstrates, those numbers have increased somewhat since then in both quota and non-quota countries.

By explicitly defining a set of conditions Htun and Jones have done the field an important service. I have one quibble with their conditions and a broader issue concerning whether conditions are necessary and sufficient. The quibble has to do with their suggesting the electoral system has to have a high average district magnitude. I believe instead the electoral system has to generate high party magnitudes. Average district magnitude is the average number of seats per district; average party magnitude is the number of seats in the party's district delegation. The two are related, but not equivalent concepts (Matland 1993). For women to get elected the parties need to go reasonably deep down on their lists. High district magnitude generally leads to high party magnitude, but it does not always do so, and when it does not, quotas can be reasonably ineffective. Party magnitude is going to be affected both by the formal rules, first and foremost district magnitude, but also by the electoral threshold, and by the form of the party system. Systems with lower effective numbers of parliamentary parties will have higher party magnitude and more effective quotas because the parties will elect more MPs from the mid range of their lists.

The distinction between high district magnitude and party magnitude is strikingly presented by Paraguay, where representation dropped precipitously after the 2003 election despite meeting all the conditions Htun and Jones set. For the 1998 election, quotas were in place, and the effective number of political parties was 2.1 as the two major parties captured a large proportion of the vote. For the 2003 election, quotas were still in place and still followed, and district magnitude remained the same. In the 2003 elections, however, minor parties did much better, and a large number of single member or dual member party delegations were elected. The effective number of parliamentary parties rose to 4.36, the average party magnitude sunk, and representation dropped precipitously (from 20 percent to 10 percent). I believe the condition of high district magnitude should be replaced by a condition requiring high party magnitude.

There is, however, a broader question. The conditions Htun and Jones describe are best understood as sufficient conditions, but not necessary conditions. In other words, if the electoral system and the quota law in a country meet all of the conditions they describe (with the modification concerning party magnitude rather than district magnitude), then increased representation is virtually guaranteed. There will be significant improvements in women's representation and representation near the level of the legal quota. They are perhaps all essential in cases where quotas are being implemented in a setting in which parties are reluctant to follow the rules and there is a limited public support for mandatory quotas, but those conditions do not always exist. It is not hard to find cases where several of these conditions are not met and quotas are still success-ful in raising representation.

Such an example is Belgium. In Belgium, the issue of women's representation became prominent in the political dialogue in the late 1980s and early 1990s when Belgium languished near the bottom of Western European democracies with less than 10 percent of the parlia-ment being women. In response, the parliament passed quota legislation in 1994 that first established that no less than 25 percent (from 1996 to 1999) and then no less than 33 percent (after 1999) of the candidates in national elections must come from the lesser represented sex. Belgium has a proportional representation electoral system, but Belgian elections did not generate high party magnitude, did not have closed lists, and there was no placement mandate in the law. In a series of simulations, Meier (1998) showed it would be relatively easy for the parties to adjust their lists to meet the letter of the law, and yet it would be possible for no increase in representation to occur. At the next election, however, representation almost doubled from 12 percent to 23 percent, just missing the quota targets. The reason was that while three of the conditions set by Htun and Jones were not met, the fourth one, reasonably good faith com-pliance from the political parties did occur.

In effect only one of the four conditions outlined was met, yet this was sufficient to lead to an increase. The Belgian case does have some import-ant elements that made it amenable to success. The women's movement, inside and outside of the parties, was well organized and active. They made it clear they were aware the parties could meet the letter of the law without meeting the spirit of the law and they expected compliance with the spirit of the law. The most important factor was that party leaders con-sistently assured women's groups they were serious about improving the position of women. The result was a significant increase in women's representation. Partially in response to the demands for greater women's representation, the Belgians redrew their electoral district lines, signific-antly decreasing the number of districts, which led directly to substantially higher party magnitude. Not surprisingly this change, in conjunction with quotas, has led to Belgium reaching its current status as one of the top ten countries in the world in terms of women's representation (Meier 2003).

The implications of the Belgian case suggest that while the Htun and Jones list describes conditions that are sufficient for effective quotas, they are not all necessary. If the conditions were to be parsed down, necessary and sufficient conditions for effective candidate quotas require a propor-tional representation electoral system, an electoral system that produces high party magnitude,[5] and good faith compliance from the political parties. Good faith compliance from political parties can occur either voluntarily, as in Belgium, or it can be coerced, as in Argentina, through the use of effective sanctions. If coercive conditions are needed, a placement mandate is almost assuredly essential. In the Argentinean case, the courts stated all lists failing to meet the legal requirements would not be allowed to field lists in the national election. After a few challenges, parties very quickly fell in line.

Note this list is a liberalization of the Htun and Jones conditions with respect to the electoral system. I believe the use of preferential voting, i.e. open lists, is unlikely to dramatically hurt women in most cases. All our studies of national voting show that party loyalties, current issues, and evaluations of national party leaders tend to dominate voter decision-making on who to vote for. The gender of the candidates is of limited importance, and even in very traditional societies there have been women leaders that have been able to rouse considerable support from male voters despite their gender (obvious examples are Indira and Sonja Ghandi in India, Megawathi Sukarnoputhri in Indonesia, and the leaders of the two opposing major parties in Bangladesh, Sheikh Hasina and Khaleda Zia).

Schmidt and Saunders (2004) have tested for the effect of open lists in Peru and argue they do not hurt women dramatically. Similar findings are found in my work on the effect of open list voting in Poland. There are cases where open lists do hurt women, but there are enough cases where women are either helped or not dramatically hurt by open list voting to suggest this is not a serious barrier. Therefore, I am confident that closed lists are not a condition that must be met for candidate quotas to be effective.

Reserved seats: quotas affecting the step from candidate to MP

The final type of quota guarantees representation by requiring a certain number of seats in parliament to be held by women. Quotas guaranteeing seats must be written either into the constitution or into the electoral law; they cannot have their basis in party rules. While there are a variety of institutional forms used, the norm is that a small proportion of seats, usually separated from the rest of the electoral system, are filled through a set of special rules. A crucial distinction among reserved seats systems is whether these seats are filled through appointment or through direct elections. We find a regional characteristic to reserved seats quotas as they are only found in countries in Asia, the Middle East and Africa. Furthermore, only one country that is defined as democratic by Freedom House guarantees women seats in parliament is Taiwan. It is worth noting that the rules guaranteeing women representation are a hold over from a period when elections in Taiwan were not considered free by Freedom House.

There are many countries that reserve a limited number of seats in parliament to specific groups to guarantee representation. They are used, for example, often to insure representation of ethnic minorities (Htun 2004).

When such rules are already in use, it is an incremental step to expand the use of this existing institution to ensure that women also receive some representation, and this has occurred in several states.

Bangladesh, Kenya, Niger, Tanzania, and Uganda all have legal guarantees of reserved seats for women. The number of seats covered ranges from six seats out of the 224 members of the Kenyan parliament to 'at least 56' of the 295 members of the Ugandan parliament. In these cases women are appointed by the prime minister, indirectly elected by the parliamentary delegations, or selected through an internal party vote. In Uganda and Rwanda, the women MPs are selected by district councils or women's councils made up exclusively of women. Importantly, these MPs do not face all voters directly. While these quotas are sometimes presented as a way to increase women's representation and therefore a way to ensure equitable representation, it is also true that the rules have often allowed the plurality party to use the women appointees to substantially increase their voting strength in parliament.

These all represent interesting cases, but Bangladesh especially stands out. Prior to the 2001 election, constitutional quotas guaranteed women held 30 out of 330 seats in the parliament. The requirement lapsed in the summer of 2001 and was not in effect for the 2001 election; women's representation dropped precipitously to only six seats out of 300. The national legislature in March 2004 reinstituted an enhanced quota for the next general election at which time 45 women will be indirectly elected to a newly constituted 345 member national assembly, as described in Chapter 9.

An initial reading of this seems to indicate a clear example of why quotas are necessary and that they work. With quotas the Bangladeshi parliament was at 9 percent representation, this dropped to 2 percent without quotas, and then will jump to 13 percent with quotas at the next election. There is, however, a more sceptical view of the same facts. These women who are elected do not have a direct tie to a district in their home province and therefore do not have an independent base of political power. They come to their positions by being elected by the male members of the parliament. In this way women are denied access to the more legitimate and directly elected seats in parliament and are at a political disadvantage within the parliament. Furthermore, women who lobby their party to be put on the ballot in single member districts are likely to be met with an argument that it is not necessary. These women will be chosen for the reserved seats after the election and therefore they should not take up a valuable slot in a single member district.[6] Under these conditions the reserved seat quotas becomes a ceiling for women's representation rather than a floor from which to build. Tripp (2000) notes a similar outcome in Uganda.

There are a few cases where effective guarantees are combined with elections to provide both guarantees for women and greater legitimacy by allowing voters significant input into the process. Among these is the case of Morocco. In Morocco, 295 MPs are elected from 92 electoral districts, and in addition 30 MPs are elected from national party lists. While these national party list seats were initially reserved only for women, the law was struck down by the courts. Nevertheless, all the major parties agreed to only nominate women on their lists and this led to 30 women being elected directly by the people. It remains to be seen whether this is a one-off action that is not repeated or whether the major parties in Morocco will continue to nominate women. The Jordanian electoral system guarantees women six of the 110 seats in parliament. In the direct election of 104 members of parliament, no woman was directly elected. Therefore, the six female candidates who ran for office and did best in terms of the percentage of the vote they won were selected for parliament.

As noted in the Arab chapter, Djibouti adopted a 10 percent quota by cabinet decree in 2002. While this quota is not formally a reserve seat quota, because of Djibouti's block vote electoral system, the cabinet's decision is in effect a reserved seat guarantee. The block vote results in the party that wins a majority of the votes in a district, winning all of the seats in the district. Each party nominates a slate of candidates that is exactly equivalent to the number of seats in the district. Because the whole slate is elected in each district, what is formally a candidate quota works effectively as a reserved seat quota. In 2003, seven women (10.3 percent) were elected to the Djibouti parliament.

Women have had their greatest success under reserve seats in Taiwan (Chou and Clark 1986; Clark and Clark 2002). In Taiwan, legislators are elected in multimember districts using a single non-transferable vote system (SNTV). The system is reasonably easy for voters to understand; each voter simply votes for the candidate they like best and the candidates with the highest vote totals are elected (if district magnitude is five then the top five candidates win). The system, however, wreaks havoc on party strategizing because the party must take into consideration how to split the party's votes to maximize the party's seats in parliament and how to get signals to the party supporters as to how they should co-ordinate to do this (Matland 2004).

On top of this extremely complicated electoral system, the national constitution requires that for each district with more than four seats a woman must be elected. This law effectively guarantees women at least 10 percent of the seats in parliament. The manner in which the law works is that if men are elected in the first four slots in a five person district then the woman with the most votes automatically wins the fifth slot regardless of whether she has the next highest vote totals. What this means is that a party may see its three strongest candidates win the first, third, and fifth highest number of votes, but they could lose the fifth slot if none of the first four elected candidates is a woman. Conceivably, if the major parties did not nominate women, a party with much less overall support could have their woman candidate elected. What this system does is quite ingeniously put pressure on the parties to both nominate and promote women candidates. Each party needs to have an effective woman candidate to make sure they have a chance at winning 'the woman's seat'. While the formal effect of the Taiwanese law only guarantees women 10 percent of the slots in parliament, representation in the Taiwanese parliament has surged well past the 10 percent level and is approaching 25 percent. Once parties were forced to nominate and promote women candidates, it turned out they were quite strong candidates, often doing better than the male candidates and getting themselves elected not to the final 'woman's seat', but much farther up the line. Furthermore, the women who are elected under these conditions have the legitimacy of having been elected directly by the voters and as such they are the equals of their male colleagues when they get to the parliament.

Reserved seat quotas, coming as they do at the very end of the recruitment process, have the opportunity to be quite effective, at least in terms of guaranteeing seats are held by women. There are, however, a couple of concerns in terms of effectiveness. First, when applied to national parliaments, the number of seats reserved is often so small that women still remain a small portion of the parliament. In addition, if reserved seats end up functioning as a ceiling rather than a floor, they can make it difficult for women to advance. Second, there is considerable concern surrounding the manner in which women gain these guaranteed seats. If they are appointed by the majority party without any direct ties to the voters, they risk the danger of not being seen as 'legitimate' or 'true' MPs. This may result in relegating the female representatives to an inferior position where they are unable to raise issues of concern to women. As Tripp, Konate, and Lowe-Morna note in their chapter women in reserve seats can be directly beholden to the president, so much so they vote for anti-women legislation.

Conclusion

Quotas can be distinguished based on the step in the legislative recruitment process they were designed to influence. While candidate quotas are the most common type of quotas, both among legal and party-based quotas, aspirant quotas and reserved seat quotas are also found. The type of quota present in a country is strongly influenced by the country's electoral system. Aspirant quotas are found only among industrialized democracies with single member district electoral systems. Aspirant quotas are a relatively weak tool, but are one of the few viable tools available given the existing institutional structure that builds upon significant traditions of local autonomy and local control of nominations (Gallagher 1988).

Reserve seat quotas are one way around this dilemma of nominations in single member district systems. Often reserve seat quotas are grafted onto an existing system so that reserve seats are selected in a different manner from the rest of the parliament. As the reserve seat system is separate, a single member district electoral system for the rest of the parliament does not cause any serious difficulties for establishing quotas. There are reserve seat quotas in states with both single member and multimember district electoral systems. Reserve seats are most frequently found in partially free polities where there has been a tradition of seats to represent special sector interests. Women can then seek to have themselves defined as a unique group worthy of guaranteed representation. Reserved seats do insure access, but because the MPs often are not directly elected by the citizens there can be a problem of legitimacy that makes it difficult for these women to wield power in the legislature.

Candidate quotas are by far the most common type of quotas, dominating among countries with multimember district electoral systems. Large numbers of parties have established self-imposed quotas especially in industrialized democracies. In addition, several polities, especially in Latin America have established formal legal quotas.

With respect to effectiveness of the various types of quotas, serious questions were raised as to whether aspirant quotas can effectively improve women's representation. The quotas affect such an early stage of the recruitment process, and still meet with such considerable resentment from local nominating committees, that there is limited evidence they have a strong positive effect on representation. Candidate quotas have the capability of being powerful tools for improving representation, but as Htun and Jones have shown, merely adopting quotas is not nearly enough. I suggested a pared down list of necessary and sufficient conditions for candidate quotas to be effective: proportional representation electoral system, an electoral system that produces high party magnitude, and good faith compliance on the part of the political parties. Good faith compliance can be generated either through party support for quotas, or through specification of regulations including a placement mandate and effective sanctions if a party fails to follow the regulations. In considering the effectiveness of reserved seat quotas, one needs to be sensitive to the possible dangers of variations in legitimacy in the parliament. Reserved seats may be effective in terms of getting women into the parliament, but exclusive mechanisms that shield women from the voters may also rob them of the legitimacy that being elected by the people gives a politician.

This chapter has argued that when attempting to establish electoral quotas there are a variety of different models that can be used. Those most commonly applied tend to vary with the electoral system that is in place. Furthermore, the effectiveness and legitimacy of these quotas also vary based on the electoral systems. When pushing for electoral quotas, it will be wise for the women's movement to consider the existing electoral structure and develop proposals that are consistent with the system in place and which include the necessary conditions making quotas an effective mechanism for increasing women's political power.

Notes

1 Electoral systems are distinguished on the basis of being either single member or multimember electoral systems, This distinction is made because of the crucial role district magnitude is believed to play in quota effectiveness. This split closely follows the distinction between plurality-majority systems versus proportional and mixed systems. Identified as single member district electoral systems are first-past-the-post, two round, and alternative vote systems. Multimember systems include list PR, STV, and mixed member proportional systems (both MMP and parallel systems). Block voting systems are a bit of an anomaly as the districts are multimember, but the party with the plurality of votes in the district wins ALL of the seats in the district, so the system is majoritarian. For the purposes of this analysis the important factor is the districts are multimember.
2 The one country is France, and in the French case the quotas written into the constitution have not been honored (see Western European chapter).
3 In fact, this is five conditions. Their electoral system component requires the system is both PR and closed list.
4 Jones would today consider Costa Rica to have also met these standards.
5 The centrality of party magnitude can also been seen in Bosnia and Herzegovina where strong quota rules were in place and were followed by the parties, but the elections produced a very low level of women's representation because party magnitude was so low.
6 Saxonberg (2003) describes a similar situation when discussing the nominating procedures of the Czech Socialist Party. The party has guaranteed a set level of representation, which it can fulfill by adding names at the national level. Under these conditions, women who would make strong candidates are rejected by the party at the local level with the explanation the party will choose you in the end at the national level so we shouldn't waste one of our slots at this level.

Bibliography

Baldez, L. (2004) 'Elected Bodies: The Gender Quota Law for Legislative Candidates in Mexico', *Legislative Studies Quarterly*, 29, 2: 231–58.

Caul, M. (2001) 'Political Parties and the Adoption of Candidate Gender Quotas: A Cross-National Analysis', *Journal of Politics*, 63, 4: 1214–29.

Chou, B. and Clark, J. (1986) 'The Political Representation of Women in a Reserved Seats System: The Application of Gender Gap Theories in Taiwan', Women's Research Program Monograph, National Taiwan University.

Clark, C. and Clark, J. (2002) 'The Social and Political Bases for Women's Growing Political Power in Taiwan', Maryland Series in Contemporary Asian Studies, No. 3 (170).

Freedom House (2004) 'Freedom in the World 2003: Tables & Charts', Online. Available at: http://www.freedomhouse.org/research/freeworld/2003/tables.htm (accessed 19 December 2004).

Gallagher, M. (1988) 'Conclusion', in M. Gallagher and M. Marsh (eds) *Candidate Selection in Comparative Perspective: The Secret Garden of Politics*, London: Sage Publications, pp. 236–83.

Htun, M. (2004) 'Is Gender Like Ethnicity? The Political Representation of Identity Groups', *Perspectives on Politics*, APSA, 2, 3: 439–58.

Htun, M.N. and Jones, M.P. (2002) 'Engendering the Right to Participate in Decision-Making: Electoral Quotas and Women's Leadership in Latin America', in N. Craske and M. Molyneux (eds) *Gender and the Politics of Rights and Democracy in Latin America*, London: Palgrave, pp. 32–56.

Inglehart, R. and Norris, P. (2003) *Rising Tide: Gender Equality and Cultural Change Around the World*, Cambridge: Cambridge University Press.

Jones, M.P. (1996) 'Increasing Women's Representation Via Gender Quotas: The Argentinian Ley de Cupos', *Women and Politics*, 16, 4: 75–98.

—— (2004) 'Quota Legislation and the Election of Women: Learning from the Costa Rican Experience', *Journal of Politics*, 66, 4: 1203–24.

Matland, R.E. (1993) 'Institutional Variables Affecting Female Representation in National Legislatures: The Case of Norway', *Journal of Politics*, 55: 737–55.

—— 'International Evidence and the Predicted Effects of SNTV on Women's Campaigns for the Indonesian DPD', paper presented at International Idea Conference on 2004 Indonesian DPD Elections, Jakarta, January 2004.

Matland, R.E. and Montgomery, K.A. (2003) *Women's Access to Political Power in Post Communist Europe*, Oxford: Oxford University Press.

Matland, R.E. and Studlar, D.T. (1996) 'The Contagion of Women Candidates in Single and Multimember District Systems: Canada and Norway', *Journal of Politics*, 58, 3: 707–33.

Meier, P. (1998) 'Vrouwwriendelijke lijsten in 1999?', *Samenleving en Politiek*, 5, 9: 3–10.

—— (2003) 'Gender Quotas or Electoral Reforms: Why More Women got Elected During the 2003 Belgian Elections', unpublished paper.

Saxonberg, S. (2003) *The Czech Republic Before the New Millenium: Politics, Parties, and Gender*, Boulder, CO: East European Monographs; New York: Columbia University Press.

Schmidt, G. and Saunders, K.L. (2004) 'Effective quotas, relative party magnitude, and the success of female candidates – Peruvian municipal elections in comparative perspective', *Comparative Political Studies*, 37, 6: 704–34.

Tripp, A.M. (2000) *Women & Politics in Uganda*, Madison: The University of Wisconsin Press.

14 Conclusion

Drude Dahlerup

All over the world, women's under-representation in politics has become a political issue, as this book has abundantly shown. During the last one-and-a-half decades, a large number of countries, although with regional variances, have chosen to introduce electoral gender quotas, an implausible prospect just three decades ago. 'Women' is being constructed as a political relevant category that has the right to representation – in spite of all philosophical and political objections.

This study has demonstrated that quotas that match the electoral system in place and are properly implemented can lead to an increase in women's representation in the political institutions. In spite of strict rules such as a requirement of 30 or 40 percent women on the lists, the actual increase is usually smaller. Whether these first increases will lead to further improvement or not, remains to be seen. Consequently, the gap between the incremental and the fast track becomes less apparent. However, in several cases electoral gender quotas have led to remarkable historical leaps in women's representation, and to jumpstarts where almost no women were elected earlier.

In Chapter 13, Richard Matland demonstrates what are the necessary and the sufficient conditions for quotas to work efficiently. It is important to note that gender quotas in many cases leave the advocates frustrated, when after vehement debates, the new quota rules result in no increase in women's representation at all, or when even a numerical increase remained purely symbolic giving the elected women no room of maneuver. However, quotas rules once installed give legitimacy to the continuing claims by the women's movements for gender balance in politics.

Regional variations

We have in this worldwide study found very interesting regional variations in the application of quota types, as Table 14.1 demonstrates. In Latin America the preferred type is legal candidate quotas, while reserved seats are the most used gender quota type in the Arab region, in South Asia and partly in Africa. Voluntary party quotas for candidates are the preferred

Table 14.1 Regional variations in preferred quota type[a]

Mandate by	Aspirants quotas	Candidate quotas	Reserved seats quotas
Legal quotas (constitutional or law)	n/a	Latin America The Balkans	Arab region South Asia Africa[b]
Voluntary party quotas		The 'West' Nordic region Africa The Balkans	

Notes
a According to the predominant type of quota. A region placed in two categories indicates that two quota types are used equally or almost equally.
b Reserved seats in one-party states are categorized as legal quotas.

quota type in the Western world, including the Nordic countries, and these are also used in Africa. This study has shown that there are clear links between the political system, the electoral system and the preferred quota types (see also Chapter 13). Chapter 8 adds a political factor: the importance of citizenship models, and the subsequent rejection of legal quotas in the liberal model. This has its parallel in the rejection of even voluntary party quotas by many liberal and conservative parties in the Western world, including the Nordic countries. The Balkan chapter tells about the move from voluntary party quotas to legal quotas, because of the limited effect of the former.

Thus this book can contribute to a better understanding of the importance of the choice of quota system.

The regional chapters demonstrate the inspiration that has traveled between countries in the same region. In Latin America, Argentina was the forerunner with its legal gender quotas. In Africa, South Africa has inspired other countries in the region to adopt party quotas, while Uganda has led concerning reserved seats. In South Asia gender quotas at the local level have been introduced in recent years in Pakistan, India and Bangladesh, even if these three countries do not openly refer to experiences made by their neighbors.

The most spectacular contagion effect is those cases where countries with different political and electoral systems take after one another, as when Latin American campaigns for quotas have wrongly argued that the legal quotas were behind the high representation of women in the Nordic countries. Maybe the most important inspiration is the evidence that male dominance in politics is no law of nature, and that active measure of some kind can lead to substantial increase in women's political representation. Even if the Nordic countries with their very high representation of women have been an inspiration for other countries around the globe, recent trends using the fast track model, especially in Latin American and Africa, has revealed that the Nordic incremental model is not the model, at any rate not the only model for increasing women's political representation substantially.

The differences between legal quotas and voluntary party quotas should not be exaggerated. In terms of increasing the number of women in politics the two systems can, as this study has shown, be equally effective – or ineffective. However, there are some important differences. Legal quotas do force all political parties to use quotas, and there can be legal sanctions for non-compliance, most effectively as this study has shown when the electoral commission has the authority, and uses it, to reject a party's lists before the election. Moreover, legal quotas are more difficult to change, whereas we see many examples of party quotas that are up for discussion during each election circle. In some few cases like in Denmark, party quotas have after a few years in action been abandoned again. But then also legal quotas can be perceived as temporary or even abandoned again like in the case of Egypt.

Women become symbol of the modern

As this study demonstrates, the wish to look modern has been one of the motives behind the introduction of electoral gender quotas in quite a number of countries around the world. This might be a strong motive for the leadership of a country in transition to democracy. This, however, rests on two factors: First, the international image of a country is of growing importance in our globalized world. Through international conferences and the regular reports to the CEDAW committee most countries in the world are up for examination, and the women's movements with increasing skill use this opportunity. To get a progressive image through gender balance and in this way attract votes is also found as a motive among individual parties as we see it today among parties that belong to Socialist International or the Global Greens.

Second, this would not work had a relatively high representation of women not been discursively constructed as a sign of modernism and progress. Just a few decades back high representation of women would not have been considered important to a country's or a party's image. Even if this motive might be questionable, the result might contribute to the empowerment of women in the long term.

We have, however, also seen cases where quotas only lead to symbolic representation of women. While the active involvement of women for some parties is seen as representing progress, fundamentalists within all major religions strive to restrict women's room of movement because women are supposed to represent and uphold the traditions. In both cases, women are reduced to objects, and deprived of their status as active citizens.

In post-conflict societies where external forces are heavily involved, we see donor countries and other forces promote gender balance in politics – provided they have a strong feminist wing like the Stability Pact Gender

Task Force for South Eastern Europe, UN in Afghanistan or the task force of the Interparliamentary Union in Rwanda. However, without the involvement of women's organizations locally, no long-term effect is to be expected. After traumatic experiences of armed conflicts, which always strengthen patriarchal forces, post-conflict societies as well as countries under major reconstructions do in some instances represent a window of opportunity for the inclusion of women or groups of women as the chapters on Balkan, Latin America and Africa have demonstrated. In the Western world new parties also represent an opening, because there are no incumbent men already occupying the seats, the main obstacle to rapid increase in women's representation.

In the introduction, symbolic policies was defined not just as politics that are intended not to have any effect, but was redefined so as to include policy measures that rest on a lack of understanding of means and ends and on a lack of interest in finding out how to get measures such as quotas to actually have an effect. While quotas have led to vehement debates in some countries, we have witnessed an astonishing lack of public debate on the issue in other countries with no discussion about how to match the proposed quota rules with the actual electoral system. This lack of match has in many cases minimized the effect of quota provisions. However, the ignorance may also turn out as to be what Gregory Smidt in the Peruvian case calls 'a blessing in disguise' (Smidt 2003: 3). This happens when the electoral commission or the courts later, pushed by the feminist movement, interprets the rules far beyond what the parliament had ever imagined like in Costa Rica and Peru.

Quota discourses

Quota discourses are surprisingly similar around the world. This is one of the unexpected results of this study. Even if the advocates of quotas do adjust their arguments to their national context and transform the international discourse to the generally accepted ideas in their society, the arguments for and against are still amazingly similar from country to country.

Do we find the fast track discourse and the incremental track discourse, discussed as ideal types in the introduction, in the actual discussions about women's representation around the globe? How close to actual discourses come to these types?

The conclusion from this extended study is that the fast track discourse as well as the incremental discourse are being used, however often in less consistent forms, especially when it comes to connection between on one hand the general assumption and on the other hand perceptions about possible actions as well as actual policy choices. *Because equality policy is usually passed in consensus, we find that parties with very different conceptions of what the problem is, vote for the same measure, here gender quotas.* As in other policy areas, in the use of electoral gender quotas such lack of clarification of goals and means weakens the implementation of the rules.

Especially among the opponents of electoral gender quotas, we found only limited discussion about the reasons behind women's under-representation. Rather, the debate focuses on *the imagined consequences of the introduction of gender quotas.* The main argument of the opponents is that quotas will have negative consequences for society and for women themselves. We will later confront these expectations with actual experiences of quota regulations.

The opponents

The traditional opposition: politics-is-a-male-business

In several countries resistance to quotas is based on traditional patriarchal perceptions of women's role in society ('the politics is a men's business'). The problem is not seen as the absence of women from the political institutions, but rather their intrusion. The argument is that political involvement of women will ruin the family, and who is then going to take care of the children? It is often said, that women do not have the capability to discuss complex issues such as foreign policy or budget matters. Stigmatization of political women and especially women elected on the basis of quotas are based on double standards (women are seen as tokens as if the men in politics were never that), and the femininity of women politicians is questioned – a women politician is a kind of she-man. The arguments may be more benevolent, stating that 'the Arab culture is not currently ready to accept political active women' (Chapter 7: 187). Or that women do not want to get involved in politics because politics is 'dirty' (Chapter 5: 127). The conservative revival in post-communist countries as well as the new fundamentalism in West as in East indicates that such negative attitudes to women in politics is not just a relic from older times that eventually will disappear. One may add that in the world today it takes active measures of exclusion by male brotherhoods to prevent women from getting any access to decision-making.

The post-communist opposition

The opposition to electoral gender quotas has been strong in the post-Soviet and post-Yugoslavia countries. In a constructed choice between 'freedom' and 'equality', freedom was a magic formula, as Chapter 6 on the Balkans records. Quotas for women were associated partly with radical feminism of the West, partly with 'forced emancipation', Soviet style. Even if quotas for women were not as widespread under communism as contemporary memory will have it, certainly not on the highest echelons in the communist parties, it has been very difficult to win acceptance for affirmative actions measures like quotas in Russia, and in Central and Eastern Europe.

The liberal opposition

Opposition to gender quotas is found to be strong within liberal discourses. Any attempt to secure women or other marginalized group, a share of the political seats through quotas is considered a violation of the classic liberal principles of 'equality of opportunity' or 'competitive equality'. Representation should be based on individuals representing different ideas, not on different groups of people. Historically, this reflects the classic liberal revolt against the previous representation of standings.

When it comes to gender, some part of the liberal opposition to quotas argue that gender should play no role in politics, here labelled *the gender blind discourse*. 'What counts, is what your have in your head, not what you have between your legs', the argument goes (Chapter 3: 68). This position is, however, not so widespread in contemporary society as one would expect. The new international discourse on women's under-representation has been influential, and today liberal opponents quotas argue from the position that gender does play a role today, even if the goal is gender neutrality in politics in the future.

According to *the incremental track discourse*, gender balance in politics is the stated goal, and this will eventually be achieved when women's resources in society increase. In the industrialized societies, which have experienced a dramatic increase in women's education and gainful employment, these arguments have lost some of their strength as explanations for women's under-representation. In countries with high representation of women like the Nordic countries, the liberal opposition to quotas do accept that there are some barriers for women in politics, but women's lower representation is also seen as a result of women's and men's different priorities. Women should not be forced into politics.

It should be noticed that in some countries, most particularly in the Nordic countries, parties who oppose quotas often work hard to recruit women through other means in order to show that quotas are unnecessary, with the result that women's representation in those parties are high seen on a global scale, however often lower than Nordic parties applying quotas.

As mentioned the main arguments among liberals and other opponents of electoral gender quotas are based on predictions about what quotas might lead to: gender quotas will, because women's lack of education, lead to the election of unqualified women. It is impossible to find a sufficient number of women to stand for election, or a sufficient number of 'qualified' women (Chapter 5: 126). It is argued that unqualified women or inexperienced women become tokens more easily.

Opponents are also worried that 'quota women' will be met with lack of respect. 'The challenge is to win an election on your own merit, not by grace' (Chapter 5: 124–5). Quotas are demeaning women and undermine the principle of merit, the British Conservatives argue (Chapter 8: 203).

The debate circles around the concept of fairness. Are quotas for women or other marginalized groups considered 'unfair', positive discrimination', or to the contrary fair because they correct present structural unfairness, as is argued in Chapter 2.

The feminist opposition

Opposition against electoral gender quotas are also found in feminist circles, that is from people who share the view that gender balance in politics is the goal and that processes of exclusion are preventing women from equal representation. The fear of tokenism is the main feminist argument against the use of gender quotas. This is especially feared when quotas are introduced as reserved seats, but also voluntary party quotas are sometimes met with suspicion.

In the Arab region some feminists warn that Arab governments use quotas to create support by 'puppet parliamentarian' (Chapter 7: 188). It is also stated that quotas might create a glass ceiling and the parties will avoid nominating any women for the free seats. Among many African feminists there is the fear that quotas will lead to tokenism 'and can become yet another mechanism in the service of patronage politics' (Chapter 5: 124). Feminist movements have also criticized the vote maximizing calculations that are often a motive behind the introduction of quotas.

Feminists who oppose quotas will advocate the use of many other measures to increase women's participation, like mentors, capacity-building, changing the competitive political culture and many other measures. The liberals among the feminist opponents share many of the liberal reservations against quotas mentioned above.

Unconstitutional

In various parts of the world legal gender quotas have been judged unconstitutional by the courts. The reason given by the judges have either been that quotas violate the principle of equality between the women and men in the constitution, or that quotas are against general principles of fairness and equality, see Chapter 2. Such judgments have been issued by courts in Morocco, France, the United Kingdom, Argentina and some other countries. The answer has varied between amending the constitution, changing the quota law or giving up on legal quota provisions.

The proponents

The ideal type of the fast track discourse presents the main cause of women's under-representation as one of discrimination and exclusion.

'The "meriocrats" use "Merit" as a gender smokescreen to keep doors to decision-making firmly shut on women' (Chapter 5: 125). Here the arguments are that quotas are not as discrimination against men, but compensation for discrimination against women, past and present. In Chapter 2, Carol Bacchi discusses the various feminist arguments of the quota advocates. These are the feminist arguments. However, this study shows that advocates of quotas seldom used this, the main theoretical argument for quotas, namely that it is discrimination that prevents women from access.

This apparently surprising finding has an explanation: because gender quotas are passed by male-dominated assemblies the politicians would in fact by such arguments criticize themselves for discrimination. It is the feminist movement and sometimes also smaller left wing parties that use the argument of exclusion, found in the Beijing Platform for Action. But also in these circles the argument of discrimination is only used occasionally in order not to offend the non-feminist support of gender quotas. Indirectly, the discrimination argument is of course present when it is said that quotas are a relevant measure because it forces the political parties to recruit more women, because men tend to select other men.

In general, those who advocate the use of electoral gender quotas tend to embed their arguments in general arguments about why gender balance in politics in general is considered important. These are the well-known arguments: (1) the justice argument that women are half the population, and have the right to half the seats; (2) the argument that women's experiences should be represented; (3) the argument that on some issues women and men have different interests, and consequently men cannot represent women; and (4) role model arguments.

Some arguments are however special to quota advocacy: the first is, that quotas make it possible for women to join parliament in larger numbers, and that this will prevent tokenism or 'the queen bee syndrome', that is the lonely women in an all-male assembly who from a non-feminist platform argues that there is no discrimination against women, and that she herself is the best example, which proves that women can make it if they strive hard enough.

Second, the argument that gender balance is important or even necessary *for the process of democratization* is more specific to the quota debate than to debates about women's representation in general. The time perspective is that of contemporary processes of reconstruction in contrast to the gradualism of established democracies.

Quota experiences

Does the actual experience with electoral gender quotas confirm the worries of the opponents or the positive prospects of the proponents? Here the qualification is important that electoral gender quotas are quite new, the research about the outcome still limited, and that eventual long-term effects are not yet recognizable. However, this comprehensive study does give some important answers to the questions raised, based research on five to ten years of experience.

Not sufficient (qualified) women

It is a general conclusion that is has been possible to find sufficient number of women candidates and elected women, even if shortage has occurred. For each parliament only few candidates in actual numbers are needed. If the political parties wanted they could probably find the limited number of women needed to fill half the seats of the world's parliaments.

In India more than one million women are elected to local councils each term, and many more stood for elections, which clearly contradicts what was being said about future lack of women candidates. It is interesting to note that under reserved seats systems many women elected for the first time tell that their willingness to stand for election increased when they did not have to compete with men, see the chapters on South Asia and Africa. Whether the elected women are sufficiently qualified, is not a factual question. The effectiveness of elected women depends more on the institutional arrangement and support than on their own resources. But obviously, historical leaps in women's representation do bring many women with limited political experience into political institutions. Consequently, capacity-building programmes for women candidates and for elected women are seen as very important in all such countries, in fact in most countries of the world.

Tokenism

Concerning the worry that quota women would be just tokens or 'proxy women', the result of this study is ambiguous. Chapter 5 on Sub-Saharan Africa concludes from African research that tokenism has not been the result in PR systems at the national level, but may be at the local level. However, quotas in plurality-majority systems, which usually are reserved seats quota systems, and in mixed systems have raised concern (p. 125). But there are also many success stories of women who felt totally isolated and powerless in the beginning, but eventually gained confidence and influence (Chapter 5: 125). During Egypt's experiment with quotas, the quota women were accused of not making a difference and being too loyal to the government. In general, the conclusions depend on what was expected, and on how dependence is measured, and further which dependency is considered legitimate, since no one is totally 'independent', especially not in politics. The feminist movement has been critical to women parliamentarians since the first women were ever elected following the enfranchisement of women, because the movement wants women politicians to be feminist, which all of them never were.

Double standards are at play, when women politicians are accused of being too dependent on their parties who own their seat, as if this was not the case for most male politicians as well. However, South Asian research tells about women who are extremely dependent on their family and whose husbands attend the meetings in their place. But it is also recorded how women by being elected have gained status in their family and in their community. Even if token women undoubtedly was the motivation behind many quota reforms, token women may not necessarily be the result, when capacity building and training by women's organizations for the elected women are available and widespread.

The motives behind the introduction of gender quotas are plentiful, as we have demonstrated in this book. The image of the countries plays an increasingly important role. The wish to maximize the votes of the party by presenting a gender balance electoral list, have also been criticized. However, this could alternatively be seen as an intended consequence of democracy that politicians feel obliged to respond to the wishes of the voters. Moreover, that women voters on a larger scale do demand women candidates is historically new, and may be seen as the result of the feminist movement pressure to construct women as a politically relevant category.

The fear of stigmatization

If women politicians in general are subject to prejudice because of their gender, then women elected by quota rules are of course also stigmatized, sometimes even more. It is the conclusion of the Arab chapter, that gender quotas may result in a jumpstart and get women elected where no women would otherwise have a chance. However, to prevent elected women from being just token, puppet women or stigmatized and thus powerless, as in the early Egypt experiment with quotas, society need to be prepared for such a gender shock, and women need to have established a prior record of visibility in the public sphere. Otherwise a jumpstart may imply that the elected women have little power base on which to act. Most cases of stigmatization seem to occur when only few women are elected, and mostly in countries marked by general hostility towards women politicians. But also the very construction of the quota regulation may in fact influence the status of women politicians. If the quota system is constructed in such a way that the 'quota women' do not have a constituency of their own, their status may diminish.

The high echelon quotas in use in some political parties in the Nordic countries, which give women 30 to 50 percent of the party fraction, does not seem to lead to any stigmatization, the Nordic chapter concludes. High echelon quotas imply that individual politicians are usually not singled out. In the case of 50–50 percent quotas with the use of a zipper system, alternating women and men on the list as in the Swedish Social Democratic party, women are no more 'quota women' than men are 'quota men'.

The fear of 'balkanization'

Opponents of the introduction of gender quotas have argued that this will result in demands from other categories for quotas for their group. This has been labeled the fear for 'balkanization' (Phillips 1995). This is of course a relevant consideration, which some will fear, while others will welcome such deliberations. In the Nordic countries considerations for gender balance in politics are now being followed up with discussion about the under-representation of immigrants. It has been criticized that so few immigrant women were to be found on the positions for 'women'. 'Immigrants', if represented at all, tend to be men, while 'women' tend to be all white. Quotas for women may lead to increased awareness of the exclusion of other groups and of women within such other groups, and the many experiments with types of gender quotas may pave the way for corrections of other types of under-representation.

Restriction on the voters

Electoral gender quotas have been criticized for restricting the free choice of the voters. This discussion rests on a naïve perception of how the electoral system works in most countries. The voters can in most systems only choose between the candidates that the political parties have selected. Because the political parties are the real gatekeepers to political positions, it is not the freedom of the voters, but rather the freedom of the party organization to choose only men candidates that is being restricted by electoral gender quotas. Gender quotas give the voters a chance to choose women as their representatives, an opportunity that is especially significant in open list systems.

Gender quotas and the empowerment of women

It is time to summarize the findings of this the first worldwide study of electoral gender quotas, based on in-depth studies in major regions of the world. It is fruitless to try to conclude whether gender quotas are good or bad for women and for democracy. Rather the task here is to conclude on what conditions gender quotas can make a change.

In terms of numbers, electoral gender quotas can be a very efficient tool to rapidly increase women's representation in political institutions, or to start a process of inclusion of women in areas where previously almost no women were present in the halls of political decision-making. However, if the rules are unclear and do not match the electoral system in place, if there are no sanctions for non-compliance and no rules about the ranking on the list, then quotas may lead to minimal or no numerical increase in women's political representation. The fear, that quotas will form a ceiling that prevents women from competing for and being elected on non-quota sets has not generally been confirmed. Voluntary party quotas can be just as efficient as legal quotas, but rely on constant good faith compliance of the party leadership.

In terms of effectiveness

Once elected many barriers still block women's ability to make use of their positions as elected politicians in the way they wish. Quotas do not remove such barriers for women politicians like the double standards women met, the lack of campaign financing, the many conflicts between family life and politics, difficulties in attending meetings, etc. But does the election by quotas in itself influence the effectiveness of women politicians? This study has demonstrated that when reserved seat systems are constructed in such a way that the elected women lack a clearly defined constituency of their own, their power base diminishes. Further, rotation systems like in India imply that many women councillors only serve one term. The conclusion is that the way the quota system is constructed influences the effectiveness of women politicians. Apart from such examples, it does not seem to cause any specific problems to be elected as 'quota women', once the political work starts, and all votes are needed in negotiations and deals within the political institutions.

It is also important to note, that a historical leap in women's representation through a properly implemented quota system with a requirement of 30 to 40 percent women like in Costa Rica, Rwanda and South Africa may imply an unknown 'gender shock'. In this case, the contested theory of a critical mass needs to be revisited, because until now this theory has been discussed on the bases of empirical incrementalism (Dahlerup 1988).

In terms of a feminist agenda

As discussed in the Introduction, political women differ tremendously in their attitudes and actions concerning feminist issues, even if research has proved that equality issues are predominantly placed on the political agenda by women politicians, and that many more female than male politicians see themselves as representatives of women or specific groups of women. But do election by means of gender quotas make women more apt to act as representatives of women? This study offers no uniform answer to this question. There are examples of women politicians who work hard and loyally to prove that they were 'real' politicians, in spite of their election by quotas. The reverse case is reported from Africa where under certain enabling conditions women politicians have made 'a marked impact on institutional culture, attitudes, laws, policies, and service delivery' (Chapter 5: 135).

That women want to be elected in order to further a new and different agenda seems to be a much more legitimate position in new democracies and in developing countries in general than in highly industrialized democracies. Whether this difference reflects the actual level of integration of women and men in different spheres of society, is an open question. In my opinion, feminism is not based on an 'identity' category, but rather on historical moves by various groups of women fighting the subjection of women in their context.

It seems to be a general feature that cross-party alliances between women politicians are a very strong tool, be it in Rwanda, Peru, Norway or the United Kingdom. Everywhere it seems to be the case that in order to further a feminist agenda in political institutions, including having quotas introduced, a combination is needed of active and critical women's movements, women politicians in the political institutions working from a feminist platform, strong public equal opportunity units and an extended and critical public debate on gender (Stetson and Mazur 1995; Dahlerup 1998).

To elect women by the fast quota track may lead to rapid results. But if these women politicians are elected with no power base in their party, in civic organizations or in their constituency, then powerless and token women can very well become the result. On the other hand, it is an open question whether the step-by-step integration of women into political institutions as in the incremental track has in fact contributed to overstated adaptation and assimilation of women in political institutions, so criticized by the feminist movement ever since the first women entered parliament.

Gender quotas, women's empowerment and democracy

Quotas are a start and have the potential to kick-start other processes of empowerment of women. But the impact of women's participation 'is rather fragile and will need further nurturing in order to be consolidated', as the South Asia chapter argues (p. 239). From the perspective of democratic deliberation, the inclusion of women where previously no women had any access does imply that the voices of at least some women are now heard.

If empowerment is defined not as a process nor as a result, but as the capacity to choose (Kabeer 2000, see Introduction), then quotas under specific preconditions do empower women. Political positions are potentially a tool to make choices, not just for the elected politician herself (carrier potential), but for society. However, no universal conclusion is possible on the basis of this book's studies. Various contexts offer different opportunities, and no gain once achieved is won once and for all. There is no one linear line of 'progress'.

Most of the chapters in this study stress the link between women's political empowerment and socio-economic changes. It is important to keep in mind, first, that without large structural changes in society the inclusion of women in political institutions will not lead to any long-term political empowerment of women. Second, public policy changes cannot alone fundamentally alter gender regimes. Third, it is fundamentally important to pay attention to the ways in which existing norms of citizenship are not only gendered, but 'classed', 'raced' and 'sexualized' (Hassim 2003; Bacchi in Chapter 2).

In terms of the redistribution-recognition debate, I agree with Iris Marion Young, that recognition in the form of political representation does mean redistribution (Young 1997). But not only of discursive power, as Young argues, see Chapter 2. Recognition of rights to political representation for previous marginalized groups involve in my mind per se a redistribution, namely of decision-making power, at least potentially.

Because political institutions have the power, although constantly undermined by internal and external forces, to make authoritative decisions for a society, then political empowerment under certain conditions may lead to cultural and social-economic changes. That the power of national parliaments is challenged because of the forces of globalization does not imply that women's political representation and gender quotas are not worth fighting for. Rather, this makes it necessary to demand access for women and other marginalized groups at all levels of decision-making, national as well as international. This ought to be the subject of many future studies.

In the fast track discourse as mentioned in the Introduction, the inclusion of women is often discussed as a move that will improve democracy, or even contribute to the process of transition to democracy. It is, however, much too early to evaluate the long-term effects of increased representation of women in political decision-making, and the use of quota provisions.

The argument that women's access will improve *the quality of politics* (less dirty and less corrupt politics, increased accountability or a broader political agenda) is widespread in post-conflict countries and countries in transition to democracy, and is often used in quota advocacy in these countries. It is an apparent paradox that these types of arguments are more frequently used in countries with more traditional gender regimes, than in countries with the highest score on the Gender related Development Index (GDI), countries such as Sweden, Denmark, United States, the Netherlands and Great Britain. *In established democracies, the argument that the inclusion of women will improve the quality of politics outside the feminist agenda is seldom heard, not even among feminists.* Here proponents are more likely to use the arguments of justice and of women's interests.

The argument that women politicians may improve democracy is usually not based on a belief in biological gender differences. Rather, the foundation is the fact that women have until now been marginalized in politics and therefore have no part of the (corrupt) establishment. Too heavy a burden may be placed on women's shoulders by such arguments. Also some women politicians can be and are corrupt. However, fundamental reconstructions of society do offer new opportunities for fast changes for good or worse, opportunities that in old established societies only exist in utopian novels.

Bibliography

Dahlerup, D. (1988) 'From a Small to a Large Minority: Women in Scandinavian Politics', *Scandinavian Political Studies*, 11, 4: 275–98.

—— (1998) *Rødstrømperne. Den danske Rødstrømpebevægelses udvikling, nytænkning og gennemslag, Vol. I–II*, Copenhagen: Gyldendal.

Hassim, S. (2003) 'Representation, Participation and Democratic Effectiveness: Feminist Challenges to Representative Democracy in South Africa', in A M Goetz and S. Hassim (eds) *No Shortcuts to Power: African Women in Politics and Policy Making*, London: Zed Books, pp. 81–109.

Kabeer, N. (2000) *The Power to Choose: Bangladeshi Women and Labour Market Decisions in London and Dhaka*, London: Verso.

Phillips, A. (1995) *The Politics of Presence: The Political Representation of Gender, Ethnicity and Race*, Oxford: Oxford University Press.

Smidt, G. 'The Implementation of Gender Quotas in Peru: Legal Reform, Discourses, and Impacts', paper presented at the Regional Workshop on The Implementation of Quotas: Latin American Experience, International IDEA, Lima, February 2003.

Stetson, D.M. and Mazur, A. (eds) (1995) *Comparative State Feminism*, Thousand Oaks/London/New Delhi: Sage.

Young, I.M. (1997) 'Unruly Categories: A Critique of Nancy Fraser's Dual Systems Theory', *New Left Review*, 222: 147–60.

Index

corporatism 61, 196–202
Costa Rica *18*, 83, *85*, 91, 93, 95–6, *99*, 100, 105, 283, 296, 304
Côte d'Ivoire *114*, 129
Craske, N. 39
'critical mass' concept 12, 304
Croatia 140–1, 146–7, *149*, 151, 154
Cuba *18*, *85*, *95*, *99*–100

Dandravate, Pramila 44
'delegate' model of representation 36
democratization and re-democratization 16–17, 22, 83–92, 99, 105, 123, 141, 228, 231, 249–50, 300
Denmark *18*, 57–9, 63–6, 70–1, 74–9, 295
Diabaté, Saran 123
Diaw, Aminata Cisse 124
discourse and discursive frames 8–9, 78, 226, 296–7
Djibouti *171*, *175*–6, 180, 288
Dominican Republic *85*, 91, 93, 95–6, *99*–101
double standards applied to men and women 13–14, 297, 302, 304

East Timor 250–3
Easton, David 15
Ecuador *85*, 91, 95–6, *99*–100, 102, 104
Egypt 113, *171*, *175*, 179, 186–90, 295, 301–2
El Salvador 88, *95*, *99*
electoral systems: overview xiv
EMILY'S List 206
empowerment 15–16, 146, 155–61, 186–91, 224–5, 228–9, 232–3, 239–40, 249, 256–7, 295, 305–6
equal opportunity units 9, 305
Equal Treatment Directive 33
equality: concepts and discourse of 5, 197; *formal* and *substantial* 143–4; of opportunity 32–4, 60, 63, 69, 124, 146, 161, 197, 298; of result 32–3, 68, 144, 197
Equatorial Guinea *114*
Eritrea 112, *115*
Ethiopia *115*
ethnic minorities 17, 139, 286
European Parliament 76–7, 154, 158, 204, 210
European Union 33, 60, 139, 158–61, 173

'fast track' to equal representation of

women 6–10, 14, 55, 65, 101, 224, 293, 296, 299, 305
feminism 3, 8–9, 12–16, 39–44, 56, 60–6, 70, 85–90, 93, 105, 139, 142–4, 158, 205, 207, 240–1, 296–305; *see also* state feminism
Finland *18*, 57–9, 62–4, 70–4, 78
'first past the post' (FPP) system xiv, 12, 129, 202, 213–14, 225, 230
France 45, *195*, *199*, 207–12, 299
Fraser, Nancy 34, 45, 240–1
Frei, Eduardo 87
frequency of quotas 275–7
Fujimori, Alberto 87, 91

Gabon *115*
Gambia *115*
Gandhi, Indira 222, 286
Gandhi, Mahatma 224
Gandhi, Rajiv 227
Gandhi, Sonja 286
Gargarella, Roberto 38
Gelb, Joyce 63
gender blindness 8, 34, 298
gender budgeting 135–6
gender neutrality 41, 57, 69–70, 78, 269–70
Gender-related Development Index 55, 306
gender shock 304
'gentlemen's agreements' 152–4, 177
Germany *18*, *195*, *199*, 200–2
Ghana 113, *115*, 118
Gibson, Douglas 124
globalization 173, 186, 295, 306
Goetz, Anne Marie 12, 36, 38–9
good faith compliance 283–6, 290
Greece *195*, *199*
Green parties 295
Guatemala *85*, *95*, *99*
Gueiler, Lydia 85
Guinea *115*, 123
Guinea-Bissau *115*

Hamadulu, Winstone 124–5
Hanoun, Louisa 175
Hasina, Sheikh 286
Hassim, Shireen 12, 38–40, 46
Hazib, Meluda 177
Herculano, Hirondina 120
high-echelon quotas 56, 75–8, 302–3
Holtmaat, Rikki 35, 46
Honduras *85*, *95*–100
Hoskyns, C. 38, 241